FOOTBALL HANDBOOK

The glory years!

Relive the beautiful game of the late 1970s
– just as though you were there

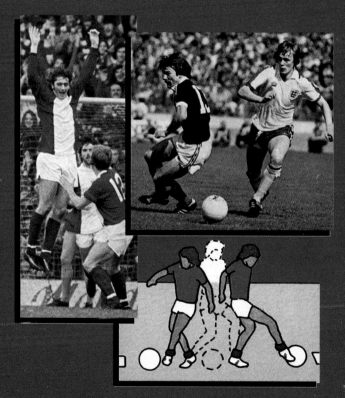

Marshall Cavendish Ltd
119 Wardour St
London
W1F 0UW

Email: footballhandbook@marshallcavendish.c
www.marshallcavendish.co.uk

©Marshall Cavendish Ltd 1978 and 2006

ISBN 10: 0 462 00681 6
ISBN 13: 978 0 462 00681 9

Printed in Malaysia by Times Offset (Malaysia) SDN BHD

Marshall Cavendish Ltd is a member of Times Publishing Ltd (Singapore)

 Marshall Cavendish Editions

GUIDE TO THE SECTIONS

Football Handbook – The Glory Years is divided into the following main sections. For specific club and player profiles, and hundreds of other great football entries, please refer to the main index at the back of the book.

Foreword by Martin Tyler

Kick off With...
A top player's snapshot views

Improve your Football
Tips and hints on how to improve your game along with fully illustrated 'Action Replay' analysis articles

Whistle Test
A referee's insights

Club Spot
Get the low down on all your favourite clubs

Pro File
In depth analysis of the top players

A Matter of Fact
Build your football knowledge with these fascinating snippets

Rising Star
The players showing most promise...did they fulfil it?

World Masters
International player focus

Quiz
Regular quiz pages feature throughout the book.
Test your knowledge...then test your mates!

FOREWORD

When I was asked to write the foreword for this book, I was slightly
reluctant. After all, in this 40th anniversary year of England's World
Cup win, were not 'the glory years' the mid-1960s? But reading the
book, I've realised that it covers far more than just the football
world of the late 1970s. Its look at club stories reminds us of how
Manchester United literally rose from the ashes of the 1958 Munich
air disaster to rebuild themselves into one of the world's top clubs.
It charts the careers of some of the great names in the football hall
of fame: Pat Jennings; Charlie George; Kenny Dalglish, and Archie
Gemmill to name but a few. And it offers insights from referees and
other football insiders of the time that still serve to throw new light
on the game. But most of all, Football Handbook takes you back to
exactly what you were doing when it was first published and how
the sport was reported then. Whether you read it cover to cover
or dip in and out, like me, I'm sure you'll find it an evocative
experience.

Martin Tyler, Sky Sports football commentator and author
of *The Story of Football* (Marshall Cavendish 1969)

Gordon McQueen

'I can't describe what a nightmare it was going to Argentina and not being able to play. But all that's in the past—a good professional looks ahead, not back.'

Gordon McQueen—a centre-half who lives up to his world-class ranking.

A collision with a Hampden goal-post leaves McQueen's World Cup dreams in tatters.

It's been a long and difficult summer for Britain's most expensive footballer. Torn ligaments in his right knee kept him out of the World Cup, and then it was the gruelling fight back to fitness.

'Football comes first with me,' Gordon explained to *Handbook*, 'and my wife Yvonne and I gave up our holiday in Corfu so that I could get my knee right by going to Old Trafford five days a week for light training.'

This determination reflects the big Scot's general attitude to the game. 'To succeed at any level a player has to show complete dedication,' he says. 'That means practising hard at the weak areas as well as sharpening up on your good skills—and listening to advice from anyone who can help.

'Every player needs a certain amount of natural ability, but you can often make up for lack of skill by giving a hundred per cent effort.'

Gordon reckons he's in for an exciting season. 'I'm sure I'll meet with a lot of success at United. I left Leeds because I didn't think the set-up would bring real success, but at Old Trafford there's bags of ability in the side and fabulous support. We're confident of lifting the title.'

A happier moment for McQueen as he heads powerfully clear in a League match against Everton.

1

Ray Wilkins on control

'Learning the basics of ball control is like learning the alphabet. You can't improve your game until you've got it right . . . and as you progress in the game you have to perfect your control.' RAY WILKINS

All concentration and determination . . . Ray Wilkins makes the kind of telling pass that results from basic ball control. 'That's the starting point,' he says.

Top pros may appear to take ball control for granted—but don't be fooled! They treat it as seriously as any other aspect of the game.

And if it looks easy that's because they perfect their control at training sessions—day in, day out for years—until it becomes a good habit.

Ray Wilkins, Chelsea's England star, is a good example of a player whose control earns him precious seconds in midfield.

'The important thing,' says Ray, 'is to keep your eye on the ball and prepare yourself to receive it.

'You need to keep your non-kicking foot firmly on the ground and use your arms to help with balance. Don't worry what you look like . . . if your control improves, that's what matters.'

If you're well balanced, you'll be more prepared for the ball that pops up unexpectedly. As the ball meets the inside of the foot, the idea is to cushion the ball, as Ray demonstrates below.

He says: 'I take the pace off the ball by letting the foot absorb the energy of the pass.

'The way to do that is to withdraw the foot slightly at impact. The more you practice, the more you get to know the ball, and the better your control will be.

'Obviously, the faster the ball is coming to you, the faster you have to withdraw the foot to absorb the pace.'

The cbject, claims Ray, is to control the ball so that it stays within a few inches of the foot.

'Control is the starting point in football,' says Ray. 'But it isn't something to get complacent about after you've mastered some of the basics. The higher you get in football, the greater the demand for perfection with the little things . . . like passing, like basic control.'

1. As the ball approaches Ray Wilkins is perfectly positioned to receive it: eye on the ball, weight on the left foot.

2. The ball is cushioned on impact by the inside of Ray's right foot. Note how he still uses his arms for balance.

Mike Busselle

Colorsport

3. The ball is now effectively controlled and Ray coaxes it down. Yet he keeps concentrating—eye still on the ball!

4. Now the ball is dead and Ray, having used the skill that has become a good habit, can concentrate on the pass.

Turning the Wilkins way

'If you learn to turn well you'll look twice the player.' RAY WILKINS

The earlier a young player is able to 'turn' with the ball, the quicker his overall game will improve.

Because turning is the skill which can switch play in a single movement.

Watch any big match—there were countless examples in the World Cup—and you'll see how important a skill it is.

You'll notice that pros,

when they have space, almost always turn in the way that Ray Wilkins demonstrates for *Football Handbook*, whereas young players tend to take the ball round in a large arc and waste valuable seconds.

'The thing to do,' explains Ray, 'is to take most of the pace off the ball and turn at the same time to follow it.

'With practice the ball will

stay in easy playing distance after the turn.'

So turning—quite an easy skill to master—can open up whole new horizons to young players who are 'blinkered' without it.

Ray rates the skill highly. He says: 'I might have to turn as many as 50 times in a match—so you can see how vital it is. And that goes for players at all levels.'

1. As Mick Mills passes, Ray prepares to turn with the ball on his right foot, his left acting as an anchor.

2. At impact Ray has already half turned and taken most of the pace off the ball.

3. The ball carries on at a slower pace; although Ray has turned quickly, it is still under his control.

Welcoming foot ... Cushioned impact ... Half-way round ... And away you go!

Improve your control

'Some kind of wall is needed if you're practising control by yourself,' says Watford boss Graham Taylor, *Football Handbook's* resident coach. 'Make sure you strike the ball with varying force so that you have different types of ball to control. And use both feet because in games the ball will come at you from different angles . . . not always how you want it to !'

'With a friend, take it in turns to control a bouncing ball. The important thing here is to mix the throws—some fast, some bouncier, some spinning and so on. Imagine you're in a game situation and split-second control is vital . . . if the ball gets away, you can call it a chance missed.'

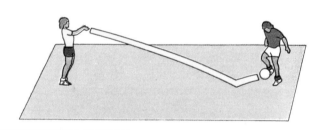

Improve your turning

'Turning has to be practised by three players,' says Graham, 'because it is unrealistic—not to mention boring—to turn without an end product. So, with three of you, one receives a pass in the middle, turns and passes to the third player. To start with, the players on the outside should play gentle passes so that the technique can be mastered by the turner. As the skill improves, the ball can be passed more firmly for slicker turns. It's also a good idea for the players on the outside to call "turn"—again because it relates to real match situations. Also, it's important for the player in the middle to meet the ball—not just stand and wait for it—because in matches a player with space to turn will suddenly find himself under pressure if he waits for the ball to arrive at his feet . . . and that's fatal.'

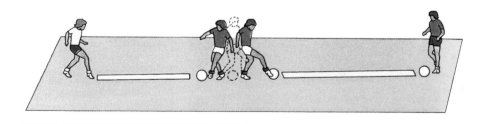

Whistle Test

'A referee must be brave . . . if he can't face up to the game's inevitable controversies he should keep right out of football.' TOM REYNOLDS

Bearded Tom Reynolds leaves the quiet life of the pub he runs in a Wiltshire village for the weekly hurly-burly of the Football League.

A big man with a booming voice, he is ideally equipped for the 'crunch' moments in big-time football.

One came in the World Cup qualifier between Austria and East Germany in Vienna last September . . .

'It was one-all with four minutes to go,' recalls Tom. 'The 72,000 crowd went mad when Austria scored—and they went even madder when I disallowed it for offside.'

The ball had been crossed into the East German penalty area and their goal-keeper and the Austrian centre-forward, Hans Krankl, clashed in mid-air.

'Both went down as the goalkeeper punched the ball outside the area, and another Austrian headed it straight back into the goal.'

But Tom ruled that the centre-forward, who had staggered back to his feet, was offside *and* interfering with play.

Tom explains: 'If he had stayed prone in the box it would have been a goal. It would have indicated to me that he wished to take no further part in the action. I also decided that the keeper would have had a better chance of saving the ball if the centre-forward had not been there.'

Tom was escorted from the pitch by 350 police . . . and Austria went on to get the point they needed to qualify by drawing in East Germany!

Ray Green

The ref's reasoning
Part of the offside law (Law XI) states a player is offside if he is *interfering with the play or with an opponent, or is seeking to gain an advantage by being in an offside position.*

Man in the middle
Originally from Battersea in South London, Tom Reynolds was evacuated to Swansea in the war . . . and stayed 20 years! He played right-half, 'a Dave Mackay-type, hard and noisy', for Newton Abbot Albion in the South Devon League. A kick in the spleen ended his playing days, so Tom turned to refereeing, joining the League referee's list in 1968. And big or small, (*left*), they all come alike to man in the middle Tom Reynolds!

Founded: 1885
Address: The Dell, Milton Road Southampton SO9 4XX
Ground: Capacity 31,000; Playing area 100.5 x 66 m
Record attendance: 31,044 v Manchester United, Div. 1,8.10.69
Record victory: 11–0 v Northampton, Southern League, 28.12.01
Record defeat: 0–8 v Spurs, Div. 2, 28.3.36 & v Everton, Div. 1, 20.11.71
Most League points: 61, Div. 3(S), 1921-22 & Div. 3, 1959-60
Most League goals: 112, Div. 3(S), 1957-58
League scoring record: 39, Derek Reeves, Div. 3, 1959-60
Record League aggregate: 160, Terry Paine, 1956-74
Most League appearances: 713, Terry Paine, 1956-74
Most capped player: 45, Mike Channon, England, 1973-77
League record: 1920 Div. 3; 1921 Div. 3(S); 1922-53 Div. 2; 1953-58 Div. 3(S); 1958-60 Div. 3; 1960-66 Div. 2; 1966-74 Div. 1; 1974-78 Div. 2; 1978- Div. 1
Honours: FA Cup Winners 1976; Runners-up 1900, 1902; Div. 3(S) Champions 1921-22; Div. 3 Champions 1959-60

Southampton

Celebrations in the stand after promotion last April. Lawrie McMenemy had quickly dismantled his 1976 FA Cup winning side—out went stars like Jim Steele, Peter Osgood and Mike Channon—and built a new team based on a blend of youthful talent (Williams, Funnell, Hebberd) and tested, experienced men.

Southampton's burden is their image: the small-time club with the small-time ground. And it'll take more than promotion back to the First Division to change that. It'll need all of manager Lawrie McMenemy's single-mindedness to point the Saints in a new and positive direction—plus a joint effort with the city council to provide a new stadium.

Everyone in Southampton knows what happened the last time their team went up in 1966. The players and veteran manager Ted Bates were geared to the big time, but that was about it. A waiting list for season tickets grew to embarassing proportions, with every seat for every home game sold

Owen Barnes

7

Owen Barnes

ABOVE *Fans greet the Saints'*
return to Division 1 after the
0-0 draw with Spurs on 29
April. The Dell itself remains
a headache—part of the
'small-time' image that
hampers the club—and it's
now 12 years since plans were
drawn up for a super-stadium
in the city centre. According
to the club, it's time for action.

before the players reported for pre-season training!

Plans were drawn up by the council for a new £3 million stadium by the central railway station with covered seats for 40,000 fans and facilities to be used seven days a week.

But ten years later . . . nothing.

McMenemy, being McMenemy, chose the civic reception for his 1976 FA Cup winners to attack the council.

Now the two sides are meeting again, with the possible result an £8 million multi-purpose stadium. The lesson could be that's what's good for the club is good for the city.

Curiously enough, Southampton is one of the half dozen

Colorsport

...vednesday	42	17	12	13	54	47	4u
Barnsley	42	17	11	14	62	51	45
Fulham	42	16	12	14	43	32	44
Southampton	42	14	14	14	40	40	42
Hull	42	14	14	14	43	45	42
South Shields	42	15	10	17	35	44	40
Derby	42	14	11	17	46	50	??
...d Cit,		??	??	13			

The 'perfect' season
In 1922-23 the Saints had (in statistical terms) the ideal record, winning 14 matches, drawing 14 and losing 14, scoring 40 goals and conceding 40.

LEFT *Former England mid-*
field dynamo Alan Ball is
perhaps Lawrie McMenemy's
shrewdest investment so far.
A great tutor for the younger
players, 'Ballie' provided a
commitment and consistency
that was lacking in earlier
London signing Peter Osgood.

RIGHT *Hero-worship among*
Saints fans is as much for the
boss as for the players. Just as
he did at Doncaster and
Grimsby, the 6 ft. 5 in.
McMenemy has created a new
confidence and atmosphere at
The Dell—a fresh approach
based on style and success.

or so clubs making money at the turnstiles—enough to keep Mike Channon at The Dell through his best years and attract Alan Ball for a reported £500 a week.

Yet before the '66 success Southampton had always been a fair-to-middling club commuting between the Second and Third Divisions.

And then, of course, there was the ground. Built at the turn of the century, it was adequate for the unambitious but a liability for the go-ahead.

McMenemy, always the realist, is fully aware that one of his tasks is to march the Saints into the modern age without dumping the sense of tradition that keeps the heart of a club like Southampton beating from day to day.

It was with a similar approach that McMenemy got his team into the First Division. Having won the FA Cup in '76 he could easily have stuck with the same players for another three or four seasons. But he went instead for consistent players who would pull in points for nine long months.

'You need workers as well as wizards,' he says. 'The Cup-winning team was magic and I still miss the players. But after turning it on for the big games, their hearts weren't really in it at places like Oldham.'

So he went for good, solid players who would give him consistency, allied to talented youngsters—'a team to take us into the First Division'. The likes of Chris Nicholl and Mike Pickering have done just that and now you can bet that McMenemy is looking at his players and asking a new question: 'Having got us here, will you *keep* us here?'

He knows that after some good years—including a couple of seasons in Europe—the '66 side grew old in the First Division and McMenemy arrived too late to stop the slide.

Now he is likely to buy or develop players to rank with the greats that stretch back to C. B. Fry and include Alf Ramsey, Ron Davies, Terry Paine and Martin Chivers.

Owen Barnes

League's lucky charm Centre-half Chris Nicholl boasts a unique record: he has won promotion in his first season with each of his four League clubs— Halifax, Luton, Aston Villa and now Southampton.

Colorsport

Saints' record breaker Terry Paine played 713 matches for Southampton and 111 for Hereford, the total being an all-time League best. Paine, who also holds the club scoring record, played in over 1,000 competitive games, including the 42 that took the Saints into Division 1 in 1966—the year he won the last of his 19 caps.

Owen Barnes

Speed off the mark: Peter Barnes

'If you let a winger as good as Peter Barnes run at you, you're really asking for trouble . . . if he wrong-foots you, you can wave goodbye.' MICK MILLS

With wingers back in favour at club and international level, surging runs down the line are again adding colour and excitement to the game.

And one of the people to thank for the revival is Manchester City's young star Peter Barnes.

But Peter is quick to point out that all players need speed.

'It's those vital first five metres that matter in football,' he says.

'Goalkeepers need to dash off their line, defenders must make last-gasp tackles and forwards have to be sharp to snap up half chances.'

Peter says most players can improve their speed off the mark by regular, short, sharp sprints.

One thing is certain. As you progress in the game, you must be prepared to improve your 'sharpness'.

And Watford boss Graham Taylor says speed of thought is just as vital as speed of movement.

He says: 'The player who can anticipate a situation and then react accordingly is better to have in your side than someone who moves fast but thinks slowly.'

Peter Barnes is aware that skill is a necessary ally to speed. 'It's no use just trying to run past a defender with the ball,' he explains. 'You must try to use skill to get him off balance first.'

And he says: 'Young players of all positions should do short sprints as often as possible. Even I should do more because it's easy to drop from a high standard.'

Peter leaves Scotland's Stuart Kennedy for dead at Hampden. 'Get them off balance first,' he says, 'then use your speed.'

Ray Green

If you're practising on your own, probably the best way to improve your speed off the mark is to lob a ball into the air, sprint to a point five metres away—marked by a stick or cricket stump—and sprint back to control the ball before it bounces twice. 'Sprint back at as sharp an angle as possible,' says our coaching consultant, Watford boss Graham Taylor, 'because that's how it is in matches—all twists and turns and short, sharp sprints. All training should relate to what happens on the pitch.'

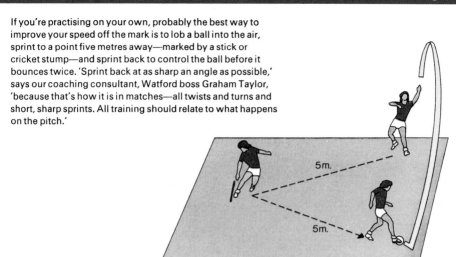

'When there are two of you, one can pass the ball through the legs of the other, who then turns to catch the ball before it crosses a specified line.'

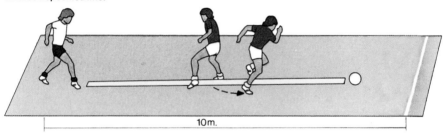

'You can get Dad or big brother to help in the third practice. He moves slowly with the ball and two of you trot either side of him—then he suddenly passes the ball forward for you to chase. This includes the vital element of competition and if Dad tries to fool you now and again—by turning, for example— so much the better.'

PRO FILE
TREVOR FRANCIS

'I wasn't sure I could make it in the First Division.'

Up and away . . . Trevor Francis heads home in England's easy 4-1 win against Hungary at Wembley in May. He formed an exciting striking partnership with Kevin Keegan after manager Ron Greenwood decided to play without a recognised 'target man' in the side.

Those words, believe it or not, come from Birmingham's England star Trevor Francis.

The same Trevor Francis who was tagged the 'golden boy' of British football after scoring four goals in a League game . . . at 16!

Trevor turned down offers to join Arsenal and Wolves because he wanted to start his career in a lower grade.

'I didn't want to go to a top club,' he explained to *Handbook.* 'I only got as far as the first England schoolboys' trial and was not selected for the team.

'So I thought I stood my best chance by going to a

12

Colorsport

Second Division side. I knew how many kids had failed to make it at really big clubs.

'Also, Birmingham had only three teams—youth, reserve and first. I could see a definite ladder there.

'I was promised a place in the youth side and I knew I would get into the reserves if I was good enough. Then, if things went well, I would get my chance in the first team. I thought I could get lost at a club with four or five teams playing every weekend.'

If Francis had his doubts, a host of admiring club scouts were convinced of his calibre. They had been eyeing him since he was an eight-year-old, but his father would not let him sign forms until he was old enough to become an apprentice pro.

That moment came in July 1969, and after a season in the Midland Intermediate League, Trevor climbed the ladder to the first team.

The 'new Jimmy Greaves' went on to score 15 goals in 15 games, including four against Bolton.

Envious noises came from other clubs as Francis signed full professional for Birmingham in April 1971, earning what was then the astronomical wage of £84 a week.

The following month Francis starred in the England side that won the European Youth Tournament. And in only his second season in the League—his first as a full pro—he played in 39 of the 42 matches which took Birmingham back into the First Division as runners-up to Norwich. His doubts began to disappear.

'That was another reason I chose Birmingham,' says Trevor. 'I knew they were ambitious and already had a First Division set-up. I had a hope they would go up.'

As well as great natural ability and speed, the young

The pain . . . Francis feels the full impact of a tackle in a League game at St Andrews.

The glory . . . Francis forgets the knocks and leaps for joy after scoring in the same match. The crowd goes mad but the Everton defender can only look on dejectedly . . . a typical reaction when Trevor is at his brilliant best.

Syndication International

13

*With the greatest of ease . . .
Francis flies through the air
during the international
against Switzerland at
Wembley last year, a
frustrating 0-0 draw.*

Francis had the indefinable 'instinct' of a great player. At his
best he was impossible to predict, impossible to mark.

The atmosphere at St Andrews was euphoric. Not only
were City back at the top; they also had an authentic star,
they kid they called 'Super Boy'.

But things turned sour as Birmingham became First
Division strugglers. Trevor managed only 12 goals over the
next two seasons. Then in 1974-75 he hit the net 13 times
in only 23 games—the start of a four-year spell that
established him among the top strikers in the country.

After a disastrous start last season, City made a remarkable recovery with Francis in sparkling form. His goal
tally: 25.

After five Under-23 caps, Francis finally made his debut
in the senior side against Holland at Wembley on 9 February
last year. Eighteen months later he has 12 caps and two
international goals—one in the 5-0 World Cup win against

Colorsport

14

Luxembourg and a header against Hungary in May.

In that game—won 4-1 by England—Francis formed an exciting partnership with Kevin Keegan, with manager Ron Greenwood forsaking the use of a conventional 'target man'.

A long international career lies ahead of Francis, but he is also hungry for success at club level. It's strange to realise that he has never won a medal or played in Europe.

Two press interviews last season broke the news to the football world that Francis was fed up at Birmingham. He made it clear that only a move to a bigger club would bring him the kind of success he wanted.

The controversy earned him club fines and eventually led to the resignation of manager Sir Alf Ramsey, who had recommended a Francis transfer to the Birmingham board.

Just when it looked like the auction had begun—with a massive £600,000 offer from Minnesota Kicks—a new man took over the hot seat at St Andrews, Jim Smith. Francis wavered. It seemed to him that Smith could be the man to lift the club out of its lethargy.

'I felt there was no ambition at the club,' he recalls. 'But when Jim Smith arrived there was a great improvement.'

Smith's arrival, plus permission to spend a lucrative summer with Detroit Express in America—£50,000 for 20 games—means Francis has started the season in a Birmingham shirt.

So is everything sorted out? 'No,' says Trevor adamantly. 'I've agreed to see out the start of the new season. Who knows, with Jim Smith in charge we could go to the top of the League and I could be here for my testimonial in two years time.'

With a style of play ideal for the American game, Francis could probably become a dollar millionaire in the States. But he doesn't want to sell out. 'Playing for my country still means more than anything to me.'

And his advice to talented young players: 'Choose the club whose standards you are sure you can match. A move up can always come later.' Sound sense from the star who had to conquer his own doubts before going on to become one of the most exciting players in Britain.

He was obviously not influenced by the teacher who saw him and said: 'That boy will play for England.'

'That boy' was then just five years old.

Control and concentration . . . Francis is perfectly poised to make a positive contribution. No sign here of the young player who doubted his own ability and chose to join a Second Division club rather than go straight into the big time with Arsenal or Wolves. 'I saw a definite ladder at Birmingham,' he says.

Colorsport

The story of a star
Trevor Francis was born in Plymouth on 19 April 1954 . . . signed as an apprentice with Birmingham City in July 1969 . . . made his debut for the club in a Second Division match against Cardiff City, coming on as a substitute for John Vincent . . . scored in his first full match the following week, in a 1-1 draw with Oxford United . . . played in the England team that won the European Youth Cup the following summer . . . gained the first of five Under-23 caps against Poland at Plymouth on 16 October 1973 . . . his first full cap on 9 February 1977 against Holland at Wembley.

Season	Div	Pos	League		FA Cup		Lge Cup		Int'nls	
			Mtchs	Gls	Mtchs	Gls	Mtchs	Gls	Mtchs	Gls
1970-71	II	9	22	15	2	–	2	–		
1971-72	II	2	39	12	5	2	–			
1972-73	I	10	31	6	1	–	5	2		
1973-74	I	19	37	6	2	1	5	1		
1974-75	I	17	23	13	1	–	2	–		
1975-76	I	19	35	17	2	1	2	–		
1976-77	I	13	42	21	2	–	1	–	4	1
1977-78	I	11	42	25	2	2	1	–	8	1
(all with Birmingham City)			271	115	17	6	19	3	12	2

How Archie kept his cool
...and gave the Dutch a fright

'It was one of those times when you just decide to go for goal and chance your luck ... if you're lucky you find yourself with only the keeper to beat.' ARCHIE GEMMILL

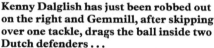

Kenny Dalglish has just been robbed out on the right and Gemmill, after skipping over one tackle, drags the ball inside two Dutch defenders ...

Gemmill 'nutmegs' another defender who makes a desperate effort to close him down. The ball goes into space with only Gemmill balanced to get it ...

One moment of magic from little Archie Gemmill is Scotland's only happy memory of their World Cup failure in Argentina.

His solo goal that gave the Scots a 3-1 lead against Holland raised the hope that they could pull off a near-miracle and qualify for the second round.

That hope lasted just 3½ minutes before Johnny Rep blasted Holland's second.

But that took nothing away from the skill and composure in the Gemmill goal.

Every goal should be seen in its context, and when you consider the pressure on Scotland, it makes Gemmill's effort all the more remarkable.

After turning towards goal and weaving his way through a cluster of players, he could have been forgiven for falling at the last hurdle with a hasty shot.

But Archie kept his cool to the extent of adjusting his body to transfer the ball to his favoured left foot and calmly slotted the ball—with the side of his foot—past the advancing goalkeeper.

'It was the sort of goal Archie tucks away in an ordinary League game,' says Graham Taylor, 'but it takes on a different significance in the World Cup.

'Archie showed that it's quite possible to nip through a crowded defence. There's the element of surprise and, in that split second, each defender is apt to think that someone else will make the crucial tackle.

'It helps, of course, if you can sell the lovely little dummy that Archie used!'

Graham Taylor's analysis
'As well as the skill and imagination that went into the Gemmill goal, there was one great—yet simple—lesson for all midfield players, and that is the importance of always being 'available' in a position to help forwards who find themselves under pressure. When Dalglish controlled a difficult through pass he was immediately closed down by two Dutch defenders. One of them got in a tackle and there was Gemmill to pick up the pieces. The Dutch 'keeper, Jan Jongbloed, did right to spread himself but Gemmill was cool enough to clip the ball over him. Note how Asa Hartford moved out of the area to avoid the possibility of being given offside. He knew that at that stage it was down to Gemmill alone ... and the little man knew it too !'

Each week *Football Handbook* will highlight the great goals and saves, moves and incidents from televised matches. We will capture the action—frame by frame—with a special diagram to show how it developed. And our coaching consultant Graham Taylor will pick out the points that made it special. By bringing alive the skills and tactics used by the professionals, 'Action Replay will pass on all the little tricks of the trade like dummies, one-twos and special free-kicks as well as the wider, tactical aspects such as marking and covering. First in the series is the Archie Gemmill goal that saved Scotland's face in Argentina—a goal that demanded imagination, a high degree of skill and determination, and, most important of all, the composure of a seasoned professional . . .

Now's the moment Archie keeps his cool. He has a split second to adjust his body and clip the ball left-footed over the advancing goalkeeper . . .

A job well done. . . Archie turns away in triumph as the ball nestles in the back of the net. Bruce Rioch's joy is just as obvious on the right.

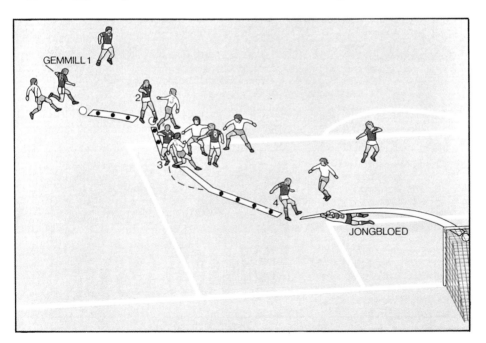

A Matter of Fact

Two present First Division sides have been forced to seek re-election in their League lives—Norwich City ('31, '47, '48 and '57) and QPR ('24 and '26).

Last February Atletico Madrid's Spanish international Ruben Cano was 'sent off' in the league match at Valencia —for pulling an opponent's hair on the way to the dressing-room at half-time!

League Champions Nottingham Forest conceded more free-kicks (632) than any other First Division side last season. The lowest tally was recorded by strugglers Wolves, with only 427.

Ted Macdougall, now back in First Division football with Southampton, scored 9 goals (an FA Cup record) in Bournemouth's 11-0 win over Southern League Margate on 20 November 1971.

In December 1976 Manchester United fielded 8 full internationals—in their reserve side in the Central League!

Colorsport

Ally McLeod was Hibs' top scorer last season with 20 goals. Ally MacLeod (no relation), Scotland's boss, also played for Hibernians.

Only 7,843 people turned up at Hampden Park (capacity 140,000) to see Scotland play Northern Ireland on 6 May 1969—the lowest ever attendance for a full home international. Lincoln City, who finished 8th in Division 4, had a better average that season.

Last season double-winners Cologne broke a 9-year stranglehold on the West German Championship by two clubs—Bayern Munich ('69, '72, '73, '74) and Borussia Moenchengladbach ('70, '71, '75, '76, '77).

Denis Law once scored 6 goals in an FA Cup tie—and still finished on the losing side. With Law scoring all their goals, Manchester City were leading Luton Town 6-2 in a 4th round match at Kenilworth Road when the game was abandoned because of heavy rain. Luton won the replay 3-1—and there are no prizes for guessing City's scorer.

During the freezing winter of 1962-63, the third round FA Cup tie between Lincoln and Coventry was postponed no less than 15 times—a record for the competition.

Seven Arsenal players appeared for England in the 3-2 win over world champions Italy, appropriately enough at Highbury, in November 1934, a record for a Football League club: (left to right) Wilf Copping, Ray Bowden, George Male, Frank Moss, Ted Drake, Eddie Hapgood and Cliff Bastin.

Press Association

All the skill in the world amounts to little unless you have the fitness to make it work.

So each week *Football Handbook* will include simple exercises you can perform in your own bedroom. Choose your exercises according to your age and spend two to three minutes on them daily . . . improved fitness can only make you a better player!

10-12 E

10-12 AGE GROUP
A. Lie on back with legs raised, hands under hips. Slow leg 'cycles', building up speed. Maximum 1 minute.
B. Lie on your front, grasping ankles behind back. Rock backwards and forwards *gently*. Maximum 15 seconds.
C. Sit up, legs wide astride, back straight. Clasp hands behind neck. Reach down and touch left knee with head. Up, then right knee. Do 5 to each knee.
D. Sit up, take body-weight on hands placed on floor a few inches behind seat. Raise legs a few inches, then lower. Raise astride, then lower. Maximum 10 times.
E. Raise arms to shoulder level. Small backward circles with arms and hands. Maximum 1 minute.

13-14 AGE GROUP
A. Assume press-up position. Keeping back straight, do eight press-ups, rest for 10 seconds, repeat.
B. Lie on your back, hands behind neck. Sit up, bringing head to knees, hooking feet under something to keep them down. Repeat 10 times.
C. Stand with legs astride, arms bent across chest. Fling arms backwards taking deep breaths. Repeat 10 times.
D. Step up and down on a box or step. Repeat 30 times.
E. Lie face down, arms along side. Raise head, shoulders, and legs as high as possible. Repeat 10 times.

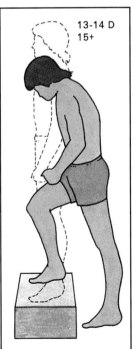

13-14 D
15+

15+ AGE GROUP
A. Stand with arms bent across chest. Fling arms backwards, and upwards strongly, taking deep breaths. Repeat 20 times.
B. Stand legs astride, trunk bending forward to touch outside of foot, head to knees. Repeat 20 times.
C. Assume press-up position. Keeping back straight and head up, do 10 press-ups, rest for 10 seconds, repeat *twice*.
D. Lie on your front, hands placed behind neck. Arch back, combined with rocking movement. Repeat 10 times.
E. Step up and down on to a box or step. Repeat 20 times.
F. Assume press-up position, legs astride. Do 'squat thrusts' with legs: knees up to body, and back. Repeat 20 times, developing a rhythm.

A KICK in THE GRASS

NASL/George Tiedemann

'Before long an American club will suddenly turn up at Chelsea with a fistful of dollars and simply say—"Now let's have Ray Wilkins" ... and there won't be much anyone will be able to do about it.' Memphis Rogues' coach EDDIE MCCREADIE

Soccer is ... 'a kick in the grass' says the Rowdies' slogan, now a national catch-phrase. Cheerleaders (above, at Tampa Bay) and electronic scoreboards (below) are just two of the differences in soccer American style. But all the changes aim at giving non-stop entertainment.

Fort Lauderdale coach Ron Newman called it 'the land of opportunity'; Italian international Gianni Rivera called it 'an elephant's graveyard'.

America provokes a variety of responses from the rest of the footballing world. There's delight: that soccer is now catching on in one of the few countries never to take to the game. There's greed: as the world's players wonder if they can earn quick bucks in their summer holidays. And there's ridicule: at American attempts to popularise the game with unrelated entertainment and gimmicks. Mostly, though,

Colorsport

NASL/George Tiedemann

Sporting Pictures JK

What's up, doc? The New York Cosmos have Bugs Bunny on their side, thanks to Warner Communications, who own the team and make the cartoons that feature the well-known carrot cruncher. Other club owners include tea manufacturers and rock stars.

American fans can take their support for their new sport to extremes . . . it can even go to their heads.

soccer in the States has the football world worried sick.

The money available to a handful of North American Soccer League (NASL) clubs is threatening to lure away our best players. And now that the soccer bandwagon has finally started to roll in the States, it seems likely that other clubs will soon match the deals offered by the super-rich New York Cosmos and Philadelphia Fury.

Cosmos' coach Eddie Firmani has warned that he has the money available to buy the whole England squad, 'if I wanted'.

He already has Franz Beckenbauer. The former West German captain was wanted by Helmut Schoen for his World Cup squad, but the Cosmos were not prepared to release him for West Germany's warm-up matches.

Now they have their eyes on Johan Cruyff. The Dutch superstar has stated that he has no wish to play in America, but, according to Cosmos' president Ahmet Ertegun, 'Cruyff's attitude is softening'. A big enough offer from the New Jersey club could see him in a Cosmos uniform by

For a few dollars more . . .
Some people suspect that British players joining US clubs are opting for big money and the easy life. The money's good, all right, but the life isn't that easy. The American thirst for success means really tough training. Says Len Cantello, summering with Dallas Tornado: 'The training's tougher than at West Brom—and we practise and play in temperatures into the mid-90s. And we have to play 30 games before we get to the play-offs.' Matches can last up to 105 minutes if the teams are level, and players are also expected to undertake demanding schedules *off* the field. A typical day for Rowdies idol Rodney Marsh involves his regular radio show, training, opening a new restaurant at lunchtime, coaching local kids after lunch and then going to an evening function. All as part of the job . . . to help promote his club and the game of soccer.

The land of opportunity
Soccer can already supply its own example of the great American success story. Ron Newman, NASL Coach of the Year for his championship with Fort Lauderdale last season, first went to the States to play for Atlanta Chiefs (now disbanded) in 1967. A veteran winger who had spent most of the previous season in Gillingham's reserves, he later took over as coach of the Dallas Tornado, then in danger of becoming the laughing stock of the League after a season when they won only two games . . . but in 1971 he led them to their only championship success.

NASL/George Tiedemann

BELOW *It was Pele, more than anyone else, who attracted the American public to soccer. He was the game's first and possibly only superstar, a player known to all whatever their level of interest. Here he salutes the crowd before his last match in October, an emotional night when Cosmos played Santos, the club he joined as a skinny kid 22 years ago.*

next summer, joining several players signed in the World Cup.

And American clubs are having an increasing influence on our Football League. Trevor Francis, on loan to the Detroit Express, could miss the start of this season at Birmingham. Three Charlton players, including England 'B' international Mike Flanagan and winger Colin Powell, jetted out to play for the New England Tea Men before the conclusion of last season. For some days it looked as though their absence could have a considerable influence on the relegation struggle in Division 2, with both Charlton and Cardiff City threatened by the drop—a prospect they might never have had to consider if the players had stayed at home.

Poaching the top players

When Fulham captain Ray Evans was loaned out to the California Surf, Cardiff manager Jimmy Andrews could contain himself no longer.

'This is further evidence of how the Americans are deciding who goes down to the Third Division,' he claimed. 'It's wicked that these loan transfers should be allowed during the most important part of our season.'

What worries European observers more, however, is the prospect that North American clubs could soon be helping themselves to our top players—not Second Division players on loan, but international stars permanently. Franz Beckenbauer, Dennis Tueart and the Cosmos' Yugoslav, Vladislav Bogicevic, could be the first of a flood.

The Cosmos' big money investments have certainly paid off. Pele and Beckenbauer led them to the championship last year, and the club averaged over 48,000 fans for their home games this season. But it's not just the star players that are attracting increasing numbers of gum-chewing

LEFT *Soccer is in direct competition with baseball for American fans. In Minneapolis the two sports share the same stadium—and the local Kicks play on a field that is part grass, part dirt.*

RIGHT *The Rose Bowl has a capacity of 106,000, but the Los Angeles Aztecs are having trouble filling it, even when George Best played. Best has now moved across country to Fort Lauderdale.*

Sporting Pictures UK

citizens to North American Soccer League games.

The American sports fan expects more for his money. He expects comfortable seats, clean, uncrowded facilities and entertainment for all the family: including short-skirted cheerleaders, autographed footballs and instant replays on flashing electronic scoreboards. Even if his team loses, he can leave the stadium feeling that at least someone was trying hard to entertain him.

If you think that British soccer could learn from this approach, then you would disagree with a great number of our soccer reporters who have been over there. The commercialisation has disturbed them and the running commentary and the scoreboard flashing '*Goal!*', '*Charge!*' and '*Did you see that?*' have come in for criticism; they are described as 'distracting', 'irritating' and 'an insult to the intelligence'.

But they work. The average attendance at last year's NASL games was 14,670. Although this is only just over half the average for the First Division in England, it represents a great improvement over 1971, when the average was only 3,850 per game.

'An offer I couldn't refuse'

And the growth of interest in the NASL has attracted the big money investors to the game. That's how a new club like Philadelphia Fury—owned by English rock stars like Mick Jagger, Peter Frampton and Rick Wakeman—can afford to spend four million dollars putting a team together. That's how a new club like Detroit Express can afford to pay Trevor Francis £50,000 for just over three month's work. That's how a new club like New England Tea Men can make Noel Cantwell 'an offer I couldn't refuse. And the taxes are superb . . .'

There lies British soccer's central problem. If our clubs try to match the salaries certain American and European clubs can offer, then our top players and managers will have to think seriously about becoming tax exiles. If they don't, then our top talent will leave anyway.

And an increasing number will be leaving for 'the land of opportunity'.

Teething troubles
National professional football in the States began with high hopes, but little success, in 1967. 'I was left,' recalls London journalist Brian Glanville, 'with a memory of much dull football, tiny attendances, violent play, weak refereeing, political bickering, impossible heat and curious errors of policy.'

In New York, the most knowledgeable fans in the country were given the choice between watching either 'a team as dull as Cerro (a Uruguayan team imported for a short summer season) or as disorganised as the unhappy Generals.' The New York Generals were a side staffed largely by Third Division players and veteran Argentinians.

Then there was the confusion of a rival league. The United Soccer Association imported 12 club teams from all over Europe and South America and renamed them for the occasion. Wolves became the Los Angeles Wolves, Hibernian became Toronto City and Sunderland were stuck with the label of Vancouver Royal Canadians. Attendances were slightly better than in the other league and the final game was a bonanza, with Wolves beating Aberdeen (or the Washington Whips as they were known) 6-5.

FOOTBALL HANDBOOK BOOTS TEST

Football is the name of the game, so what you wear on your feet is all important. *Football Handbook* **takes a close look at some of the most popular boots on the market and makes its own recommendations . . .**

Buying boots is like buying any other commodity—generally speaking, you get what you pay for. Quality costs, but if you've got the cash to pay for the best, do it.

Dr John Williams, a specialist in sports injuries, pointed out to *Football Handbook* that badly made or ill-fitting boots can not only ruin performance, but also cause injury. He explained that the sole forms the contact between pitch and foot; movements in the foot that give balance and control are passed through the sole to the pitch, and if the sole is rigid this will not happen. So make sure the boot is flexible in *all* directions when buying.

As far as size goes it's important to get the width right—even if the boot is a little long. The uppers should be supple and strong.

Studs should be the type for the ground you are playing on. This is where screw-in studs score: the alternative is two pairs.

None of this, however, stops you looking around for decent boots at a reasonable price.

Adidas and Puma have led the field for years and earned a reputation for high-class boots, and certainly anyone who buys a pair in their upper price range—like the Adidas '2000' at £22.95—knows he's got boots that can't be bettered.

But that hasn't stopped other firms, notably Gola and Mitre, competing with some success for the market. And a striker could argue that he scores hat-tricks as regularly with Gola 'Speedster' (£7.49-£8.49) as someone with Puma 'Inter' (£11.95).

Boots supplied by Hawkinsport

FOOTBALL HANDBOOK VERDICT

For the player who is determined to get the best boots to suit his needs and his pocket, the variety available (a typical selection is shown above) can lead to confusion. Now, Football Handbook *has examined many popular makes, and recommends 'best buys' in cheap, medium and expensive price ranges. They are (top to bottom in the picture below): the Adidas '2000' at £22.95, leaders in the all-weather screw-in league. Cheaper, but similar, is the Puma 'Meister' (not shown). In the middle range we chose the Mitre 'Milan', a classy boot with unusual trimmings—£11.95, size 6 and upwards only. For the younger player an ideal choice is the Adidas 'Kid'—at £5.99 (5½ and under) or £6.99 (6 and over), it's very good value indeed.*

Michael Edwards

Care for your boots
1. Loosen laces properly to remove boots.
2. Clean boots after each match, remove all dirt with a soft brush, wipe with damp cloth.
3. Never use oil or detergents on boots.
4. Stuff boots with newspaper to hold shape.
5. Never dry boots by applying heat. Ideal drying takes place at room temperature.
6. Apply polish or Kiwi Wet-prufe when dry.
7. Grease screw-in studs to stop rusting.
8. Never mix different types of studs.
9. Never play with broken studs.

RISING STAR STAN CUMMINS

One of the few highlights of a dismal football year in the North-East was the way a lad called Stan Cummins burst upon the local soccer scene.

Last November Middlesbrough were languishing dangerously near the bottom of the First Division. In spite of the arrival from Wrexham of Billy Ashcroft, the team were still short of goals. And the side seemed certain to lose its star midfielder—Scottish international Graeme Souness, who was eventually sold to Liverpool for £352,000.

New manager John Neal came up with the solution. Dropping David Mills back into midfield, he introduced a pint-sized 19-year-old flyer to his front line. Stan Cummins justified Neal's faith immediately, scoring the goal that gave Middlesbrough a shock 1-0 win at Aston Villa on 12 November.

It wasn't quite Durham-born Cummins'

Cummins is hardly built like a typical target player, but his form last season suggests that he soon could be numbered among the top strikers in the League. Manchester City's Paul Power had a good first-hand look at his speed and control in a League game at Maine Road last season, when Cummins again proved a handful for the defence.

> **'What a ridiculous tag for the kid to live up to. It isn't fair on the lad and it doesn't help him. He should be left alone to develop naturally.'**
>
> Middlesbrough boss JOHN NEAL

Club	Season	League		FA Cup	
		Mtchs	Gls	Mtchs	Gls
Middlesbrough	1976-77	2	–	–	–
	1977-78	25	6	5	1
		27	6	5	1

first game for the senior team. He had made his League debut as an apprentice pro on a less happy occasion the year before, when Boro lost 2-0 at home to Ipswich. And to complete Stan's misery he was substituted by David Mills.

But the youngster had already attracted some attention. First for his size, which, at 5' 3½" and 9½ stone, was very small for a professional footballer; and secondly for a claim that Jack Charlton made about him, which was very big for anyone.

'He'll be the first million-pound footballer in Britain.' That was what Charlton, the man who first picked Stan for the first team, predicted for Cummins. It was a prediction that did not please Charlton's successor John Neal at all.

'What a ridiculous tag for the kid to live up to,' he said. 'It makes me shudder. It isn't fair on the lad and it doesn't help him at all. He should be left alone to develop naturally.'

The tag may have proved to be a handicap to Cummins, but so far his size has not. He may lack size, but he does have speed, vision, tactical awareness and an instinct for goals that put him second equal among Middlesbrough's League scorers last season.

And he has an honesty that most people will find refreshing.

'At my size,' he says, 'it would be easy to play-act, making every tackle from a big defender look far worse than it is. I could kid on the ref that I'd been badly injured, even when a foul hadn't been committed.

'But I don't want to be labelled a cheat. Even when I've been fouled I try to get off the deck as quickly as possible. I never try to feign injury.'

Stan, then a Sunderland supporter, was first spotted by Middlesbrough as an 11-year-

old. He signed associate schoolboy forms for them as a 14-year-old in June 1973 before making it on to the full-time staff at the end of 1976.

'I tried a few other clubs, but none of them came up to Boro,' he recalls. 'Chelsea was one, but I didn't like the set-up there. They treated me great at Ayresome Park and I liked everyone at the club.'

Cummins spent part of the summer of '77 playing in North America with the Minnesota Kicks, but this year did not return.

'The manager won't let me go—and that's fine with me. It'll do me a lot more good to stay at home.'

But watch out this season when a thoroughly rested Stan Cummins once again takes on those big First Division defenders.

Cummins being closely marked by QPR's England international Ian Gillard, who at 5' 11" has a clear seven-inch height advantage over the young forward.

Syndication International

27

Test your football knowledge and...
WIN THE TRACKSUIT TREVOR BROOKING WEARS!

20 Super Impala tracksuits to be won from

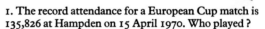

Gola

in this week's great
FREE ENTRY quiz

1. The record attendance for a European Cup match is 135,826 at Hampden on 15 April 1970. Who played?

2. Which goalkeeper did not captain his country in the World Cup: Emerson Leao, Sepp Maier, Dino Zoff?

3. Match the player to the club: (1) Rodney Marsh, (2) Mike England, (3) Dennis Tueart, (4) George Best, (5) Peter Osgood; (a) Seattle Sounders, (b) Philadelphia Fury, (c) Fort Lauderdale Strikers, (d) New York Cosmos, (e) Tampa Bay Rowdies.

4. His team took off well in Argentina but failed to make the final. Name the manager (*below*).

5. When was a penalty last awarded in an FA Cup final: 1954, 1962, 1970 or 1974?

6. Which present Fourth Division club has won 3 League Championships?

7. Which one of these men never won a full England cap: Jack Charlton, Brian Clough, Ron Greenwood, Joe Mercer, Gordon Milne, Alf Ramsey, Don Revie?

Bob Thomas

Colorsport

8. A despairing leg fails to stop the ball going in the net. Name the teams, the year, the venue and the score.

HOW TO ENTER
List your answers to the questions on a postcard, add your name and address, cut the 'Part 1' flash from the cover and attach it to the postcard (entries that do not bear the flash will be ineligible), then mail to: Football Handbook, 600A Commercial Road, London E14 7HS. Entries must arrive by September 11, 1978, the closing date. The senders of the first 20 correct answers scrutinised after that date will each be awarded a GOLA SUPER IMPALA TRACKSUIT like the one Trevor Brooking is wearing in the picture. Please specify the colour and chest size of the tracksuit you'd like, if a winner. *Colours:* Royal blue/white, red/white, sky blue/navy blue, white/navy blue. *Sizes:* 24″, 26/28″, 30/32″, 36″, 38″. The Editor's decision on all matters relating to the competition is final and binding. All winners will be notified as soon as possible and a full list of prize winners to date will be available from *Football Handbook* on request.

John Gidman

'This could be the greatest year of my career. I feel that Villa are poised to go out and win honours and I hope to be part of the England set-up which will win through to the final stages of the European Championship next summer.'

Those bold words come from John Gidman, and are backed up by some fine displays last season. Gidman got the taste for European football when Villa reached the last eight of the UEFA Cup before losing to Barcelona.

'Playing in Europe is a marvellous experience,' John told *Handbook*. 'The atmosphere is tremendous. Villa must make a bid to get back into that class of the game.

'And I reckon we can. Last season we lost Alex Cropley, Andy Gray and Tommy Craig for long spells, and I was out injured too. If we steer clear of that sort of bad luck we'll be up there challenging for the Championship.'

John's tough break came at the end of the season when he was ordered to rest a niggling groin injury and miss the England 'B' squad summer tour.

He explains: 'I was really disappointed about that. I think that England are on the brink of great things, and it was a chance to stake my claim for a regular place in the full side. But I can have a good season with Villa—and I'm hoping international honours will follow.'

Once a free transfer from Liverpool, John Gidman is now looking to add to the England cap he won in 1977.

ABOVE *The sight the fans love—John on a surging run down the right flank. His adventurous play makes him one of the most exciting full-backs in Europe.*

LEFT *John is training hard to shake off the groin injury which made him miss the England 'B' tour.*

Dave Watson on power heading

'When you're in the last ten minutes of a big match and the other team is pressing for an equaliser, a firm header out of defence is a real life-saver.' DAVE WATSON

Colorsport

A string of great displays has made the England centre-half shirt Dave Watson's personal property.

And if you had to pick one quality which makes the Manchester City star stand out above the rest, it would have to be his exceptional power in the air.

Dave is not the biggest man in the world, but he has all the qualities to be a great header of the ball . . . timing, agility and determination.

It's not always defensive, either. Dave is always a danger when he goes up for set pieces.

And who will forget that amazing 40-yard header that led to England's first goal in the 4-1 win against Hungary at Wembley in May?

But before you even think about headers like that one, you've got to master the basics of a good technique.

Dave explains: 'It's important to avoid the temptation to close your eyes when you head the ball. You're more likely to hurt yourself and get headaches if you close them because the ball could hit you higher on the head or on the nose.'

So first, says Dave, you should just practise simple, standing headers with the ball lobbed to you.

'Concentrate on heading the ball squarely on the forehead—as with most skills it's a question of getting to know the feel of the ball.

'When you're confident of heading consistently well from a standing position, move on to the header on the run—the one that matters most in matches.'

'Don't get caught standing' is the order to professionals when it comes to heading—in defence or attack.

That's because the player who moves to head the ball will always have an advantage over the one who stands. His momentum means that he'll get height and power.

Timing will almost certainly prove the biggest problem for young players who practise headers on the run.

There has to be great co-ordination between the legs, arms, shoulders and neck—as Dave demonstrates on the following pages.

At first you'll probably find yourself coming down to the ground as the ball is still rising in the air!

But don't worry about it. The more difficult the skill the more you have to practice —a simple but golden rule essential for success.

The two-finger test . . . Dave says: 'Head it here and it won't hurt.'

Dave shows exactly where the forehead is supposed to strike the ball.

Ray Green

Ray Green

Dave prepares for take off, his eyes on the ball and his body leaning forward ready to gain maximum height.

Just before impact, Dave arches his back for maximum power, using his arms for height and balance.

If you're on your own, throw the ball against a wall and follow up to head the rebound. 'Head upwards,' says Graham Taylor, 'because the object is to get distance.'

'Head tennis for two or four is a useful way to practise power heading. You can use a goal in the local park if possible. The important thing is to set a mark which the ball must cross, so

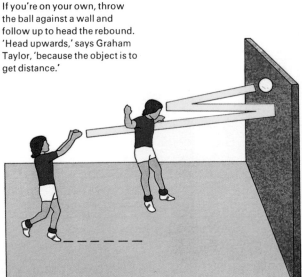

From the front you can see how Dave's shoulders, neck and arms all combine for power—eyes still fixed on the ball.

Perfect landing . . . Dave curls his body to cushion his return to the ground and sees the ball cleared into the distance.

that you have to head a good distance. If you make it competitive, the practice will be that much more enjoyable— and if you enjoy it you're more likely to keep at it and improve.'

'Three players can take turns as piggy in the middle, throwing the ball to the players on the outside and then attempting to catch the ball as they try to head it back over his head.'

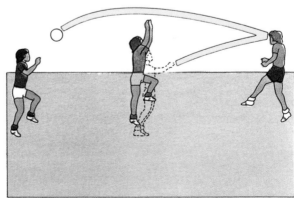

A Matter of Fact

The oldest player to appear in the Football League was Neil McBain, who played in goal for New Brighton against Hartlepool in Division 3(N) on 15 March 1947. He was then aged 52 years and 4 months.

Real Madrid were unbeaten at home for more than 8 years, from February 1957 to March 1965. In that time, they won 114 and drew 8 games—and won the European Cup 4 times.

During the game against Malta at Wembley on 12 May 1971 England keeper Gordon Banks not once received the ball direct from a Maltese player, and the ball not once crossed the English goal-line.

The World Cup in Argentina produced 102 goals, an average of 2.64 per game. Though slightly better than 1974, it is still the second lowest average of all time.

When Chelsea manager Ken Shellito signed keeper Bob Iles from Southern League side Weymouth for £10,000 in June, it was the first time in three years the London club had paid out a transfer fee.

Scotland's 3–2 win over Holland in Argentina was only their second in 11 matches in the World Cup finals. They didn't record a victory in 1954 or 1958, and the only other win was over Zaire (2–0) in West Germany in 1974.

Year	Games	Goals	Ave.
1930	18	70	3.89
1934	17	70	4.12
1938	18	84	4.67
1950	22	88	4.00
1954	26	140	5.38
1958	35	126	3.60
1962	32	89	2.78
1966	32	89	2.78
1970	32	95	2.97
1974	38	97	2.55
1978	38	102	2.64

Syndication International

Kenny Burns with the 'Footballer of the Year' trophy at the Football Writers' Association dinner in May. Kenny is the first Forest player to win the award in its 30-year history.

The smallest ever attendance at a Football League game was recorded at Old Trafford. Just 13 people saw a Second Division match there between Stockport County and Leicester City on 7 May 1921. Stockport were banned from playing on their own ground at the time.

Joe Craig of Celtic managed to score a goal for his country without ever having kicked a ball for them. Coming on as substitute in the friendly against Sweden at Hampden Park last year, he dived full length to head home a cross with his first touch.

Roy Clarke, the former Manchester City winger, played in three divisions in consecutive League games. Roy appeared for the new Third Division Champions Cardiff City in the last-but-one week of the 1946-47 season; he was then transferred to Manchester City in time to figure in the last match of their promotion-winning season from Division 2; his next game was for City the following August—in the First Division!

Glasgow Rangers won every single game they played in the Scottish League in 1898-99, the only time a British club has finished the season with a 100% record. The Scottish First Division of the time had 10 clubs and Rangers played only 18 games.

Ground: Capacity 60,500; Playing area 106 x 69.5 m
Record attendance: 76,962 Wolves v Grimsby T., FA Cup, 25.3.39
Record victory: 10–0 v Anderlecht, European Cup Prel. rd., 10.9.56
Record defeat: 0–7 v Aston Villa, Div. 1, 27.12.30
Most League points: 64, Div. 1, 1956-57
Most League goals: 103, Div. 1, 1956-57 & 1958-59
League scoring record: 32, Dennis Viollet, 1959-60
Record League aggregate: 198, Bobby Charlton, 1956-73
Most League appearances: 606, Bobby Charlton, 1956-73
Most capped player: 106, Bobby Charlton, England, 1958-70
League career: 1892 Elected to Div. 1; 1894-06 Div. 2; 1906-22
Div. 1; 1922-25 Div. 2; 1925-31 Div. 1; 1931-36 Div. 2; 1936-37
Div. 1; 1937-38 Div. 2; 1938-74 Div. 1; 1974-75 Div. 2; 1975-Div. 1
Honours: European Cup Winners 1968; Div. 1 Champions 1908,
1911, 1952, 1956, 1957, 1965, 1967; FA Cup Winners 1909, 1948,
1963, 1977; Div. 2 Champions 1936, 1975

Manchester United

Gordon McQueen and Bob Latchford, representing nearly a million pounds worth of talent, clash at Old Trafford. McQueen became Britain's most expensive footballer ever when he joined United in February for £495,000.

When Bobby Charlton curled a right-foot shot into the top corner of the Benfica net, the final flourish of Manchester United's extra time destruction of the Portuguese champions, it gave millions of people all over the world cause to rejoice. United had clinched the European Cup.

But there was a lot more to it than that. Ten years before, the United team that was the outstanding club side of its era had been destroyed by a plane crash at Munich airport. The heart of a team that promised to be one of the greatest

Ray Green

Matt Busby, a Scottish international wing-half with Manchester City before the war, was United's manager throughout their best years, from 1946 to 1969. He was later knighted and appointed to the board of directors.

Ray Green

Red-shirted railwaymen
United were founded as Newton Heath Lancashire and Yorkshire Railway in 1878, shortened the name to Newton Heath in 1885.

Bombed out
For three seasons after the war United played all their home games at Maine Road while bomb damage at Old Trafford was re-paired. But they still man-aged to finish as runners-up in the League in four out of the first five post-war seasons.

Bobby Charlton, football's greatest ambassador, started as a winger with the 'Busby Babes', developing into a classical midfield general with a stunning shot, an inspiration in England's World Cup winning side.

the world has seen was ripped out.

The Wembley crowd roaring its joy at United's triumph were both paying tribute to those dead 'Busby Babes' and celebrating the triumph of the survivors—the men who had come through the wreck, formed the basis of the rebuilt team, then nursed it back to health and greatness.

Men like Bobby Charlton, who scored two of the goals in that 4–1 win; like Bill Foulkes, the centre-half who had played in all of Manchester United's European Cup campaigns; like Matt Busby, manager for 23 years, who had spent a harrowing nine weeks in a Munich hospital bed, immobilised and for some days close to death.

The greatness of Manchester United—and consequently their massive popularity—is largely a result of Matt Busby's vision and ability. It was his belief in attacking football that gave the team its style . . . his judgement that took players like Tommy Taylor, Denis Law and Pat Crerand to the club . . . his far-sightedness that brought youngsters like Duncan Edwards and George Best to Old Trafford and gave them an early chance in the first team.

His great ambition finally fulfilled, Busby, soon to become Sir Matt, resigned as manager. He stayed on at United, first as general manager, then as a director. His presence, though, proved unsettling to his successors, faced with the task of

Ray Green

36

Ray Green

Colorsport

LEFT *Denis Law and George Best, extravagantly skilled artists of United's great sides of the 1960s, both became European Footballer of the Year. Law's career embraced 55 Scotland caps and spells with Huddersfield, Manchester City, Torino and United. Best won 31 caps for Northern Ireland, but his frequent and well-publicised exploits off the field eventually wrecked his career. He now plays in America.*

filling the great man's shoes while he was still around to step back into them. Neither Wilf McGuiness nor Frank O'Farrell lasted very long and Tommy Docherty's reign began disastrously. United's problems had been allowed to grow until they threatened to swamp the club.

First of all, the playing careers of Denis Law and Bobby Charlton were drawing to a close and both McGuiness and O'Farrell were faced with the task of replacing the irreplaceable. The club seemed to be constantly in a turmoil over what to do about George Best, who allowed the excesses of his private life to destroy his concentration, fitness and finally his genius.

It seemed as though all United's problems came to a head in the 1973–74 season. Charlton had left to manage Preston; Law had moved across the city to Maine Road on a free transfer; Ian Storey-Moore, an expensive singing from Nottingham Forest only the season before, was forced out of the game by a persistent ankle injury; Best flitted back for 12 undistinguished mid-season games.

Finally, in the last home game of that season, United's relegation was sealed by a goal from Denis Law, of all players, and a large number of their young fans immediately disgraced themselves. Invading the pitch, they succeeded in their futile intention of having the game abandoned.

United spent only one season in the Second Division, emerging as impressive champions. The team contained only one major new signing, but was unrecognisable from the squad that had struggled so desperately the season before. Under Docherty they had found a rhythm—a feverishly fast rhythm that left opponents often breathless,

Tommy Docherty's career with United peaked with the Cup win of 1977, but he was soon to leave the club in dubious circumstances. Stuart Pearson, coach Tommy Cavanagh, Docherty, Lou Macari and Gordon Hill show off the Cup at Wembley.

Hill fails his exams
Gordon Hill went to Derby complaining that 'you need an O-level or a degree to understand tactics at Old Trafford', and claiming that he had 'become a scapegoat for the club's lack of success'. 'I've been accused of not doing my share of the work, but I've got 20 goals,' he said. 'They can't have their cake and eat it.'

Sexton disagreed. 'Ask any player whether they would rather attack or retrieve and they would all prefer to attack,' he said. 'But the retrieving has to be done and everyone has to do it.'

usually beaten. Stuart Pearson, the new signing, fitted in well with the new mode of play. Quick, deft and strong, he topped United's scorers with 17 League goals.

The style proved almost as successful in the First Division. United led the League into February of 1976, finishing in third place, and also reached the final of the FA.Cup, where they lost disappointingly to Southampton.

Like Busby, Docherty was not scared to make changes in a successful team. Steve Coppell had been signed from Tranmere for a bargain £40,000 during their promotion season and he was later joined by Gordon Hill from Millwall and Jimmy Greenhoff from Stoke. Together with Pearson, they formed the attack that revived memories of the great sides of the past. United scored exactly 100 goals in League, League Cup and Cup games in 1976-77 and reached the Cup final for the second successive season.

This time they won: Liverpool's great dream of the treble—League, Cup and European Cup—was destroyed.

The Doc's joy was short-lived. At the height of his success and popularity with the fans, he was sacked for reasons that have little to do with football. His successor at United turned out to be the same man who followed him

Popperfoto

Popperfoto

Tragedy at Munich
On 6 February 1958 a British European Airways aircraft crashed on its third attempt to take off from Munich airport, ending the lives of 23 of the 44 people aboard. On board was the Manchester United team that had just won through to the semi-finals of the European Cup. Eight of that team died; two were never to play again.

Among the dead were Tommy Taylor, Duncan Edwards and Roger Byrne, three of the players that had made England one of the favourites to win the World Cup that summer.

United line-up 10 months before Munich. *Left to right, back row:* trainer Tom Curry, Duncan Edwards, Mark Jones (all died), Ray Wood, Bobby Charlton, Bill Foulkes, manager Matt Busby (all survived). *Front row:* John Berry (never played again), Bill Whelan, Roger Byrne, David Pegg, Eddie Colman (all died).

The survivors formed the basis of the side that astonishingly took United to the Cup Final. Matt Busby, after ten weeks in a Munich hospital bed, returned to England in time to see his new side lose 2–0 to Bolton.

Dave Sexton, quiet spoken and modest, with a formidable reputation as a tactician, had a difficult first season as United manager, facing mounting criticism of his methods. But the former West Ham wing-half has an excellent managerial record, including FA Cup and European successes with Chelsea.

into the manager's tracksuit at Chelsea—Dave Sexton.

Sexton's reputation as a coach and tactician was formidable, but United started the season poorly, and showed no improvement when he bought £495,000 Gordon McQueen and £350,000 Joe Jordan. The new signings provoked some controversy among the fans. Jordan, in particular, was the subject of much argument among supporters. Those who liked his style of play reckoned he was the most complete centre-forward to play for the club since Tommy Taylor in the middle 1950s. Others pointed to Jordan's poor disciplinary record, the surprisingly small number of goals he scores—and the fact that United already had England's centre-forward on their books.

Dave Sexton is under pressure. Manchester United are used to success. Their fans expect it. Sexton has had other problems—finding a replacement for Alex Stepney, for instance—besides coming across resistance to his ideas, but he must solve them soon . . . and solve them brilliantly.

Sexton's most controversial signing was the big Leeds and Scotland centre-forward Joe Jordan. Arriving in January for £350,000, Jordan took some time to settle in a team already well equipped with top-class forwards.

For genuine supporters the fencing around Old Trafford must seem like an ugly scar on an unhealed wound.

The exercises featured in Part 1 were a basis to start you off. The course will gradually get harder, but try not to ease up. Extra effort can only mean better results.

10-12A

UNDER-12 AGE GROUP
A. Warm up with upside-down cycling. Max. 30 secs.
B. Stand with legs astride and raise arms to shoulder level. Turn body to face backwards. Start gently, and build up to maximum effort. Repeat 10 times.
C. Lie on your front, grasping ankles behind your back. Rock gently back and forth. Max. 30 secs.
D. Sit up, legs straight, hands behind neck. Raise legs a few inches, then lower. Repeat 10 times.
E. Do 5 press-ups. Rest for 10 seconds. Repeat twice.

13-14 AGE GROUP
A. Standing astride, arms above your head, reach down to touch the floor between your feet, then to the side of each foot. 1, 2, 3, up. Repeat 10 times.
B. Lie face down, arms by your side. Raise head, shoulders, and legs as high as you can. Repeat 10 times.
C. Sit up, arms raised to shoulder level. Keeping head up, lift legs, then lower. Repeat 10 times.
D. Assume press-up position. Move legs apart, then together, up to body, and back. Repeat 10 times with a 'bounce'.
E. Standing, raise knee to chest, then relax. Shake arms and shoulders loosely.

15 & OVER AGE GROUP
A. Warm up with upside-down cycling. Max. 30 secs.
B. Assume press-up position. Move legs apart, then together, up to body, and back. Repeat 10 times with a 'bounce'
C. Lie on your back, legs straight. Raise right leg, then drop it across body and reach for right foot with left hand. Repeat 10 times, alternating legs.
D. Lie on your front, hands clasped behind neck. Raise head and feet as high as possible. Repeat 10 times.
E. Sprint on the spot for 5 seconds, then drop to crouch, spring up, then run again. Repeat 10 times.

15+

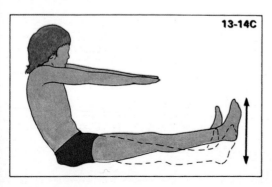

13-14C

The NASL is aiming at 'big league' status—and that means bigger attendances, bigger money and bigger names.

SOCCER CITIES USA

AMERICAN CONFERENCE WESTERN DIVISION

San Diego Sockers, the most travelled club in the league—they were originally known as the Baltimore Comets, then as San Diego Jaws, then Las Vegas Quicksilvers—produced the biggest surprise of the season when they opened up a big lead in this division. British players include Ade Coker (West Ham)

Oakland Stompers went short of goals this season. Alec Lindsay, the former Liverpool and England full-back, is one of their players.

San Jose Earthquakes have built up a large and enthusiastic following, but they started the season disappointingly. Paul Child, ex-Villa reserve, has been their major scoring threat since they were formed five years ago.

California Surf is the most American team in the league, though coach John Sewell, the former Palace defender, can also call on experienced pros like Ray Evans (Fulham), Peter Wall (Palace), John Jackson(Orient), Malcolm Lord (Hull).

NATIONAL CONFERENCE CENTRAL DIVISION

Colorado Caribous have former Northern Ireland manager Dave Clements as player-coach.

Dallas Tornado, champions in 1971, are the oldest surviving club in the 10-year history of the NASL. Players include Len Cantello (WBA), Jim Ryan (Norwich) and Jeff Bourne (Palace).

Tulsa Roughnecks, a new club, have British players like Jim Redfern (Chester), Colin Boulton (Derby), Doug Collins and Colin Waldron (Burnley).

NASL

Pat McMahon, once of Villa, trendsetting with the Caribous.

Minnesota Kicks have done well again this season. Former Birmingham manager Freddie Goodwin could field an all-English XI if he wanted. For instance: Geoff Barnett (Arsenal); Ron Webster (Derby), Steve Litt (Luton), Alan Merrick (WBA), Tony Want (Birmingham); Mike Bailey (Wolves), Chico Hamilton (Sheffield U.), Alan West; Ron Futcher (Luton), Alan Willey (Middlesbrough) and Charlie George (Derby County). Scottish international winger Willie Morgan also plays.

NATIONAL CONFERENCE WESTERN DIVISION

Los Angeles Aztecs started the season with six internationals and finished with a lot of problems. George Best walked out and the coach was sacked, leaving Tommy Smith, veteran of Liverpool and England, in charge.

Portland Timbers chose Don Megson, former manager of Bristol Rovers, as the coach to put them back on top . . . and he succeeded with help from Jimmy Conway (Manchester City), Clyde Best (West Ham) and Graham Day (Bristol Rovers).

Seattle Sounders reached the Soccerbowl final last year with a team of exiles from the English south coast. Jimmy Gabriel is still the coach, and Mike England and Jimmy Robertson (both ex-Spurs) play on.

Vancouver Whitecaps, coached by former Plymouth manager Tony Waiters, made a good start to the season. On the staff are Phil Parkes (Wolves), Kevin Hector (Derby), Mick Lambert (Ipswich), Jon Sammels and Steve Kember (Leicester).

NORTH AMERICAN SOCCER LEAGUE

NASL

1968	Atlanta Chiefs
1969	Kansas City Spurs
1970	Rochester Lancers
1971	Dallas Tornado
1972	New York Cosmos
1973	Philadelphia Atoms
1974	Los Angeles Aztecs
1975	Tampa Bay Rowdies
1976	Toronto Metros
1977	New York Cosmos

MINNESOTA Kicks

SEATTLE SOUNDERS

VANCOUVER WHITECAPS

PORTLAND TIMBERS

Vancouver Whitecaps

Seattle Sounders

Portland Timbers

Oakland Stompers

Los Angeles Aztecs
California Surf

San Jose Earthquakes

Colorado Caribous

San Diego Sockers

OAKLAND Stompers

CALIFORNIA SURF

HURRICAN

EARTHQUAKES SAN JOSE

L.A. AZTECS

SAN DIEGO SOCKERS

the Caribous of Colorado

CHICAGO STING

DETROIT EXPRESS

NEW ENGLAND TEA MEN

Toronto Metros-Croatia
Detroit Express
Rochester Lancers
Minnesota Kicks
Chicago Sting
New England Tea Men
New York Cosmos
Philadelphia Fury
Washington Diplomats
Tulsa Roughnecks
Memphis Rogues
Dallas Tornado
Houston Hurricane
Tampa Bay Rowdies
Fort Lauderdale Strikers

TORONTO METROS-CROATIA

COSMOS

ROCHESTER LANCERS

PHILADELPHIA FURY

ROUGHNECKS

ROGUES

ROWDIES

DIPLOMATS

TORNADO

Strikers

43

AMERICAN CONFERENCE EASTERN DIVISION

Philadelphia Fury, backed by rock stars Peter Frampton, Mick Jagger, Rick Wakeman and Paul Simon and staffed by a mixture of young Irish players and experienced League pros, did not start well in their first NASL campaign. England internationals Alan Ball and Peter Osgood and Eire internationals John Dempsey and Johnny Giles were on the staff this season, as well as Pierce O'Leary, younger brother of Arsenal's David. Alan Ball took over as player-coach when Richard Dinnis, former Newcastle manager, resigned.

Fort Lauderdale Strikers' dismal start to the season forced Gordon Banks into retirement again, but they have recovered since. British players include Ray Hudson (Newcastle), Tony Whelan (Rochdale), David Irving (Everton), Norman Piper (Portsmouth) and latest signing George Best.

New England Tea Men are a club with a strong British flavour. Their controverisal deal with Charlton brought them Lawrie Abrahams, Colin Powell and England 'B' international Mike Flanagan and they also signed Roger Gibbins (Norwich), Gerry Daly (Derby), Peter Simpson (Arsenal), Brian Alderson and Keith Weller (Leicester). The coach is Irishman Noel Cantwell, formerly manager of Coventry and Peterborough.

Tampa Bay Rowdies are coached by Gordon Jago, former manager of QPR and Millwall. Rodney Marsh, once the languid idol of Loftus Road, is the star, but the line-up is well stocked with highly respected players like Paul Hammond (Palace), Davie Robb (Aberdeen), Jim Fleeting, Mike McGuire, Graham Paddon (all Norwich) and Australian Adrian Alston (Cardiff).

NATIONAL CONFERENCE EASTERN DIVISION

New York Cosmos, the club that signed Pele, still bristles with famous names, including internationals like Chinaglia (Italy), Beckenbauer (West Germany), Carlos Alberto (Brazil) and Dennis Tueart (England). Coach Eddie Firmani, the South African who played for Italy, also has Steve Hunt (*right*, with Beckenbauer), a young striker who never made the Villa first team, but whose pace and finishing power could be seen in the First Division this season. Cosmos are owned by Warner Communications.

NASL/George Tiedemann

Rochester Lancers: are a small town team that continue to get by in the big time.

Toronto Metros, staffed largely by Yugoslavs, have not made much of an impression this year.

Washington Diplomats have British players like Paul Cannell (Newcastle); Ray Graydon (Coventry City); Mike Dillon (Spurs) and Bobby Stokes and Jim Steele from Southampton's Cup winning side of 1976. The coach is Gordon Bradley, once of Carlisle.

AMERICAN CONFERENCE CENTRAL DIVISION

Chicago Sting, after a disastrous start, signed former Preston striker Gerry Ingram. They play in two different stadiums

Detroit Express are partly owned by Jimmy Hill's World Sports Academy. Trevor Francis scored the winning goal in his first match and sent the Express steaming away at the top of the division. Other Britons include Steve Seargeant (Everton), Graham Oates (Newcastle), Steve Earle (Leicester) and coach Ken Furphy's son, Keith (QPR).

Houston Hurricane have brought soccer back to the breathtaking Astrodome with Stewart Jump and Mark Lindsay (Palace), John Dowie and Bobby Lennox (Celtic).

Memphis Rogues, under former Chelsea boss Eddie McCreadie, started with a string of defeats, but have looked better since. Bobby Thomson, Jimmy Husband and John Faulkner, all of whom have played for Luton, are on the staff, together with Tony Burns (Palace) and Alan Birchenall (Leicester).

Bowing out . . . Ramon 'El Loco' Quiroga admits his guilt to ref Pat Partridge in the Peru-Poland match at Mendoza.

Colorsport

'Players expect a ref to have a sense of humour—and it is important. But that doesn't mean using a laugh or a joke to shirk your responsibility.' PAT PARTRIDGE

The little man who made millions laugh during the World Cup—Peru's eccentric keeper Ramon Quiroga—had top English referee Pat Partridge grinning, too.

But that didn't stop Pat showing the yellow card to 'El Loco' (the madman).

Pat was in charge of the Peru-Poland game in which El Loco kept charging out of his goal to make tackles . . . sometimes by the half-way line.

The experienced Partridge had seen nothing like it in 25 years of refereeing.

'The first time he did it I thought someone from the crowd had leapt on to the pitch,' says Pat. 'Then I realised who it was . . . the one and only El Loco.

'Twice he made really good tackles. But in the second half he came out and chopped down Lato—in his opponents' half!'

The crowd loved it—and Pat admits he saw the funny side of it, too.

'But, even with him standing there with his head bowed in apology, I still had to caution him for ungentlemanly behaviour.

'If I'd let him get away with it, other players who use similar tactics would have been entitled to say: "Hold on a minute, ref—look what you allowed that character to do in the World Cup".

'So I'm saying it's important for refs to keep thinking in amusing situations as well as the controversial ones. And El Loco provided another good lesson . . . be ready for the unexpected!'

Man in the middle . . . Co. Durham farmer Pat Partridge is one of Britain's top three referees. Aged 45, he's been 'through the card' since joining the League referees' list in the 1966-67 season. He was in charge of the West Ham-Fulham FA Cup final in 1975; the Nottingham Forest-Liverpool League Cup final last season; the SV Hamburg-Anderlecht European Cup Winners Cup final last year, and the Cruzeiro-Bayern Munich World Club Championship match of 1976. Most players dream of making Wembley once during their careers . . . Pat's been there five times. Not bad for a full-back—'I never used to get into trouble'—who had to pack up playing because of injury at the age of 18.

45

PRO FILE

PAT JENNINGS

If ever they construct a bionic goalkeeper, most of the parts could be modelled on Arsenal's Pat Jennings.

Pat's perfectly proportioned for the job between the posts . . . tall, solid—and with those massive hands.

In 15 years of top-class football, Pat has never suffered an injury when handling (although once he fractured a knuckle punching a player's head instead of the ball in a youth match!). Those hands measure nearly a foot from the tip of the thumb to the tip of the little finger and were developed felling trees in his home town of Newry. He also played Gaelic football, with its greater emphasis on handling the ball.

Calmness is the other great Jennings characteristic. Even after a stunning save, he has the air of a man who has flicked an insect from his forehead.

Born in Newry on 12 June 1945, Pat was about five when he first started playing football in the streets.

'There was no chance to play organised football at school,' he recalls, 'because there was only Gaelic football. So we formed street leagues.'

By the time he was 11, Pat was playing against boys twice his own size in an under-19 side.

By 1963 he was in the Northern Ireland youth side that came to England for the Little World Cup. He starred in the battle through to the final and, although they lost 4-0 to England, Jennings was snapped up within days by Watford for just £6,000.

If that seems a bargain, Tottenham manager Bill Nicholson would never regret the £27,500 he laid out to take Jennings to White Hart Lane in June 1964—the start of 12 years of outstanding consistency.

And by the end of the 1976-77 season Jennings had set a new Spurs' appearance record of 472 League games.

He had also topped the Northern Ireland caps list with 68, a record previously held by the man whose path he keeps crossing . . . Terry Neill.

As for honours, Pat has picked up his fair share—winners' medals in the FA Cup, League Cup and UEFA Cup. And cream on the cake came when he was voted Player of the Year by both the Football Writers' Association in 1973 and the Professional Footballers' Association two years later, a unique double.

Among his more unusual achievements

The save of the 1978 FA Cup Final . . .
Jennings dives full length to palm away for a corner a fierce header from Ipswich Town's young full-back George Burley.

Colorsport

The moment the TV slow-motion men love ... a spectacular one-handed save by Jennings in an ideal setting—Wembley—during one of Pat's record 71 appearances for Northern Ireland.

was the goal he *scored* at Old Trafford, a huge kick bouncing over stranded Alex Stepney's head. Then there were the *two* penalty saves he made in one game at Anfield.

Last summer Spurs shocked the football world by selling their famous goalkeeper to Arsenal for £40,000.

Jennings was less than happy at being made available, but Spurs boss Keith Burkinshaw decided to give a chance to the younger Barry Daines, his constant shadow.

At least Jennings was happy to be rejoining Neill, his one-time international colleague and manager.

Neill says: 'I was delighted to get the chance to buy Pat. I had no hesitation in deciding he was the man who could give stability to our defence.'

And he did. Arsenal looked a classy side last season, chasing the championship and making the FA Cup final against Ipswich.

One of the first men to spot Jennings' potential was Pat Welton, Spurs' youth team coach who managed the England youth side that beat Northern Ireland in 1963.

Syndication International

You need hands . . . and Pat Jennings has got them—measuring almost a foot from thumb to little finger!

Club	Season	Div	Pos	League	FA Cup	Lge Cup	Int' nls
Watford	1962-63	III	17	2	—	—	—
	1963-64	III	3	46	3	1	2
Tottenham	1964-65	I	6	23	—	—	6
Hotspur	1965-66	I	8	22	3	—	5
	1966-67	I	3	41	8	1	2
	1967-68	I	7	42	5	—	3
	1968-69	I	6	42	4	6	6
	1969-70	I	11	41	4	1	4
	1970-71	I	3	40	5	6	5
	1972-72	I	6	41	5	7	5
	1972-73	I	8	40	3	10	6
	1973-74	I	11	36	1	—	4
	1974-75	I	19	41	2	1	6
	1975-76	I	9	40	2	6	7
	1976-77	I	22	22	1	1	7
Arsenal	1977-78	I	5	42	6	7	3
				562	52	47	71

Welton says: 'Pat plays so much within himself and is therefore able to stretch himself when necessary. His influence on the younger players at Spurs was enormous.

'Even though he is now at Arsenal, you can still see what the young 'keepers here think about him—they all try to catch the ball one-handed like big Pat does.

'But that's something you can do only after years of experience . . . and if you've got hands like Pat Jennings!'

We'll meet again . . . Jennings saves at the feet of Terry Neill—now his manager at Arsenal.

Colorsport

49

Talbot and Wile: total commitment

'It was one of those balls you just have to go for. You can't stop and think about getting hurt.' JOHN WILE

Owen Barnes

Bloody hero . . . West Brom's John Wile after the clash of heads with Brian Talbot.

The goal that set Ipswich Town on their way to their first FA Cup final was a classis in terms of commitment.

It was the header by Brian Talbot in the semi-final victory over West Bromwich Albion . . . a goal that led to Talbot leaving the pitch with double vision and left Albion's John Wile with blood pouring from a head wound.

Wile carried on with his head bandaged—the gutsiest performance of the season and one seen by millions on television.

Both he and Talbot showed the kind of commitment that comes from the true professional. It would have been easy for either of

them to 'chicken out' of the crunch situation on the edge of the Albion six-yard box.

But both went all the way . . . and both can take different kinds of satisfaction from the incident. For Talbot it must rank as one of the most important goals of his career; Wile can remember it as the moment when he really did go in 'where it hurts'.

Quite apart from the commitment angle, it was a memorable goal for other reasons.

The build-up was neat: Paul Mariner picked the ball up in midfield and slipped it to Clive Woods. Full-back Mick Mills then made a great run down the left on the overlap.

Woods played the ball into Mills' path and the Ipswich skipper crossed it inside first time . . . the hard-hit 'early ball' dreaded by defenders.

Colorsport

Crunch . . . the ball flew into the top left-hand corner of the net and the two heroes hit the ground—and stayed there.

If ever a goal showed the courage needed to be a top-class footballer, this was it.

Make no mistake, anyone who dreams of becoming a pro should realise that it's as much about taking the knocks as showing the skills.

The crunch goal of last season . . . John Wile and Brian Talbot hit the ground as the ball hits the roof of the Albion net despite keeper Tony Godden's touch.

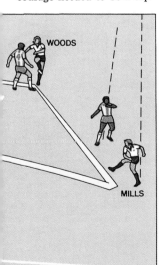

WOODS

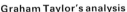

MILLS

Graham Taylor's analysis
The clash of heads must have made a few TV viewers wince— I bet some even avoided the slow-motion replays ! It was a clash between two of football's winners. This is a physical game and there's no way of softening that fact of life. Certainly, Wile and Talbot knew all about commitment before that incident.

What else did the goal have ? Well, on top of Mick Mills' great overlap, I liked the way Clive Woods put his foot on the ball and looked around for the alternatives. From where he was he could have been expected to chip the ball to the far post. But he thought : no,

let's have a look. It was the look over his left shoulder that encouraged Mills to make such a positive run.

Woods also showed that football doesn't always have to be played at 100 miles an hour. He had the composure to stop and assess a situation, knowing that a telling pass would possibly be superior to a run. And what a pass it was—just stroked into the path of Mills, perfectly weighted in time with the speed of the full-back.

In those few seconds you had so much of what is good in football—the smooth skills of Woods, the perception and energy of Mills . . . and the commitment of Wile and Talbot.

RI SING STAR **BOB HAZELL**

'When I couldn't even get in the reserves at Molineux I thought about packing it up. But I pushed myself to the limit and it brought results.' BOB HAZELL

Club	Season	League		FA Cup	
		Ms	Gs	Ms	Gs
Wolves	1977–78	20	1	3	–
Bob was voted Wolves Player of the Year last season					

While Cyrille Regis was hogging the headlines at West Bromwich, down the road at Wolves another black player was taking the first few tentative steps to football fame.

And at one stage the strapping Bob Hazell doubted he would ever make it.

Molineux seemed full of central defenders better than him and his bags were half packed. But he stuck at it—and now people are saying he could be the first black man to play for England in a full international.

Hazell, 6′ 2″ of menacing muscle, would like nothing more than to pull on the England shirt.

He says: 'I would be happy if I could improve my game enough to get a chance in the Under-21 side.'

The emergence of Hazell was one of the few things for Wolves fans to cheer last season.

Boss Sammy Chung had so much confidence in the 19-year-old that he was able to sell the experienced Scottish international Frank Munro to Celtic.

Unfortunately for him, the first many people saw of Hazell was the FA Cup tie against Arsenal at Highbury, where he was sent off for swinging a punch.

But Chung says: 'He's young, inexperienced and he buckled down well after I fined him.'

Wolves fans have always loved big, no-nonsense number fives and Hazell is in the mould.

'It's no good being a continental type of centre half in the Football League,' he explains. 'I like to stick close to a striker and get there first when the ball is played up to him.

'If you don't get tight with someone, close them down, they can turn and run at you and the advantage is with them.

In the thick of things . . . Wolves defender Bob Hazell puts himself about in a League match against Manchester United last season.

'Abroad you can get away with being weak in the air but not here because so many balls are played to the head of the target man.'

With the effervescent Chung relying on youth to take Wolves places this season, a ton of responsibility will rest on the broad shoulders of his young central defender.

Hazell knows his inexperience is likely to lead to mistakes, but he also knows the only way to learn the game is out on the pitch.

And one thing he's sure of: 'At my height and weight no one will push me around.'

Pretty soon Hazell could be doing his own pushing . . . for international honours.

Bob Thomas

53

See the play Trevor Brooking's way

'Young players who can grasp the importance of receiving the ball sideways on, the way Trevor Brooking does, will see their game improve almost overnight...' Watford boss GRAHAM TAYLOR

Colorsport

It's worth spending a whole game studying the style of West Ham's England midfield star Trevor Brooking.

He's one of those special players who seem to have plenty of time while everyone around them is hustling and bustling.

And he possesses the kind of balance that makes it almost impossible for opponents to get in an effective tackle.

'If I look well balanced it's not because of any special exercises, like walking on beams,' says Trevor.

'The secret, as far as I am concerned, is getting into the right position to receive passes sideways on.

'If you stand too square when you get the ball, it cuts down your vision. For example, you would find it hard to play a first-time ball to a striker simply because you couldn't be sure where he was.

'But sideways on you get a much better picture of what is going on—where your team-mates are and where there is space you can use.'

Trevor's sideways on approach helps to explain a lot of the many subtleties of his game . . .

The way he shields the ball from opponents, for example. With his greater vision he is able to get the ball on to the outside of the foot furthest away from the opponent.

Sideways on, Trevor is perfectly positioned to take the ball in a different direction as it reaches him.

He is also able to 'ride' tackles the way he does by being sideways on. By seeing the danger early he can let the ball run a little further—which surprises the opponent—or meet it a fraction of a second earlier, which also catches the defender out.

And the Brooking feint, which has left many a defender flat-footed, is another result of the sideways on method.

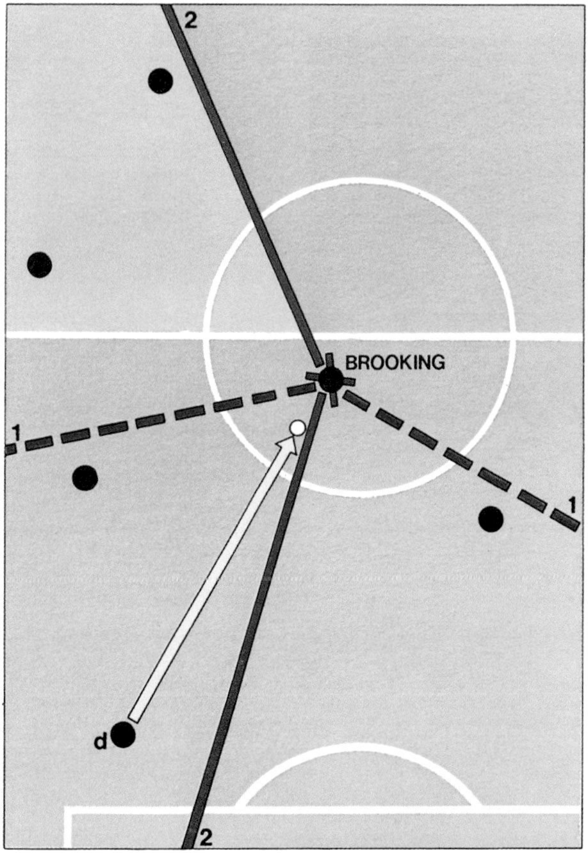

'This diagram shows the great advantage of seeing play the Trevor Brooking way. The area inside the two red lines is Trevor's range of vision if he receives the ball sideways on, while the two broken blue lines show how he would be 'blinkered' if he positioned himself too square to receive the pass from the defender. It's from positions like this that Trevor turns without even touching the ball and so switches play from defence to attack in a second or two . . . all because he is seeing things sideways on. Obviously, it's a great advantage for midfield players who are constantly turning and changing direction, but the Brooking method can improve players of all positions. For example, if a goalkeeper rolls the ball to a full-back—as happens in virtually every game —the full-back can start an attack from his own penalty area if he has the kind of vision shown in the diagram. Anyone who starts doing this in games will soon notice the difference it makes. Try it yourself this season !'

**Test your soccer knowledge and . . .
WIN THE BALL THAT ENGLAND
AND SCOTLAND USE!**

10 'Max 25' balls to be won from

in this week's great
FREE ENTRY quiz

1. When England played West Germany last February—at 'B' level on the 21st and full level on the 22nd—one player scored in both games. Who was he?

2. Match the club to the city: (1) Grasshoppers, (2) Bohemians, (3) Rapid, (4) Torpedo, (5) Crusaders, (6) Corinthians; (a) Moscow, (b) Zurich, (c) Sao Paulo, (d) Dublin, (e) Vienna, (f) Belfast.

3. Which present First Division manager once led the Second Division scorers in three successive seasons?

Ray Green

Sporting Pictures UK

4. Who is hidden—and what is his present club?

5. Where was the crucial goal on the left scored?

6. Which company sponsors the (Ulster) Irish League – Texaco, Bass, Fiat or Schweppes?

7. Which one of the following players has never played for Luton Town: Don Givens, Ray Graydon, Derek Hales, Malcolm Macdonald, Bruce Rioch?

8. Shielfield Park is the most northerly League ground in England. Who plays there?

Steve Perryman

'I think it's the duty of professionals to pass on what they've learned to youngsters . . . we do well out of this game and it's up to us to give a bit back.'

One-club man Steve Perryman has had to develop all kinds of different skills for the various roles he's played at Tottenham.

And he says: 'It's right to specialise in the qualities needed for your own position, but you must also look at your game from a wider point of view.

'For example, a midfield player who makes a run down the line should be able to cross the ball like a winger.'

Steve's a great admirer of the way Liverpool play. Their players have all-round abilities—forwards who tackle like full-backs and defenders who finish like strikers.

'That's their secret, I think,' says Steve. 'So youngsters who want to improve should practise *all* the skills and exercises. And never get complacent about practice: a skill neglected in training is always the one that lets you down in matches.

'Look at me: I play sweeper for Spurs and have obvious height problems. In matches I try not to get into situations where I have to head the ball, but in training I'm put under that pressure . . . if only to find ways to put the big men off!'

Still only 26—but Steve Perryman has earned his testimonial season at Spurs.

A telling pass . . . Steve in action for Spurs against Birmingham.

Jimmy Case on shooting

'That moment when the ball bulges the back of the net is what it's all about for strikers . . . and if you score from 25 or 30 yards, that's the icing on the cake.' JIMMY CASE

The hotshots of the World Cup—Haan, Nelinho and Cubillas—were an inspiration to every player who loves to let fly from 25 yards or more.

And no professional does that better than Liverpool's young star Jimmy Case.

Like Bobby Charlton and Peter Lorimer before him, the young Liverpool forward strikes the ball with exceptional power.

Jimmy told us: 'Shooting hard has always come naturally to me, but I still have to concentrate on the basics.

'I can sky the ball over the bar as easily as the next bloke, so my advice to young forwards is to avoid the temptation of trying to burst the net with shots.

'But even then you can't forget the golden rule—keeping your head over the ball—because you're just as able to balloon the ball at 29 as you are at nine.

'One thing's for sure—you'll see me do it again before my playing days are over!'

'The important things are to strike the ball cleanly and keep it down. To do that you must keep your eye on the ball and your head over it until the very last moment. If you lift your head you'll lift the ball—believe me.'

Timing, balance and kicking 'through' the ball are also vital ingredients of a good shot, explains Jimmy.

'It's better to hit fairly firm, accurate shots in training, otherwise you will be blasting the ball all over the place, which can be very disheartening for someone who really wants to do well.

'When you feel that you're hitting the ball cleanly and accurately, that's the time to start thinking about power.'

Ray Green

1. The Case approach . . . eye on the ball and arms out for balance, Jimmy is perfectly set for a power drive.

2. Just before impact, Jimmy still watches the ball. Throughout the movement his left leg acts as an anchor.

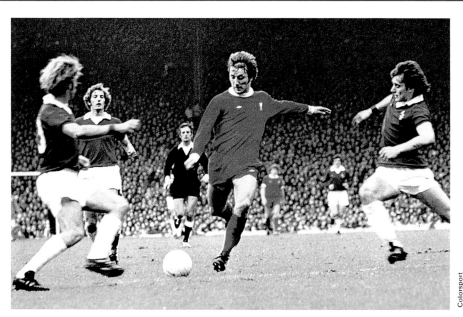

Colorsport

The moment top defences dread . . . Liverpool's Jimmy Case draws back his lethal right foot in a League match against Merseyside neighbours Everton.

3. Even after kicking the ball, Jimmy keeps his eye on it—to make sure that the shot stays down.

4. Away it goes and Jimmy ends in the classic pose, perfectly balanced on his left leg. And his head is still down!

Ray Green

A close-up of the keeper's view of the Jimmy Case shot . . .

Close-ups of Jimmy Case's shooting boot—his right is the one that really worries the opposition—shows clearly how it should be done. Notice how his left foot gets close to the ball.

See, too, how he strikes the ball with the correct part of the foot—the instep. That gives the shot accuracy as well as power, whereas a 'toe poke' is likely to fly off at any height and in almost any direction. And the instep provides that magic 'feel' that is common to all ball games—even in rugby you'll notice that more and more players are using the instep for penalties. Ask them why and they'll all come up with same answer . . . 'it gives me greater accuracy'. As Jimmy emphasises, it's accuracy that comes first and power later . . .

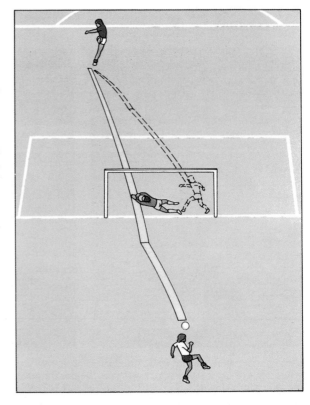

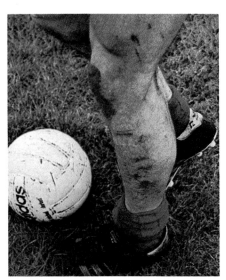 

and what the technique looks like from the side . . .

Training : three players

'Three of you can have one of the most enjoyable of all practice sessions,' says Graham Taylor. 'You need a goal in your local park— without a net !—and you each take a turn in goal while the other two shoot from either side of the goal. It's best to start with shooting a stationary ball and then progress to a moving ball.

'Again it's important to stress the importance of accuracy over power. So, if you have a competition between the three of you, it's a good idea to award one point for hitting the target—even if the shot is saved —and two for a goal.

This is the sort of practice you can keep up for half an hour or more without getting bored. And if the end product is a new level of consistency it'll be more than worthwhile.

If you dream of scoring goals like some we saw in the World Cup, it starts here. You keep on shooting till it comes naturally.'

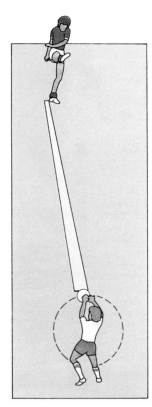

Training : two players

A good practice for two players is simply shooting over different distances—but it's important to impose one very necessary restriction. And that is that the player receiving the ball should not have to move from his spot to save the ball—as the broken circle shows in the diagram. This has the effect of forcing the shooter to concentrate on accuracy.

'There's no point in blasting the ball all over the place,' says Graham Taylor. 'But this restriction doesn't have to take out the competitive element. You can earn a point, for example, for every firm shot that hits the target, i.e. the area immediately around the other player.

'It's not as easy as it sounds but when you start hitting the target consistently then the thing to do is increase the distance. If you begin to get power and accuracy over, say, 20 yards, then you're really on the right road.'

Whistle Test

'Feigning injury is one of the most common kinds of time-wasting. It may look clever but it's not. It's a low form of cheating.' JACK TAYLOR

Jack Taylor has no time for football's actors—players who go down as if poleaxed and the next minute run— about like two-year-olds.

Britain's best-known butcher puts it bluntly: 'It's calculated cheating. They do it simply to waste time, usually to take the heat out of a period of sustained attacking. I get them off the pitch as soon as I can.'

What pleased Jack most about the World Cup this year was the way refs insisted on minor injuries being treated off the pitch.

He says: 'Hopefully we'll see more of this from British refs this season. There was a FIFA directive in 1971 for this to happen but, well, let's say the standard slipped a little.

'In Argentina there was a blatant case of cheating in the Italy-France match. It was towards the end, with Italy leading 2-1, and Rossi was knocked off the pitch by a tackle.

'It was no conincidence, in my opinion, that his writhing and rolling in agony just happened to take him back on to the field of play.

'And, as we all noticed on our television screens, there seemed to be very little time added on for this kind of blatant time-wasting.

'Of course, you've got to use your common sense. It would be criminal to drag off someone who's badly injured.'

But how can you tell if a player is really hurt or after an Oscar?

'It's not the easiest task in the world,' admits Jack, 'but a general rule is that if a player remains still on the ground you can be pretty sure he's badly hurt. And I always call on the trainer if there's been any kind of head injury—they're the ones you've got to be careful about.'

As for the actors, Jack says: 'They soon get back on their feet if their side is in trouble.'

Man in the middle . . . Jack Taylor, OBE, is Britain's most famous ref. He was widely praised for his handling of the 1974 World Cup final when he gave a penalty to Holland against the host country two minutes into the game. His prized possessions include the players' union merit award.

'Come on, son, I'm a referee, not a film producer' . . . Jack sorts out a resting German during the 1974 World Cup final against Holland in Munich.

Syndication International

Founded: 1874
Address: Tynecastle Park, Gorgie Road, Edinburgh 11
Ground: Capacity 49,000 ; Playing area 100.5 x 69.5 m
Record attendance: 53,496 v Rangers, Scottish Cup 3rd rd, 13.2.32
Record victory: 15–0 v King's Park, Scottish Cup 2nd rd, 13.2.37
Record defeat: 0–7 v Hibs, Div. 1, 1.1.73
Most League points: 62, Div. 1, 1957-58
Most League goals: 132, Div. 1, 1957-58 (Div. 1 record)
League scoring record: 44, Barney Battles, 1930-31
Record League aggregate: 206, Jimmy Wardhaugh, 1946-59
Most capped player: 29, Bobby Walker, Scotland, 1900-13
League career: Div. 1 1891-1975 ; Premier 1975-77 ; Div. 1 1977-78 ; Premier 1978-
Honours: Scottish League Champions 1895, 1897, 1958, 1960 ; Scottish Cup Winners 1891, 1896, 1901, 1906, 1956 ; Scottish League Cup Winners 1955, 1959, 1960, 1963

HEART OF MIDLOTHIAN

The knockers are already saying that Hearts are in for a season of struggle after winning back their place in the Scottish Premier Division.

All the usual criticism has been flung at the Tynecastle club: not enough skilful players to live with Rangers, Aberdeen and Celtic; no strength in depth; no real money to buy star players.

But the fans are convinced that one man has the ability to make the club the force it once was—Willie Ormond.

Ormond, ironically a former Hibs player, was enticed away from his role as Scotland soccer boss to take charge of Hearts after they had suffered the indignity of relegation for the first time in their 103-year existence. That was in May

Colorsport

Heart of Hearts
Hearts' best years were under the managership of Tommy Walker, when they won the Cup in 1956, then ran away with the League in 1958, finishing 13 points clear and scoring a record 132 goals. Walker has been associated with the club since the 1930s, first as a player, then as manager and now as a director.

The Scotsman Publications Ltd

Willie Gibson, unlucky this time, still scored 20 League goals for Hearts last season to help take the Edinburgh club back into the Premier Division —the second year running he had finished as the club's top marksman.

Colorsport

Willie Ormond was lured away from his job as Scotland team boss to take over a Hearts team that had just been relegated for the first time in their history. Now one season later they are back in the Premier Division.

Early success
Hearts made 6 Scottish Cup final appearances between 1891 and 1907—winning 4 of them, including the 1896 defeat of Hibs in the only final ever played outside Glasgow—but they have only won once since.

Graham Shaw keeps control of the ball even though he loses his footing against Ayr at the beginning of the 1976-77 season—Shaw scored in a 2-2 draw. Hearts were in the middle of a 10-game winless run. Later they were to go through a worse spell (12 games without a win) and were relegated at the end of the season.

1977 . . . and a year later Hearts were back in the top grade. But will they stay there?

The burden will inevitably fall on experienced players: centre-half and captain Jim Jefferies, strikers Drew Busby, Graham Shaw and Willie Gibson, top scorer for the past two seasons.

With 'old hands' providing the backbone, Ormond will look to talented youngsters to provide the flair—like left-sided midfield player Lawrence Tierney and former Celtic free transfer Walter Kydd, a full-back of genuine promise.

Pick of the crop, however, must be Eamonn Bannon, who is already knocking on the door of the international side. Ormond's headache—especially if Hearts make an indifferent start—is the cheque-book brigade ready to make a beeline for Bannon. Ormond says: 'Fans of a club as big as Hearts expect success . . . they demand it. Last season we gave them something to shout about by winning promotion.

'But they aren't going to settle for mediocrity in the Premier Division. We must be seen to be offering a strong challenge.'

Apart from their Scottish FA Cup final appearance two seasons ago (Rangers won 3-1) and in 1968 (Dunfermline won 3-1), Hearts have not made a squeak since being nipped on goal average for the League in 1965.

Today's problems are a far cry from the heady days of the 1950s when a dynamic inside-forward trio of Alfie Conn, Willie Bauld and Jimmy Wardhaugh was the most feared in Scotland.

The results speak for themselves: two League titles ('58 and '60), three League Cup triumphs ('55, '59, '60) and the end of a 50-year wait to regain the Scottish Cup, beating Celtic 3-1 in 1956. The Hearts side of that period also

The Scotsman Publications Ltd

64

included a young half-back by the name of Dave Mackay and the seemingly indestructible John Cumming.

So what caused the decline? Perhaps the rot set in after the team's failure to get a point off Kilmarnock at Tynecastle to clinch the title in 1965.

Seventeen months later the legendary Tommy Walker was sacked as manager. He was replaced by his coach, the popular John Harvey, but he too was eventually removed in favour of Bobby Seith.

Seith was a fine tactician and had a pleasant personality, but he lacked the drive to shake Hearts out of their lethargy. A young unknown, John Hagart, took over in 1975, saved Hearts from relegation and guided the side along a shaky path to the Scottish Cup final. But then he made way for Ormond who, with a shortage of cash, went for bargains and found two—goalkeeper Ray Dunlop and defender Dave McNicoll for £15,000 apiece.

Older fans still blame the board for getting rid of a man of the calibre of Tommy Walker. Now back at Tynecastle as a director, Walker knows the kind of pressure that 51-year-old Ormond is under to get results.

A club with Hearts' deep-seated traditions can only be satisfied by possessing trophies.

Jailhouse theft
Heart of Midlothian's name was chosen by their first captain, Tom Purdie, when the club was formed in 1874. It was taken from the local nickname for the old prison — demolished more than 50 years before but made famous by a novel of the same name by Sir Walter Scott.

Dave McNicoll, signed from Montrose last season, clears from Hibs winger Arthur Duncan. The Hibs-Hearts rivalry should hot up again now that both clubs are in the top grade. Hearts have drawn more support than their local rivals in recent seasons, though Hibs have had most of the playing success.

Sportapics Ltd

RISING STAR GLENN ROEDER

Chance can change the course of a footballer's career . . . like it did with 22-year-old Glenn Roeder, QPR's £200,000 signing from Orient last month.

An injury to Orient's Phil Hoadley last Christmas forced manager Jimmy Bloomfield to bring in reserve Nigel Gray to play alongside Roeder in the back four. And, with Gray doing well, Bloomfield faced a three-into-two-won't-go problem when Hoadley was fit again.

Bloomfield's solution was to play all three of his talented young defenders—with Roeder operating as a sweeper.

The move had much to do with Orient's marvellous run to the FA Cup semi-final and won Roeder wide acclaim.

But aren't sweepers supposed to be crafty

Roeder robs Arsenal's Frank Stapleton in last season's FA Cup semi-final. 'We wern't flexible enough to recover after Arsenal's two crazy early goals. We switched systems too late to save the game,' says Glenn.

'Playing against top teams in Orient's Cup run was a real confidence booster for me ... but I've always fancied playing in the First Division.'

Club	Season	League		FA Cup		Lge Cup	
Orient	1974-75	6	—	—	—	—	—
	1975-76	25	2	1	—	1	—
	1976-77	42	2	4	—	4	—
	1977-78	42	—	8	—	3	—
		115	4	13	—	8	—

old pros who use their vast experience to make up for lack of pace?

'Usually, but I don't find it difficult to play there,' Glenn told *Handbook*. 'I enjoy playing this way, which helps make it easy.'

Anticipation is central to the sweeper's role, so that he can be in the right place at the right time. Glenn says: 'I have to be able to judge which balls are likely to come through and know exactly where I should be.

'The same goes for players. If one gets through the main line of defenders it's my job to be there—and stop him.

'I do a lot of shouting because where I am, 20 or 25 yards behind the play, I get a good view of what's going on. My talking helps other defenders who may not see quite so much.'

Every system can come unstuck, of course. 'It had been working well in the Second Division and FA Cup run,' says Glenn. 'But then we played on a quagmire at Stoke and lost 5-0. I was waiting for the ball to come through, but all it did was stick in the mud. We got well stuffed!'

A typical manoeuvre for the sweeper is to block up holes that open up, then drop back to cover one of the two centre-backs as the opponents try a different approach.

'Funny thing is,' says Glenn, 'you can have a good game without touching the ball. You put people off by being where they want to go.'

One game that gave Glenn great satisfaction was the Cup replay win against Chelsea. 'Ray Wilkins kept looking up for a space to play the ball into—and kept seeing me. Ray was good enough to check and play the ball somewhere else, but it held up their attacks.'

As a boy Glenn played for juniors teams linked with Arsenal. But on leaving school at 16 he was small and light and looked unlikely to make the grade.

Orient's chief scout, Len Cheesewright, took him to Brisbane Road. At 18—and now 6' 1" and 12 stone—Glenn signed pro.

It'll be interesting to follow the progress of a young player at Queen's Park Rangers who thinks about his football.

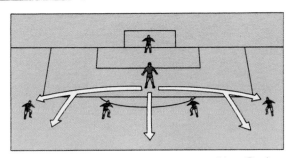

Sweeping the Roeder way
'There are three main things to master,' says Glenn. 'One, learn to read the game and spot the potential danger. Two, make sure you play the ball accurately out of defence —otherwise you will be straight back in trouble. Three, be patient about going forward—if you do it too often you lose the element of surprise. When the ball is with the opposition's midfield players, look for gaps in your half of the field and move into one of them to reduce the options for your opponents. Once the ball is coming towards one of your defenders, drop back to cover your centre-backs and watch for the ball or an opponent coming through into dangerous positions. That's the strange thing about playing as a sweeper: you spend much of the game using your head and your eyes instead of the ball.'

 WORLD MASTERS MARIO

Peter Robinson

In Argentina in June, at the age of 23, Mario Kempes, the quiet-spoken young man from 'next door to the back of beyond', reached the pinnacle every footballer is aiming at—but only a handful can ever achieve . . .

Mario Kempes has been back to Argentina during each of the two summers since he left Rosario Central for Valencia for £340,000 in 1976.

But each time the reception has been completely different. This year Kempes returned home to the most glorious moments of his career, scoring two goals and making a third in Argentina's World Cup final win, finishing as the tournament's top scorer with six goals and winning the best player award.

But last year it was very different. When Kempes returned home to the little town of Bell Ville, midway between Buenos Aires and Cordoba and next door to the back of beyond, only close friends came round to say hello.

This was where Kempes learned his football, far from the jam-packed sophisti-cation of the giant River Plate stadium.

From the start he was a centre-forward 'Everyone thinks it's the glamour posi-tion,' said Kempes once. 'But if you miss couple of chances, then you've got everyon on your back wanting to know why.'

It didn't take Kempes long to attrac attention and at the start of 1973 he joine Instituto Cordoba, where he had bee studying economics.

But Kempes didn't stay long wit Instituto; just 15 games, in fact, in which hi 11 goals earned an immediate move on t Rosario Central. They were in desperat need of someone to score goals, yet even s were stunned when this tall raw newcome smashed a hat-trick in one of his early game against former world club champion Estudiantes de la Plata.

A matter of weeks later Kempes wa thrown into Argentina's World Cup squa preparing for the high-altitude qualifier wit Bolivia in La Paz.

Argentina won 1-0 but in the rarifie atmosphere Kempes burned himself out wit his enthusiasm and had to be substituted a half-time. That was to prove the first of 3 internationals which would bring 20 goals t add to the sackfuls he has collected in th league.

One of Kempes' finest displays was a Wembley against England, yet he playe only because a calf muscle injury had side lined Hector Yazalde, the then Sportin Lisbon striker who had just won the 'Golde Boot' as Europe's top scorer.

After 53 minutes Argentina were 2- down, but five minutes later Kempes too full advantage after Emlyn Hughes and Pete Shilton tied themselves in knots in defence and with two minutes remaining he con verted the penalty to equalise after Hughe tripped him going into the box.

He scored against Rumania in anothe pre-World Cup game, and then played in a six of Argentina's finals matches in Wes Germany.

Two years later Kempes returned t Europe to join Valencia.

'I'd have quit soccer if I hadn't been abl

68

KEMPES

The River Plate stadium . . . 25 June 1978 . . .
the World Cup final . . . Mario Kempes on the
attack once again. The unenviable Dutch
defenders are Ruud Krol and Ernie Brandts.

to move,' he said later, even though he
explained that his motive wasn't financial.
'The basic pay rates for top players in Spain
are similar to those in Argentina, though in
Spain the bonuses are far higher. But I didn't
come to Spain just to make money . . . I came
to make my name as a footballer.'

He also went to Spain to score goals, and
was Valencia's leading marksman both in
1977 (24 goals) and last season (28).

But that transfer very nearly cost Kempes
his World Cup place. Cesar Menotti was for
a long time determined to use only home-
based players, and it wasn't until his forwards
were found wanting in the 1977 series of
international friendlies that he decided to
recall Kempes.

Everyone knows now what a good move it
turned out to be.

Gilt-edged star

Valencia must be congratulating themselves on
signing Kempes to a multi-year contract before
the World Cup pushed his market value
through the roof. The contract guarantees him
£110,000 a year plus a monthly salary and
bonuses for five years—which means he
probably will be playing for Valencia when the
World Cup comes to Spain in 1982. Kempes
also cashed in on a deal with a Danish
company that offered him £700 for every
World Cup goal he scored—and a bonus of
£1,000 if he finished top scorer . . . which
means that Mario collected a cool £5,200 for
his rapid-fire scoring burst.

Kempes the Goal King

Kempes captured the imagination of World Cup watchers by his direct approach to goalscoring. He was constantly prepared to take on defenders, especially around the penalty area. And although he did not score in the first round of three games, he finished as the tournament's top scorer with six goals—two against Poland, two against Peru and two in the final against Holland. Here he takes on Hungary's Gyozo Martos, Italy's Mauro Bellugi and Gaetano Scirea and Holland's Willy van der Kerkhof.

Kempes tormented the Hungarians . . .

Pictures by

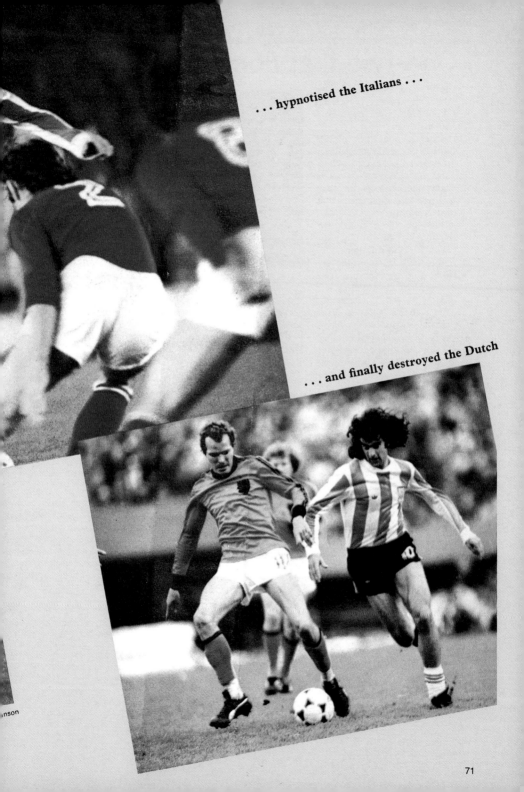

... hypnotised the Italians ...

... and finally destroyed the Dutch

nson

71

One-two that floored the champs!

Once again the World Cup left many observers tearing their hair out over the Italians.

One moment they played football of the highest calibre. The next . . . back in their shell.

But let's look at the Roberto Bettega goal that beat Argentina.

It was a classic, if only for the magical touch play between Rossi and Bettega.

But look at it frame by frame and even more is seen . . . all kinds of subtleties.

It started harmlessly from a throw-in on the left.

Rossi battled well to win the ball, then shaped to cross it. But he slipped the ball inside to Giancarlo Antognoni. He, too, disguised his clipped pass to Bettega.

From there it was pop, pop. . . and goal! Bettega flicked the ball past his marker then flashed past him for a brilliant return from the heel of Rossi's right boot. Fillol tried to narrow the angle but Bettega finished with a low shot—perfection!

Peter Robinson

Argentinians everywhere . . . but none of them could cope with the superb one-two which was finished by the triumphant Bettega.

ROSSI 1

ROSSI 2

ANTOGNONI

'If you have to be beaten, perhaps it is better to be beaten by a great goal.' ARGENTINA MANAGER CESAR MENOTTI

Graham Taylor's analysis

'That's one you could look at again and again, all day long, without getting bored.

'But it's not enough to just sit there admiring it—there are always lessons to learn from a goal like that.

'The skill involved in the one-two between Bettega and Rossi is there for everyone to appreciate, and the way both Rossi and Antognoni disguised their passes shows how even the simplest things can be cloaked by a little subtlety.

'But I would say the number one lesson is not so obvious—and that's the few yards Rossi covered to make himself available for Bettega's one-two.

'It's so easy for someone on the line to think their part is over once they've played the ball inside. But Rossi kept involved by going inside to take up a useful position.

'If he hadn't we wouldn't have witnessed a great goal.'

BETTEGA 3

TARANTINI

GALVAN

BETTEGA 2

BETTEGA 1

73

PRO FILE

TONY CURRIE

'He has got everything England needs—skill, stamina and pace. He's the best midfield player in the country on current form.'
FORMER LEEDS MANAGER JIMMY ARMFIELD

Although Currie set the game against Wales alight with a long range goal—'special enough to win a game anywhere in the world,' said Welsh manager Mike Smith—he had less scoring success in the League last season, netting only 3 in 35 full appearances for Leeds. Manchester United's defenaer Jimmy Nicholl blocked this effort.

'Cut out some of the showmanship!' That was one of the first things former Leeds United manager Jimmy Armfield told Tony Currie when he arrived at Elland Road in the summer of 1976.

'It seems daft looking back at it,' the 28-year-old Londoner told *Handbook*, 'but I could understand how he felt. He had paid Sheffield United his highest-ever fee for me—and he wanted to show the fans that he'd bought an action man, not a playboy.

'So I got stuck in, trained hard and tried to fit into the Elland Road pattern. But no matter how hard I tried, my instincts led me to let my hair down on the pitch.

'You know what I mean—I was blowing kisses and waving to the fans, exchanging backchat with them at throw-ins and corners and generally letting them know that I appreciated their presence!'

Despite making himself a firm favourite with the Leeds fans—they voted him their 'Player of the Year' last season—

Colorsport

it seemed that this likeable, gifted craftsman was destined to pay dearly for the qualities that lifted him head and shoulders above most of his contemporaries.

It looked as though the once-promising England career was over. 'After being discarded by Sir Alf Ramsey and being given only one game by Don Revie I feared the worst,' he says, with less bitterness than you would expect. But Currie persevered. 'I knew everything would turn out well,' he says. And so it proved. He was rewarded with his recall against Brazil at Wembley last spring.

Looking back with relish to that memorable evening when he produced a world-class performance, he comments: 'I was proud to be a member of an England side that had matched—and often bettered—some of the best players in the world for pure skill.'

Perhaps because the game is second nature to him, he has often been resentful of his being overlooked by England at the expense of less well-equipped players. 'Now England have a manager who believes in skill first and strength second; obviously work-rate is important, too, and despite being labelled lazy and inconsistent I think I do more than my share of work. It infuriates me when I hear folk accuse me of lack of effort. It means they don't appreciate the amount of thought that goes into my game. Maybe that's the result of my clowning. It possibly gives them the impression that I'm not taking the game seriously. But I think a lot about football. I analyse every game—and I try to learn from my mistakes.

'But one thing I'm dead against is dossiers. Don Revie often used to fill his players' heads with useless information.

Don Masson—and Trevor Francis—are left wrong-footed by Tony Currie's impertinent skill in last season's international at Hampden. 'I believe I'm a naturally gifted player—if that doesn't sound immodest,' Currie says. 'But over the years I've been left out of the England side in favour of donkeys in terms of vision and football skill.'

Currie's career
After failing to impress in trials with QPR and Chelsea, Tony was spotted by Watford playing Sunday league football . . . scored twice in his first full League game at the age of 17 and joined Sheffield United for £26,500 later that same season . . . made his full England debut in 1972 against Northern Ireland, but Alf Ramsey took him off as England went down to a 1–0 defeat . . . joined Leeds for £240,000 in June 1976.

Kenny Dalglish gets a close look at Currie's control in the match against Scotland. Looking on are (top) Don Masson, Dave Watson, Martin Buchan and (above) Ray Wilkins. Currie's international come-back call-up came against Brazil. 'Tony showed skill, and composure .. and he controlled the game,' said Ron Greenwood. 'He outdid the Brazilians in both strength and flair.'

Praise from Greenwood
Currie's international recall certainly pleased England manager Ron Greenwood. 'Tony showed skill, composure and controlled the game,' he said. 'It wasn't an easy baptism because, for most of the time, we took the risk of letting Brazil outnumber us in midfield ... but he screened the ball with all the strength of the Brazilians.'

'Ron Greenwood will give individual tips on your opposition, but generally he sends you out with a clear head, and that gives you confidence. It's a terrific morale-booster to know that the manager has faith in you. If a boss treats you like an adult it gives you a greater sense of responsibility. And when he tells you to go out and enjoy yourselves, as Ron Greenwood does, pointing out that you can take the credit while he'll take the blame, it relieves players of a lot of pressure.

'I think too much attention can be paid to pre-planned tactics. Once out on the park footballers have to be prepared to improvise for the simple reason that you really don't know what the opposition will do'.

No one improvises better than Tony Currie. He is a master at catching opponents on the wrong foot, either with his deft dribbling, his snaky body-swerve or his accurate long passes.

'Tony is almost as accurate as the world's No. 1 passer, Johnny Giles,' says Trevor Cherry, the Leeds skipper and Currie's England colleague. 'He can switch play with a pinpoint diagonal pass and his corners and free-kicks are perfection.'

If Currie had a fault last season it was his shooting—despite his 30-yard stunner against Wales and the cracker against Hungary. 'I honestly don't know what went wrong at club level,' he says. 'I was inhibited by a foot injury. Every time I whacked the ball I found I was in pain for the rest of the game so I tended not to try long distance efforts. And as I was playing deeper than usual in midfield for long periods I wasn't getting much chance near goal. 'I'm not quite in the Peter Lorimer class when it comes to cracking in thunderbolts, but I've a fair shot so I ought to hit the back of the net more often.

'This winter I'm hoping to recapture the scoring habit and I'll be disappointed if I don't total at least a dozen. During the summer I went to Elland Road at least three times a week to practice. Frankly, I don't think we pay enough attention to this important aspect of the game. After all, you can't win games without goals.

Club	Div	Pos	Season	League		FA Cup		Lge Cup		Int'nls	
				Ms	Gs	Ms	Gs	Ms	Gs	Ms	Gs
Watford	III	3	1966–67	1	–	–	–	–	–	–	–
	III	6	1967–68	17	9	2	–	1	–		
Sheffield	I	21	1967–68	13	4	–	–	–	–		
United	II	9	1968–69	35	4	1	–	1	–		
	II	6	1969–70	42	12	2	–	2	–		
	II	2	1970–71	42	10	1	–	2	1		
	I	10	1971–72	38	10	1	–	5	1	1	
	I	14	1972–73	39	1	2	–	5	1	2	
	I	13	1973–74	29	6	1	1	1	–	3	1
	I	6	1974–75	42	7	2	1	4	–		
	I	22	1975–76	33	1	1	–	2	–	1	
Leeds	I	10	1976–77	35	1	5	–	1	1		
United	I	9	1977–78	35	3	1	–	5	1	5	2
				401	68	19	2	29	5	12	3

'I think it's time our footballers had the confidence to try their luck with more surprise shots outside the box. I'll certainly be on the lookout for "sleepy" goalkeepers!'

So Ray Clemence, Peter Shilton, Joe Corrigan, and the rest have been warned! Tony Currie has the bit between his teeth. And his big ambition this season is his first major medal.

Jimmy Armfield has parted company with Leeds after rebuilding the team following Don Revie's departure and Currie was sorry to see him go. 'Jimmy showed that he wanted to change the Leeds image when he signed me,' says Tony. 'He made us an attractive side. But we didn't achieve success under him. We were short of perhaps two quality players who would have enabled us to compete more favourably.

'This time, I think we can make that slight improvement which will win us the League or a cup. When I left Sheffield I thought I was moving to a club which would go places— and I haven't changed my opinion.

Tony Currie, the self-assured, crowd-pulling superstar with a flair for the unexpected, has shown that the fiercely competitive, point-chasing First Division can be fun for players and fans.

The question he wants answered with a resounding 'Yes', is: can it be successful? He's convinced that it can. But no matter what happens, he'll still involve the fans in his display. 'After all, where would we be without them?' he asks.

Balance, power, the ability to find space ... Tony reveals these qualities in one of his first games for Leeds—against Spurs at White Hart Lane— and John Pratt is left a vital few feet adrift. Nevertheless Spurs won 1-0.

Increase your stamina: Kevin Keegan

'I've always enjoyed cross-country running . . . it's amazing what you can think and daydream about as you run. And there's no doubt it builds up your stamina.' KEVIN KEEGAN

Sporting Pictures UK

If Muhammad Ali stings like a bee, then Kevin Keegan certainly buzzes like one.

On top of his undoubted skill, Kevin is able to zip about at an amazing rate for 90 minutes.

And for that he needs stamina . . . tons of it.

'I'm lucky,' says the SV Hamburg and England star. 'I've always enjoyed cross-country running—you can even say that I find it relaxing!'

But, Kevin says, there's no substitute for pushing yourself to improve stamina.

'You have to go through what we call the pain barrier,' he says. 'When you've run for a long time and it begins to hurt, you must force yourself to keep on running.'

'Pain barrier' is not as bad as it sounds—if you have the determination to keep running the pain disappears and you can actually feel exhilirated. 'You find you can run for miles,' says Kevin.

'I still get the stitch in big matches but I just ignore it and keep going—it soon disappears.'

It's vital, he says, to mix long runs with sprints.

'Long distance runs help you to get through the 90 minutes but the sprints are essential for the five or ten-metre bursts you get in games.'

Kevin has always realised the need to push himself to new limits of endurance.

He says: 'With long runs I used to run against the clock to see how much I could knock off my previous best.'

'Then I'd do the same run in boots or in extra clothing to make it harder.'

There's no need to find 'country' for long runs. Lots of players have built their stamina by running round the streets and local parks.

A good way to push yourself when it begins to hurt is to set yourself targets . . . first a telegraph pole, then a pillar box and so on. 'It really does work,' says Kevin.

Stamina is also linked to a player's mental attitude. If he knows he can last 90 minutes it makes him more confident to use his skills and to make runs for the benefit of his team.

But if he is uncertain about his ability to last a match, he is tempted to 'hide' from the action and save what energy he has.

And, once tired, his contribution is virtually nil . . . he stops thinking as well as running.

So keep at it. Who knows, you might reach the stage where, like Kevin Keegan, you actually enjoy it!

'There's no set kind of running for football,' says Graham Taylor. 'During a game you'll sprint, jog and even walk, so that's what your training should include. If there's a running track near where you live, you can alternate walks, jogs and sprints. You can use posts or clothing as markers and, as a general rule, the sprint should be shorter than the walk and jog.

Once you have your circuit planned out, stick to it because that's how you can test yourself—either by doing more circuits or by doing them faster. If there isn't a track near you, a large triangle in a park or open space will do just as well.'

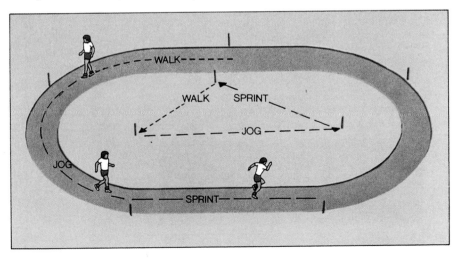

A Matter of Fact

Ballymena United, Ulster's representatives in this season's European Cup Winners Cup, were bottom of the Irish League in May, finishing 4 points adrift with only 10 from 22 matches. They qualified for Europe by being double champions Linfield's victims in the Irish Cup final.

Aston Villa full-back Peter Aldis scored his first ever League goal in September 1952 from 35 yards—with a header!

Arsenal can claim the longest current unbroken run in Division 1; they have not been relegated since they first were elected in 1919, 59 years ago.

Chris Nicholl, the former Aston Villa centre-half now with Southampton, scored all four goals in the 2-2 draw earned by Villa against Leicester City at Filbert Street on 20 March 1976. The only other player to record this feat was Sam Wynne, playing for Oldham Athletic against Manchester United in Division 2 on 6 October 1923.

Charlton Athletic lost an FA Cup tie in the 1945-46 season —and still reached the final. It was the only time the competition has been played on a two-legged basis, and in the third round Fulham beat Charlton 2-1. Charlton won the other leg 3-1 to go through on aggregate, eventually losing the final 4-1 to Derby County.

When Forest won the League title last season, midfielder Martin O'Neill became the first Northern Ireland international to win a championship medal in seven years. The last was Arsenal's Pat Rice in 1971.

The highest score in the Olympic Games is 17-1, when Denmark beat France in 1908. The same margin was recorded when Germany trounced Russia 16-0 in 1912.

For their first visit to the World Cup finals—in Switzerland in 1954—Scotland took only 13 players, including two goalkeepers. They lost both their games, 1-0 to Austria and 7-0 to Uruguay.

In 1937-38 Manchester City were the First Division's leading scorers with 80 goals—and still got relegated!

Colorsport

Billy Meredith, who played 670 League games with the two Manchester sides, was chosen 71 consecutive times for Wales from 1895 to 1920, though released by his clubs for only 48.

Syndication International

WOULD FRANCESCO BOGLIONE FROM TORINO PLEASE NOTE HIS WIFE HAS HAD A SON

All part of the superb Wembley service ... at least one Italian fan had something to cheer about during his side's 2-0 World Cup defeat by England last year.

80

Founded: 1873 (oldest club in Wales)
Address: Racecourse Ground, Mold Road, Wrexham
Ground: Capacity 30,000; Playing area 107 x 68.5 m
Record attendance: 34,445 v Manchester United, FA Cup 4th Rd,
26.1.57
Record victory: 10-1 v Hartlepool United, Div. 4 3.3.62
Record defeat: 0-9 v Brentford, Div. 3, 15.9.63
Most League points: 61, Div. 4, 1969-70 & Div. 3 1977-78
Most League goals: 106, Div. 3(N), 1933-34
League scoring record: 44, Tom Bamford, Div. 3 (N); 1933-34
Record League aggregate: 175, Tom Bamford, 1928-34
Most capped player: 22, Horace Blew, Wales, 1899-1910
League record: 1921 Original members of Div. 3 (N); 1958-60 Div.
3; 1960-62 Div. 4; 1962-64 Div. 3; 1964-70 Div. 4; 1970-78 Div.
3; 1978- Div. 2
Honours: Div. 3 Champions 1978; Welsh Cup Winners (21) 1878,
1883, 1893, 1897, 1903, 1905, 1909, 1010, 1911, 1914, 1915, 1921,
1924, 1925, 1931, 1957, 1958, 1960, 1972, 1975, 1978

WREXHAM

'We'll be very disappointed if we don't have some kind of success in our first-ever season in the Second Division.'

Those are the words of Wrexham's little dynamo of a player-manager, Welsh international Arfon Griffiths.

'I think everyone who gains promotion tends to think they are going to do just as well as they did the previous season. We know it's going to be different. It will be more competitive and we are going to need consistency.

'The last two Third Division champions—Mansfield and Hereford—both came straight back down . . . but on the other hand, Brighton proved a good Third Division side, a fine Second Division side . . . and almost a First Division side.

'We have a good record against top opposition, but I'm the first to admit that these were one-offs. That's why I'll be looking for consistency next season.'

Griffiths is obviously confident of building on the excellent start he has made as Wrexham manager. Not only did he lead the club to the championship in his first season in charge, but also added the Welsh Cup, the Welsh Youth Cup, the 'Reveille' Giant-Killers Cup, the Border Counties Floodlit League Cup, the Northern Floodlit League Challenge Cup and a five-a-side championship organised by the local evening paper to Wrexham's groaning display of trophies.

Just one season ago, however, Wrexham's morale was at rock bottom. They needed to beat Mansfield at home in the last game of the season to gain promotion . . . and lost 1-0. The next day manager John Neal decided to accept an offer to take over at First Division Middlesbrough.

'Missing out on promotion and John's departure had a shattering effect on the club,' recalls Griffiths. 'But I looked at the players and I thought "You don't become a bad side overnight" . . . so I agreed to take over as manager. But I

Bob Thomas

Prince of Wales
At the age of 19 Arfon Griffiths was transferred to Arsenal for a then record fee for the Welsh club of £15,000. With Arsenal he ran into injury problems and 18 months after his arrival he was back at Wrexham. It was 10 years before he gained his first full international cap in April 1971, but it wasn't until 1974 that he got another chance, establishing himself as a midfield regular, scoring 9 goals in 15 games.

knew we needed a couple of players to make up the squad.'

Almost immediately, he paid out a club record fee of £38,000 for Coventry City's midfield-winger, Les Cartwright. But Wrexham made a poor start to the season and were in the bottom four of the table in September.

Griffiths moved fast. Billy Ashcroft joined Neal at Middlesbrough for £130,000, and, in the space of a week, Griffiths spent a bargain £8,000 for Everton's Welsh international goalkeeper Dai Davies and a record £70,000 for Hereford's high-scoring Dixie McNeil.

Wrexham began their climb up the table. Top managers flocked to their games and made no secret of their admiration for dazzling winger Bobby Shinton, the midfield play of Mickey Thomas and the brilliant displays of full-back Alan Dwyer.

And if there were any First Division managers who didn't know about the quality that ran right through this Wrexham side, then the cup results soon enlightened them. Newcastle, Bristol City and Leicester were among the clubs Wrexham knocked out. And it took Liverpool to put them out of the League Cup with a flattering 3-1 scoreline in the fifth round and the Welsh club were very unlucky to lose 3-2 at home to Arsenal in the quarter-finals of the FA Cup.

Right after the Arsenal defeat came the match that Griffiths regards as the key match of their League campaign —against Swindon Town at the County Ground.

Dai Davies was out. Dixie McNeil had injured a heel and would not play again that season. Griffiths put young Eddie Niedzwiecki in goal and played John Lyons up front . . . and Wrexham won 2-1. Lyons scored both goals and Niedzwiecki saved a penalty.

'That's the game that did it . . . I fancied Swindon myself. Then we went on to win the next seven games on the trot. It confirmed to us that you have to have a good squad. The previous season we had a good side but when we were hit

It took two of Britain's top teams to put Wrexham out of the major trophies last season. Arsenal came to the Racecourse in the FA Cup 6th Round and, after a disastrous start, Wrexham worried them. Dixie McNeil (above) headed past Pat Jennings, despite the close attention of Willie Young, and Arsenal were relieved to come away with a 3-2 win.

by injuries we never had anyone to come in and do a good job. This season it was different.'

Wrexham made sure of promotion on 22 April, hammering Rotherham 7-1 in front of 17,000 at the Racecourse Ground, and they became Third Division champions the following Saturday after drawing with Hereford.

The icing on the cake came in the Welsh Cup. After beating Second Division Cardiff City 2-0 at Ninian Park in the semi-final, they saw off Northern Premier League side Bangor City in the final.

Now Wrexham are set for their third venture in the European Cup Winners Cup . . . against Yugoslav unknowns NK Rijeka. Last time they qualified, in 1975, they shook the continent by reaching the quarter-finals, only going out to the eventual winners—Anderlecht—through a late goal from a player who had had a frustrating time against

the Wrexham defence . . . a fellow by the name of Robbie Rensenbrink.

Wrexham are now giving their Racecourse Ground a £300,000 face-lift: bringing the floodlights up to European standards, ringing the ground with a 'cage' and building a new stand at one end of the ground. When the improvements are completed, the club will once again have room for 30,000 spectators—the capacity of the ground before the Ground Safety Act regulations cut it to 15,000. And the behind-the-scenes facilities are already good enough to have impressed visitors like Arsenal and Liverpool.

Then Wrexham will have a ground and a team that should impress Europe—as well as the Second Division.

Like Nottingham Forest, Wrexham signed an experienced keeper early last season . . . Dai Davies.

Ray Green

Record your magic soccer moments by winning one of this week's star prizes

Six 'freeze-the-action' Ektra 12 camera outfits to be won from

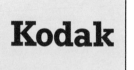

in this week's great free-to-enter quiz

1. Whose term as a national team manager ended in April 1974 after 113 matches with only 17 defeats?

2. Part of Magpies striker Peter Withe's career has been spent with Arcadia Shepherds—in the league of which country?

3. Two League clubs play at St James' Park. One is Newcastle United, but who is the second?

4. Who secured a winner's medal at Wembley in 1971 at the fifth attempt?

Bob Thomas

5. A fair exchange . . . which teams have just played, where, and what was the result?

6. John McGovern has played under Brian Clough at four League clubs: Derby County, Leeds United, Nottingham Forest and . . . name the fourth.

All-Sport

7. Pictured here in his playing days with West Ham, he won 17 Welsh caps with the Hammers and Aston Villa between 1959 and 1963, and is now Commissioner of the North American Soccer League. Who is he?

8. The record points total in the First Division is 67. Which club, and in which season?

9. Which Scottish player was sent off in the World Cup qualifier against Czechoslovakia in Prague on 13 October 1976?

HOW TO ENTER
List your answers to the questions on a postcard, add your name and address, cut the 'Part 3' flash from the cover and attach it to the postcard (entries that do not bear the flash will be ineligible), then mail to: Football Handbook, 600A Commercial Road, London E14 7HS. Entries must arrive by September 25, 1978, the closing date. The sender of the first 6 correct answers scrutinised after that date will each be awarded a Kodak 'Ektra' 12 camera outfit as illustrated in the picture at the top of the page. The Editor's decision on all matters relating to the competition is final and binding. All winners will be notified as soon as possible and a full list of prize winners to date will be available from *Football Handbook* on request.

KICK OFF WITH...

Duncan McKenzie

'In some ways I'm like a golfer with an unusual grip, and if I'd been forced to change my style I think I might have ended up as Joe Average—or perhaps not had a career in football at all.'

Even though he is so often labelled as unorthodox and individualistic, Duncan McKenzie is quick to emphasise the value of coaching . . . and he has strong views on it.

'I prefer to think of the teaching of youngsters as "organising" them—giving them a framework in which they know how to use their skills . . . and are encouraged to express them. I believe that the coach's role is to make sure that natural abilities aren't lost as youngsters move from schoolboy into senior football. And to do that all coaches should try to make their sessions enjoyable: that's the way to get the best response.'

Duncan has this tip for young players: 'Listen to all the advice you're given, but if you're blessed with a special gift don't neglect it. If you're a bit different stick with it . . . as long as it works.'

Duncan's chequered career has seen him at several clubs—including Anderlecht—but wherever he plays he always displays his own special brand of virtuosity.

Sporting Pictures UK

Colorsport

Joe Corrigan on handling

'When going for high balls, it's vital to keep your eye on the ball. Get distracted and you could be picking it out of the net.'

Colorsport

Competent handling is just about the number one requirement of a goalkeeper—there's no substitute for 'a good pair of hands'.

But there's a lot more to it than that, simply because your hands will have to take the ball in any number of different positions—from around your ankles to high over your head.

And Manchester City's international star Joe Corrigan has some useful tips for youngsters who play their football between the posts.

'Basically, shots will come at you from three different heights,' says Joe—'around your feet, between your stomach and chest, and at or above head height. And each one requires slightly different approaches and techniques.

'Most keepers tend to go down on one knee to save low shots or collect the ball. But I prefer to keep my weight on both feet and bend down for them.

'It's up to each individual goalkeeper to find out which they find most comfortable—and safest!'

With shots to the stomach and chest, Joe says: 'Get your body firmly behind the ball and form a cradle with your hands and arms.'

Thumbs play a vital part in shots at and above the head. 'They just about touch,' says Joe, 'to stop the ball going straight through the hands, and the fingers are spread out as far as possible to make a net for the ball.'

It was with this catch that Joe had an important piece of advice for you keepers.

'Whatever you do,' he says, 'you must avoid the temptation to take your eyes off the ball.

'It's a mistake to look for what you might do with the ball while it's still in the air. Catch it first, then decide.

'The same goes for opponents challenging for high balls. Ignore them—just concentrate on getting the ball. And don't let anyone tell you not to lead with a leg. You get a lot of momentum that way and it makes you a safer catcher of the ball. All you should avoid is being dangerous by raising your knee too high or by showing your studs.'

Big Joe shows how it's done under pressure in a League game against Queens Park Rangers . . .
'Everything you do on the park has its roots at the training ground,' says Joe.

The ball no forward can get . . . when Joe Corrigan catches the ball and holds it aloft (left), that's it—it's his! A close up from behind his hands (above) shows how the thumbs almost touch and the Corrigan fingers are spread as wide as possible to make sure the ball's going nowhere. 'It's not a difficult catch,' says Joe, 'but distraction is the big danger— you've got to ignore the forward rushing in and concentrate on just one thing . . . that ball!'

Ray Green

Ray Green

As you can see in the picture, Joe Corrigan prefers to go down to low balls from a standing position as opposed to going down on one knee (as shown in the diagram). Joe chooses that way because, he says, he is much more able to retrieve the ball quickly from that position if it gets away from him. Other goalkeepers prefer kneeling because, they argue, it gets more of their body behind the ball—they feel a lot more secure that way.

'Choose the position that gives you most confidence,' says Graham Taylor. 'But, as a general rule, I would advise young keepers to start with the kneeling method. The first priority is to stop the ball and an inexperienced keeper may find trouble with Joe's way. What you can do is try out both in training and see how it goes. It's not a good idea to experiment in matches !'

Safe as a baby . . . Joe shows how to save the ball that comes at you in the region of the chest and stomach. 'Use your hands, arms and body to form a cradle for the ball,' he says. 'It's almost as if your body is swallowing the ball—and these are the kind of saves you should make consistently to boost confidence—not only on your own but also for the rest of the team. If you're looking safe and sound it helps your team-mates with their game.

Ray Green

Ray Green

Eye on the ball, Joe jumps off his right leg to catch the ball. Note the wide spread of his fingers.

Got it ... Joe grabs the ball but still keeps his eye on it —if not it could easily slip to a waiting forward.

From the side you can see how Joe bends his arms to cushion the impact of the ball as it drops.

Get someone to throw a ball to you at different heights and try to remember the points Joe makes—thumbs just about meeting and the fingers well spread. The thrower should change the trajectory because that's how it is in matches, especially with crosses from different angles.

For shots to the stomach it's best to get someone to shoot hard from a few yards. This is a practice you can't do too much of because it's the one that makes you familiar with the ball. And, as Joe says, if you catch the ball consistently well in that region it gives a great boost to your overall confidence.

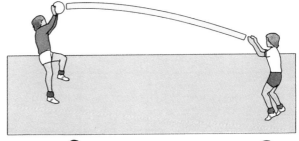

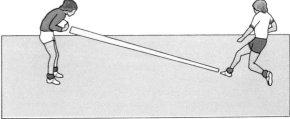

FOOTBALL FITNESS TRAINING PROGRAMME

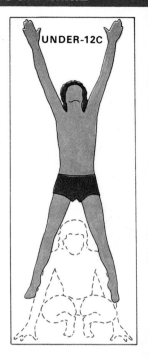

UNDER-12C

UNDER-12 AGE GROUP

A. Running on the spot, slow at first, getting faster, raising knees high. Max. 30 secs.

B. Stand with legs astride. Place hands on chest, palms down. Fling arms outwards and upwards, combined with deep-breathing. Do 10 times, rest for 5 secs, then repeat.

C. 'Star jumps'. Assume crouch position. Place hands on floor palms down. Spring up, flinging arms upwards and legs apart, closing legs before landing. Breathe in as you spring, out as you crouch. Repeat 10 times.

D. Try 7 press ups. Rest for 10 secs. then repeat as many as you can—but no more than another 7.

E. Lie on your front, with hands clasped behind your neck. Raise head, trunk and legs as high as possible. Then back to lying position. Repeat 10 times. Rest for 5 secs. and repeat.

13-14 AGE GROUP

A. 'Upside down' cycling for a maximum of 30 secs, starting with small fast circles and slowing down to large ones.

B. Sit up with legs straight, Place hands on chest, palms down. Fling arms backwards and slightly upwards, combined with deep breathing. Max 30 secs.

C. Stand with one leg raised. Bend other knee and lower body, then raise as slowly as possible. Repeat 3 times on each leg.

D. Do 10 press-ups. Rest for 5 secs, then repeat.

E. Sit up with legs straight arms behind you, palms on the floor. Raise legs a few inches, then apart, together, then down. Repeat 10 times, rest, then repeat.

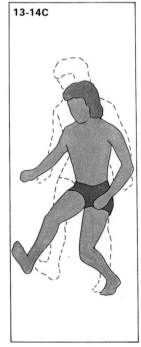

13-14C

OVER-15 AGE GROUP

A. Step up and down on to a low box or stool. Repeat 30 times, alternating legs.

B. Lie on your back, hands behind your head, elbows on the floor. Keeping your legs straight, place feet under a piece of furniture. Sit up, then twist trunk so that you touch the left knee with your right elbow, and back. Repeat with the left elbow to the right knee.

C. Do 10 press-ups. Rest for 10 secs. and repeat twice.

D. Kneel to face a chair. Place hands on arms of chair at an arms length. Press chest towards chair (as in press-ups). Repeat 10 times.

E. Assume press-up position. Move legs apart, then together, up to body, and back. Repeat 10 times with a 'bounce'.

PRO FILE WILLIE MILLER

'What have I got to complain about when dozens of players go through their whole careers without achieving anything? But I sometimes wonder whether I would have ever made it if I had continued as a striker . . .'

One week in the life of Willie Miller gives the ultimate example of the ups and downs in a pro footballer's career.

The day after his 23rd birthday on May 2, the Aberdeen captain waited expectantly to be named in Ally MacLeod's World Cup squad . . . he wasn't.

Then, a couple of days later, Willie led out his side against Rangers in the Scottish Cup final . . . and Aberdeen gave their worst performance of the season to lose 2-1.

Miller could have been forgiven for cursing the cruelty of it all.

But instead he reflected: 'There will be other chances for me to win things. What have I got to complain about when dozens of players go through their whole careers without achieving anything?'

And MacLeod has said: 'Willie will captain Scotland in the Spanish finals in 1982.'

Someone else who has no doubts about Miller's abilities is the experienced Aberdeen goalkeeper Bobby Clark.

He says: 'It was always obvious to me and a lot of other people that Willie had the potential to make it big.

'He showed he was willing to work hard at improving his skills and learning new ones.'

It was as a striker that Miller was signed by Jimmy Bonthrone from Glasgow amateur side Eastercraigs. And it was in that role that he was farmed out to Highland League club Peterhead, where he won an Aberdeenshire Cup to add to the Amateur Cup medal he

Willie Miller—the player who became a sweeper almost by accident and is now being tipped by many as the future captain of Scotland. Yet at one point he could hardly hold down a reserve team place as a striker and thought he'd never make it . . .

Disappointment ahead . . .
Willie shakes hands with
Rangers captain John Greig
before the Scottish FA Cup final
defeat in May—a bleak day
for the Aberdeen skipper.

won with Eastercraigs.

Back at Pittodrie, Miller found it hard to hold down a reserve team place and began to doubt whether he would ever make the grade.

It was then that fate worked in his favour. He was converted to sweeper almost by accident.

He recalls: 'The team was short of someone to play at the back, so I volunteered to play there. I thought it was better to get involved than kill time on the sidelines.

'Well, I've been there ever since and needless to say I don't regret the move one little bit.'

In 1974 Miller was a fully-established first team player and his form soon won him a place in the Scottish Under-23 side.

It was at this level that Miller fell under the influence of Aston Villa's Tommy Craig, the man with the great left foot.

Miller says: 'Tommy is an inspirational player and a bloke who shows great confidence on the park. Watching him closely I learned a lot of the qualities needed to captain a side and I also became more aware tactically.'

A happier moment for the unlucky Miller as he
whacks the ball past Partick Thistle's
international keeper Alan Rough. No—the
effort was disallowed. But if anyone can survive
such setbacks, Willie Miller can.

Even with his new-found success, Miller kept working hard at his game—even returning in the afternoons for extra coaching from George Murray.

It paid off. Miller was picked for his international debut against Rumania in a European Championship tie in Bucharest.

Honours
Scottish League Cup winners medal 1977
Scottish Cup runners up medal 1978

Club	Season	Div.	Pos.	League Ms Gs	FA Cup Ms Gs	Lge Cup Ms Gs	Int'nls Ms Gs
Aberdeen	1973-74	I	4	31 1	1 –	9 –	
	1974-75	I	5	34 1	4 1	6 –	1 –
	1975-76	P	7	36 –	2 1	6 –	
	1976-77	P	3	36 –	3 –	8 –	
	1977-78	P	2	36 2	6 –	6 –	1 –
				173 4	16 2	35 –	2 –

Captain Miller
Apart from his two International caps, against Rumania and Bulgaria, Willie has won 12 Scotland Under-23 caps. He captained the side in their match against Holland in Breda, when the Dutch won 2-0. Miller is also the Aberdeen captain, leading his side to second place in League and Cup last season.

Amazingly, Miller had to wait three years for his second cap—in the 2-1 friendly win over Bulgaria at Hampden Park in February.

Experienced players—like Tom Forsyth and Martin Buchan—have kept Miller on the international sideline, but he is not despondent.

He argues: 'I have age on my side. Four years from now I'll only be 27, so if I keep my form I could figure in the next two World Cups. I'd be a liar if I said I wasn't disappointed at not making Argentina, but it was impossible for Ally MacLeod to please everyone.'

Like Buchan before him, Miller is lured by the thought of football south of the border.

Two years ago he asked Aberdeen for a move but—despite talk of a big-money deal —nothing materialised and he settled his differences with the club. Beating Celtic 2-1 in the League Cup final also helped to smooth things over.

But Miller admits: 'I would still like to play in England if the chance came. Besides the money in the move, I feel players get more recognition in England.

'It doesn't matter how good you are in Scotland– if you don't play for Celtic or Rangers you don't get noticed in a big way.

'And another thing: they say the Football League is the toughest in the world . . . well, I want to find out if it's true.'

Sportapics

How green is my valley!

'Sometimes I wake up during the night before a big game—there's never anything to worry about but that's how this job gets you.'

Goalkeepers who scratch a mark through the six-yard line at The Valley—home of Charlton Athletic—might fool the ref if his back is turned.

But one man always notices—soft-spoken Maurice Banham. And at half-time, he'll have a quiet but firm word in the keeper's ear: 'Don't do it at the other end, son.'

It's not so much the illegality that irks Maurice. It's the damage to his preci‹ grass.

For Maurice is one of the unsung her‹ who are never known by their names ‹ simply as 'the groundsman'.

And he's widely acclaimed as one of ‹ best in the business. Most seasons his Val looks as green and inviting in April as it ‹ in August.

Lucky for some . . . managers may come and go but Lucky the cat—found by Maurice in the centre circle nine years ago—is one of soccer's survivors.

Duncan Raban

That's because he looks after every blade of grass himself. No one else is allowed within trimming distance.

'Grass is life,' says Maurice, 'and you can't go hacking and chopping it about as you like.'

So his is a painstaking job. 'But it gives me great satisfaction,' he says. 'My attitude is this: the players want a pitch that's right for skill and the fans want one that's right for entertainment.'

Then there's the succession of managers during his 14 years at the club. They've been 'boss' to the players but when it comes to the pitch . . . what Maurice says goes.

Divots are his main concern—'I wince every time there's a slide tackle'—and, as with everything else, he takes care with the task. 'It's no good just stamping them back willy-nilly,' he says. 'You've got to get the ground open to help them re-root.

'And it's the same with cutting. I'll top the grass two or three times a week, half an inch a time, to thicken it up—not take four inches off once a fortnight.'

Rejuvenation is the word he constantly uses when talking about his grass. He always seeds, never puts down turfs, and the grass feeds on a ton of fertilizer put down in small quantities three times a year.

Rain is rarely a problem at The Valley because over the years Maurice has 'crowned' the pitch from the centre circle to the goalmouths.

That work unearthed no less than 28 barrel-loads of bricks and an old tin bath!

Maurice's record is impressive—only two first team games, against QPR and Aldershot, postponed since the 1964-65 season.

The holder of two certificates for 'turf culture', 56-year-old Maurice has moved with the times and uses chemicals on the pitch. But it amuses him that modern science has yet to find a killer to rid him of a hardy little weed, the cabbage-like plantain . . . 'he'll outlive the lot of us'.

Eight o'clock every working day sees Maurice surveying the grass inside the vast, empty Valley.

And, depending on the time of year, he's quickly out there seeding, feeding, harrowing, spiking or topping.

It's his baby. And it makes him shudder every time young fans spill on to the pitch after a game . . . 'if only they knew the effort that goes into preparing that field of grass.'

A man and his pitch . .
Maurice gets to work on the
grass that's the envy of many First Division
clubs. His secret—knowing every blade of
grass and treating each one as something special.

McDermott's master move

'The goal Terry McDermott scored against Borussia was a real Liverpool goal. It wasn't just about fitness and skill . . . it was also full of enthusiasm for the game.' GRAHAM TAYLOR

The stunning goal that put Liverpool on the road to their first European Cup triumph showed in a few marvellous seconds what that club is all about.

A typically sharp Liverpool build-up down the right led to a delightful through pass by Steve Heighway for Terry McDermott, who had made an amazing 60-yard run from his own half of the pitch into the Borussia penalty area.

McDermott's finishing matched the rest of the move —a sweet shot across the Borussia keeper and into the far corner of the net.

Callaghan, as ever, started the move after winning the ball by the half-way line. He played a quick pass to Heighway and followed up to support him on the outside.

This gave Heighway what every player needs: alternatives. He took the ball inside, and as two Borussia defenders came at him he played one of the most devastating balls in football—the one between two defenders which puts them out of the game.

So it had just about everything: Callaghan's tigerish tackle to win the ball in the first place, followed by his unselfish run.

Heighway showed skill and confidence to bring the ball inside and then needed to play the ball at the perfect weight for McDermott's run.

And what a run! It demanded a level of awareness for which Liverpool, with their great traditions of strength and character, are not given enough credit.

Looking back, this goal was the one that helped to establish McDermott as a goalscoring midfield player.

He followed up with a hat-trick against Kevin Keegan's SV Hamburg in the second leg of the Europe Super Cup at Anfield.

Graham Taylor's analysis

'Liverpool at their best—when you've got players as honest as that, your problems are few. By honest, I mean players who make the kind of runs that Callaghan and McDermott put in to make that move possible— not only once, either, but whenever it's needed in a match. I'll tell you one thing—if McDermott had shot wide, he would have made the same run three minutes later !

'And don't just put it down to the standard of fitness that Liverpool demand. There's another quality that doesn't get enough attention . . . real enthusiasm. They made those runs because they've got it— they love the game and they want the ball, a very basic requirement but one that keeps Callaghan running about like a teenager. If you're finished when you stop enjoying the game, Callaghan will carry on for ever. He's a great example to every youngster.

Heighway's through pass puts two defenders out of the game and McDermott has time to check on the keeper's position after his 60-yard run . . .

Perfectly poised, the midfield man becomes a striker to put Liverpool on their way to their first European Cup final victory . . .

It's in the back of the net and McDermott feels up to doing another 60-yard run in triumph.

Colorsport

A Matter of Fact

Albert Iremonger, keeper for Notts County and Lincoln from 1904 to 1925, is believed to be the League's tallest ever player—at 6′ 5½″.

Northampton made the trip from Division 4 to Division 1—and back—in just 8 years. The Cobblers won promotion in 1961, 1963 and 1965; they were relegated in 1966, 1967 and 1969! By 1972 they were applying for re-election.

Peter Shilton kept a clean sheet in 24 of his 37 League games for Forest last season—the best record in the First Division.

Argentina's manager, the long-faced Cesar Luis Menotti, was one of the first players to defect to American soccer, back in 1967. He played for the now disbanded New York Generals under coach Freddie Goodwin, who later managed Brighton and Birmingham.

Clackmannan's 1921-22 season was the only one they spent in the Scottish League. They finished last in the Second Division and were not re-elected.

Manchester City once missed three penalties in a match—against Newcastle United in the First Division on 27 January 1912.

Whistle Test

'It's useful to be able to laugh at some of the things that happen to you in this game—at times you've got to!' TOM REYNOLDS

Anything can happen—and often does—to top referees who travel the world to take charge of games played in all kinds of different atmospheres.

Wiltshire's Tom Reynolds is a ref with a sense of humour—he allows regulars at his pub to stick derogatory newspaper reports up in the bar—and he is able to look back and laugh at one or two alarming experiences.

Like the one in 1974 when he went to Sweden for a 'Little World Cup' match between Yugoslavia and Greece, on the face of it a very pleasant excursion to a new part of the world for a game that few people knew about.

But it was one the intrepid Tom would never forget!

'It was a very average sort of game,' he recalls; 'nothing to get heated up about. But after the match, which Yugoslavia won 1-0, there was a riot by about 3,000 Greek waiters—who else would have been working in Sweden? There hadn't been a particularly controversial decision in the match. They just seemed to think that losing was a good enough reason for a spot of aggro.'

A ring of ten policemen protected Tom as he left the pitch—each of them with a vicious looking dog that made Tom feel a whole lot better.

'But then this Greek with an eight-foot flag-pole tried to clobber me,' says Tom. 'So I backed off to the far side of the police cordon.'

The pole-waving Greek couldn't quite reach him, but Tom still felt a sharp pain . . . when one of the police dogs bit him!

Arsenal reached the final of the FA Cup in both 1971 and 1972 without being drawn at home.

Only one club outside the Northern Premier League has won the FA Challenge Trophy in its 9-year history—Southern League Telford United in 1971.

Hull City used 42 players during their 1946-47 season in Division 3 (North).

In 1888 FA Cup winners West Bromwich Albion played Scottish Cup holders Renton for the title of 'Champions of the World'. Renton won 4-1.

The 1934 Welsh Cup replay was played in England between two English clubs, when Bristol City beat Tranmere Rovers 3-0 at Chester.

Bob Thomas

Trevor Francis—here putting one past Memphis Rogues—equalled the NASL record this summer with five goals in Detroit's 10-0 win over San Jose.

Colorsport

You're guessing, ref!'
Tom tells of another time when a sense of humour came in handy. 'In one game a defender thought a throw-in should have been given in his favour after a fifty-fifty tackle by the line and he told me: "You're guessing, ref!" I needed to say something fast, so I said: "Good guess, though, wasn't it?" And I can remember when Derek Dougan (current chairman of the Professional Footballers' Association) demanded a corner he didn't get and asked: 'What's this ref, your first game?' This kind of banter is all part of the general pace of the game that refs have to fall in with. If you do you create a rapport with the players.

Sheik up in the Middle East

Oil money is financing a soccer revolution in the Middle East . . . and British coaches are helping talent to bloom in what was once considered to be a football desert.

Frank O'Farrell, the son of a Cork engine-driver, earned £40,000 a year during his spell as team manager of Iran.

Ajman take on Al Arabi in a UAE Second Division game. Sand pitches are rapidly being replaced by new stadia with real or artificial grass.

Iran may not have had as successful a World Cup as they were hoping for, but in their three matches they gave notice that they are now a force to be reckoned with.

Before the game with Scotland they were not given much chance by the experts. Even their former.manager, Frank O'Farrell, considered that 'they won't have the sustained fitness, the pace and the class.' But they went out and hammered another nail in the coffin of the ragged Scots. And it wasn't lack of fitness or class that robbed them of a memorable victory. It was a single moment of panic in an otherwise sound defence.

This game may have been the first sign of soccer progress in the oil-rich countries of the Middle East, as far as we are concerned, but Britain can take some pride in their rapid development and growing success.

For though great names such as Ferenc Puskas (in Saudi Arabia) and Mario Zagalo (in Kuwait) have worked in the Middle East in recent years, it is with men like Don Revie, Jimmy Hill, Bill McGarry, Ronnie Allen and Frank O'Farrell that football in the oil-rich nations is taking off.

When the Saudis offered to provide Jimmy Hill with £25 million to develop their football it sounded as if the BBC

man had found the proverbial crock of gold at the end of a rainbow. But as he has been at pains to explain, a country with only one grass pitch needed to invest a great deal of money in facilities alone before it could start to think much about its players making much progress in the arts, skills and tactics of the game.

When Bill McGarry, Hill's original choice for national manager, left to take over at Newcastle last November, his place was taken by Ronnie Allen, whose experience working through interpreters at Atletico Bilbao and Sporting Lisbon was obviously invaluable.

Allen was enjoying an outstanding season with West Bromwich Albion, but he had not yet been offered a contract. It was an oversight that was to prove costly for the West Midland club. After an interview with Prince Faisal in Saudi Arabia, Allen announced that he 'was so impressed with the ambitious approach and the terms I decided to accept then and there.'

Saudi Arabia's first ambition must be to qualify for the World Cup finals. Last time they were put out by Iran, the major power in Middle East football.

Even though Iran's national league—divided into a number of regional divisions—has been in operation only half a dozen years, they first took the Asian Games soccer title in 1968, winning it again in 1972 and 1974. That third triumph made a national hero out of Irishman Frank O'Farrell, who worked sensibly and steadily for a two-year spell to lay the foundations for Iran's World Cup success.

'The administration and structure of football out there is very good,' said O'Farrell—formerly manager of Torquay, Leicester, Manchester United and Cardiff—after returning to England at the end of his stint. 'The main thing is it's no use thinking about the things you get in Britain. That's no good to you. It's no use thinking it's like home. But my time out there didn't seem like two years. But then, the job

Don Revie limbers up the United Arab Emirates national team before a trial match. Nicknamed 'The Godfather' by English critics, Revie is better known as 'Captain Don' in the UAE.

Allen of Saudi Arabia
All 10 first division clubs. have new stadia and work has begun on six football complexes, all with synthetic turf. Ronnie Allen, 47, who played over 500 games for WBA before spells as manager of Wolves, Bilbao, Sporting Lisbon, Walsall and WBA, is now national manager.

Hammer of the Scots
Iran spent £30 million on facilities for the 1974 Asian Games, in which they took the gold medal for football. Frank O'Farrell was the manager then, but his assistant, Heshmat Mohajerany, took over the side that qualified for the World Cup finals in Argentina, where they damaged Scotland's hopes almost beyond repair by holding them to a 1-1 draw.

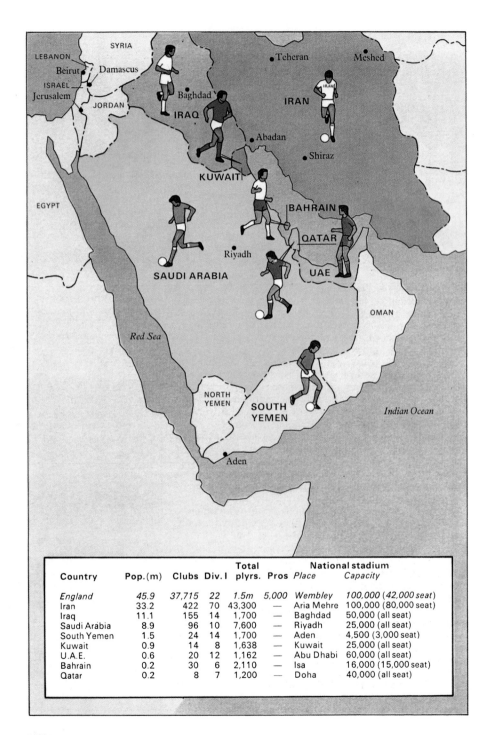

Country	Pop.(m)	Clubs	Div. I	Total plyrs.	Pros	National stadium Place	Capacity
England	*45.9*	*37,715*	*22*	*1.5m*	*5,000*	*Wembley*	*100,000 (42,000 seat)*
Iran	33.2	422	70	43,300	—	Aria Mehre	100,000 (80,000 seat)
Iraq	11.1	155	14	1,700	—	Baghdad	50,000 (all seat)
Saudi Arabia	8.9	96	10	7,600	—	Riyadh	25,000 (all seat)
South Yemen	1.5	24	14	1,700	—	Aden	4,500 (3,000 seat)
Kuwait	0.9	14	8	1,638	—	Kuwait	25,000 (all seat)
U.A.E.	0.6	20	12	1,162	—	Abu Dhabi	60,000 (all seat)
Bahrain	0.2	30	6	2,110	—	Isa	16,000 (15,000 seat)
Qatar	0.2	8	7	1,200	—	Doha	40,000 (all seat)

All-Sport

Colorsport

Nasrullah Abdullahi plays for Shahbaz, one of the top clubs in Iran's regionalised league.

Jimmy Hill, a success at everything he has turned his hand to since he was a £7 a week Brentford forward, now has overall charge of soccer in Saudi Arabia.

went very well. Nowhere's very beautiful if you keep getting beaten 4-0 . . .'

Why—apart from the money—did he go out there? 'It was simply a challenge,' O'Farrell replies. 'The challenge of helping an emerging soccer nation.'

Another man to take up that challenge was Don Revie, English soccer's most famous—or infamous—export.

Revie walked out on the England manager's job after three unsatisfactory years in the summer of 1977, accepting a £340,000 four-year contract in the little-known United Arab Emirates. With him went Les Cocker, his assistant for most of his reign with Leeds and England.

Revie was struck by the players' natural ability and ball skills developed on oil-rolled sand pitches. 'They seem to lose confidence very quickly if they try something different and it doesn't come off,' he adds. 'But they liked being disciplined and organised because, as I told them, it's all part of being a professional.

'I think we must keep things very basis, very simple, at least until we get them into the camps. They love practising dead-ball moves because most of the teams here do the same things at throw-ins, corners and free-kicks.

'I'm making as few changes to the squad as possible and drilling and drilling them as Sir Alf Ramsey did with the England team when he was manager . . . and as I did at Leeds in the days when I had no money to buy players.'

Already it's clear that those youngsters who have had the opportunity to watch the top European stars on television have a far greater appreciation of the game than the established players.

The UAE entered the 1978 World Cup, but, drawn in a group with Qatar, Bahrain and Kuwait (Kuwait went through to the next round), they withdrew before a ball had been kicked. It'll be interesting to see what happens next time—not just to them but to all the oil-rich nations.

`Nicking´ the ball: Brian Flynn

'If he shows you a piece of the ball, go in and get any part you can to it. Knock it away—to a team-mate if it's possible.'

You need all-round skills to make it in football these days. Attackers must know how to defend . . . and defenders—even goalkeepers—have to know how to use the ball once they've won it.

Even more is expected of midfielders. They've got to be great at both jobs.

Take Brian Flynn. He's the little fellow who keeps things moving in the Leeds and Wales engine-rooms . . . playing one-twos, appearing in support of the player with the ball . . . always looking to find space or to make it.

But nobody's job finishes when the other side has the

In like Flynn . . . Brian puts the pressure on, trying to force the loss of control that will give him his chance.

ball. Brian is constantly harrying opponents and denying them the space and time to set up their own moves.

And he's especially good at getting back to 'nick' the ball—putting in a foot to knock the ball away.

'I get my share,' admits Brian. But he points out that there is a time to nick . . . and a time *not* to nick.

'You've got to wait for a mistake . . . when your opponent has lost just that little bit of control. There's no point in just diving in. The level of skill in the First Division is so high you're just left looking like a fool.

'And you're out of the game if you're on your backside.

'If he shows you a piece of the ball, go in and get any

part you can to it.

'But if he shows you all the ball then you've got to go into the tackle . . . all the way.

'When it's a 50-50 ball with an opponent, then you've got to go in with everything—or you're likely to get hurt.

Don't go trying to get just a toe to the ball . . . or you'll get it knocked back at right angles.'

Brian is the kind of quick-witted player who can make opponents pay for those small mistakes: a momentary loss of control and he's pinched the ball.

'A lot depends on how sharp you are,' he says. 'Being small helps . . . and lots of short sprints in training. If you're that bit quicker over five metres, it makes all the difference.'

'Speed and determination—these are the vital factors,' says *Handbook's* coaching consultant Graham Taylor. One of you (B) should

concentrate on nicking the ball while the other two take it in turns to dribble towards the centre spot. After a while, change over.

'Wait for the moment when the ball has just left the dribbler's foot . . . then get in there quickly before he can gain control of it again.'

RISING DEREK
STAR STATHAM

When people like Ron Greenwood, Brian Clough and Bill Shankly are piling on the praise, you've got to have something going for you.

And that's the happy position Derek Statham, West Bromwich Albion's exciting young left-back, finds himself in.

Shankly says: 'Statham is the best prospect since Ramon Wilson was a youngster—and he'll get better and better with experience.'

Clough enthuses: 'If I needed a left-back I'd go for Statham. He's young, dedicated and willing to learn. He's a credit to the game and will go a long way.'

Greenwood says: 'He's one for the future.'

Enough to turn the head of most youngsters, but Statham—still only 19—keeps his feet firmly on the ground.

He says: 'It's nice to have people who have achieved so much in the game saying these things about me, but I know I've got a lot to learn. I'm working hard at improving my positional sense off the ball. It's easy to be caught out if you're not alert to everything that's going on around you.'

Off the pitch Derek is a quiet teenager from the heart of the industrial Black Country just outside Birmingham.

On it he is a bold attacking defender, a stocky athlete with tremendous speed and a cool head under pressure . . . all the qualities for an international future.

Last season was an exciting one for Derek, with WBA in the First Division title chase and the semi-final of the FA Cup.

Defeat against the eventual winners, Ipswich, was an important lesson for the Wolverhampton-born youngster.

He says: 'At first I thought it was the end of the world. To be so near Wembley and then see it disappear left me with a dreadful feeling.

'But football is a game of ups and downs. Everyone can't be a winner all the time and there's always another day. For us at Albion

that day was when we clinched a place in the UEFA Cup.

'The boss said we had to get our heads up and go all out for Europe. He drove us. He made sure nobody lost belief in themselves.'

Ron Atkinson repays the defender's tribute. 'Derek works hard in training and is always willing to listen to advice. He's dedicated to becoming a better player. That's a must for youngsters. It's not enough just to have potential; you have to keep working to make sure it comes to something . . .'

Amazingly, Derek has already played under three different managers at West Bromwich. The first was Johnny Giles. In those days the route to the top looked long and twisting for the young defender.

The left-back position was held by Scottish Under-23 player Ray Wilson, and when he was injured midfield man Len

Derek's left foot clears from Manchester City's Peter Barnes. There are many people in the game who would like to see this duo together in the England team, providing a young, talented and eager left-sided thrust.

106

'Derek Statham is undoubtedly the England left-back of the future. He's one of our greatest prospects . . . I believe he is ready now for the full England team.' BOBBY CHARLTON

Club	Season	League		FA Cup		Lge Cup	
		Ms	Gs	Ms	Gs	Ms	Gs
WBA	1976–77	16	1	–	–	–	–
	1977–78	40	–	6	–	3	–
		56	1	6	–	3	–

Cantello droppped back to fill the breach.

Then Wilson was forced to quit the game, Cantello was sidelined with cartilage trouble, and Statham stepped in.

He recalls: 'When I came into the side Johnny Giles really nursed me along. He was playing on the left side of midfield and was always there to help out.'

At that time Albion played a slow, deliberate, continental type of game, passing square or back to probe for an opening, then swiftly cutting into the defence. But under Atkinson they are more direct, which suits the overlapping style of Statham.

His link with Willie Johnston gives Albion a lethal left hook . . . and there are a few people around who can envisage a similar partnership with Peter Barnes—for England.

Derek, here taking on Arsenal full-back Pat Rice, is a defender who loves to attack . . . and has the speed, control and judgement to make it pay off. He scored on his debut, against Stoke, and his touchline bursts and one-twos with Willie Johnston have since worried even the best organised defences.

Founded: 1883
Address: Highfield Road, Coventry
Ground: Capacity 48,000; Playing area 100.5 x 68.5 m
Record attendance: 51,457 v Wolves Div. 2, 29.4.67
Record victory: 9-0 Bristol City, Div. 3 (S), 28.4.34
Record defeat: 2-10 v Norwich City, Div. 3 (S), 15.3.30
Most League points: 60 Div. 4, 1958-59, Div. 3, 1964-65
Most League goals: 108, Div. 3 (S), 1931-32
League scoring record: 49, Clarrie Bourton, Div. 3 (S), 1931-32
Record League aggregate: 171, Clarrie Bourton, 1931-37
Most League appearances: 486, George Curtis, 1956-70
Most capped player: 21, Dave Clements, N. Ireland, 1965-71
13 with Sheffield Wednesday, 12 with Everton, 2 with Cosmos)
League record: 1919 Elected to Div. 2; 1925-26 Div. 3 (N);
1926-36 Div. 3 (S); 1936-52 Div. 2; 1952-58 Div. 3 (S); 1958-59
Div. 4; 1959-64 Div. 3; 1964-67 Div. 2; 1967- Div. 1
Honours: Div. 2 Champions 1966-67; Div. 3 Champions 1963-64;
Div. 3 (S) Champions 1935-36

COVENTRY CITY

Bob Thomas

Manager Gordon Milne takes a breather from his duties at Highfield Road.

Coventry in Europe
Coventry have qualified for Europe only once—in 1970 when they played in the Fairs Cup. After convincingly beating the Bulgarians of Trakia Plovdiv, they went to Munich to take on Bayern . . . and were beaten 6-1.

Only a year ago Coventry were licking their wounds after just escaping relegation in their last game of the season. But now, following a campaign which saw them finish a fraction away from a place in this year's UEFA Cup, they are bursting with confidence and ready to go chasing honours.

It is a tremendous credit to team manager Gordon Milne and the man recalled to the club to help them lay the financial foundation for lasting success—Jimmy Hill.

Hill was the man in charge for the six years when the club advanced from the Third Division to the First—for the first time ever—and the whole city caught sky blue fever.

Highfield Road was often filled to capacity. Trainloads of fans would travel to away matches on the 'Sky Blue Special' and on one famous occasion 10,000 fans turned up at Highfield Road when the team were playing away—but they did not miss the match. It was relayed back to Coventry on close-circuit television . . . and three giant screens showed City beating Cardiff 2-1.

When things got tough for Coventry, with falling gates causing a cash crisis, Hill returned in the role of unpaid managing director.

And he and Milne came up with a buying and selling scheme aimed at putting the club's finances right.

Now Coventry have money to spend again . . . and Milne is convinced that the club is on the brink of the big time.

The former Liverpool wing-half has a set of players who are young, skilful and improving all the time.

'They're a young team without much First Division experience,' says Gordon. 'It was their first full season together as a team. And they did well. Now they've got to build on what they've learnt.'

One of Milne's shrewdest buys was Ian Wallace, who cost only £50,000 from Dumbarton. It was his partnership with

the tall Mick Ferguson up front that gave Coventry much of their goal thrust—with 37 in the League.

Ferguson grabbed his chance when Milne was forced to sell David Cross to West Bromwich Albion for £120,000, and his ability in the air proved to be the ideal foil for the speedy, darting Wallace.

Wallace has already played for the full Scotland side, while Milne believes that Ferguson's qualities will soon be recognised by Ron Greenwood.

'If he continues to play as well as he has been doing then international recognition is bound to come,' says Milne. 'I believe he's capable of 30 goals a season.'

Milne has had other successes as well. Bobby McDonald was a reserve midfielder at Aston Villa before his £45,000 move to Highfield Road. Milne moved him to left-back and he hasn't missed a game for two seasons.

Jim Blyth was signed for £20,000 from Preston . . . now there are many who believe that he should be Scotland's first choice goalkeeper.

Mick Ferguson, who emerged from Coventry's reserves to score 17 goals in 30 League games last season, gives Ian Bowyer and the Forest defence a tough time. Larry Lloyd looks on.

Going for goals
Coventry used a bold new strategy last season. Gordon Milne explains: 'Our strengths lay in attack . . . so we decided to go for goals whatever the consequences.' Coventry scored 75 League goals; only Everton (76) scored more in the First Division.

Reg Matthews won his first England cap as a Coventry player in 1956, when City were in the Third Division. He was the first Coventry-born man to play for England.

Colorsport

Then there is Don Nardiello, who forced his way into the side and won a cap for Wales, and Barry Powell, who added bite and consistency to his game . . . 'his best season ever,' says Milne.

Add to these the experience of internationals Tommy Hutchison and captain Terry Yorath and of senior professional Micky Coop and the ingredients were there for a successful side; a side that, but for a faltering spell at the end of the season, would have qualified for European competition for the second time.

One problem Coventry have faced since Hill resigned the manager's job to become a television personality is a fall-off in support. The days of regular full houses at Highfield Road seemed to have gone for good.

But that is changing now. Towards the end of last season attendances improved and this summer there have been encouraging signs that the fans are coming back. More season tickets have been sold than ever before.

The Coventry board of directors, which includes former England manager Joe Mercer, can take some credit for the Sky Blues' revival. They stepped in when Coventry were in danger of relegation and offered Milne and his right-hand man, Ron Wylie, new two-year contracts.

That took a lot of the pressure off the two men and allowed them to work for success in the only way that is worthwhile . . . by planning for the long-term future of the club and being willing to take the setbacks in the meantime.

They are lucky to have someone like Jimmy Hill around. He knows the pitfalls of taking the easy way out and sacking the team boss. He has a wide experience of football as a player, administrator and observer and his word carries a lot of weight in the Coventry boardroom.

And his return to Highfield Road has gone some way to reviving sky blue fever in Coventry.

Syndication International

Sky Blue revolution
Derrick Robins provided the foresight and Jimmy Hill the flair for a glorious six years at Coventry in the 1960s. They took the club to the Third and Second Division championships, before Hill resigned in 1967. Many of their ideas were dismissed as gimmicks, but the fact remains that support for the club reached a peak never achieved before . . . or since. Hill said: 'Gimmick is a word used by jealous people to describe an idea they wished they'd thought of first.'
Said Robins: 'When I first began my association with this club, all they ever thought about was getting back into the Second Division. Now that would be considered a disaster.'

Owen Barnes

LEFT *Jimmy Hill, the manager who, backed by chairman Derrick Robins (above), took City to the First Division for the first time in their history.*

Terry Yorath, captain of Coventry and Wales, whose will to win, experience and example have proved invaluable to a side rich in young talent.

Ian Wallace—20 League goals last season—takes on Scottish international team-mate Kenny Burns.

Colorsport

Test your soccer knowledge and WIN A SET OF ENGLAND KIT—OR KIT FROM THE TOP TEAM OF YOUR CHOICE!

20 sets of super-modern strip from

to be won in this week's FREE-TO-ENTER QUIZ—choose from the list at the foot of the page

1. Which is the only country to appear in all 11 World Cup final series?

2. Which *three* of these clubs were *not* among the founder members of the Football League in 1888: Aston Villa, Blackburn Rovers, Bolton Wanderers, Derby County, Everton, Liverpool, Manchester City, Notts County, Sunderland?

3. Joe Payne holds the record for most goals scored in a Football League match—10 against Bristol Rovers on 13 April 1936. Which club did he play for?

Syndication International

4. LEFT In 1964 he became the youngest player ever to appear in an FA Cup final. Who is he?

5. Match the club to the town: (1) St Mirren, (2) St Johnstone, (3) Raith Rovers, (4) Queen of the South; (a) Perth, (b) Dumfries, (c) Paisley, (d) Kirkcaldy.

6. Which team are known as the 'Loons'.

7. Who is the odd man out, and why: Zoff, Cabrini, Gentile, Tardelli, Benetti, Rossi, Causio, Bettega?

8. Which club lost four Irish Cup finals in five years, 1973-1977?

Trevor Cherry

'I try and spend a few minutes with kids who come to me for advice ... I believe we professionals have a duty to help them.'

Trevor Cherry is one of those players who just seems to get better and better. With Huddersfield, he was just another unspectacular wing-half; when he first joined Leeds, he struggled to get into the side; now he's an England squad regular and the captain of a Leeds team that should be challenging for honours this season.

'The three words that have been my inspiration since long before I joined my local club—Huddersfield Town—as a 15-year-old were: 'Never stop trying!'

'There were times when I thought I'd never achieve my ambition of becoming a full-time professional. I eventually made the grade through sheer hard work.

'Then I had to justify Don Revie's belief in me. I must

Trevor Cherry ... aiming for a second championship medal.

Left-back for England, defensive midfielder for Leeds ... Trevor Cherry's hard work and 100 per cent effort have made him a success in whatever role he tackles.

have proved something to him, because when he took over the England job he gave me my first cap.

'It's a fact that if you have faith in yourself—if you train hard and always give 100 per cent effort—you can virtually work miracles.

'And dedication is not something restricted to footballers. It's something you need in every walk of life.'

113

Gary Hamson on passing

'If you can't pass the ball you can't play football—it's as simple as that.' GRAHAM TAYLOR

Colorsport

It's probably the first thing you ever do as a kid in the school playground. And it's certainly the first thing you are liable to take for granted . . . the pass.

Yet it's passing and control that the likes of Ron Greenwood are pointing to as the weaknesses of English players compared with the best in the world.

And our coaching consultant Graham Taylor says: 'A pass doesn't only involve the player making it but also the player who receives it. So you can say that a good pass is one that presents no problems to the receiver.'

That means the pass must be accurate and hit with the right 'weight'—it's no good passing straight to someone's feet if the ball is going at 50 miles an hour!

One of the best young passers in the game is Sheffield United's brilliant young midfield player Gary Hamson.

Gary demonstrates the pass that is used most often in matches—the push pass.

'I've been playing League football for two seasons now, but I still practise passing regularly.'

Gary is naturally left-footed but can pass well with his right as well.

For players whose weaker foot is 'just for standing on' there's no substitute for practice—and then more practice.

Find a wall and keep at it . . . until the weak foot passes like a machine. Even if it's only good for a five- or ten-yard pass—that's something.

The push pass is played with the inside of the foot—as Gary demonstrates—because it's the best place to give a good, accurate ball. There's a nice wide area to strike with, and you'll find that it's a good position for balance.

A final word to anyone who still thinks it's all a bit too easy: see how many times in succession you can hit the perfect 10-yard pass to a friend—one that's accurate and hit with the right 'weight'.

And use both feet!

Ray Green

Gary approaches the ball for a pass with his left foot. Note how, even for a simple pass, he still uses his arms for balance.

Just before impact you can see how he will pass the ball with the inside of the foot—which is best for accuracy.

At impact Gary still has his eye on the ball—he's nicely positioned for the pass that presents no problems to the receiver.

Ray Green

The Hamson pass seen from behind . . . Gary gets his non-kicking foot as near to the ball as is comfortable and the left —the one he uses most on the left side of Sheffield United's midfield—makes the pass that is stroked but not lashed.

Graham Taylor on passing

'It's encouraging that British football is starting to look again at the little things—like control and passing,' says Graham.

'This is the area where we've fallen behind the continentals but now hopefully we're beginning to catch up—at least we're recognising the problem !

'Every so often you have to stop and take stock—which can mean going back to the basics. And you can't get more basic than the need for good passes.

'The tendency is to pass to a team-mate and not bother to think whether it was a good one or not—just think : "Oh, well, he's got it", and leave it at that.

'But was it a pass that he controlled without too much trouble ? Was it a pass that enabled him to carry on a move in the way he wanted ?

'Or was it a pass that put him in trouble—perhaps the dreaded "hospital ball", which is fifty-fifty between team-mate and an opponent ?

'A good practice for two is shown in the diagram below. One player receives passes from the other as he runs backwards, which means the passes must be hit with the correct weight.'

Solo practice

'A good pass always feels right,' says Graham Taylor. 'It's that indefinable communication between foot, ball and brain. But what you can say about it is that the "feel" comes from constant practice—getting to know the ball, what it will do and what you can make it do.

Behind every good pass in a match are literally thousands of passes in training—not all of them good ones, either ! So, unless you can get dad out of his chair, it's back to the wall for passing practice. A wall is not much of a team-mate, so imagination must play a part in terms of the "weight" of the pass.

Concentrate on the points that Gary demonstrates— passes hit with the inside of the foot and arms used for balance. Keep at it and you'll begin to get that magic "feel".

A Matter of Fact

Hans Krankl, Barcelona's £750,000 buy from Rapid Vienna this summer, was Europe's top First Division scorer last season with 41 league goals . . . out of a Rapid total of 76! The Austrian's nearest rival was Carlos Bianchi, of French club Paris St Germain, with 37.

Celtic once played two League games in one day, beating Raith Rovers 6–0 and Motherwell 3–1 on 15 April 1916.

Billy Minter of St Albans City scored 7 goals in an FA Cup tie against Dulwich Hamlet in November 1922 . . . and still finished on the losing side: St Albans went down 8–7!

Charlton Athletic's Bert Turner scored twice in the 1946 FA Cup final—once for each side! Charlton lost 4–1 to Derby.

The youngest team boss in British senior football is 27-year-old Dave Clarke (above), player-manager of East Fife since February. He replaced former Hibs and Coventry star Roy Barry—but couldn't help the club avoid relegation.

The hottest day on which a full League programme has been played is thought to have been 1 September 1906, when nowhere in the country recorded an afternoon temperature of less than 32 C (90 F). That same afternoon George Hilsdon, in his League debut for Chelsea, scored five goals against Glossop North End.

Of the 22 clubs that formed the original Third Division in 1920-21, only Merthyr Town are no longer in the Football League. Of the 20 clubs that formed the original Third Division (North) the following season, eight are no longer in the League. They are (with the date they dropped out of the League): Stalybridge Celtic (1923), Durham City (1928), Ashington (1929), Nelson (1931), Wigan Borough (1931), Accrington Stanley (1962), Barrow (1972) and Southport (1978).

Portsmouth once 'held' the FA Cup for 7 years. They won the trophy by beating Wolves 4–1 in the 1939 final and, because there was no competition during the Second World War, retained it until they lost to Birmingham City in the third round in 1945-46.

Benfica finished last season unbeaten in the Portuguese League, conceding only 11 goals in their 30 matches. Yet Porto still beat them for the championship on goal difference!

The only brothers from the same professional side to play for England were Fred and Frank Forman of Nottingham Forest, way back in 1899.

All of Uruguay's 12 First Division clubs play in the capital, Montevideo.

Newcastle United's Billy Foulkes (no relation to the former Manchester United player) scored with his first kick on his international debut, for Wales against England at Cardiff in October 1951.

Ladislav Kubala played at full international level in the 1950s and 1960s for three countries—Hungary, Czechoslovakia and finally Spain.

PHILIPS

Simply points ahead could be the motto for PSV, Dutch champions for three out of the last four seasons . . .

P.S.V.

Ralf Edstrom, one of the world's greatest headers of the ball, in his days as PSV's centre-forward.

If you took a typical British fan to watch a PSV Eindhoven game, he'd feel at home straight away.

For the Dutch champions play a very English type of game—fast with long balls and high crosses. Up front they've got a bustling centre-forward who's known as Harry. And when their supporters burst into song, it's 'You'll Never Walk Alone' . . . in English.

It's largely because of television. Fans in the south of Holland can watch both 'Match of the Day' and 'The Big Match'.

But the style of the team is down to their manager coach Kees Rijvers, a former international winger with Feyenoord.

Rijvers has known nothing but success as a manager. He joined PSV in 1973 after steering unfashionable FC Twente of Enschede to a high spot in the Dutch 'Division of Honour'.

In Rijvers' first season, PSV finished fourth and rattled in 96 goals in 34 league games.

The following season (1974-75) PSV were champions—and by this time Rijvers had bought some big names.

He brought the lanky Ralf Edstrom from Sweden for £100,000 and snapped up the Van der Kerkhof twins, Rene and Willy, for a bargain £30,000 each.

Already in goal was Jan van Beveren—bought from Sparta Rotterdam for the then world record fee of £175,000

ANP Photos

Willy van der Kerkhof beats St Etienne keeper Curkovic in a European Cup semi-final in April 1976.

EINDHOVEN

—and he is still rated the best goalkeeper in Holland. Van Beveren was first choice for his country but lost his place in the team for refusing to go to Argentina World Cup for political reasons.

Six PSV players were in the World Cup squad—the Van der Kerkhof twins, centre-back Ernie Brandts, midfielder Jan Poortvliet, sweeper Adrie van Kraaij, who all played, and 'Harry' Henricus Lubse.

Last season Edstrom returned to Sweden but Rijvers—instead of going for a new superstar—re-organised his side . . . and won the championship for the third time in four years.

If you add the Dutch Cup in 1976 and the UEFA Cup last season, it's clear that PSV have taken over as the number one club in Holland; not bad for a team once branded as 'pirates'.

That was in 1954 when PSV was one of a group of clubs who broke away from KNVB—the Royal Dutch FA—to form their own professional league. Peace was restored after two years with a deal on semi-professionalism.

The 'Division of Honour', started in 1956-57, was fully professional by the 1960s and PSV were soon champions—in 1962-63—with centre-forward Pierre Kerkhoffs the league's top scorer with 22 goals.

Ernie Brandts . . . surprise success in the World Cup.

Willy van der Kuylen's fierce volleys have been a feature of Dutch football for more than a decade. Now a veteran, Willy is the side's midfield general—but defences still try to keep him off his lethal left foot.

Big guns of the PSV attack are Lubse and Gerrie Deijkers, who shared 32 goals in last season's title winning side. Their approach is very English, with many of their goals headed 'knock-downs' by one for the other.

PSV clinched the title with several games in hand and among their victories was a 4–1 thrashing of the once-great Ajax in Amsterdam. In the UEFA Cup final they beat the team Dutch World Cup star Johnny Rep plays for, Corsican club SC Bastia.

Among the PSV reserves is yet another British connection —Welsh international striker Nick Deacy. Although he makes only rare appearances in the first team—and there isn't a reserve side—Deacy did score a vital goal away to Barcelona in the semi-final of the UEFA Cup.

Capacity at the PSV ground is still only 23,500—but more often than not that was the gate last season

They had the best attendance figures in Holland, averaging 22,235, ahead of Feyenoord (18,412) in second place. Ajax managed only 11,177.

With loyal supporters like that, there's no chance that PSV will ever walk alone.

Popperfoto

Ford goes to Philips
Trevor Ford, a hard, direct, shoulder-charging centre-forward who scored 23 goals in 38 internationals for Wales, played for PSV for three seasons from 1957. Always a controversial figure in a career that included spells at Swansea, Villa, Sunderland, Cardiff and Newport, Ford was banned from the League after his autobiography, 'I Lead the Attack', revealed that illegal payments were being made to League players whose maximum wage was meant to be a mere £15 a week. Ford went into exile in Eindhoven, where he earned good money both as a player and as a public relations officer for Philips. In a career that spanned 16 seasons he scored 177 League goals—and was never sent off.

Peter Robinson

Continuing PSV's Welsh connection is Nick Deacy. A striker signed from Hereford United, Deacy has since broken into the Welsh international squad, but he is still not a regular in the Eindhoven team.

120

FOOTBALL FITNESS TRAINING PROGRAMME

UNDER-12 AGE GROUP

A. Fast 'upside-down' cycling for 20 secs.

B. 10 press-ups, 10 secs rest, then 5 press-ups.

C. Stand with legs astride. In a backwards direction, make large circles with your arms. Start slowly, building up speed. Do 20 secs with each arm.

D. 'Star jumps'. Assume crouch position, hands on floor. Spring up, flinging arms upwards and legs apart closing legs before landing. Repeat 10 times.

E. Lie on your back, arms raised upwards. Sit up, reaching forward to touch your toes, bringing head as close to your knees as possible.

F. Lie on your front and take the body weight on your elbows. Raise body from the floor by straightening it from head to heels, then down. Complete as many as possible in 20 secs.

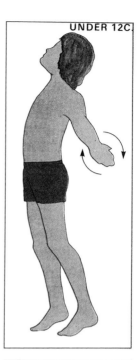

UNDER 12C.

13-14 AGE GROUP

A. Running on the spot. Start slowly, getting faster. Max. 30 secs.

B. Do 10 press-ups, rest for 5 secs, then repeat.

C. Lie on your back with arms by your sides. Raise both legs a few inches, then lower slowly. Do as many as possible in 20 secs.

D. Sitting up, place arms across chest. Fling your arms backwards and slightly upwards, combined with deep breathing. Max. 20 times.

E. 'Upside-down' cycling. Start slowly, building up speed. Max. 30 secs.

F. Stand with legs astride, and toes pointing slightly outwards. Clasp fingers under chin, and drop to a squat, with seat as close as possible to your heels. As many as possible in 20 secs.

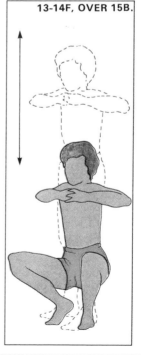

13-14F, OVER 15B.

OVER-15 AGE GROUP

A. From the crouch position spring up, stretching upwards. On landing, go back to crouch. As many as possible in 20 secs.

B. Stand with legs astride, toes pointing slightly outwards. Clasp fingers under chin. Bend knees and drop to squat, then stand up slowly. Max 20.

C. Do 15 press-ups, rest for 5 secs, then do 5 more.

D. Lie on your back. Reaching forward, touch your toes bringing head as close to knees as possible. Repeat 15 times.

E. Place both hands on the wall a shoulders width apart. Allow your nose to touch the wall with a 'vertical' press-up. Repeat 10 times.

F. Sit on the edge of a chair with your feet resting on another about 4 feet in front of you. Take hold of the sides of the chair, and raise the body. Bending the arms at the elbows, lower the upper body as low as possible, then up again. Repeat as many as possible in 20 secs. If after 20 secs. you still feel strong, do as many more as you can. But don't overdo it—this is a demanding exercise.

Working the triangle: John Robertson

'John Robertson is a great example of a right-footed left winger who is a constant danger just because he can move inside naturally by using his better foot.' GRAHAM TAYLOR

Ray Green

Players who are naturally left-footed are looked upon as gold dust in the football world —and the search for them goes on daily.

Their importance is simply the ability they have to use the ball well after getting into good positions on the left side of the pitch.

But there's one great example of a predominantly right-footed player who works

wonders out on the left— John Robertson, the number 11 with champions Nottingham Forest.

Time and again Robertson brings the ball inside with his right foot and causes panic among the opposition.

'It's very difficult for the full-back marking him to make a tackle because, being right-footed, Robertson keeps the ball away from him

Inside he goes ... Robertson sets off on the run that causes panic in defences—this time against Birmingham.

naturally,' explains Graham Taylor.

'As he comes inside he also has a good view of the pitch ... and therefore has lots of alternatives. If it's on, he can hit a long ball to the opposite flank, but more often you'll see him work the triangle along the left.

'All it needs is a touch off to someone in midfield and a run by Archie Gemmill into the space that Robertson and his marker have left. Then pop—a chipped pass puts Archie away for a move that is one of Forest's sharpest weapons.

'Left-footed left wingers tend to hug the line and if the service to them is cut out they can be shut out of the game.

'Then, of course, he can play a one-two into the heart of the opponents' defence or hit the kind of shot that gave him a great goal in the Charity Shield match against Ipswich at Wembley. So often you see a left-footed winger come inside and not have the alternative of a shot simply because his right foot is not good enough.

'So you can see that having a right-footed left-winger is no great handicap, as long as you have a left-sided player to make the runs outside him.

'And Robertson is not the only example, is he ? Look at Clive Woods at Ipswich and Liverpool's Steve Heighway —both favour their right foot and both are always making the runs full-backs dread—on the inside.'

The Robertson magic thrilled 68,000 at the Charity Shield match against Ipswich and earned him high marks from the Sunday People . . .

FOREST Shilton 8 — Anderson 7, Lloyd 7, Burns 7, Barrett 7— O'Neill (w'drawn), 7, Gemmill 8, McGovern 7, — Woodcock 7, Withe 7, ★ROBERTSON 9. Sub.1 Needham.
Ref: P. Reeves (Leic⌐ ⌐r) 8.

Robertson began it, jinking in from the left touchline. His attempt to find a shooting position was crowded out so he turned the ball back towards the left. Barrett lobbed it forward

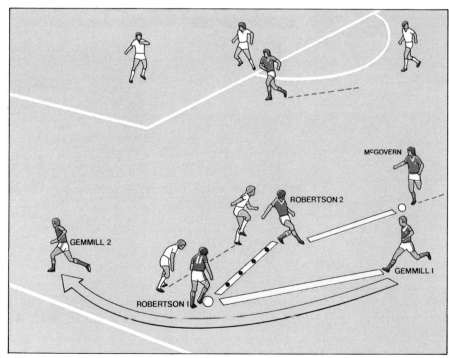

Our diagram shows how a typical Forest move develops down the left wing and makes use of John Robertson's natural asset of a strong right foot. Archie Gemmill plays the ball to Robertson and follows the pass to go outside Robertson as the winger brings the ball inside. From there Robertson has the choice of a touch pass to a midfield team mate—often John McGovern—who can chip the ball into the path of Gemmill. If it's on, Robertson can chip the ball to a striker, who can use Gemmill or Robertson again.

For years it was British clubs, and now the Americans are coming. But with Johnny Giles making a full-time job out of football in Ireland, there's hope that—in the south at least—they can start . . .

RESISTING IRELAND'S
SOCCER
RAIDERS

Johnny Giles, whose results with the national team and Shamrock Rovers have revived interest in the game in Eire.

Football in Ireland is in every way a subsidiary of the British game. Its talent is proved by the fact that no less than seven of the 22 that started the FA Cup final in May were Irish, its poverty by the fact that less than £6,000 was paid to Irish clubs for them.

Arsenal centre-half David Leary, for example, was just 13 years old when he went to Old Trafford for a trial. United wanted him there and then, but he chose not to sign professional for two years . . . and he picked Arsenal. His story is typical, though his success isn't; the majority of teenagers come back rejected.

All Irish clubs are part-time and gates average 1,000. So they offer little competition to even the lower divisions in England and Scotland, where an ambitious player has a better chance of being spotted by the big clubs. Even though Scotland is a similar breeding ground for English clubs, it does have full-time professional clubs. Most of the native talent passes through these clubs, which means that they receive a substantial transfer fee if the players later move on to England.

Not so in Ireland. Last season centre-forward Paul McGee left Sligo Rovers and walked into the first team at QPR, the fee a ludicrous £15,000. Sligo's manager Billy Sinclair explained to *Handbook* why the fee was so small: 'QPR offered us £15,000. I turned it down as too little. But Paul made it very awkward. He wanted away. I don't blame him. He's in his twenties and it was his last chance. So what do you do if the player won't play for you? I had no choice.'

The recently formed American league offers another destination for Irish players. About a dozen were playing there this summer on a temporary basis, while three were transferred permanently to Philadelphia Fury.

> **Two Irelands**
> Ireland was split into two in 1921, when the Irish Free State was founded. Prior to that, there was one national league and cup competition. The league, founded in 1890, was dominated by northern clubs—no southern club ever won the title, although Shelbourne & Bohemians both won the cup . . . For a while the new Southern cup admitted clubs from the north—and Alton United of Belfast won the trophy in 1923 . . . Linfield's double last season brought their total of league championships to 31 and their total of cup wins to—31 . . . Shamrock Rovers' cup win in the south was their 21st, well ahead of their rivals.

Arsenal's Northern Ireland international full-back Pat Rice on the attack against Ipswich's George Burley and Roger Osborne in last season's Cup final. Rice was one of 7 Irishmen playing that day . . . their total transfer value to Irish clubs: less than £6,000.

124

The three all came from Bohemians for a fee variously quoted between £28,000 and £100,000. Most people think they will be the first of many for a league with a lower standard and better wages than England. One 18-year-old Dubliner was earning £1,000 a month with a free car and a free flat playing for the Fury this summer.

But there arrived in Ireland last summer a man who plans to change the face of Irish football. Johnny Giles shocked the football world by resigning the managership of West Bromwich Albion and buying a half of—and becoming player-manager of—Shamrock Rovers in Dublin. At the same time he turned down the job at Old Trafford and £80,000 tax free to manage the Saudi Arabian team.

Giles moved not because of the pressure but because of a system which prevents a manager getting due reward for his success. 'The season before I went to West Brom, they lost £120,000; the first season I was there, they made a profit, including transfers of £40,000. But that makes no difference to my salary.

'For another thing, you could give an English club ten years, build up the team—then a few bad results and you could be fired by a businessman who's been on the board for a few months.' This can't happen at Shamrock Rovers. With a half share in the club, Giles gets half of every penny of profit.

His first year has been successful. Rovers won the Irish

Danny Blachflower, former Spurs captain and a perceptive football writer, is now manager of Northern Ireland.

Ireland's league clubs

NORTHERN IRELAND

Season	League	Cup winners
1968-69	Linfield	Ards
1969-70	Glentoran	Linfield
1970-71	Linfield	Linfield
1971-72	Glentoran	Distillery
1972-73	Crusaders	Coleraine
1973-74	Coleraine	Glentoran
1974-75	Linfield	Ards
1975-76	Crusaders	Coleraine
1976-77	Glentoran	Carrick Rangers
1977-78	Linfield	Coleraine
		Linfield

1. Ards (Newtonards)
2. Ballymena United
3. Bangor
4. Cliftonville (Belfast)
5. Coleraine
6. Crusaders (Belfast)
7. Distillery (Belfast)
8. Glenavon (Lurgan)
9. Glentoran (Belfast)
10. Larne
11. Linfield (Belfast)
12. Portadown

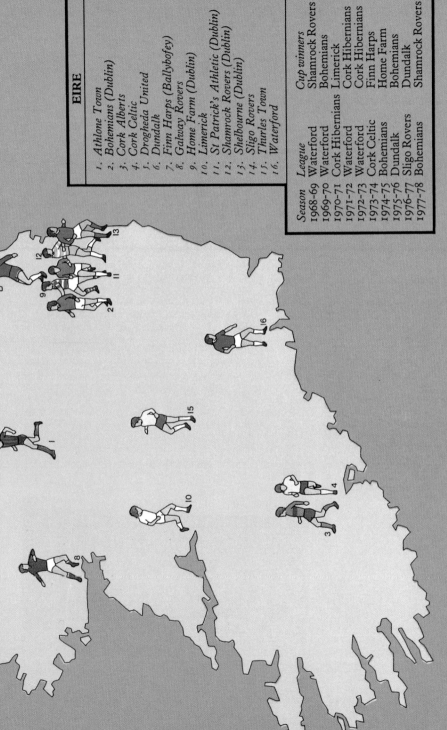

EIRE

1. Athlone Town
2. Bohemians (Dublin)
3. Cork Alberts
4. Cork Celtic
5. Drogheda United
6. Dundalk
7. Finn Harps (Ballybofey)
8. Galway Rovers
9. Home Farm (Dublin)
10. Limerick
11. St Patrick's Athletic (Dublin)
12. Shamrock Rovers (Dublin)
13. Shelbourne (Dublin)
14. Sligo Rovers
15. Thurles Town
16. Waterford

Season	League	Cup winners
1968-69	Waterford	Shamrock Rovers
1969-70	Waterford	Bohemians
1970-71	Cork Hibernians	Limerick
1971-72	Waterford	Cork Hibernians
1972-73	Waterford	Cork Hibernians
1973-74	Cork Celtic	Finn Harps
1974-75	Bohemians	Home Farm
1975-76	Dundalk	Bohemians
1976-77	Sligo Rovers	Dundalk
1977-78	Bohemians	Shamrock Rovers

Colorsport

Manchester United full-back Johnny Carey played 28 games for the Republic and 7 for Northern Ireland in the days before 1949 when it was not unusual for players from the south to be dual inter-nationals. On one occasion he represented both sides in the space of three days.

Eire's Liam Brady lets fly past France's Marius Tresor in a World Cup qualifier last year. Brady scored the only goal in a 1–0 win.

Cup and the Tyler Cup and finished fourth in the League. Attendances more than doubled. More important, his name and reputation has attracted to the club exactly the kind of player who would have gone straight to England in the past. For example, Pierce O'Leary, younger brother of Arsenal's David, is his left-back. Philadelphia Fury offered £60,000 after watching him play one match. Within two years he'll be worth £150,000 or more.

Although an All-Ireland League is unlikely in the foreseeable future, an All-Ireland national side is more of a possibility after two meetings this season between the two associations. 'I'd say the will is there on both sides,' Harry Cavan, president of the Northern FA, told *Handbook*.

Ireland already fields a single national team in hockey, cricket and rugby; and the players and supporters are all in favour. They point to how close the Republic's team, with Giles as player-manager, came to reaching the World Cup finals, beating France 1–0 in Dublin. With the Northern players to select as well, Ireland might have qualified. Most people believe it is a question of the association officials agreeing to give up their perks. 'Either way,' says Cavan, 'it won't happen till after the European Championship in which the two parts of Ireland are drawn together—along with England, Denmark and Bulgaria. It'll be the first time the two parts have played each other. None of us want to miss that.'

So soccer in Ireland is an uphill struggle—against poor attendances, the troubles, competition from Gaelic sports, from Britain and now from America. Probably fewer than half a dozen of the professional clubs are in the black. If it weren't for the loyalty of their fans and the interest of sponsors, professional soccer in this island would pack up altogether. But Johnny Giles, who holds two FA Cup winners medals, was moved to say after his club's win in the Irish final in May: 'It's just as much satisfaction to me to win this one as the ones at Wembley.'

GLEN ABBEY

Sporting Pictures UK

Whistle Test

'If a player does well to ride a foul tackle, he's right to get annoyed if the referee brings him back.' PAT PARTRIDGE

Referees who play the advantage rule well win a lot of respect from players and spectators alike.

There's nothing more irritating for a player who has survived a foul to hear the whistle blow for a free-kick. The stoppage means that his progress has been halted and the opponents have the chance to get back behind the ball.

And fans prefer the ref who waves play on to the one who keeps bringing the play back—'whistle happy' is their polite word for him.

'I'm a great believer in playing advantage,' says Durham's World Cup ref Pat Partridge. 'Fans pay good money to watch 90 minutes of football and if they can see continual play, so much the better.

But, adds Pat, there is another school of thought which says that referees should show their authority in the first few minutes of the match—a point of view opposed to the use of advantage.

'I don't go along with that,' says Pat. 'In my view the first minute of a match is the same as the last or any of the minutes in between. You should allow the play to flow at all times—and you're more likely to win players' respect that way than by any heavy-handed methods.

'In any case, if you feel that a particular foul deserves a caution, you can let the play go on and then caution the player at the end of the move.'

Pat puts his theories into practice. At the Leeds-Liverpool League game last season, one sharp-eyed journalist noted that Pat didn't blow his whistle once in the first 18 minutes of the match.

It's not only Pat Partridge who thinks that advantage should be played more often—it says as much in the laws.

Law V(b) says that *the referee shall refrain from penalising in cases where he is satisfied that, by doing so, he would be giving an advantage to the offending team.*

Surely the point is that every free-kick is potentially an advantage for the offenders and that referees should always adopt the policy of 'wait and see'.

Playing advantage can have one detrimental effect . . . on the ref! Puffing Pat keeps up with Everton's Duncan McKenzie and Brian Greenhoff of Manchester United.

Ray Green

129

PRO FILE
PETER REID

'The next thing on my list is a full England cap . . .'

County Press Photos

Peter Reid, the Koppite who preferred a career at Burnden Park to one at Anfield, will relish his visit to the Liverpool ground this month.

If Bolton Wanderers are Peter Reid's first loyalty these days, there's no doubting his second—Liverpool FC.

Born and bred on Merseyside, Reid has supported Liverpool for almost as long as he's been able to kick a football.

So it's hardly surprising that when Reid and his Bolton

Peter Reid in action against the Scots in typical buzzing style. Despite being a Second Division player, Peter was a regular member of the England Under-21 team, providing both skill and hard work in the run to the semi-finals of the European Championship against Yugoslavia. He also skippered the side against Finland: 'It was a tremendous honour,' he says, 'and I shall always remember it vividly.'

team-mates troop back to the dressing-room after a game, it's the Liverpool result he wants to hear first.

There won't be any need to make the usual inquiry this Saturday though—because Bolton, back in the First Division after 14 years absence, are playing at Anfield.

Whatever the result on Saturday, it's unlikely that Reid will have such a disappointing experience as he had on his previous appearance on the ground where, as a young fan, he used to stand regularly on the famous Kop.

'It was an utter disaster,' Reid explained to *Handbook*. 'I was playing for Bolton Reserves in a Central League game . . . and I got sent off.

'It was stupid really. I was very raw then and playing at Anfield meant so much to me that I foolishly let it go to my head.

'It won't be that way this time, that's for sure. I've been looking forward to it since the fixtures were published in July. I know all my family will be there and when I see the

Peter Robinson

Peter gets in a header against Notts County. Though renowned for his work rather than his scoring, he improved last season to 9—Bolton's third highest tally.

crowd and feel the fantastic atmosphere, there's no way I'm not going to enjoy it . . . for the whole 90 minutes.'

If things had worked out differently Reid could have been playing for Liverpool.

He says: 'As a schoolboy I played for Huyton Boys. We were very successful and caused something of an upset when we won the English Schools Trophy in 1970.

'Naturally plenty of scouts came to our games and chances arose to join various clubs as an apprentice. I had the choice of joining Liverpool or Everton, but when I went over to Bolton to look round Burnden Park my mind was made up.

'There was something about the club that attracted me. I think it was the family atmosphere of the place. Everyone is so friendly and get along through thick and thin.

'I owe so much to Ian Greaves. He had only just taken over from Jimmy Armfield when he gave me my debut . . . as a substitute at home to Orient in October 1974. I was 18.'

Reid soon established himself in the side and was ever-present for the next two seasons—when Bolton just missed out on promotion. And his cultured midfield play and his intense desire to be involved all the time were features of Bolton's championship side of last season.

'Last year we changed our pattern of play somewhat. Once I realised our game had benefitted I believe we would go up.

'We were much more solid than we had been in the previous two years. To some extent throwing caution to the wind was part of our downfall in the two seasons we

Peter the Great

What's Reid aiming at now he's in the top grade? 'Naturally I want to see Bolton do well in the First Division,' he says. 'And I think I'll do well this season.

'I'm a confident person . . . I believe in my own ability. You've got to if you are going to be successful in football.'

'From a personal aspect the next thing on my list is a full England cap. I think I'm good enough to win one.

'Don't think I'm being big-headed when I say that. I reckon you've got to aim at the top and have that bit of arrogance. Besides, I'm fiercely patriotic . . . I'd be thrilled to win a full cap.'

A first team regular at 18, Reid has always shown impressive maturity. He's a consistent performer . . . and a determined competitor.

Club	Div.	Pos.	Season	League		FA Cup		Lge Cup	
				Ms	Gs	Ms	Gs	Ms	Gs
Bolton	II	10	1974-75	27	–	2	–	–	–
Wanderers	II	4	1975-76	42	2	6	1	1	–
	II	4	1976-77	42	5	1	–	9	1
	II	1	1977-78	38	9	4	–	3	–
				149	16	13	1	13	1

went so close but just missed out.

'But in hindsight it could have been a blessing in disguise that we didn't go up earlier. I don't think the side would have been ready. There were too many youngsters with only limited experience.

'Failure—and that's what it was whichever way you look at it—helped me grow up . . . and it made success that much sweeter when it came.'

Reid pays tribute to the fans' contribution to Bolton's revival. 'Having the crowd behind you is half the battle,' he says. 'When I used to watch Liverpool I always considered myself part of their success whenever they won honours.

'That's the way it should be. At Bolton the fans stayed with us when we had gone so near to promotion. They deserved our success last season as much as the players — and they deserve First Division football.'

Reid will be looking to those same fans to make themselves heard over the Kop on his extra special day at Anfield.

133

Founded: 1867
Address: Hampden Park, Glasgow
Ground: Capacity 88,000 ; Playing area 105 x 68.5 m
Record attendance: 149,547 Scotland v England, 17.4.37 (*Club record 97,000 v Rangers, Scottish Cup 2nd rd, 18.2.33*)
Record victory: 16–0 v St Peter's, Scottish Cup 1st rd, 1885-86
Record defeat: 0–9 v Motherwell, Div. 1, 26.4.30
Most League points: 57, Div. 2, 1922-23
Most League goals: 100, Div. 1, 1928-29
League scoring record: 30, Willie Martin, Div. 1, 1937-38
Most capped player: 14, Watty Arnott, Scotland, 1883-93
League career: 1900-1922 Div. 1 ; 1922-23 Div. 2 ; 1923-48 Div. 1 ; 1948-56 Div. 2 ; 1956-58 Div. 1 ; 1958- Div. 2
Honours: Scottish Cup Winners 1874, 1875, 1876, 1880 1881 1882, 1884, 1886, 1890, 1893 ; Runners-up 1892, 1900 ; Div. 2 Champions 1923, 1956 ; FA Cup runners-up 1884, 1885

QUEEN'S PARK

Gilroy's babes
'We've proved we can attract good young players,' says manager Joe Gilroy, the former Clyde and Fulham forward. 'A few years back the average age was about 26. Last season it was 19½.'

Hampden Park empty . . . a home game for Queen's Park is played before an average of about 140,000 empty spaces.

One week Hampden Park is full of the game's most fanatical supporters . . . when Scotland are at home.

The next it's virtually empty . . . when Queen's Park are at home—the club that goes it alone as amateurs in a world full of professionals.

And the inevitable result is mediocrity.

Only eight or nine hundred people bother to watch Queen's Park stick to their principles in Scotland's Second Division. But it wasn't always so.

On a cold February day in 1933 no fewer than 97,000 people watched Queen's Park face Rangers in a Scottish Cup second round match.

And there was a time when Queen's were *the* team to beat, having won the Scottish Cup ten times before the turn of the century.

All, alas, in the past—so what lies ahead?

Joe Gilroy, manager for the last two seasons, says: 'Of course it's a great challenge finding high-quality players who are prepared to play for nothing.

'The committee and I accept that our best players will join other clubs. In my first season I lost eight players to the pro ranks; last season it was three.

'Somehow I have to produce a team capable of winning promotion without ignoring style or destroying the principle that football should be played for the enjoyment of the game.

'What purpose does a club like Queen's Park serve? Well, we must be the greatest "feeders" in Scottish football. I could fill an exercise book with the names of players who have become stars elsewhere—like Danny McGrain.'

Many people feel Queen's Park should give up Hampden, a 'ghost ground' for home games. But Joe argues: 'For players from clubs like Forfar and Brechin it's probably the only chance they'll ever get to tread on the same turf as the greats of the game.'

Queen's in 1874, first winners of the Scottish Cup. They were unbeaten for the first nine years of their existence.

The good old days
Founded on 9 July 1867, Queen's Park have won the Scottish Cup 10 times, but their last success was against Celtic way back in 1893! They also appeared in two FA Cup finals, losing to Blackburn Rovers in both 1884 and 1885.

Hampden Park full . . . for last season's Scotland-England international. Safety regulations kept the gate down to 88,000.

Ray Green

Right place-right time...Kaltz foils a Bettega beauty

For sheer drama, the Manfred Kaltz save against Italy in the World Cup was impossible to beat.

The picture of Roberto Bettega—the man robbed by Kaltz's last-ditch effort—holding his head in his hands said it all.

The save was instinctive. And it was made even more memorable by the beauty of the build-up it ruined.

Bettega took charge of the move from start to finish, going out to meet defender Antonio Cabrini and taking the ball.

From there it was a quick turn and a ball played forward to Paolo Rossi.

And, just as he did to provide the Bettega goal that beat Argentina, Rossi laid on the perfect return, allowing the ball to pass between his legs and flicking it on with his right heel.

Bettega still had a long way to go but made it look easy against the defending world champions. Two German defenders converged on him but Bettega skipped over both tackles.

Out came the experienced Sepp Maier to dive at Bettega's feet—and miss.

Bettega must have thought that was that. But his 'finishing touch' didn't have the desired result, his swivel kick from a rapidly narrowing angle being blocked by the outstretched leg of Kaltz.

The German sweeper had raced back to cover his exposed keeper and, even though he was off balance as he ran towards the near post, Kaltz still managed to keep the ball out with his heel.

The alert Herbert Zimmermann got up to head the loose ball to safety . . . Bettega held his head in disbelief.

If the ball had gone in, and if Italy had gone on to beat the Germans—instead of drawing 0–0—Italy would only have had to draw with Holland to reach the final.

But it wasn't to be. One moment of German discipline—after all, Kaltz is trained to get back in such situations—was enough to cancel out an Italian move full of skill and invention.

'When Bettega went past Maier it seemed a certain goal . . . I was not so surprised to see Kaltz covering, but I never thought he would save the situation.' HELMUT SCHOEN

The moment Bettega couldn't believe . . . he cuts through the entire West German defence only for Kaltz to get back behind the stranded Maier and keep the ball out of the net with an outstretched leg. The ball was then cleared by the alert Zimmermann . . . as the unlucky Bettega held his head in his hands.

Graham Taylor's analysis
'You had to feel sorry for the Italians—Bettega in particular—but you had to admire the Germans' discipline and organisation. It's not often you see a move that slices the German defence open—but even when that happened there was someone's heel to keep the ball out. Kaltz could have frozen as Bettega got clear, but he didn't. He kept his head and did all that was left to him —get back and cover the empty goal. It may seem funny, but you need character to do that, a never-say-die attitude that says a goal is not a goal until the ball is buried in the back of the net.'

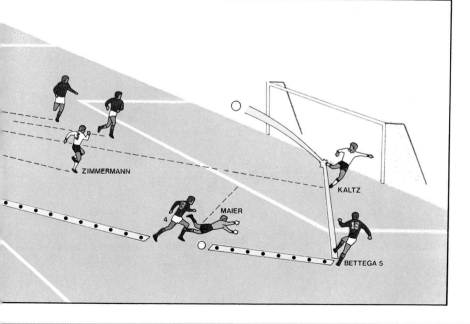

Sporting Pictures UK

RI**S**ING PAUL
STAR RANDALL

Paul Randall's one ambition in life was to be a manager—to run his own team and to buy and sell as he pleased.

A manager, that was, of a supermarket. Last year, when Britain's professional footballers were returning to their clubs for pre-season training, Randall was filling shelves in a discount store.

Six months later he was in the £200,000 class and being watched by Manchester City, Everton and Spurs.

It started when he played against Bristol Rovers in a pre-season friendly for Western League Frome Town.

Rovers boss Don Megson thought this stringy 6' 1" 19-year-old might have something to offer. He was brave, quick, and had remarkable close control ... and always seemed to be in the box when the ball arrived.

Colorsport

138

'The lad's really got an eye for goals ... a priceless asset.'
Rovers' manager BOBBY CAMPBELL

Club	Season	League Ms Gs	FA Cup Ms Gs	Lge Cup Ms Gs
Bristol Rovers	1977-78	31 20	4 2	– –

Paul was invited to join Rovers. Two weeks later he was thrown into the first team for the first League match of the season at Cardiff.

He galloped around Ninian Park, not quite sure of what his colleagues were doing. But when Rovers' Dave Williams shot and the keeper parried, Randall popped up to tap the ball over the line from a few yards.

He couldn't believe his luck.

'At 19 I thought my chance had passed me by. I'd had trials with Bristol City and Manchester City—and two periods with Rovers—and each time I'd been turned away,' remembers Paul.

'It was very different: the big crowds, training all week, learning to work much harder on the field instead of hanging around up front to score goals.'

He scored three times in the next five

In the air or on the ground ... Paul gave Everton a tough time in a pre-season friendly. Though manager Bobby Campbell points out that 'he needs to improve his work in the air', he has proved a dangerous handful for defences.

games but at the beginning of October, with the club struggling, he was dropped.

He was written off as a one-month wonder. 'But I knew different. I knew that I would go through bad patches ... but I also knew I could get back and be successful,' says Randall.

Coach Bobby Campbell took over at Rovers and began to add some polish to the rough diamond Megson had unearthed.

Campbell, a former Scottish international winger, believes in attacking football. 'That suited me fine. Everything was geared to going forward and scoring,' Paul explains.

The highlight of the season for the club —and for Randall—was a stirring FA Cup run. He scored both the goals that sank Southampton in the fourth round and one of them was voted third in ITV's 'goals of

the season' competition.

No wonder Campbell thinks highly of him: 'The lad's really got an eye for goals, a priceless asset. He has his weaknesses—he needs to improve his work in the air—but I'm a believer in playing on people's strengths and trying to eliminate the weakness without spoiling the natural game.'

Randall is pleased with his progress—and with that of the team. 'We're doing well here now and building a really good side,' he says.

'And when I hang up my boots I think I'd like to go back to the shop business and run my own store ... as I was planning to do last year.

'It's a great life at the moment, but I'd love to play for England one day. Stranger things have happened—look what's happened to me in the space of a year ... '

Supermarket to superstar?
Paul was assistant manager at a Glastonbury supermarket when he made his first team debut—scoring in a 1–1 draw at Cardiff.

TO BE WON...
ANOTHER GREAT
FREE COMPETITION
50 COPIES OF

A - Z OF MANCHESTER FOOTBALL – 100 YEARS OF RIVALRY,

the publication packed with everything you need to know about soccer, Manchester-style

1. Only two men have led *two* clubs to League Championships. One is Brian Clough, who is the other?

2. Three players were sent off during the World Cup finals. Two were Hungarians, but who was the third?

3. Who lost their League place to Hereford in 1972?

4. The record run of undefeated matches at home in League and Cup stands at 52, set between 9 April 1963 and 10 April 1965. Which Football League club holds that record?

Ray Green

5. LEFT What have Liverpool just won, when, and who did they beat?

6. Who missed the penalty which cost West Germany the 1976 European Championship final against Czechoslovakia?

7. Match the club to the city: (1) Olympique, (2) Olympija, (3) Olympiakos; (a) Marseilles, (b) Ljubljana, (c) Piraeus.

8. When did England last qualify for the World Cup finals?

9. Which *two* of these countries have never enjoyed a success by its representative in the European Cup: Spain, England, France, Portugal, West Germany, Poland, Holland, Italy, Scotland?

10. Stair Park is the most southern of the Scottish League grounds. Who plays there?

HOW TO ENTER
List your answers to the questions on a postcard, add your name and address, cut the 'Part 5' flash from the cover and attach it to the postcard (entries that do not bear the flash will be ineligible), then mail to: Football Handbook, 600A Commercial Road, London E14 7HS. Entries must arrive by October 9, 1978, the closing date. The sender of the first 50 correct answers scrutinised after that date will each be awarded a copy of A-Z OF MANCHESTER FOOTBALL. The Editor's decision on all matters relating to the competition is final and binding. All winners will be notified as soon as possible and a full list of prize winners to date will be available from *Football Handbook* on request.

KICK OFF WITH...

Ray Clemence

'I didn't want to be a keeper. I played in the back four until a youth club final at Scunthorpe, when my sportsmaster told me I was in the team . . . but only if I played in goal.'

Ray Green

You need natural ability to be a top keeper . . . and then you have to work at every detail, says England's Ray Clemence.

Ray Green

As a schoolboy Ray played as a left-winger, then as a defender, before being reluctantly converted into a goalkeeper at the age of 15.

'I've been lucky with help all through my career,' Ray told *Handbook*. 'When I first joined Scunthorpe just over a year after that youth club game I started in the third team. It wasn't a very good team and I was letting in three, four or five goals a match. I became disenchanted with the game . . . I began to feel I was right and my schoolmaster was wrong.

'But there were two people there—Jack Brownsword and the late Alan Bushby—who got a grip of me . . . told me that if I was willing to work at it I could make the grade.

'They were prepared to stay behind with me two or three afternoons a week, working on everything, in a sandpit under the stand. By the end of that season I'd played four first team matches.'

Ray emphasised to us that the agility and the reflexes were already there. It was the other aspects of the game that needed work on them.

'So much of goalkeeping is just instinct. You have to be born with the basic ability, then you have to work at every little detail.

'Even when I arrived at Liverpool I was still a poor kicker of the ball. Now I reckon I'm as good as anyone.

'I've been at the club so long now, I know what my own needs are. So if I don't feel I've been doing well on crosses or angles or whatever else, I'll take a couple of the young players, maybe a couple of coaches, and practise away from the rest of the team.'

Whistle Test

'I worked hard at refereeing—no professional could be more dedicated ... you could say I was a professional referee and an amateur butcher.' JACK TAYLOR

Zico heads home ... but referee Clive Thomas says it's too late.

Man in the middle
Local butcher Jack Taylor was a Wolverhampton Schools left-back before turning to refereeing. In 1966 he became the youngest ever FA Cup final referee; he was in charge of the 1971 European Cup final and the 1974 World Cup final. He was awarded the OBE in 1974, but he considers the Meritorious Award he was presented with by the players union his greatest honour.

Jack Taylor was the television panellist whose predictions about the last World Cup were the most accurate. But he came in for a lot of criticism when he disagreed with one of Clive Thomas' decisions in the Brazil-Sweden game.

With the score at 1-1, Brazil dithered about taking a corner. When the ball finally came over, Zico headed home ... but Clive Thomas was already walking off. He'd blown for full-time—so the goal didn't count.

'It's an unwritten law that you don't blow the whistle for full-time when the ball is in the danger area,' says Jack, 'because there's no way you can tell exactly when time is up. I learnt this the hard way: I made exactly the same mistake myself once.

'It was Bolton against Sheffield Wednesday, a Second Division game on 14 September 1974. Bolton were losing 1-0 when they won a corner in the last minute of time. And I blew when the ball was coming over—identical to the Brazil match. Paul Jones, the Bolton centre-half, got up well and the ball hit the back of the net. And nobody knows whether it's a goal or not.

'Believe me, I've had plenty of letters reminding me of this match since I said I disagreed with Clive's decision. But the lesson for young referees is this: never blow for full-time when the ball is in the danger area.'

Mick Mills on tackling

'Your determination in the tackle is one way of showing your commitment to the game ... it's great for confidence, both yours and your team-mates.' Ipswich skipper MICK MILLS

One of the qualities that makes Mick Mills 'the pro's pro' is his strength and determination in the tackle.

The Ipswich and England full-back is one of the last players that most opponents would choose to meet in a 50-50 situation.

'It's all about enthusiasm —wanting the ball,' says Mick. 'I've always gone for the ball wholeheartedly. I suppose it's my way of saying how seriously I take the game.

'Everyone wants to show what he can do with the ball, but half the time that means winning it first—and that's something that younger players are sometimes not too keen on.'

So determination is the first requirement—without it you're on a loser. But confidence to tackle is something that can be built up.

'The thing to do,' says Mick, 'is find a way of tackling that you find most comfortable and gives you confidence.

'Not all players tackle in the same way. My Ipswich team-mate Allan Hunter nearly always uses a sweeping tackle, while I normally go for a scooping, up-and-under type. And some players tackle in a very upright way —all are right for the individual player because that's how he likes to do it.'

What about the simple fear that a hard tackle is going to hurt?

Mick says: 'You're more likely to get hurt if you pull out of a tackle at the last moment than if you attack the ball and really mean it.

'And it's a great feeling to go for the ball 100 per cent and come out of a tackle with it.'

Although Mick has his own individual tackling style, he offers advice on basic technique which youngsters should bear in mind whatever their style.

'You must put your weight behind the tackle,' says Mick. 'You tackle with your body, not just your foot. If you just stick out a foot, a determined opponent will go straight through you.

'So, at the moment of impact, make sure your body is over the ball, not back from it.

'If you duck your shoulder as you tackle, that's another way of making sure your weight is fully behind it.

'And if there's a stalemate, with the ball stuck between boots, try to roll it over your opponents' foot.

'Don't always expect to win the ball—more often than not it will run free.'

Owen Barnes

Full of determination—Mick Mills about to demonstrate the block tackle against Ray Wilkins during an England training session at Bisham Abbey ...

Just before he makes his move, Mick gets his weight on his left foot ready to tackle with his right. 'It's all about wanting the ball,' says the Ipswich and England full-back. . .

At impact (above right) Mick gets all his weight behind the ball, his left foot solidly anchored in front of it. By keeping his eye on the ball, Mick makes sure that he keeps over it as well. . .

The ball runs free and Mick is favourite to get it. 'Sometimes you don't win the ball cleanly,' he says, 'but if you've unbalanced an opponent or made the ball run loose, that can be good enough.'

In close up you can see that both Mick and England team-mate Ray Wilkins went for the ball with equal determination.

It's at this point—with the ball locked between boots—that you try to roll the ball over your opponent's foot.

145

A Matter of Fact

Ipswich Town must be wishing they'd never heard of the FA Charity Shield. Forest beat them 5–0 at Wembley in August, and in their only previous appearance in this fixture they were thrashed 5–1 by Spurs at Portman Road in 1961.

Only 4,554 people turned up at Highbury to see Arsenal play Leeds in May 1966, although the visitors were chasing the title. Heavy rain and TV coverage of the Liverpool–Dortmund Cup Winners' Cup final were blamed for the poor crowd.

Peter Withe's travels have taken in Wolves, Birmingham, Nottingham Forest and Newcastle. Yet he made his bow in League soccer as an amateur with Barrow and Southport, both now in the Northern Premier League.

The first player to appear as a substitute was Charlton's Keith Peacock—still turning out for the Londoners—at Bolton on 21 August 1965.

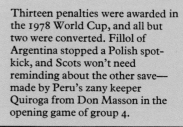

Thirteen penalties were awarded in the 1978 World Cup, and all but two were converted. Fillol of Argentina stopped a Polish spot-kick, and Scots won't need reminding about the other save—made by Peru's zany keeper Quiroga from Don Masson in the opening game of group 4.

In 1962 Wales' representatives in the European Cup Winners' Cup were tiny Bangor City from the Cheshire League. They shook the soccer world by beating the crack Italian side Napoli 2–0, and only lost 3–1 in the away leg—which would have been enough to clinch the tie under the present 'away goals' rule. Bangor finally went down 2–0 in a play-off.

Colorsport

LEFT *'Hey mister, can we have our shirts back please?'—QPR's Stan Bowles seems to be trying to reclaim the Rangers' away strip worn by Henry Newton, then with Derby, after a mix-up over colours in a match in February 1975.*

Perhaps Bristol Rovers got off lightly when Spurs trounced them 9–0 last year. In an FA Cup replay in 1960 Spurs beat Crewe Alexandra 13–2 after a 2–2 draw at Gresty Road. The teams met in the Cup the following year, and Spurs won 5–1.

During Brian Clough's stay as Brighton manager his team crashed 8–2 to Bristol Rovers. However it wasn't the Seagulls' record defeat: that was a 9–0 humiliation by Middlesbrough on 23 August 1958. Boro's centre-forward that day? None other than Brian Clough, who went on to head the League scorers that season with 42!

Hull City have never been in the top flight, but in August 1971 a First Division match was staged at their Boothferry Park ground, when Leeds and Spurs drew 1–1 there. Elland Road was closed following crowd trouble, so Leeds had to play their first four 'home' games at Hull, Sheffield Wednesday and Huddersfield.

Founded: 1883
Address: Feethams Ground, Darlington, Co. Durham
Ground: Capacity 20,000 ; Playing area 100.6 x 67.7 m
Record attendance: 21,023 v Bolton Wanderers, League Cup 3rd round, 14.11.60
Record victory: 9–2 v Lincoln City, Div. 3 (N), 7.1.28
Record defeat: 0–10 v Doncaster Rovers, Div. 4, 25.1.64
Most League points: 59, Div. 4, 1965-66
Most League goals: 108, Div. 3 (N), 1929-30
League scoring record: 39, David Brown, Div. 3 (N), 1924-25
Record League aggregate: 74, David Brown, 1923-26
Most League appearances: 442, Ron Greener, 1955-67
Most capped player: None
League career: 1921 Div. 3 (N) ; 1925-27 Div. 2 ; 1927-58 Div. 3 (N) ; 1958-66 Div. 4 ; 1966-67 Div. 3 ; 1967- Div. 4
Honours: Div. 3 (N) Champions 1924-25

DARLINGTON

Peter Madden's first job when he took over as manager of Darlington was to stop all the laughing.

A joke started by a David Frost TV programme threatened to send the club, laughing hysterically, into extinction.

The programme saw the news—and humour—value of focussing on a team that applied for re-election more often than Richard Nixon.

And it took the anger of the big, bluff, bull-necked Madden to pull the club back from the brink of elimination.

'It sickened me, that programme,' says Madden, who was coach at Rochdale at the time it was televised seven years ago.

'The attitude of the players was totally unprofessional. They laughed at themselves and they laughed at Darlington FC.

'Needless to say, not one of them has survived since I arrived at the club.

1923—and a game against Aldershot has to be played on the cricket ground because of snow.

'It'll take a long time to recover from a programme like that, the shame of it, but we'll get there. That's a promise.'

Darlington's pretty little Feethams ground in County Durham is owned by the amateur cricket club that plays behind the covered goal.

And that really sums up the club's continuing crisis . . . cash. But, like the jokey image, that unhappy situation is also being attacked.

Mrs Alice Burton—now that her son has joined the air force and her daughter is set to become a WPC—is the woman employed to feed the club with finance.

Her first job as commercial manager was to start an ambitious £1,000 lottery, a brave step for a small Fourth Division club.

As for new blood on the pitch, manager Madden says: 'You either buy players or produce them. I'm trying to do a little bit of both.

'It's consistency I'm after, a team that's hard to beat.'

Madden, 44, was a no-nonsense stopper at Rotherham for 14 seasons and played in the very first Football League Cup final against

Mike Cowling

ABOVE *The man who's trying to stop the laughing—manager Peter Madden.* BELOW *The team that played as Northern League amateurs before joining the professional ranks in 1908 . . . and reaching the FA Cup last 16 in 1911.*

Courtesy of Mawers & Sons

Giant-killers
It's in cup games that Darlington have hit the headlines in their 95-year history; and none more so than the 4–1 replay win against Chelsea in the FA Cup in 1958 (team left). Two years later they sent Crystal Palace and West Ham packing in the Football League Cup. But in the League their record is dismal. After winning promotion from the Third Division (North) in 1925 they dropped down again two seasons later. And after promotion from Division 4 in 1966, they spent only one season in the Third.

Aston Villa in 1961.

His coach, 34-year-old Len Walker, spent 12 years in Aldershot's midfield after spells at Middlesbrough and Newcastle.

'We've got to change the thinking around here,' says Len. 'People seem obsessed with the bottom four and re-election. We've got to get them thinking about the top four and promotion.'

Two seasons ago the side finished tenth in the division and appeared in no fewer than 12 Cup ties. Hopes were high last season but they were back down among the dead men, sixth from bottom . . . 87th in the Football League.

If they finish in the top four this season, it'll mean more than just promotion . . . it'll bury a joke.

Over the years Darlington have produced a string of fine goalkeepers. Best known is Ray Wood, who went on to play for Manchester United in the 1957 Cup final, spending most of the game on the wing after being injured between the posts: United lost 2–1 to Aston Villa. Another fine keeper at Feethams was Andy Greig, who was deaf but more than made up for it with a great pair of hands. The two Harrys, Holdcroft and Walker, were both with Darlington before moving on to Everton and Portsmouth respectively . . .

Formed in 1883, Darlington played as Northern League amateurs until joining the professional ranks in 1908. In 1911 they reached the last 16 in the FA Cup and in the first Cup competition after the first war they beat First Division Sheffield Wednesday at Hillsborough—the last time a non-League side knocked out a First Division club on its own ground for 60 years. The feat helped Darlington become a founder member of Division 3 (N).

The first apprentice at Feethams in seven seasons—16-year-old Donald Ball—could be in at the start of a new era for the Durham club.

ARCHIE GEMMILL

'This season could be a little different because teams always want to beat the champions. They'll be gunning for us from the start. There certainly won't be any easy matches.'

Archie Gemmill, the diminutive midfield man who added character, experience and skill to Nottingham Forest's Championship drive, is in no doubt that his current team-mates are a match for the title-winning Derby sides in which he figured before his £130,000 move.

But the Scottish ace will reserve judgment for just a while on whether Brian Clough's Forest are better than Brian Clough's Derby.

He explains: 'It's an important season for us to try and build on what happened last year. I think we're capable of going from strength to strength . . . but only time will tell.

'There can be no question that this side at Forest is as good as the one we had at Derby.

'We play the same 4-3-3 way that we did under the boss and Peter Taylor at Derby. Instead of Alan Hinton we have John Robertson, for Kevin Hector there's Tony

Archie hits one of the three League goals he scored last season . . . beating Pat Jennings by a whisker in January. Archie—who began that move well inside his own half—is a direct, hard-running midfielder who is prepared to take on defenders . . . but he doesn't score many goals. Nevertheless, he is a calm and efficient finisher— as he proved in the World Cup against Holland.

Woodcock and you can go on like that throughout the side.

'I had some great times at Derby, winning two Championship medals, but there's no reason why I shouldn't go on to have an even better time with Forest. It's as if nothing has changed.

'The attitude is the same as it was at the Baseball Ground because the boss and Peter wouldn't have it any other way. The basic organisation and discipline is the same . . . we defend when we have to and go forward in numbers.

'Everybody knows what they have to do and we just go out and do it. That's the way it was throughout last season and I must admit I was even more impressed by Forest having played with them.

'Early on last season I came to Forest with Derby and for 25 minutes at the start we played all the football. They hardly got a kick and I had doubts about how good they were.

'But once they had scored they looked a different team, while some of our lads just jacked it in. At the end Forest won 3–0—and deserved to.'

Forest's impressive start continued after Peter Shilton and Gemmill, later to be winner

Bob Thomas

151

and runner-up in the PFA Player of the Year poll, had been signed within the space of a fortnight.

It took the abrasive little Scot some weeks to knit into a midfield that had previously been made up of John McGovern, Martin O'Neill and Ian Bowyer, with Bowyer eventually the odd man out.

Gemmill's presence emerged as an invaluable factor in Forest's pursuit of the First Division title. His aggression, verve and pace often provoked fresh impetus on the rare days when the side dropped below their best.

Archie is, however, quick to hand the tributes around the Forest dressing-room.

'Everybody has heard about the part that the likes of Peter Shilton, Kenny Burns and Tony Woodcock played last season but not so much about some of the others.

'Martin O'Neill had a great season and he really didn't get the credit he deserved. I reckon I work hard but he went through a spell when he literally ran himself into the ground for the club. Now he's accepted as a top class midfield player.

'Colin Barrett is another who didn't get the recognition he deserved. He came on a ton as the season went on and he's now one of the best full-backs around.'

But how does Gemmill view Forest's prospects of capitalising on their exciting success last season after winning promotion? Can they go on to establish themselves as a major force for several years?

'It'll be harder this year,' he argues. 'I'm certain that when last season started a lot of teams took Forest a little bit lightly. They had just come up from the Second Division and I don't think many other clubs thought they were Championship material.

'But if that was the case they underestimated us—and paid the penalty. We only lost three League games last season . . . and that's an incredible record.

'But we had a preview of what to expect in the last six or eight weeks of last season when everybody woke up to the fact that we looked like winning the League.

'Teams set out to make it harder for us, but we showed our ability by going to places like Anfield, Maine Road, Villa Park and Highfield Road in the last few weeks of the season and not conceding goals.

'That was no fluke and as far as I was concerned we won the League because we proved ourselves the best team over the season. Nobody can say otherwise.'

Archie, like his City Ground team-mates Kenny Burns and John Robertson, has had to overcome the disappointments of Scotland's ill-fated World Cup trip to Argentina this

We're number one, says Archie . . . though he admits that when he played at the City Ground with Derby early last season he 'had doubts about how good Forest were'. But he had changed his mind by the end of a match that Derby lost 3–0.

Electric Archie
Archie signed for his home town pro club, St Mirren (of Paisley), from Glasgow junior club Drumchapel Amateurs. When Preston signed him, he had established himself in the side as a left-winger or half-back, even though he was only a part-timer still qualifying as an electrician. He was a deep-lying left-winger playing in the Third Division when Brian Clough persuaded him to sign for Derby—in the face of high-powered competition from Everton—for a fee of £63,000. Within a year, Gemmill played in his first full international.

summer before embarking on the fresh challenges of a new season.

But he declared: 'Forest pay my wages and what happened in South America will not affect the way I play here.

'The Scotland business was something that didn't work out. One or two things were not right from the start. It was a big disappointment after we had built ourselves up for so long to see it all suddenly turn sour.

'But I'm sure the three of us who were out there will put it down to experience and concentrate on winning more trophies for Forest.

'We had eight or nine great months together last season and you can't expect things to be rosy all the time in your career.

'I'm ready to put the Scotland thing behind me. The boss certainly won't allow it to affect our form.'

Owen Barnes

Archie in space in last season's Scotland-England international, with Tony Currie and Paul Mariner closing fast. Dalglish and Greenhoff look on.

Archie and Brian
Brian Clough has never disguised his admiration for his midfielder. 'He has what every team needs,' he says. 'He has tremendous pace, he gets involved and he engages opponents.' When he was trying to sign Archie for Derby, Clough spent a day and a night at the Gemmills' home before finally clinching the deal.

Honours: League Championship medal 1972, 1975, 1978; Football League Cup winners medal 1978

Club	Div.	Pos.	Season	League Ms	League Gs	FA Cup Ms	FA Cup Gs	Lge Cup Ms	Lge Cup Gs	Int'nls Ms	Int'nls Gs
St Mirren	I	15	1964-65	19	4	1	–	–	–		
	I	16	1965-66	17	–	1	–	–	–		
	I	17	1966-67	31	5	3	1	4	–		
Preston	II	20	1967-68	31	4	2	1	1	–		
N.E.	II	14	1968-69	21	3	1	–	1	–		
	II	22	1969-70	39	6	2	–	1	–		
	III	1	1970-71	7	–	–	–	2	–		
Derby	I	9	1970-71	31	3	3	1	–	–	1	–
County	I	1	1971-72	40	3	5	–	2	–	6	1
	I	7	1972-73	34	3	5	–	3	–	5	1
	I	3	1973-74	38	1	4	3	3	1		
	I	1	1974-75	41	–	3	–	2	–		
	I	4	1975-76	42	6	5	–	2	–	5	1
	I	15	1976-77	30	1	3	–	6	–	9	–
	I	12	1977-78	5	1	–	–	1	–	1	–
Forest	I	1	1977-78	35	3	4	–	–	–	7	3
				461	43	42	6	28	1	34	6

The chip that had Jennings groping...

'He really does pull them out of the top drawer . . . a lovely turn— all in one movement.' BBC commentator BARRY DAVIES

It was one of those moves that seemed to have a lot of build-up left in it.

But quite suddenly Kenny Hibbitt turned and hit a chip so sweet that it had a world class goalkeeper—Pat Jennings—groping helplessly.

The golden goal came in the FA Cup fourth round match between Arsenal and Wolves last January.

A long ball by Wolves goalkeeper Paul Bradshaw bounced off an Arsenal defender and into space— nothing much to really worry about.

Hibbitt called for the ball even before substitute Martin Patching picked it up.

He got it, turned, pushed the ball square to make room for a shot—all in a split second.

Alan Hudson tried to get in a tackle and Willie Young made an attempt to close in on Hibbitt, but the Wolves midfield man was too quick.

Jennings was left cold just outside his six-yard box by the suddenness and accuracy of the shot. Any other kind of shot would probably have been saved because Jennings had narrowed the angle—but the chip did the trick.

It was a remarkable goal because it came completely out of the blue. Hibbitt could have been expected to lay the ball off and go looking for a shooting position nearer goal. But, no, an amazing turn and a beautiful left-foot chip . . . from a player who favours his right foot.

As well as the skill involved, Hibbitt needed imagination and belief in his own ability: he had both.

The acclaim . . . Hibbitt is mobbed after his wonder goal —but Wolves still finished up 2-1 losers to Arsenal.

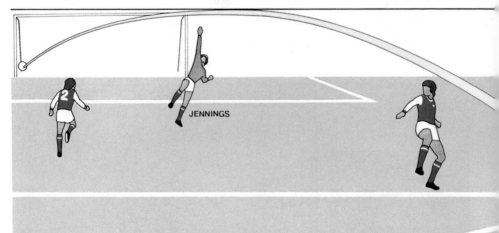

JENNINGS

All in vain
Kenny's great goal didn't get Wolves through to the 5th round. They were sunk by a shot from former club-mate Alan Sunderland and, following a disputed corner which led to young Bob Hazell being sent off by Clive Thomas, a header from Malcolm Macdonald. Wolves were left to fight against relegation.

Graham Taylor's analysis
'Well, it was all about instinct, wasn't it? You could see quite clearly on television that Hibbitt asked for the ball before Patching had actually controlled it—which tells me that Hibbitt had already decided he was going to have some sort of go at goal. The fact that he pulled it off in the way that he did only added to the greatness of the goal.

'But let's get back to instinct. You could call it a constant question that buzzes in your head during a game: what can I do in this situation? If you're not asking yourself that, you're unlikely to score this kind of goal.

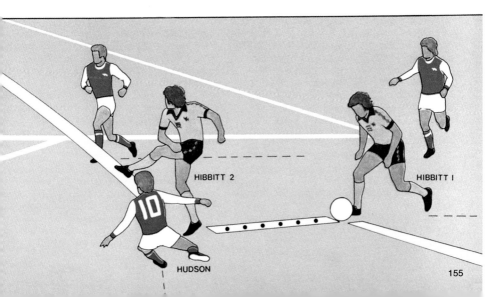

HIBBITT 2

HIBBITT I

10

HUDSON

RISING STAR CARL HARRIS

It's time for Carl Harris to put his foot down.

The Neath-born winger made his international debut three years ago at the age of 18. His breath taking speed and devastating skill have consistently unnerved some of the best defences in the League . . . and excited spectators throughout Britain. But in four seasons he has made only just over 50 first team appearances for Leeds . . . featuring in less than half of their games last season.

'I love Leeds, but I want first team football,' Carl explained to *Handbook* on the dawn of the new season. 'So by the end of the year I shall want to have a better idea of where I'm going than I did under Jimmy Armfield.'

Harris, a modest, self-effacing young man, feels he would have been more successful under a different manager.

'I'm not complaining,' he says almost apologetically, 'but I've often felt that I would have developed more quickly if I hadn't been in and out of the side all the time . . .

An established international star, yet in and out of the first team at Leeds, Carl demonstrated his quality in the Home International tournament. In these pictures, he leaves Mick Mills tackling thin air, then, perfectly balanced, shoots hard and low.

'I've never felt the manager had complete confidence in my style of play. One week I'd be in the team, the next I'd be on the subs' bench. It was a bit unsettling. And it wasn't good for my morale.'

This continual changing led to a classic chicken-and-egg situation at Elland Road. Several team-mates urged Carl to have more faith in his abilities; but warming the bench only eroded that confidence.

Perhaps if Leeds had won something recently all would have been well. Managers of successful teams are more likely to field a formation that includes two wingers than those who are struggling to keep their jobs.

At Leeds Jimmy Armfield was always under enormous pressure to steer his team to a title or into Europe. He wasn't always

> 'His speed is tremendous, and even though opponents know all about it it's difficult to counteract because of his great dribbling skill.'
> Leeds defender PAUL MADELEY

Club	Season	League		FA Cup		Lge Cup		Int'nls	
Leeds	1974-75	3	1	–	–	–	–	–	–
United	1975-76	14	3	–	–	1	–	2	–
	1976-77	16	3	–	–	1	–	–	–
	1977-78	19	2	1	–	4	1	4	–
		52	9	1	–	6	1	6	–

prepared to go into a game with only two accepted midfielders . . . and he clearly felt that the granite-like Arthur Graham was a greater asset to the side than the more fragile Carl Harris.

Harris disagrees. 'I'm certain that I can fit

into any formation. No-one can say that I don't work hard. I can forage with the best and defend all afternoon if necessary.'

Carl certainly convinced a lot of people with his displays in the Home International tournament. His incisive ` runs, launched on either flank or at the heart of defences, will remain in the memory of Welshmen for as long as Tony Currie's thunderous goal . . . which settled the match.

'I decided to prove to the manager that he would be stupid to leave me out so often.'

But he had already convinced most people connected with the club.

'I reckon he's as tricky a winger as you'll find in Britain,' reckons Paul Reaney, now at Bradford City. 'It's a pity he's not English!'

With tributes like that a player could be in danger of getting swollen-headed. But Carl Harris won't.

As he says: 'My first Leeds manager—Don Revie—taught me to work hard, practise day in and day out and make the most of any breaks that came my way.

'I've tried to follow that advice, Leeds United have been good to me and I want the opportunity to repay them with my skills.'

Wriggling out of troubl

'It's all about control and confidence . . . and no matter how much skill or flair you might have you've really got to work with that ball in training, especially on your weaker foot.'

Few sights in football turn the crowds on like a player using skill to leave opponents floundering.

And there's nobody more likely to win out in tight situations than Aston Villa's Brian Little, one of the best 'wrigglers' in the game.

Brian seems to have all the qualities needed to throw defenders. He can check, turn and change direction with bewildering speed and without warning; and his two-footed stop-start technique—often using the sole of the boot—is tailor-made for shaking off close markers.

'You know when you're going to be up against it,' explains Brian, 'and if you're to beat your man you've got to know where he is. The thing is, you must keep your eye on the ball, so it's important to have a quick look round before the ball arrives. From there on it's down to skill and confidence.'

Colorsport

Brian Little

Brian reckons it's vital to be able to use and trust both feet. 'It's not often you can wriggle out of trouble without calling on skill from both feet,' he says, 'and that means

Little by Little . . . 'The first thing is to know where your opponent is,' says Brian, 'and then use your skill. Getting out of tight situations needs the control that comes from balance and ability in both feet.'

working hard with your weaker foot in training.

Like most pros, Brian lays great emphasis on practice. 'It's the only way you'll become sure enough of your ability to try it on the pitch . . . and you don't always need a friend. You can sharpen your control and increase your confidence just by tight dribbling, using both feet and throwing in jinks and changes of direction.

You just can't get enough practice with the ball.'

Brian's ability to stay out of trouble is reflected in his lack of injury problems—only a couple of League games missed in the last two full seasons.

But he sounds one note of warning about playing to the gallery for the sake of it. 'It's not easy to wriggle out of trouble . . . but very easy to get into it.'

'Any practice with the ball is good practice, no matter how many of you there are,' says Graham Taylor, 'but these exercises for "mobility on the ball" are some that you can easily do on your own.

'The one on the left sharpens up control with one foot : you dribble left to right using the inside and then outside of

your foot. Don't just use your best one—the sort of ability Brian Little has comes from constant practice on the weaker foot, and you must use both

'The other one sharpens up two-footed control. Run along a line pushing the ball from one foot to the other, occasionally "jumping" over it or improvising routines.

THE

The failure rate among footballs young hopefuls is startling ... when Bertie Mee was manager of Arsenal's double-winning side he discovered that, of all the boys watched by his scouts, one in 160,000 made the grade. Becoming an apprentice professional is further than most boys get— but there's still a long way to go. So *Football Handbook* will follow the progress of two youngsters who have just signed on the dotted line—starting with one of Watford's 'new boys'.

APPRENTICE

Apart from the grunts and groans, he's very quiet during training . . . a raw recruit in a strange new world.

And when most of the hard work is over and it's his group's turn for some three-a-side, he plays lots of 'easy balls'—respectful of the senior pros around him.

Just two weeks after his 16th birthday Steve Terry is playing football for a living.

He's left his family and two dogs in Cheshunt for 'digs' with the Paveys in Watford: 'It was a bit strange at first but they're a friendly family.'

The fact that most apprentices finish as failures doesn't bother him. 'There's no point in thinking about failing,' he says. 'Sometimes I worry after a bad game, but when I have a good game it's okay again.'

The good games already outnumber the

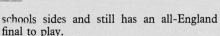

tuff ones. Last season, while still at Riversmead School, Cheshunt, he played half a dozen games for Watford Reserves and, according to coach Tom Walley, 'he came on a bundle'.

He finished a game against Charlton with a black eye and needing three stitches in a cut mouth. 'I didn't mind,' he says. 'I had quite a good match.'

At 6' 1" and 12½-stone Steve is—not surprisingly—a central defender. He starred in the Lee Valley district and Herts county schools sides and still has an all-England final to play.

But school football is very different from the real thing and Steve and the other three Watford apprentices had a week with Walley to prepare for the training with the seniors.

It helped. But the lads still found Graham Taylor's session a bit of a shock. 'Tough!' was Steve's verdict at the end, with the hand-clapping press-ups 'a real killer'.

For improving his game, Steve says: 'I need to get sharper all round, in everything

I do. That's the big difference from school football.'

Like most young players, Steve was spotted by 'scouts' who watch hundreds of junior and schoolboy games all over the country.

He's had brief spells with West Ham and Spurs, whose training ground is at Cheshunt, but he's happy to be a 'Hornet'.

'There are so many boys at bigger clubs

hat you hardly get noticed,' he says. 'Here
here is always someone to concentrate on
'our weaknesses.

'And it's great to be at a club that's just
won promotion and makes the headlines. I
don't think it would've been so good if
hey'd have stayed down.'

Extra encouragement for Steve comes from
his dad, PC Peter Terry, who played as an
amateur for Enfield and Walthamstow
Avenue and won two international caps.

'He was a hard man,' says Tom Walley,
and there's a lot of him in young Steve.'

Chores for the new apprentices—Watford
had none last season—include cleaning the
plunge bath after training, putting tracksuits
away and cleaning the floors and passages.

'But it's not bad, when there's four of
you,' reckons Steve.

Even so he's fit for nothing by the time he
gets back to the Pavey home in Oxhey
Avenue . . . 'only a bit of television.'

After a strange first week 'meeting
different people all the time', Steve went
home for the weekend.

His two dogs—Taff, who was bought in
Wales, and Prince—almost knocked him
over with their welcome.

The following week the young apprentice
already seemed a little more confident, those
first few awkward days behind him.

The new boy is on his way . . .

Steve Terry's 'boss', Watford manager Graham
Taylor, is critical of the scheme. 'We have to
make a yes-or-no decision three months before
a player's 18th birthday,' he says, 'and that
could be as little as 16 months after he's signed
as an apprentice—which isn't long enough.

'I would prefer a straightforward, three-
year apprenticeship which gives a boy time to
learn his trade. As it stands now, the period is
determined by the boy's date of birth and when
he is able to leave school. So most boys have
to make the grade in a tough profession in a
lot less than two years.

'Steve is one of the lucky ones. He was 16 in
June, which means that he gets the benefit of
the full two-year period.

'A three-year scheme would lay clubs less
open to accusations of using cheap labour, and
the boys themselves would get a better
opportunity of becoming a pro.

FOOTBALL FITNESS TRAINING PROGRAMME

This programme is a little harder because it's designed to carry you through several weeks. Attack these exercises, and it af the end of the time or number of repetitions you feel that you can keep going, then do so: it can do you nothing but good. Use this routine in alternation with previous ones.

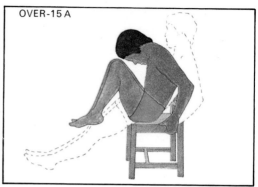

OVER-15 A

UNDER-12 AGE GROUP
A. With two chairs placed a shoulder width apart, place one hand on each chair. Take weight on toes and, keeping your back straight, do 10 press-ups.
B. Stand up, toes pointing slightly outwards, with your legs apart. Reach for the left foot with your right hand, then up straight; and then your right foot with your left hand. Repeat 10 times to each foot.
C. Lie on your back, arms by your sides. Sit up to touch your toes, trying to keep your legs and feet on the ground. Repeat 10 times.
D. Lie on your front with your hands behind your neck. Raise your legs, head, and shoulders as high as possible, and then down. Repeat 5 times.
E. Stand straight with arms at your sides. Keeping each arm straight, raise them to shoulder level, then up above your head and back to shoulder level. Hold for a few seconds, then down. Repeat 10 times.

13-14 AGE GROUP
A. 'Upside-down' cycling for 30 secs.
B. Lie on your back with hands behind your neck and your feet under a piece of heavy furniture to keep them down. Raise the upper body from the waist and then lower. As many as possible in 20 secs.
 C. Stand an arms length away from a wall. Place hands on the wall, palms down. Bend your arms so that your nose almost touches the wall, then straighten. Repeat as many times as possible in 30 seconds.
D. Lie on your back, arms by your sides. Raise legs a few inches, then move apart, back together, and down. Repeat as many times as possible in 20 secs.
E. Jog on the spot, letting your arms hang loosely by your sides, and your chin drop close to the chest.

OVER-15 AGE GROUP
A. Sitting on the edge of a chair, lean back and grip the sides for control Raise both knees towards chest, allowing your back to bend and the chin to drop so that the head nearly touches the knees. Then lower. Repeat 10 times, breathing out as the knees are raised and in as they go down.
B. Standing straight, raise your arms forward, keeping them a shoulders width apart. Keeping them at shoulder level, bring them round to the side. Then lower. Repeat as many times as possible in 20 secs.
C. Lie on your back, palms down. Raise your legs a few inches, then part them, back together and down. Repeat as many times as possible in 30 secs.
D. 'Upside down' cycling for 30 secs, starting with large slow circles and working up to small faster ones.
E. Jog on the spot, letting your arms hang loosely by your sides, and your chin drop towards your chest. Max. 30 secs.

Founded: 1908
Address: Leeds Road, Huddersfield HD1 6PE
Ground: Capacity 48,000 ; Playing area 105.5 x 68.5 m
Record attendance: 67,037 v Arsenal, FA Cup 6th round, 27.2.32
Record victory: 10–1 v Blackpool, Div. 1, 13.12.30
Record defeat: 0–8 v Middlesbrough, Div. 1, 30.9.50
Most League points: 64, Div. 2, 1919-20
Most League goals: 97, Div. 2, 1919-20
League scoring record: 35, Sam Taylor, Div. 2, 1919-20 and
George Brown, Div. 1, 1925-26
Record League aggregate: 142, George Brown, 1921-29
Most League appearances: 520, Billy Smith, 1914-34
Most capped player: 31, Jimmy Nicholson, Northern Ireland,
1964-72 (+ 10 with Manchester United)
League career: 1910 Elected to Div. 2 ; 1920-52 Div. 1 ; 1952-53
Div. 2 ; 1953-56 Div. 1 ; 1956-70 Div. 2 ; 1970-72 Div. 1 ; 1972-73
Div. 2 ; 1973-75 Div. 3 ; 1975- Div. 4
Honours: Div. 1 Champions 1924, 1925, 1926 ; Div. 2 Champions
1970 ; FA Cup Winners 1922, Runners-up 1920, 1928, 1930, 1938

HUDDERSFIELD TOWN

Leeds Road, the scene of past triumphs and recent decline. The record attendance is 67,037—but last season's average was only 4,507. Huddersfield provide a stark illustration of the plight of northern town clubs: chasing dwindling audiences in competition with big city clubs and Rugby League.

Huddersfield fans old enough to remember the 1920s must be shattered to find their team in the middle of the Fourth Division. 50 years ago Huddersfield Town was the most famous side of the day ; now the club seems to have no hope of living up to its traditions.

Huddersfield won the Football League Championship three years in a row (in 1924, 1925 and 1926) after winning the FA Cup in 1922. They did all this on crowds of about 18,000—but were able to maintain a team with a sprinkling of star players partly because, in the days of the maximum wage, they could afford to pay their players the same as the

Peter Robinson

165

Huddersfield Town in desperate defence of their First Division status in 1972. On the post is full-back Dennis Clarke—behind him is Trevor Cherry.

bigger, more profitable clubs. If neighbours Leeds were a team of the 1970s, Huddersfield were undoubtedly *the* team of the 1920s. But in Yorkshire now a generation gap has evolved which Huddersfield cannot hope to close.

During the 1950s the club seemed to find a new level for itself, halfway up Division 2—a position more in keeping with the size of the club's support. The gates were adequate at that time in that division to keep the club going, together with occasional income from the sale of locally developed talent like Denis Law, Ray Wilson and Bob McNab.

Ian Greaves, appointed manager of Huddersfield in 1968, was not one to settle for mediocrity. 'I suppose I had stars in my eyes when I took over. I imagined we could become a top club even though we had no money.'

Huddersfield were promoted in 1970, but looking back Greaves says: 'The biggest mistake was to shift them from the Second Division, though there's no way a manager can think like that at the time. In fact we bit off more than we could chew—on crowds of around 15,000 there was no way we could sustain First Division football.'

Town survived just two seasons in the top division before they re-appeared on the Second Division fixture lists.

'I don't feel guilty,' says Greaves. 'We really didn't belong there, even though we did deserve our promotion. But dropping from the Second really sticks in my throat. In the end we were undone by the mass psychology of losing. If you're winning you get a snowball of the right attitudes. The average player becomes a good player and the good player becomes excellent. When you fail it's the same

Ray Green

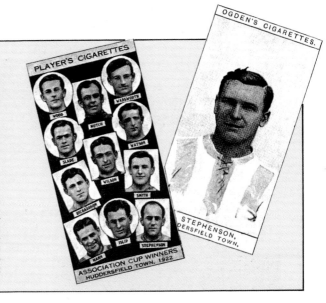

Town's triumph
Clem Stephenson and the Huddersfield Cup winning team of 1922, as portrayed by cigarette cards at the time. Stephenson, a clever scheming inside-forward, had already won Cup winner's medals with Aston Villa—and he is still the only man to have played in three Cup winning and three League championship sides. The 1922 Cup win was Town's first major success, but the final was not a great game. Billy Smith, who still holds the club record for appearances, was tripped in the penalty area midway through the second half and scored the only goal of the game from the resulting spot kick.

The greatest manager
Herbert Chapman was the most brilliantly effective manager of all time—the man who inspired both Huddersfield and Arsenal to 3 successive League championships. Born in Yorkshire, he spent most of his playing career as a Spurs reserve. After serving his managerial apprenticeship with Northampton Town and Leeds City, he took over at modestly successful Huddersfield, led them to two championships, then left for Highbury in 1925 when Town were well on the way to a third. It was to be their last major honour.

principle in reverse. The good player becomes average and the average becomes a very, very poor player.'

Greaves became involved in a much-publicised dispute with three of his best players early in 1972—allegedly Worthington, Ellam and Cherry asked for a cash bonus to help keep the club in Division 1. The manager refused the demand and sold all three players, a decision which he knew could contribute to the club's relegation and put his own job in jeopardy.

Using some of the proceeds of the sale of these players, Greaves went back to his old club Manchester United to make Huddersfield's record signing—the £65,000 purchase of Alan Gowling. Gowling contributed 58 goals in 128 League appearances for his new club, and was top scorer for each of his three seasons before moving to Newcastle.

Huddersfield's fall from First to Second Division was followed by falls to Third and Fourth. Crowds dropped to the 3,000 mark. Ian Greaves was followed by Bobby Collins, Tom Johnston and John Hasleden—with Johnston recently resigning the managership a second time.

Huddersfield are in something of a dilemma. The squad has recently had a number of very promising young players—young men constantly being reviewed by bigger clubs. Men like Dick Taylor, a goalkeeper thought by many clubs including Manchester United, Sunderland and Wolves to be the best in the lower divisions, midfield starlet Martin Fowler and versatile defender Peter Hart. But these young men have not been able to lift Huddersfield above the middle of the Fourth Division. Johnston achieved considerable success with a similar club—York City—taking the club briefly up to the Second Division.

It is difficult to forecast a future any higher than that for the Pennine club that was once the country's top team.

THIS WEEK'S FREE-TO-ENTER COMPETITION...

10 sets of SUBBUTEO table-top soccer (World Cup Edition) to be won!

Ray Green

3. George Best, then with United, breaks clear of four City defenders during a Manchester 'derby'. Can you name the four Manchester City men in hot pursuit?

1. Argentinian international defender Osvaldo Piazza and France's World Cup striker Dominique Rocheteau played on an English Third Division club's ground on 5 October 1977. Whose ground, which teams played, and what was the score?

2. When England met West Germany last February—at 'B' level on the 21st and full level on the 22nd—who were England's centre-halves in the two games, and which club do they have in common?

4. Match these Dutch internationals to their clubs: (1) Robbie Rensenbrink, (2) Wim Jansen, (3) Ernie Brandts, (4) Johnny Rep, (5) Rudi Krol; (a) Bastia, (b) Feyenoord, (c) Anderlecht, (d) Ajax, (e) PSV Eindhoven.

5. Which of these players has never won a full England cap: Peter Taylor, Larry Lloyd, Alan Hudson, Jimmy Greenhoff, Phil Boyer, Frank Lampard, Ian Gillard?

6. Who were the last club other than Rangers or Celtic to win the Scottish League, and when?

7. Former England midfielder Keith Weller has played for three London clubs during his career Which are they?

8. Glan Letheran and Mark Kendall have represented Wales at U-21 level in recent seasons. Which clubs do they play for?

Martin Peters

'At West Ham Ron Greenwood used to keep on at all the young players about learning a "feel" for the ball. That was responsible for developing good touch in my control.'

Twelve years after playing a magnificent part in England's World Cup triumph, Martin Peters is still one of the most skilful players in the First Division.

Yet he might never have fallen in love with football. 'I only really started playing after my family moved from the East End out to Dagenham, in Essex,' explains Martin. 'I was about eight and till then I was a mad speedway fan.

'Because I was on the tall side I got into the school team, but I don't remember receiving much coaching till I went to West Ham. It was there I developed my touch.

'Basic techniques are all important, so you must work at them. But don't lose your sense of individuality. Coaching isn't black and white: it's about making the most of what you're good at and harnessing that to basic skills.'

Sporting Pictures UK

Colorsport

Colorsport

Martin became the first £200,000 footballer when he moved from West Ham to Spurs in 1971. He's always been a great header of the ball, particularly dangerous on blind-side runs.

With 67 caps and over 600 League appearances behind him, Martin opened the 14th season of his League career with a 3-0 win over newly-promoted Southampton at Carrow Road.

Terry McDermott on the chip

'That goal against Everton in the semi-final of the Cup was probably the best I've ever scored . . . it's certainly the best I've scored with a chip.'

McDermott lays on a chipped centre. Since joining Liverpool from Newcastle four years ago, Terry has developed into a top-class midfielder with a great range of skills.

Chipping the ball is a delicate skill that can have a devastating effect in matches.

And there's no better example than the Terry McDermott goal for Liver-

pool against Everton in the 1977 FA Cup semi-final.

His beautiful chip from the edge of the penalty area was so good that it was judged BBC 'Goal of the Season'.

Colorsport

174

Terry demonstrates the chip for Handbook. *Note the slight lean back and the position of the non-kicking foot, which is slightly withdrawn rather than right alongside the ball.*

'It was probably the best goal I've ever scored,' says Terry. 'It's certainly the best I've scored with a chip.'

After receiving the ball from Kevin Keegan, Terry feinted to shoot with his right foot and turned it on to his left as a defender moved in to challenge.

'I sensed the keeper was moving off his line, so I decided to chip him,' says Terry.

The ball floated past the groping David Lawson and into the top left-hand corner of the net.

So goalkeepers who do the right thing and come out to narrow the angle as a forward shapes to shoot, dread the chip—the one skill that can leave them in 'no man's land'.

And all players—particularly defenders—hate to be the victim of a well-placed chip. It's often more dangerous than a ball played inside them because of the split second that's wasted as they wonder if they can get up to the ball . . . that's why there are so many handballs —and bookings—just outside the area.

Terry slows it right down to show how to get under the ball to create lift and backspin.

'You need to get your foot right under the ball,' Terry explains. 'The kick itself is a jabbing motion that gives the backspin.'

'It's a bit like golf. You've got to strike through the underside of the ball to get the lift.

That goal against Everton was hit with the left foot . . . same balance. same concen-

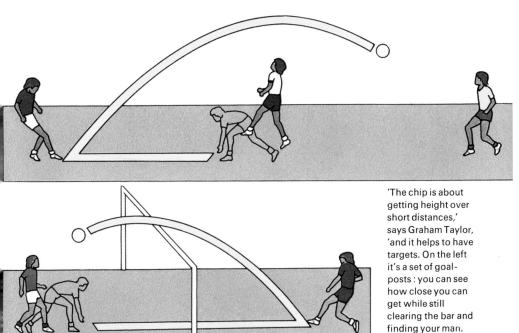

'The chip is about getting height over short distances,' says Graham Taylor, 'and it helps to have targets. On the left it's a set of goalposts : you can see how close you can get while still clearing the bar and finding your man. At the top it's a pal in the middle. And if he's a keeper then so much the better.'

tration . . . same result. But Terry warns: 'Keep your head down, eye on the ball.'

173

PRO FILE
GLENN HODDLE

'Glenn has really turned it on.
Ardiles thinks he's wonderful . . . a
must for England.' PETER TAYLOR

The arrival of Osvaldo Ardiles and Ricardo Villa has taken some of the pressure off Glenn Hoddle in what is a particularly important season for him. His ability has never been in question, with his sure touch and exceptional balance for a tall player. But for the Argentinians he might have been expected to provide much of the class in Spurs' midfield. Now he's just one of a pedigree trio . . .

At Spurs' training ground in Cheshunt Glenn was answering questions about his new team-mates with the same kind of quiet patience he signed autographs. You sensed he'd been asked the same things several times already.

'There's no doubt he's a great player,' he said in answer to a *Handbook* question about Ardiles. 'He's got great vision—he sees things so quickly—and he's very busy.'

How do he and Ardiles fit into the same midfield? 'It's true we're both naturally right-footed, but I really don't mind which side of the midfield I play on.

'So we started off with me in the centre and Osvaldo on the right. But we switch around during the game.'

And what are the problems of playing alongside team-mates whose English is just good enough for them to be puzzled by a shout of 'square ball!'? 'It takes time to build an understanding with any player. I think we have established that understanding —with Ricky as well. It's come along quicker than anyone could have thought.'

Que . . . ? Hoddle and Ardiles discuss tactics at Forest. It was a blazing start to the season for Glenn, with Spurs earning a good draw.

Bob Thomas

Young hopeful Hoddle
Glenn attended Burnt Mill school in Harlow and represented Essex Schools . . . He joined Spurs as a 16-year-old apprentice and signed as a full professional in April 1975 . . . He made his debut at home to Norwich on 30 August 1975, coming on as a substitute for full-back Cyril Knowles, and scored in his first full game— a 2–1 win over Stoke . . . Aged 20, he is an Under-21 international.

But then Glenn Hoddle has had to be a quick learner. In his brief career he has already played with a variety of midfielders and a constantly changing selection of target players. And he's experienced life in both the First and Second Divisions.

'I expected it to be tough this season,' he admits, 'and not just while the new lads were settling in. There were some good footballing teams in the Second Division, but they're all difficult in the First. They're better all round. You tend to have more time to play, but then it's harder to get the ball back once you've lost it.'

Spurs have been changing their style, too. In the recent past they've been criticised for ending their cultured midfield play with too many high balls into the penalty area.

'Our club's changing that,' claims Hoddle. 'We've been looking to play more in the continental style . . . play from the back.'

Spurs' new continental style will suit Glenn Hoddle, whose vision and accuracy should insure that the First Division newcomers get plenty of goal chances this season.

Glenn himself has been scoring more regularly and 12 goals made him Spurs' second top marksman last season.

Now he's progressed physically from the stringy youngster of Spurs' relegation side two years ago. And he's more self-assured—his confidence helped by his England Under-21 experiences: 'I played against Finland at home, Italy at home and away and Yugoslavia at home. That was disappointing, because we only drew when we needed a win.

'The Italian games were pretty rough. They went into every challenge very hard. But it was good for me. It sounds funny, I know, because they were a very, very physical side. But the experience is valuable. Playing in these games you pick up a lot of little things, insights into European styles.'

And that could be especially valuable now that, as Glenn points out, 'the continentals—and South Americans—are having an increasing influence on our football.'

By the season's end Ardiles' English may be good enough to answer the question: 'What's it like to play with Glenn Hoddle?'

Club	Div	Pos	Season	League		FA Cup		Lge Cup	
				Ms	Gs	Ms	Gs	Ms	Gs
Tottenham	I	9	1975-76	7	1	–	–	–	–
Hotspur	I	22	1976-77	39	4	1	–	2	1
	II	3	1977-78	41	12	2	1	2	–
				87	17	3	1	4	1

Glenn Hoddle with Trevor Lee, two of the scorers in the Spurs-Millwall game last season, which ended 3-3. Glenn's goal was one of his 12 in the League: 'I was getting into the area more,' he esplains, 'especially on the blind side.'

Whistle Test

'I took terrible stick in the press. One journalist said I'd lost all credibility, my common sense, the lot . . . He never apologised.'

*Who loves ya, ref . . . ?
Tom Reynolds starts the
new season at Dean Court—
a first round League Cup
game between Bournemouth
and Exeter. A top ref will
take some lower division
games during a season . . .
'as well as plenty of stick',
says Tom. 'The Kojak?
Nothing to do with image—
just an irritating rash.'*

Trial by television

'It doesn't bother me,'
says Tom, 'especially
if you're found Not
Guilty! In another
match Brian Moore
said I was wrong
during his comment-
ary but was big
enough to admit he
was wrong after see-
ing the incident in
slow motion. Of
course a ref can be
wrong, but all he can
do is stick to the
decision he makes at
the time.

Sometimes it's the watching thousands who need glasses—not the poor, pilloried referee.

Wiltshire ref Tom Reynolds was bang in the middle of a disallowed goal row last season. Even his linesman was convinced Tom was wrong!

But Tom was right, as the TV cameras proved.

The incident came in the exciting Wrexham-Arsenal FA Cup-tie, with the game beautifully poised at 1-1.

A Wrexham forward broke clear and Arsenal keeper Pat Jennings rushed out to narrow the angle.

And, as an Arsenal defender raced back to cover the empty goal, the Wrexham player passed forward to a team-mate, who beat the defender on the line.

A major Cup shock seemed on the cards—until Tom disallowed the goal for offside.

Quite right, too! The defender on the line fooled most people, including the linesman.

But the law states, quite clearly, that a player is offside unless there are TWO players between him and the goal when he receives the ball.

Tom says: 'No-one would have complained if it had been the goalkeeper on the line and not the defender. For once, trial by television found someone innocent!

'But I took terrible stick in the Press. One journalist said I'd lost all credibility, my common sense, the lot.

'But he never apologised after the TV programme. Still, that's a referee's lot, I suppose!

**Handbook's consultant
Martin Tyler on the
man who led Holland
in Argentina**

Syndication International

RUDI KROL

'The night lights of Buenos Aires make an impressive view from the 22nd floor of the Sheraton Hotel but Rudi Krol was not admiring them. Instead he stared emptily through the windows, his eyes haunted after coming face to face for the second time with a living nightmare...

Forty-eight hours earlier he had confided to me that whatever happened in the 1978 World Cup final he would avenge the agony of Munich: 'I once went to watch the re-run of our game against West Germany in the 1974 final. It hurt so much that I had to walk out before half-time. We were so much the better side I could not understand how we lost. I am lucky to have the chance to make amends.'

Those words rebounded with a vengeance. History now records that Kempes replaced Muller as the torturer of Holland; that Fillol's brilliance equalled that of Sepp Maier; that 90 seconds from the end of normal time a goalpost stopped Robbie Rensenbrink's shot from becoming a winning goal ... when once again Holland had been the better side against the overwhelming odds of passionate home support from their opponents.

I intruded into Rudi Krol's grief that evening with the timidity of a casual acquaintance attending a funeral within a close family.

I needn't have worried. The reception was warm and friendly, just as it had been throughout the tournament; the Dutch captain had made sure that he and his squad were available to the world's press ... an exercise in public relations that was never strained even when Holland began so poorly against Peru and Scotland.

Originally a left-back and later a sweeper —where he exhibited a clinically impressive calmness in Argentina—Rudi joined Ajax at 17. He bounced into the first team at the

Colorsport

ABOVE *Policing Bertoni in the World Cup final— the second in which he'd finished a runner-up.*

OPPOSITE PAGE *Tangling with Joe Jordan in Holland's surprise 3-2 defeat at Mendoza.*

start of the 1969-70 season, but a broken leg kept him out of Ajax's first European triumph, against Panathinaikos at Wembley.

In the 1974 World Cup Rudi's fluent style fitted glove-like into the total football that enchanted the watching world and he contributed greatly to Holland's attacking output, scoring in spectacular style against Argentina. That time the Dutch completely dominated the meeting, winning 4-0.

Great players are hardly plentiful, but those who retain a charm and dignity to their personality in the face of the pressures of their profession are scarcer still. Rudi Krol

179

is one of that breed, a genuine gentleman, and as articulate in German and English as in his native language.

When I first met him, he went to great lengths to assure me that whichever member of the squad I wished to interview in Argentina he would make them available. He was as good as his word, leaving a team meeting to answer my desperate call from the only antiquated public phone in the foothills of the Andes 40 miles from Mendoza, and happily being woken up at eight o'clock in the morning after Holland's extravagant 5-1 win over Austria in Cordoba.

Krol's integrity also shines through on the field, where his disciplinary record has been almost impeccable; the yellow card in the River Plate stadium was only the second caution of his long career.

While most footballers are adept at side-stepping awkward questions, Rudi's candour is refreshing. For example, he put into honest perspective comments about the Dutch fearing a kicking match against Scotland in Mendoza: 'We have no worries about playing against Scotland because their players have a European style. Sure they will be aggressive, but you can knock them down and they will get up and still shake your hands.

'We are more worried about Brazil and the South American style. Their players seem to attack you off the ball.'

LEFT *Krol is the only survivor from the brilliant Ajax side who dominated the European club scene with their hat-trick of Champions Cup wins in 1971, 1972 and 1973, though he missed the first of those finals—against Panathinaikos at Wembley—because of a broken leg. Unlike Johan Cruyff, Johnny Rep, Gerrit Muhren, Arie Haan and Wim Suurbier, he has not jumped on the gravy train to West Germany, Spain and all points south . . . though he says he would like to play for an English club if the right offer from a big side could secure his release.*

Colorsport

Colorsport

His frankness has obviously been an asset in his flourishing business career; Rudi runs two popular snack bars in Amsterdam. He's dabbled in interior design, and his ruggedly masculine looks have been in demand for modelling sessions.

This contact with commerce has developed a shrewdness so respected by his fellow internationals that they are happy to let him negotiate their financial dealings with newspapers, television or other fringe enterprises.

Krol's business acumen will surely be brought into play when his contract with Ajax is up in two years' time, when he is likely to finally opt for a transfer: 'I just think that I will need new inspiration then and that is more likely to come from abroad. I would very much like to face a new challenge.'

Though the position of his Ajax club will probably dictate otherwise, Rudi Krol would love to come to England, a desire based on a traditional respect for our people and our football. 'I watch English games on the television all the time, and I am excited now with the way that England are playing under Ron Greenwood. As a defender I know how dangerous wingers are and I never understood why you played without them. Now you have chosen men like Peter Barnes you are again a team to be feared.'

If Krol did opt to play in England there would be few objections. Professionals remember his interest and his courtesy when he flew over to play in Jack Taylor's testimonial at Villa Park; an ITV film crew fondly recall his offer of a lift in the Dutch official aircraft in Argentina; a producer could not believe that his christian name was remembered even though he was just one of a thousand who had requested an interview. Little things, yes . . . but indicative of an exceptional character. 9

ABOVE *Rudi slots a pass through the Argentinian attack. As in 1974, he starred in a side which lost the final to the host nation. By 1982 he'll be 33 and could still be around to tilt once more for the game's ultimate honour. Many neutrals will hope he makes it third time lucky.*

RIGHT *Krol made his debut for Holland—after only 10 first team games for Ajax—in a 1-0 defeat by England in 1969. A remarkably consistent player, he has missed only one international since returning after injury in 1972.*

Syndication International

Johnstone's header

'You can argue about luck playing a part . . . but the key factors are timing, judgment and positioning.' DEREK JOHNSTONE

There weren't many highlights in Scotland's summer —but Derek Johnstone's goal against Wales was one.

After hitting 37 goals for Rangers last season, the reluctant attacker did enough in this one appearance to suggest that Scotland would

have need of him in Argentina . . . but in the event he wasn't called upon at all.

It was a Welsh mistake that began it all . . . and they were swiftly punished by the efficient Scots.

With Kenny Dalglish in possession 40 metres from

goal, the Welsh defence was cruelly spread-eagled. Johnstone was goal-side of the central defenders . . . and stayed that way throughout the move.

Dalglish's pass inside the full-back was perfectly weighted for Archie Gem-

Bob Thomas

DAVIES

punishes the Welsh

mill's well-timed run. Dave Roberts moved across to challenge, but Archie played the ball first time . . . a neat 'out-of-step' cross with the outside of his left foot . . . right on to the head of the charging, unmarked John-stone. And the ball rocketed past a bewildered Dai Davies between the Welsh posts to give the Scots a 1-0 lead.

Graham Taylor's analysis

'The Scots reacted and thought faster than the Welsh . . . and made them pay for their mistakes.

The first mistake was giving away the ball—that's criminal in your own half—but the second was equally vital. The Welsh defenders didn't come out together. If they had then Johnstone, on the goalside of the central defenders, would have been off-side when Dalglish played the ball forward.

Dalglish and Gemmill played their parts well—Gemmill's cross was perfect—and Johnstone's header looked a good one to me. It had power, direction and it finished in the net. You can't ask for more.'

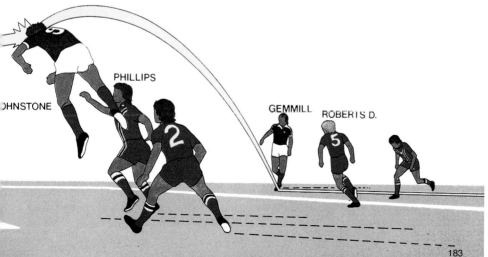

JOHNSTONE   PHILLIPS   GEMMILL   ROBERTS D.

Founded: 1874
Address: Burnden Park, Bolton BL3 2QR
Ground: Capacity 51,000; Playing area 103 x 69.5 m
Record attendance: 69,912 v Man. City, FA Cup 5th rd, 18.2.33
Record victory: 13-0 v Sheffield United, FA Cup 2nd rd, 1.2.1890
Record defeat: 0-7 v Manchester City, Div. 1, 21.3.36
Most League points: 61, Div. 3, 1972-73
Most League goals: 96, Div. 2, 1934-35
League scoring record: 38, Joe Smith, Div. 1, 1920-21
Record League aggregate: 255, Nat Lofthouse, 1946-61
Most League appearances: 519, Eddie Hopkinson, 1956-70
Most capped player: 33, Nat Lofthouse, England, 1951-59
League career: 1888 Original members of Football League;
1892-99; 1899-1900 Div. 2; 1900-03 Div. 1; 1903-1905 Div. 2;
1905-08 Div. 1; 1908-09 Div. 2; 1909-1910 Div. 1; 1910-11 Div. 2;
1911-33 Div. 1; 1933-35 Div. 2; 1935-64 Div. 1; 1964-71 Div. 2;
1971-73 Div. 3; 1973-78 Div. 2; 1978- Div. 1
Honours: FA Cup Winners 1923, 1926, 1929, 1958, Runners-up
1894, 1904, 1953; Div. 2 Champions 1909, 1978; Div. 3
Champions 1973

BOLTON WANDERERS

The centenary men
Wanderers celebrated two centenaries in the 1970s. They were founded as Christ Church FC in 1874 —when players were fined 1p for swearing and 2½p for failing to play if selected! The club was renamed Bolton Wanderers in 1877. In 1988 they will notch up 100 years in the League as one of its founders.

Nat Lofthouse, Bolton's great No 9, opens the scoring in the 1958 Cup Final. Bolton beat Manchester United 2-0.

'The story of Bolton Wanderers is all about people. The club is really part of the town. I feel that the function of the Board of Directors is to act as custodians of the club for everyone—and we aim to keep Wanderers at the forefront so its activities will reflect well on the town. The club's first hundred years have had moments of glory as well as moments of sadness, but I hope the club will go from strength to strength as it moves into the second hundred years of its existence.'

With these words, Wanderers' chairman George Warburton summarises the hopes and dreams of many once-great Lancashire clubs who have suffered lean years since the abolition of the maximum wage for players in 1961.

Clubs with a proud tradition of success—like Bolton, Blackburn and Preston—soon found themselves engaged in a fight for survival. Traditional support eroded away as newly-mobile fans with cars chose to travel to the glamour

clubs like Manchester United, or stay at home and watch television soccer.

As far as Bolton were concerned, a healthy average gate around the 27,000 mark gradually evaporated and in 1964 the club were relegated after 22 consecutive seasons in the First Division.

Worse followed in 1971 when, after a number of indifferent seasons and a series of traumatic managerial changes, they went down again. After one season in Division 3—they finished seventh—the tide turned. Jimmy Armfield, the former Blackpool and England full-back, in his first managerial job, put together an exciting attacking side that stormed to the sixth round of the FA Cup in 1973 —and won the Third Division Championship with a club record points haul of 61.

The Second Division place was consolidated in the season before Armfield was lured to Leeds, in October 1974, to take over after Brian Clough's stormy 44-day reign. Luckily Wanderers had a ready-made successor in assistant manager Ian Greaves.

After another season in mid-table, Wanderers suddenly emerged as serious promotion candidates. They became an attractive footballing side, much praised by the critics.

They shunned the big boot up the middle so characteristic of the lower divisions—'route 1', as Greaves dismissively describes it—and concentrated on short first-time passes and patient build-up, often (though not as often as the fans may have wished) culminating with sharply-taken goals inside the box.

In the likes of Roy Greaves (no relation to manager Ian), England Under-21 midfield man Peter Reid and ex-Scotland star Willie Morgan, they had the players with the drive and

Sponsorship's fizzing! Wanderers players Sam Allardyce, Roy Greaves, Mike Walsh and Frank Worthington pose in their Cambrian shirts—Cambrian being the local soft drinks firm that has entered into an overall sponsorship arrangement with the club. In addition, individual matches are sponsored by other local firms. With the extra revenue springing from pools activity, Golden Goals etc., the club benefitted to the tune of £60,000 last season—a vital contribution to a club that can't survive on gates.

Wanderers' most expensive signing, £120,000 Alan Gowling—here seen in action against Oldham in the Anglo-Scottish Cup—started the season with a spectacular goal.

Dynamic duo
The partnership that has brought success to Bolton—manager Ian Greaves (left) and coach George Mulhall (ex-Sunderland). Greaves admits that the club has turned his hair grey, though he knows all about the tough facts of managerial life after a six-year spell with Huddersfield. He took them to the First, saw them slump to the Third, while his pleas for cash to buy new players was ignored, and was then made the scapegoat for failure. He must be hoping that history doesn't repeat itself!

The disaster game
Burnden Park was the scene of the worst-ever disaster in English football. On 7 March 1946, during an FA Cup 6th round tie against Stoke City, 33 spectators among the 60,000 capacity crowd were killed and 400 injured when crush barriers collapsed on the Manchester Road side. As a result, tighter controls were introduced on British grounds —and Wanderers were among the first clubs to meet the additional safety measures required of Division 1 and 2 clubs after the disaster at Ibrox in January 1971, when 66 died at the end of a Rangers v Celtic derby, which led to the Ground Safety Act.

skill to create the chances, while up front prolific scorer John Byrom (since retired), Neil Whatmore and Steve Taylor (now with Oldham) were on hand to convert.

The defence was the rock on which the club's revival was built. Canny ex-United full-back Tony Dunne combined with Paul Jones—one of the country's best uncapped centre-halves—and club skipper John Ritson to set an example to fine young players like Sam Allardyce and Mike Walsh. These players added skill to the ruggedness that has always characterised Bolton defenders; indeed, it used to be said that you needn't apply for the job unless you had thighs like tree-trunks!

Success returned to Burnden Park, with gates regularly nudging the 20,000 mark. In 1976 an epic FA Cup run was ended by Newcastle United—then high in Division 1— after three fifth round matches watched by 139,245 people live, and more on television. The next year, in the League Cup, a single-goal defeat by Everton in the two-legged semi-final cost Bolton their first Wembley trip in 20 years.

But the most important prize—promotion to Division 1 to reclaim the place the club regarded as their right— proved frustratingly elusive. In 1976 they finished fourth,

Hard training
In the days of steam this was a common sight at Burnden Park—an engine driver stopping his train for a sneaky bit of match action, though the passengers probably didn't complain! Bolton secured the site of Burnden Park in 1893 for an annual rent of £130—it was land previously earmarked for an extension to the gas works—and have been developing it into the fine ground it is today ever since that date. It is the club's third ground, which may explain the Wanderers in their name. The railway end terrace is now divided to provide a segregated area for visiting fans, aimed at minimising crowd violence.

pipped at the post for the third promotion place by West Brom, despite an effortless 4-0 win at Charlton on the final Saturday of the season.

In 1977 it happened again. After leading the table for long periods, last-minute jitters saw them slide into fourth place once more—this time on goal difference to Brian Clough's Nottingham Forest, who so nearly didn't make it and earn their brilliant League Championship.

Last year, the fans must have felt that their team was going to fail again. The season that Ian Greaves described as 'lasting ten years' began well, with Bolton making the running—establishing mastery over main rivals Spurs in both League and Cup—until bad luck with the weather and Wanderers' seemingly inevitable Christmas slump.

Suddenly, a late challenge from Southampton and Alan Mullery's high-flying Brighton threatened Wanderers' promotion hopes—and Ian Greaves is honest enough to admit that they countered the threat by tightening up their game.

'After all,' says Greaves, 'mistakes we'd made in trying to play attractive football from the back had cost us promotion twice. Everywhere we went in the Second Division they told us we were the best footballing side they'd seen . . . but I made myself sick wondering if we were a West Ham that everyone loved, and loved taking points off.'

He needn't have worried. Though the race remained tight to the end, Wanderers clinched their promotion place at Blackburn with a nervy 1-0 win in the last week of the season—eight years to the day after Greaves' Huddersfield

Giants of the FA Cup
Wanderers have a fine FA Cup record, having lifted the trophy in 1923, 1926, 1929 and 1958 and finishing as runners-up in 1894, 1904 and 1953. They share the distinction, with West Ham, of having played before the largest crowd to watch a live football match in Britain. No actual figures are available for the first Wembley Cup final—in 1923—because excited fans stormed the gates, invaded the pitch and had to be cleared before the match could commence. It is estimated that well over 150,000 spectators were inside the ground. Bolton also shared the highest-scoring final—1953's seven-goal thriller against Blackpool.

All-action Roy Greaves, now team captain, shoots for goal against Chelsea. The No 10 is John Byrom, since retired, a regular scorer for Bolton.

Ray Green

Ray Green

One of Wanderers' exciting youngsters is Neil Whatmore, here showing the control that makes him an integral part of the team's short-passing style. He has been top scorer for the past two seasons.

Bob Thomas

Mike Walsh, a determined, versatile young player, started the season at left-back, but he has also played in midfield and as a central defender.

team clinched *their* Division 2 Championship on the same Ewood Park pitch.

This time it should be different: the club have waited too long for First Division football to let it slip, and have shown their willingness to spend with the successive records transfers—Frank Worthington for £90,000 then Alan Gowling for £120,000—that helped to clinch promotion.

As he celebrated at Blackburn, Greaves was like a man who has been pardoned after three years on death row.

'I doubt I could have climbed another mountain,' he admitted as he sipped champagne. 'The tension of these last few weeks has been horrific, impossible to explain to anyone . . . but we've won the Championship tonight. There can be no way now that we won't win our last game against Fulham on Saturday . . .'

In the event, Wanderers drew that game 0-0, but it was enough to clinch the Championship for Bolton. When he heard the news, Lawrie McMenemy, manager of rivals Southampton, only had to swallow his disappointment for a second before saying 'so Greavsie's nicked the Championship, has he? It couldn't have gone to a nicer bloke. Good luck to him.'

And Wanderers will need luck. It's never easy to step straight from the top of Division 2 to success in the first—particularly without buying big—and with a gate of just 21,000 in their opening match the size of Bolton's problem was obvious. They have the basis of a good team, which probably needs one or two experienced men to complement the youngsters—but even then they may well be fighting for First Division survival as so many promoted teams have before them.

A Matter of Fact

In a First Division match at The Valley in 1957, Charlton were down to 10 men and trailing 5-1 to Huddersfield. Then Johnny Summers—who has since died from a tragic illness—decided to take a hand, slamming five goals past Town's stunned defence as Charlton stormed to an amazing 7-6 win.

Only five of the Spurs side which clinched promotion at Southampton in April held their places for the first game of the 1978-79 season at Forest: Daines, Perryman, Hoddle, Taylor and McAllister.

Alan Willey has scored just 7 goals in his Football League career. But when Minnesota Kicks crushed defending champions New York Cosmos 9-2 in a North American League play-off in August, the ex-Middlesbrough striker banged in 5 goals! His team-mate Charlie George scored after 52 seconds to start off the fun.

When Manchester United's Duncan Edwards won his first England cap against Scotland in April 1955 at the tender age of 18 years and 183 days, he became the youngest ever England player—a record that still stands. Edwards died from injuries he received in the Munich air crash of 1958.

Even though he spent two years in Switzerland with Servette, only one current First Division striker has more League goals to his name than Martin Chivers. That man is his predecessor at Norwich, Ted Macdougall. Up to the start of the present season they'd notched 402 in 901 games—just under a goal each every two games. But even their aggregate total was 32 less than the record holder, Arthur Rowley, who finished his career with Shrewsbury, scored on his own!

RIGHT 'Pop' Robson and Bobby Moncur, pictured tussling for the ball in a West Ham v Newcastle United match at Upton Park, were team-mates when the Geordies defeated the Hungarian aide Ujpest Dozsa in the 1969 European Fairs Cup final. Moncur, who now manages Carlisle, scored twice in a great 3-0 victory in the first leg at St James Park and followed up with another goal in United's 3-2 triumph in the second leg in Budapest. Moncur's performance was all the more remarkable because in those two matches he doubled his tally in 9 years with the Tyneside club.

Colorsport

'We would give any

The other Saints, winning the 1973 cup final . . . with commitment and powerful shooting.

190

rourth Division side a good game'

They've won the cup six times. They've got seven internationals in their side and last season they swept all before them . . . winning the league, cup, league cup and European Cup Winners Cup.

Any player they lose is not through a fat transfer . . . but because of babies.

They're Southampton WFC—shining stars in the expanding world of women's football.

Today, the Women's Football Association has no fewer than 21 regional leagues, 260 clubs and a national side that plays all over Western Europe.

And WFA secretary Pat Gregory is confident in her claim that 'the England ladies team would give any Fourth Division side a good game.'

She adds: 'We play good, plain football. Football at its most basic. We use wingers. When men watch our games they always admit to being pleasantly surprised at seeing "pure" football again. And we don't have any "aggro".'

But Pat, like the FA, doesn't believe that women should play in or against men's teams. 'Men are stronger, so what enjoyment do you get from a game if the players don't start off reasonably equal?

'We want to keep on working at our own standards and developing our own skills.'

The England side's skills compare well

Heading for equality? Spectators are 'pleasantly surprised', says WFA's Pat Gregory. 'Our standard really impresses them.'

Syndication International

191

with other European teams. They've won 17 out of 23 international matches—losing twice to Italy, twice to Sweden and once to Wales.

Yet very little is still known in this country about women's football. 'When we played Italy in Rome there were 10,000 people watching,' says Pat. 'The biggest crowd we've ever had here was 4,000 when England played Switzerland at Hull City.

'We have a lot of old prejudices to overcome . . . and the fact that everything in England changes slowly. The WFA is trying to get football taught to girls at school. But at the moment it's an uphill battle.'

Pat herself wasn't allowed to go to a football match until she was 15 years old—a victim of the old 'football is for boys' attitude.

'It was a home game at Spurs. There were loads of women watching, and it struck me how unfair it was that none of them ever had the chance to play.'

According to the FA, girl's teams were 'illegal'. A cob-webbed rule dating back to 1921 had effectively banned women from

Legs Eleven
Blinkers United—a decorative publicity stunt—with David Sadler, Alan Ball and George Best back in the 1960s. . . Just the image the WFA are struggling to avoid—of players more worried about their hairstyles than their skills.

Yes, it's Birmingham City . . . a Blues player attempts a tricky bit of control in a match against the Amersham Angels. Also among the big guns: QPR Ladies.

playing organised football.

But teams were springing up all over the country, including one that Pat founded in North London, and in November 1969—despite opposition from the FA—they formed the WFA. It wasn't until three years later that the FA 'legalised' them.

Now the breach is healed, women can share club facilities and use registered coaches and referees. Pat feels there is still resentment towards women's football from some of the top FA officials, though, she emphasises, 'the staff are very helpful.'

So what caused the upsurge of interest in women's football?

'There was special interest after the 1966 World Cup,' explains Pat. 'It's a bit like the recent interest in gymnastics following the Olympics and Olga Korbut.'

PE teacher Sue Lopez, midfield player for Southampton and England, says: 'Football is just a good game. It's attractive because it gives the player a chance to express her individuality as well as a team effort.'

What is it that makes Southampton the country's top team?

'Some of us have been playing together for almost ten years,' suggests Southampton captain and England goalkeeper Sue Buckett. 'And we have a good bunch of young players. It's this combination that's made us so successful.'

There won't be any shortage of skilled youngsters at Southampton in the future either. So many show an interest that former international Lynda Hale has started a junior side.

Julie Clarke, 13-year-old daughter of trainer Charlie, has already made the grade, and the latest recruit to the first team is 15-year-old centre-half Heather Kirkland.

The club has some well-known fans. Lawrie McMenemy, of that other Southampton club, lets them use The Dell's five-a-side facilities. And some Saints have been in the 500-strong crowds that attend the floodlit home games in the Home Counties League, the strongest in the country.

And they're impressed with what they see . . .

Southampton WFC undergo an exhausting pre-season fitness programme. The Saints have won the WFC Cup 6 out of the 8 years it has been in existence, and they're back in Europe this season.

Theresa tackles the FA
12-year-old Theresa Bennett of Newark brought female football into the limelight when she fought the FA for the right to play in a boy's team. But the WFA are also opposed to mixed football, even for 12-year-olds.

Tight marking at set pieces: Stuart Boam

'Free-kicks around the box are the times when every defender has got to be extra alert to the dangers . . . it's the worst time to get caught ball-watching because one touch from an outstretched leg could finish you off.' STUART BOAM

Ray Green

Stuart Boam marks Denis Law . . . 'He was very difficult to mark because his close control was so good,' says Stuart. 'He was one player you couldn't give a yard to because he'd turn and come at you. He never needed two touches—one was always enough.'

'Basically, a defender marking at set pieces has three things to worry about,' says Graham Taylor. 'Most obvious is the pass to the feet of the player he is marking. Second, and possibly the most dangerous these days, is the ball played into space in front of the forward. A glancing header or outstretched foot can send the ball flashing goalwards.

'And then there's the ball hit to the far post, beyond both players. A good forward might feint to come short and then check to get behind his marker into that dangerous area. So, as Stuart says, it's very much a question of not getting caught ball-watching.

'A good practice is for three of you to work a free-kick as shown in the diagram. If you keep mixing them—deep, short and to feet—you'll find it a very useful and enjoyable exercise. And if you can find someone to go in goal, so much the better!'

Free-kicks around the box always give defenders the jitters—they know that just a touch from a sharp forward can plant the ball in the back of the net.

That's why a defender like Middlesbrough's king-pin Stuart Boam takes special care in training to keep this aspect of his game—tight marking at set pieces—at a peak.

'These days most teams try to do something special from free-kicks,' says Stuart, 'and it's in these situations that we have to be really alert.

'To be honest, I don't mind the balls played to the big fellas at the far post so much. I certainly prefer them to the quick, possibly curling free-kicks which nippy strikers are looking to get on to.

'Opponents try to get as many people into the box as possible and try to put defenders off by constant movement.

'So our orders are clear: keep on your toes and make sure you keep looking about you.' The big danger for defenders, explains Stuart, is the temptation to ball-watch.

'It's more than just picking up someone and keeping an eye on the ball. You've got to watch for anyone getting in behind you—say, for a simple header.'

The nearer goal the free-kick is the tighter you have to get, says Stuart.

If the kick is taken a fair way out, defenders can give forwards a yard or so because

the danger is not so great and it gives them that extra space to size up the situation.

'Exactly the same rules apply for corners and long throw-ins,' says Stuart, 'but the danger is not quite so great because, we're more used to the routines.

'No, it's those free-kicks that cause the ulcers—so keep on your toes and don't ball-watch!'

Stuart Boam didn't sign pro until he was 19. He was in Mansfield's first team at the time, but his dad insisted he get a trade behind him before signing on the dotted line. Transferred to Middlesbrough for £50,000 in 1971, he now holds a full FA coaching badge.

20

copies of the greatest ever book – in sensational colour – on the World Cup

WORLD CUP '78

to be won in our great free-entry competition

1. Match the player to the club: (1) Hans Krankl, (2) Rainer Bonhof, (3) Hansi Müller, (4) Klaus Fischer, (5) Allan Simonsen; (a) VfB Stuttgart, (b) Barcelona, (c) Borussia Moenchengladbach, (d) Valencia, (e) Schalke 04.

2. With which clubs did these players begin their League careers: Don Masson, Paul Hart, Terry McDermott, Stewart Houston?

3. Peter Coyne played for Los Angeles Aztecs last summer. Which Fourth Division club does he usually play for?

4. Which of these Scotland players did not play, even as a substitute, in the last World Cup: Joe Harper, Derek Johnstone, John Robertson, Tom Forsyth, Jim Blyth.

5. Number 13 is marking Manchester City & England winger Peter Barnes. Who is he—and what is his present club?

7. Which present Fourth Division club gave both Denis Law and Frank Worthington their League debuts?

8. Which one of these clubs has Tommy Docherty never managed: QPR, Rotherham, Chelsea, Preston North End, AstonVilla?

9. Which current First Division clubs have played in the Third Division since 1970?

10. England have only beaten Brazil once in 11 full internationals between the countries: was it in 1956, 1963, 1970 or 1978?

10. Last season Nottingham Forest won the League Championship in their first season after promotion. Who were the last club to perform this feat, and when?

HOW TO ENTER
List your answers to the questions on a postcard, add your name and address, cut the 'Part 7' flash from the cover and attach it to the postcard (entries that do not bear the flash will be ineligible), then mail to: Football Handbook, 600A Commercial Road, London E14 7HS. Entries must arrive by October 23, 1978, the closing date. The sender of the first 20 correct answers scrutinised after that date will each be awarded a copy of 'WORLD CUP 78', *the* book on this years finals in Argentina. The Editor's decision on all matters relating to the competition is final and binding. All winners will be notified as soon as possible and a full list of prize winners to date will be available from *Football Handbook* on request.

Gerry Ryan

'The new defensive patterns with a man spare at the back mean more and more coaches are looking to attack from wide positions, and wingers are back with a bang.'

Brighton's new touchline terror Gerry Ryan is one man who is pleased to see what was a dying breed back in demand.

'Wingers win matches,' Gerry explained to *Handbook*. 'Defences are left trying to turn and close down on the ball, plus pick up players running at them into space from deep when the winger gets it across. It's more difficult for them to provide cover.'

Few managers utilise the winger more than Tommy Docherty. 'He's a great believer in attacking football,' says Gerry. 'He was always making the point at Derby that our job was not just to win but to win in an entertaining way.

'And wingers are great entertainers. There's a tradition of wingers being the men loved by the crowd, from Stanley Matthews to Peter Barnes.

'But in the old days they operated in a restricted area and relied on service. Now that isn't on. I have to drop back into midfield and help out when the opposition have the ball. Today's wingers have not only got to turn on the skill and beat defenders; they must be as involved as any midfield ball-winner.'

Gerry made his Eire debut in a 4-2 win over Turkey in Dublin last April.

Alan Mullery seems to have made an £80,000 bargain buy for Brighton in September.

197

Phil Parkes: throwing and distribution

Phil Parkes has made over 350 appearances for QPR since joining them from Walsall, and he has always been regarded as among the top handful of keepers in England. The brilliance of Ray Clemence and Peter Shilton has restricted his full England experience to a single game: he kept a clean sheet against Portugal in Lisbon in 1974.

There's far more to this aspect of goalkeeping than just clearing to an unmarked player.

'It really breaks down into two parts,' explains QPR's Phil Parkes, 'the actual techniques of throwing and a sense of distribution.

'Getting the throws right with lots of practice comes first, and learning how to use the ball best comes mostly with match experience.

'A good keeper should not just be the last defender; he should also set up attacks.

'Obviously the more power and distance you get the more effective you can be—but accuracy must come first. Too many youngsters try to heave the ball 40 yards before they've got it right over 20.'

Colorsport

Like a javelin thrower, Phil puts everything into a big clearance.

Owen Barnes

'The overarm is like bowling,' says Phil.

'Line up with your leading arm . . .

'Bring the ball over, arm extended . . .

. . . and follow through in the same line.'

For this distance practice the middle person should jump from a specified position.

Above Solo training, using a wall. 'Accuracy first, then go for distance,' warns Phil.

Below This gives the keeper distribution and catching practice. The roll must be accurate.

Owen Barnes

'The underarm is the "safest" technique, but it can only be used for short distances says Phil. 'A good follow through is vital.

'The short-arm technique is great for the quick throw,' says Phil. 'This is the one to use when an attack has broken down.

'A good example is in the shot on the right, where one Coventy player is behind me and that quick throw I'm putting in could well take out others.

'The best time to use it is after collecting a cross when your momentum takes you past the opposing players.'

Colorsport

Owen Barnes

Phil shows the short-arm technique.

'It's a movement from the shoulder . . .

'with a "flick" at the moment of release

. . . and a strong follow through.'

201

The Bonhof

The World Cup in Argentina produced few of the spectacular free kicks which characterised the 1970 and 1974 finals, but some were worthy of note: goals by Cubillas and Dirceu, for example, and a German near-miss . . .

Müller Free Kick

It came in the last match of Group A—with the Germans having to beat Austria by five goals to make the final.

Rainer Bonhof (6) was expected to take the free kick, as he had done (with a certain lack of success) throughout the tournament. Hansi Müller (20), on as substitute for Erich Beer, waits innocently near the end of the Austrian wall [1]; as Bonhof comes in, Müller begins a run across the wall [2]; Bonhof runs in front of Müller and is picked up by Strasser (14) as Müller prepares to shoot [3]; his left-foot shot needs less of a swerve than Bonhof's right-footer would have done, but Friedl Koncilia is well positioned [4]; Koncilia dives to his right to parry the shot away [5].

All Photos by Colorsport

While refs get more coverage—good and bad—the linesmen remain on the sidelines. *Handbook* **followed match day in the life of one of the forgotten men in black . . .**

He stands in line with Newport County's last defender, red flag resting by his side—the ball at the other end of the pitch.

Someone in the crowd shouts out: 'Come on, linesman, keep on the move. Get rid of some of that flab.'

Mr M. K. Bevan (Melksham) just smiles . . . the same as he does at Arsenal or Aldershot, Torquay or Tottenham.

Mick Bevan travels hundreds of miles and gets £12.50 to be insulted. But he loves every minute of it.

'You've got to have a sense of humour in this game,' says Mick. 'I never take offence and I've got to admit I could do with losing a few pounds!

'The best ground for wit is Upton Park. Some of those West Ham fans could write a script for Morecambe and Wise. I have to chuckle to myself—but I never show it to the crowd. That would be fatal. Concentration is everything with a linesman and once you allow yourself to get distracted, you're finished.'

Inside every linesman there's a referee raring to get out and take charge, and Mick admits he prefers reffing to lining.

'There's nothing like being out in the middle, but I can't complain. I've refereed at Wembley, the Oxford-Cambridge match in 1975, and I've been on the line for some big League games. I've had my moments.'

Nowadays, Mick is making every moment count. He's on his way out. This is his last season.

'There's a new rule that if you reach 42 and haven't made it as a League referee after six seasons you have to pack up,' says Mick—'and I fall into that category.

'I don't really mind. I'm getting older and find it more difficult to train regularly.'

Mick, supplies manager at the Avon Rubber Company in Bradford-on-Avon, Wiltshire, had two seasons on the League's supplementary list of referees. He handled nine or

ten games each season but never reached the required standard.

'Looking back, I think I worried too much and stopped being myself. If you get uptight, the players soon see it and it can cause problems. I think I've got the ability to be a top class referee but perhaps not the dedication. Maybe I thought it would all somehow happen naturally.

'I'm definitely a pusher—you don't get anything unless you ask for it—but I've never stepped on anyone else's toes.'

Mick is talking as he drives across the Severn Bridge on his way home to the Wiltshire village of Melksham. He's just given a competent display on the line of a

League Cup tie between Newport County and Swansea City.

'That went okay,' he says, 'but it's the odd bad one that keeps nagging you. Last season I had a bad game at Millwall when they played Blackpool. I apologised to the ref afterwards. I just wasn't with it. I don't know why. I felt really sick about it.

'The year before I cocked it up for 22 players when refereeing in the Western

League. Being a referee is like being a goalkeeper . . . you can be great for 89 minutes and ruin the match with one mistake.'

He used to be a goalkeeper until he broke a finger playing for Melksham Town. Then a friend suggested he should become a ref. Mick thought he was joking; he couldn't stand referees.

Nevertheless, he took charge of a Trowbridge and District fourth division match between Rowde Reserves and Druids—in the pouring rain—and got hooked.

The following season he refereed in the Chippenham and District Saturday League and felt like packing it in after abandoning his third match because of a brawl.

His wife Ann kept on at him to keep going, so she's largely responsible for the happy memories Mick will treasure 'into old age' . . . and the unpleasant ones.

'I've been struck by a penny and, of all things, a Mars bar,' says Mick, 'and at an Arsenal-Chelsea match I was hit on the ear by an apple core. It stung but I kept going. If there'd been an off-side goal, who would have got the blame . . . ?'

So, come April, it'll be curtains for Mick. No more abuse. No more apple cores . . . yet he'll be sorry!

RI**S**ING **STEVE** **S**TAR **PHILLIPS**

Steve Phillips started out as a mate of Trevor Francis at Birmingham. They were apprentices together, they made their first team debuts the same year and they both played in European Youth Tournament winning sides.

But it was Trevor Francis who went on to achieve stardom, Steve Phillips who plunged into obscurity.

One of Steve's problem's was his size. At 5' 6", no one believed he would make it as a striker. So he played in midfield.

But he made a convert of Bill Dodgin, then manager of Northampton, when he joined the club at the end of 1975. And when Dodgin's new club, Brentford, were at the foot of the Fourth Division he signed Phillips for a bargain £4,500.

And last season Brentford were promoted.

'I started quite well last season and it just went on from there,' says Steve. 'The first goal in our 3-0 win over Northampton gave me a lot of pleasure because I left there in a bit of a controversy . . . But I think the two I got at Southport in March were the best.'

Gordon Sweetzer had just been sold to Cambridge, so Steve was at last taking on the role of out-and-out striker.

'If we hadn't won the boss would have come in for a lot of stick because he had moved me up. But I got a couple of almost identical goals. Both came from one-twos and I hit both from the edge of the box. That was really the turning point of the season. Everything seemed to go right after that.'

Starting at Southport, Steve hit 16 goals in the last 15 games of the season.

'When I passed the 20-goal mark and defenders went out to clobber me, I still scored goals,' says Steve. 'Big men don't like to mark me because I beat them on the ground. They give you lots of stick and threaten you.

Colorsport

'I've always scored regularly, but everyone seemed to think I was too small to do well consistently ... Birmingham City thought I wasn't big enough to be a success.'

BELOW LEFT *'Even when Steve isn't scoring goals he's busy trying to create them for others,' says Brentford manager Bill Dodgin about his bargain buy, here taking on Huddersfield.*

RIGHT *'If the ball is played to my feet, then defences are in trouble,' says Steve Phillips, the striker who came from nowhere to top the League scorers last season.*

Bob Thomas

'I shout back. I'm not usually the quietest person on the ground.'

But Steve, born in the shadow of White Hart Lane, does pay tribute to one big man — his striking partner, 6′ 2″ Andy McCulloch.

'Andy makes a lot of difference to my game. He always causes trouble up front and takes the pressure off. It's a lot worse for me when he doesn't play.'

Steve is still only 24 ... and he may yet make it in a representative side alongside his old mate Trevor Francis. If confidence was the key factor, he'd walk it.

Club	Div.	Pos.	Season	Lgue Ms	Lgue Gs	FA Cup Ms	FA Cup Gs	Lge Cup Ms	Lge Cup Gs
Birmingham City	I	2	1971-72	7	–	–	–	–	–
	I	10	1972-73	3	–	–	–	–	–
	I	19	1973-74	4	1	–	–	2	–
	I	17	1974-75	2	–	–	–	–	–
Torquay U. (on loan)	IV	14	1974-75	6	–	–	–	–	–
Birmingham City	I	19	1975-76	4	–	–	–	–	–
Northampton Town	IV	2	1975-76	34	6	–	–	–	–
	III	22	1976-77	17	2	1	–	3	–
Brentford	IV	15	1976-77	19	7	–	–	–	–
	IV	4	1977-78	46	32	2	3	2	1
				142	48	3	3	7	1

209

Liverpool's 'new boys'

**'You've nearly always got more time than you think you have ...
and a good player will often make time.'** GRAHAM TAYLOR

The European Cup final may have been something of a disappointment, but the goal that won it was worthy of the occasion.

Nothing looked on when Terry McDermott, in possession, seemed trapped near the right-side corner flag.

But he kept his head, kept the ball, and finally found space for a little chip to Dalglish. Then it seemed as though the move had broken down when Kenny Dalglish's overhead flick was headed clear by Bruges's Vandereyken.

But Souness, on the edge

of the box, controlled the ball and calmly played it between two defenders for Dalglish to run on to. Dalglish shot coolly over the falling Jensen to give Liverpool a lead they never looked like losing. The European Cup was theirs for the second year in succession.

strike Wembley gold

Graham Taylor's analysis
'A goal that showed the positive side of what everyone talks about in connection with Liverpool—professionalism. In spite of the great pressure of the situation, Souness found the time for control and telling pass and Dalglish coolly waited until the Bruges keeper was going down before clipping over him. That's flair *and* professionalism.'

SOUNESS 1

FAIRCLOUGH

Surrounded, Souness makes the pass . . .

Jensen spreads himself well, but . . .

. . . Dalglish has clipped over him—and Liverpool retain the European Cup.

PRO FILE

ANDY GRAY

'I'd worked out all the boss's permutations for the Austria game and included myself in one of them . . . the right one.'

The most staggering fact about Andy Gray must be his age—22. Not only because he's so good so young, but also because of what he's already been through.

Top scorer in the First Division in 1976/77 with 29 goals . . .

Unique double the same season when he was named the PFA's Player of the Year and Young Player of the Year . . .

The 'numbing experience' of being left out of Ally MacLeod's Scottish squad for Argentina . . .

Such ups and downs are normally the memories of a player at the end of his career—not someone whose best years still lie well ahead of him.

But all that's happened convinces Andy that football really is a 'funny game'.

He says: 'One minute you can be up on cloud nine and the next you have a real attack of the miseries.'

Rejection in June dumped him in the depths.

'At no time did I take it for granted that I would be in,' he says, 'but I was desperate

Great in the air but no slouch on the ground . . . a determined Andy Gray shows the style that makes him one of the most popular strikers in the country—except with Division 1 defenders.

Peter Robinson

to go. It meant so much to me.

'I know it's not a new thing to say, but it's all part of football. I'm still young and there's plenty of time for all sorts of things to happen, and I believe that a lot of good things are going to happen at Aston Villa.

'I'll fight hard to get back in the Scotland side, too,' Andy told *Handbook* before his selection against Austria.

Andy, one of football's most likeable lads, is not the sort to sit around and wait for things to happen. Few of the game's big names practise harder than the striker that cost Villa £150,000 from Dundee United three years ago.

Andy admits: 'I'm not overloaded with skill but I make up for it. I've never thought I can leave any part of my game.

'It's no use living on what you've done. I know I've got a reputation as a goalscorer but that means opponents will stick closer.

'That means I've got to be able to cope

Champagne time for Gray and John Gidman after Aston Villa's Football League Cup victory—after three games—against Everton last year ... a taste of things to come?

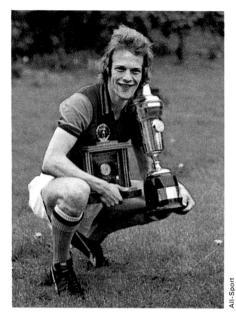

Player's pride ... Andy with the two PFA trophies he received last year—Player of the Year and Young Player of the Year.

with the greater pressure. Which means practice. I often go back for extra training in the afternoon to sharpen up any part of my game that troubles me.'

It's that attitude—plus a quality called courage—that gets Gray into great positions in the box. He goes where it matters, where it hurts.

Some say he's a throwback to past great number nines like Lawton and Lofthouse.

But Andy says: 'I don't know about

The injuries that niggle ...
Andy accepts that he'll start almost every match with an injury of some kind. 'If you want to get goals, you have to face the fact that you'll get knocks,' he says, 'and there's never time to get 100 per cent between matches.

'Usually it's a niggling injury, like a knock on the back of the thigh or ankle. Referees used to give us more protection but I think they've started to relax again.'

Andy always wears shinguards because it's the difference between a bruise and six or seven stitches.'

Eminence Gray

A Rangers supporter, Andy grew up in Drumchapel and represented Glasgow Schoolboys . . . He stayed on at school for 'A' levels, but then signed for Dundee United at the age of 17 . . . He joined Villa on 27 September 1975 and made his debut the following Saturday in a 0-0 draw at Middlesbrough . . . He made his full international debut the same year on 17 December in a 1-1 draw with Rumania in a European Championship match at Hampden . . . He has won 4 Under-23 caps and 4 full caps for Scotland . . . He has scored twice for the full international side, both goals coming in the 6-0 defeat of Finland.

ABOVE *An army of admirers accompany Andy as he takes his dog Ben for a walk near his mother's home in Glasgow.*
BELOW *Andy's kilt complex.*

trying to play like the old-timers. I can't remember them. I just attack the ball, run at defences and chase everything.

'Never give a centre-half a minute during a game and, sooner or later, the chances will come.'

As for Villa's future, Andy is adamant. He says: 'We've got a superb young side. We've grown up and matured together. Now I think we could be on the brink of becoming one of the really top sides.

'Our League Cup victory last year only whetted our appetite for more success. With huge support filling our marvellous stadium, we've got everything going for us.

'When I was a kid in Scotland, after I started playing for Dundee United, it was my ambition to join one of the really big clubs in England and play in Europe.

'We had a taste of it last season before

Keeping your cool

All strikers take stick as part of their job but there's always the danger that they'll retaliate against an opponent whose attention is a little too close for comfort.

Andy himself was sent off playing for Scotland and admits he was stupid. He says: 'You've got to turn the other cheek—it's not easy but you've got to do it. If you get known as a player who retaliates, it's easy for an opponent to take advantage of it. In the long run it's best to stay cool.'

A few memorable seconds in the life of striker Andy Gray . . . he gets his head to the ball before Everton's Mick Lyons and, even as he falls, he can see that another goal will be added to the tally of Gray A. Afterwards, of course, the reactions are the same as ever: Gray, arms aloft in triumph; the Everton defenders, heads down in a picture of dejection.

Colorsport

That worst of all moments in football—when the stretcher is called for. Andy Gray is carried off in a League game against Derby County at the Baseball Ground last season.

going out to Barcelona in the quarter-final of the UEFA Cup. I'm dying to play in the European Cup but there's the small matter of winning the championship first!'

Is that beyond Villa?

'No, not if we get the breaks,' says Andy. 'We'll be there at the finish if we can steer clear of the kind of injuries that crippled us last season.'

Andy himself has been crocked more often than he would have liked, but he refuses to listen to claims that he's injury-prone.

He says: 'Every striker takes a lot of knocks. It's the way the game is played. I don't take any more than anyone else. I had trouble last season but not as much as some

people make out.'

Others have it that Gray, a real 90-minute galloper, will burn himself out before he makes it big.

But Andy says: 'I train hard and look after myself, and my style of play is the one that suits me best.'

And his great disappointment—the Ally announcement—did'nt do any lasting damage, either, as he proved against Austria.

He says: 'In a way I knew it was all a sort of test. I knew that how I came out of it would determine the rest of my career.'

Could be—but it's more likely that the Gray career was determined long before that . . . by the kind of displays that crowds see week in, week out.

Handy tips from Andy
Andy Gray offers sound advice to young players who lack confidence in their game when he says: 'Not everybody can play like Pele and there is no point going out and trying what you're not very good at. It's far better to play to your strengths during matches—and work on weaknesses during training sessions.

Honours: Scottish FA Cup losers medal 1974 ; League Cup winners medal 1977 ; PFA Player of the Year and Young Player of the Year 1977

Club	Season	Div.	Pos.	League		FA Cup		Lge Cup		Int'als	
				Ms	Gs	Ms	Gs	Ms	Gs	Ms	Gs
Dundee	1973-74	I	8	26	16	5	1	2	1	—	—
United	1974-75	I	4	33	20	3	2	6	4	—	—
	1975-76	P	8	3	—	—	—	6	2	—	—
Aston Villa	1975-76	I	16	30	10	2	1	1	1	2	—
	1976-77	I	4	36	25	3	1	9	3	2	2
	1977-78	I	8	32	13	1	1	3	4	—	—
				160	84	14	6	27	15	4	2

Founded : 1894
Address : Ashton Gate, Bristol BS3 2EJ
Ground : Capacity 37,000 ; Playing area 105 x 68.6 m
Record attendance : 43,335 v Preston North End, FA Cup 5th rd,
16.2.35
Record victory : 11–0 v Chichester, FA Cup 1st rd, 5.11.60
Record defeat : 0–9 v Coventry City, Div. 3(S), 28.4.34
Most League points : 70, Div. 3(S), 1954-55
Most League goals : 104, Div. 3(S), 1926-27
League scoring record : 36, Don Clark, Div. 3(S), 1946-47
Record League aggregate : 315, John Atyeo, 1951-66
Most League appearances : 597, John Atyeo, 1951-66
Most capped player : 26, Billy Wedlock, England, 1907-14
League career : Div. 2 1902-06 ; Div. 1 1906-11 ; Div. 2 1911-22 ;
Div. 3(S) 1922-23 ; Div. 2 1923-24 ; Div. 3(S) 1924-27 ; Div. 2
1927-32 ; Div. 3(S) 1932-55 ; Div. 2 1955-60 ; Div. 3 1960-65 ;
Div. 2 1965-76 ; Div. 1 1976-
Honours : Div. 2 Champions 1906 ; Div. 3(S) Champions 1923,
1927, 1955

BRISTOL CITY

Alan Dicks, Bristol City's shoestring budget specialist, has recently had a new management problem on his hands— spending half a million pounds.

That may sound like the best kind of headache, but the sudden transformation of the club's resources could provide Dicks with his biggest test yet in his 11 years at Ashton Gate.

How he deals on the transfer market will decide the future of the ambitious club. Quite simply, he can't afford to fail.

Paul Cheesley and Gerry Sweeney celebrate City's first Division 1 goal for 65 years . . . a Cheesley header at Highbury in August 1976 in a 1-0 win. It was Cheesley's last League goal before injury destroyed his career.

Colorsport

217

Colorsport

International City
Peter Cormack, one of several experienced internationals Alan Dicks has signed for the club since City won promotion.

Chairman Stephen Kew, a Bristol solicitor, says: 'We're very close to establishing ourselves as one of the country's major clubs.

'The money is there for the managers to strengthen the side if he feels it's necessary . . . but I know Alan Dicks won't be spending money for the sake of it.'

A big new share issue and money-spinning promotions have raised the kind of cash that anabled Dicks to bid £400,000 for Gerry Francis.

'The present squad is the strongest City have had in our three years back in the First Division,' says Dicks. 'I'd like to strengthen it still further but the players just haven't been available.'

His only summer signing was another addition to City's clutch of ex-internationals—Terry Cooper for a modest £20,000.

Dicks rates experience highly. 'The advice I would give to any club coming into the First Division would be to go out and sign players who have experience at the highest level. They help settle the other players in the side and buy the time for them to develop.'

That's why Dicks paid £50,000 for Peter Cormack and £40,000 for Norman Hunter two seasons ago.

Cormack settled the midfield and Hunter, then 32, threw himself into the new challenge of establishing City in the

Colorsport

Vintage years
City have never won a major trophy. The closest they came was 70 years ago when they finished as runners-up in the League in 1907 and in the Cup in 1909. It remains their only Cup final appearance . . . and it wasn't at Wembley.

John Atyeo was an inside-forward at City throughout his career, during which he made over 600 first team appearances and scored 350 goals for the club. In 1955 he became the first City player for 41 years to play for England, making his debut and scoring in a 4-1 win over Spain at Wembley. He won six caps, but never played in the First Division. He was a regular in two Third Division promotion-winning sides (1955 and 1965), retiring in 1966 to become a schoolteacher.

Sporting Pictures UK

Boss Robin
Alan Dicks, 44, once a defender who played with Chelsea, Southend and Coventry, has been City's manager for the last 11 years. He was assistant to Jimmy Hill at Coventry when they won promotion to the First Division in 1967 ... then was in charge at Bristol City when they went up in 1976.

First Division with the same kind of enthusiasm he tackled a similar task with the newly-promoted Leeds side of over a decade ago.

Last season he played in constant pain with an achilles tendon injury and only rested when City were safe from relegation. A close season operation successfully restored him to full fitness . . . and he says: 'I'm good for a couple of seasons yet.'

Hunter's injury was just one of the many that destroyed City's high hopes last season.

Chris Garland, for instance, played only a handful of matches before he became the latest victim of an astonishing crop of knee injuries.

So once again Dicks was forced to buy a player. He obtained Joe Royle on loan from Manchester City . . . and the former England centre-forward scored all four goals in a 4-1 win over Middlesbrough on his debut. After that, Dicks just had to sign him.

City went from strength to strength for a while, but with mounting injury problems they fell away badly and again finished just above the relegation zone. Their only consolation: victory in the Anglo-Scottish Cup.

That first glimmer of silverware in the Ashton Gate trophy cabinet has made the club hungry for more success. The fine ground, capable of holding almost 37,000, has been too quiet for far too long.

Colorsport

Careless talk cost Dicks
It was through a remark made by Jimmy Hill, then manager of Coventry, that Alan Dicks first came to the notice of Bristol City. 'I've no need to worry,' Hill told City director Stephen Kew on the morning of a crucial Second Division promotion battle against Cardiff in 1967, 'I've got a very good assistant.' The assistant was Dicks . . . and within 6 months he was manager of Bristol City.

Tom Ritchie, closely marked by West Bromwich's Alistair Robertson. The Edinburgh-born striker has been City's top scorer for the last three seasons, and City will be relying on the Ritchie-Royle partnership for most of their goal thrust . . . unless Dicks spends some of the half million pounds he has available on a new striker.

219

A Matter of Fact

Following in father's footsteps . . . there 16-year-old Mark Hateley of Coventry City. Dad is Swindon winger-coach Tony Hateley, who notched over 200 goals in a career which took him to Notts County (twice), Villa, Chelsea, Liverpool, Coventry, Birmingham and Oldham.

In 1953-54 Port Vale conceded just 21 goals (only 7 of them at Vale Park) in 46 Third Division (North) games—the League's best ever record for a season involving 42 matches or more.

Andy Gray's penalty against Ipswich on 9 September was Villa's first in the League since 16 May 1977.

When Stoke played away to West German club Kaiserslautern in the 1972 UEFA Cup, striker John Ritchie was sent off . . . only 40 seconds after coming on as a substitute.

LEFT *Billy McNeill, appointed Celtic manager in May, appeared in 12 Scottish FA Cup finals (16 including replays) and 9 Scottish League Cup finals for the club between 1960 and 1975—both British records.*

Whistle Test

'With a name like mine, I'm there to be shot at.' *Durham ref* PAT PARTRIDGE

One of the most controversial goals of last season was the one Nottingham Forest scored to beat Liverpool in the replayed League Cup final at Old Trafford.

Liverpool dominated the goalless final at Wembley and again took charge in the replay.

But Forest battled tenaciously and there was always the possibility that one of their quick breaks would produce a goal.

Then it happened. John O'Hare was brought down by Liverpool defender Phil Thompson and referee Pat Partridge pointed to the spot.

> Another controversy first brought Pat Partridge into the limelight. He added on seven minutes for time-wasting and said afterwards: 'I would have played until midnight if necessary.'

John Robertson put the ball away and Forest took the trophy with a 1-0 win.

But it didn't end there. Liverpool players complained bitterly that O'Hare was brought down outside the box—and slow-motion replays during the TV highlights seemed to prove it.

'As far as I'm concerned there's no controversy,' says Pat. 'I thought it was a penalty—and my linesman agreed.'

So is Pat, a World Cup referee in Argentina, a critic of 'trial by television'?

'Oh, no,' he says. 'It's just an occupational hazard. Sometimes they say nice things about you, so you have to accept the bad.'

West Brom keeper Tony Godden gives his forceful opinion of a Pat Partridge decision. Willie Johnston, no stranger to ref's notebooks, this time acts as peacemaker.

RIGHT Less than 250 yards separates Dundee's Dens Park ground from their neighbours Dundee United at Tannadice Park—the shortest distance between any of Britain's senior clubs.

Dino Zoff regained his place between Italy's posts soon after the 1970 World Cup and went an international record 1,143 minutes without conceding a goal.

All change! Doncaster Rovers have now been through 16 managers since the war, among them current Southampton boss Lawrie McMenemy.

Joe Baker, whose career took in spells with Arsenal, Forest and Italian club Torino, won five England caps in 1960—when he was starring for Scottish club Hibernian.

Scotsman Publications Ltd

The great Francisco Gento played a staggering 94 games in top European competition for Real Madrid, 88 of them in the European Cup. His nearest challenger is Liverpool's Ian Callaghan, with 89 up to this season. Bayern's Sepp Maier is next with 83, but his club aren't in Europe this year.

Peter Robinson

'Closing down' the Brian Talbot way

Closing down . . . pressurising . . . getting tight . . . hustling. Call it what you like but it's what makes the Football League such a hard place to survive in.

From the top of the First Division to the bottom of the Fourth, it's the pressure players are put under as they receive a pass.

And if you're playing

Getting tight . . . Brian Talbot puts pressure on Don Masson —denying him space—in the England-Scotland game at Wembley in 1977.

opposite Ipswich Town international Brian Talbot, never expect the luxury of dwelling on the ball.

'That's what it's all about —denying people space,' says Brian. 'You want them to play ordinary, negative balls, and they're more likely to do that if you deny them space.

'Most midfield players in the First Division are pretty skilful and if they get space they can all do something useful with the ball.

'It's about confidence as well. If you close down an opponent well early on, his

head might drop—although most good players won't let it affect them.

'It's important not to get too tight because good players like Trevor Brooking and Graeme Souness will dummy you or shield the ball and turn you with their bodies—a yard or yard and a half is about the right distance.

Does 'getting tight' prevent young players from showing their skills? 'No, I don't think so,' says Brian. 'If you've got the right attitude your skill will always get you through.'

'The whole point about closing down an opponent is that you do it as the ball is passed to him,' says Graham Taylor. 'If you do it when he has control he can easily knock it past you. So a good practice for two players is a 15- or 20-yard pass played and followed to get tight. You should try to close within a couple of yards of the receiver to shut down his chances of a forward pass without selling yourself.'

'A practice for three players shows clearly the importance of closing down without committing yourself. As A passes to B, C gets tight. You'll notice that he closes down at an angle so that a pass into space in front of A is cut off—a return pass square or behind A is not so dangerous. So C is dictating the play. He could, for example, be a full-back forcing a winger wide, where he is less of a threat. That's the whole point really. While an opponent has the ball he is dictating play just by being in possession, so your job is to take the initiative away from him if you can.'

Colorsport

1. Manchester United celebrate their FA Cup final win over Liverpool in 1977. Which two players pictured here missed the previous year's Wembley defeat?

Owen Barnes

2. Which of these clubs has Stan Bowles never played for: Crewe, Stockport, Bury, Queen's Park Rangers or Carlisle?

3. Which club did German international Paul Breitner join in August?

4. With which clubs did the following players make their League debuts: Graham Paddon, Steve Kindon, David Webb and Stewart Barrowclough?

5. Who is the only player ever to win the Scottish Footballer of the Year award on two occasions?

6. Which was the first British club ever to enter the European Cup?

7. Which club won the Texaco Cup in 1975: Southampton, Newcastle or Birmingham?

8. Which one of these Northern Premier clubs has never played in the Football League: Stafford Rangers, Gainsborough Trinity, Northwich Victoria?

9. Two players who took part in the Brazil v Sweden match during the 1978 World Cup have since joined Saudi Arabian clubs. Name one of them.

10. Who was the first player ever to appear as a substitute and score in an FA Cup final at Wembley?

11. Match the club to the ground: (1) East Stirling, (2) Stirling Albion, (3) Raith Rovers, (4) Motherwell, (5) Partick Thistle; (a) Firhill Park, (b) Annfield Park, (c) Firs Park, (d) Stark's Park, (e) Fir Park.

David Hay

'My vision in that eye will never be quite the same . . . And there's always the chance —with the kind of knocks you can get during a game—that it'll go again . . .'

David shows Liverpool the determination and control that made him a World Cup regular in 1974.

Sporting Pictures UK

Last season David Hay faced the possibility that he might never play football again.

He went through three operations—and a year out of action—before returning to the Chelsea side.

'It was depressing, of course,' David told *Handbook*. 'I spent a lot of that year in hospital . . . then, when I was finally out, I had to do a lot of work on my own to get properly fit again. Mostly I did running to build up my stamina before I could think of rejoining the first team squad.'

What effect has the injury—caused by an elbow in the eye against Bristol Rovers in Chelsea's promotion season—had on David's game?

'I've found that in the games I've played since I came back in March I think I've played better in defence. I don't know if it's the eye or the fact that I was out for so long, but I now feel happier with the play in front of me.

'But I don't dwell on it. I'm always being asked about my eye but I don't like to be reminded of it. You've got to put your injuries behind you . . . and get on with playing.'

Colorsport

Bob Latchford on chest control

'Good control on the chest is vital to playing up front as a target man . . . because you need it so often.' BOB LATCHFORD

In every game you'll see mid-field players and defenders trying to 'hit' the target man with long passes.

And that means the man up front needs a wide variety of skills to kill balls that come at him from various heights and angles.

Often—with passes chip-ped to by-pass opponents—it's a case of sticking the chest out.

No one does that better than Everton's England star Bob Latchford.

Time and again he takes the ball on his chest prior to laying it off.

'Really, it's like any other kind of control,' says Bob. 'You've got to make the ball yours—and that means cush-ioning the impact. The last thing you want is for the ball to pop out of reach.'

'It's mine' . . . Latchford keeps Gordon McQueen at bay after killing the ball on his chest.

Ray Green

Bob shows the technique that has helped him become the ideal target player. Every player who receives the ball chest heigh is vulnerable simply because of the time needed to control the ball, But Bob shows how you can make the ball yours by presenting a good, wide target.

'You've got to use your whole body, almost to welcome the ball, make it feel at home,' says Bob. 'Keep your eye on the ball and let it fall like a pancake on the platform created by the chest. If you do it right the ball will fall nicely at your feet.'

Photos by Ray Green

Bob is just the person to find in the chest region—not only because he's a big lad but also because he kills the ball so well and rarely encourages his marker to come round and try to pinch it.

He uses his arms both for balance and to make it even more difficult for anyone to get in front of him. Also, for that vital second that the ball 'hits' him he effectively hides the ball, and it would be risky for his marker to go for a ball that he can't really see.

'As the ball is played to you, the idea is to show as much of your chest to it as possible,' explains Bob—'a nice, wide target. And at impact you withdraw your chest slightly to cushion it.

'As with most skills, if you can mix your game it's a good idea. For example, if you lay the odd ball off with your chest there's no way you'll become predictable.'

The Latchford method ... Bob 'presents' a big area for the high ball, which falls for a volleyed pass.

Photos by Ray Green

'The ball never comes to you exactly how you want it,' says Bob, 'so you have to be prepared to meet the ball in all sorts of ways. Sometimes, if a defender is trying really hard to get to the ball first, you have to attack the ball in the air. You can flick it on with your head if you've got support, but if you're isolated, you can control it with your chest—and by the time you've done that there should be someone coming to help you out.'

The pictures on the left show Bob doing just that —an advanced form of chest control but the principles are the same.

'The point about chest control is that you're using it to get the ball to your feet,' says Graham Taylor. 'So you should judge your practice by the ease with which you're able to make a pass after the control. If the ball keeps getting away from you there's something wrong.

'The practice for two players is simply the chip—or throw— for the control and pass. For three it's a chip (throw), control and pass to the third player. A fourth player marking the receiver will help create the sort of pressure you'll get in match situations.'

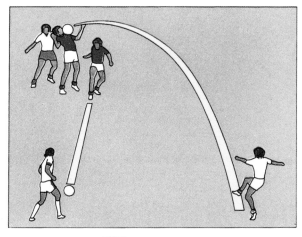

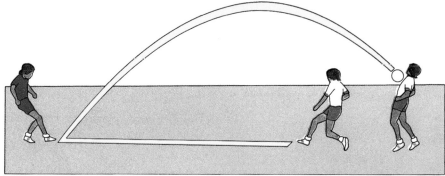

Whistle Test

'There were two classic examples of what I believe to be blatant penalties . . . and the more I see them the happier I become.' JACK TAYLOR

Jack Taylor was the referee in the 1974 World Cup final, when West Germany beat Holland 2-1—and Jack awarded two penalties, one in the opening moments of the game.

'People talk about the Dutch penalty being a brave decision to make in the first minute . . . but refereeing's about concentration,' Jack told *Handbook*. 'I'd started to think long before that, well before the first whistle.'

'When I came to start that match, for instance. I'm about to blow the whistle for the kick-off and I look around and there are no corner flags.

'Can you imagine what would have happened if I hadn't spotted that? Holland would have kicked off—17 passes without a German touching it—and they get a penalty and there'd have been no corner flags. Just think of it, a thousand million people watching and the referee has had to restart the game with one team just about to go 1-0 up in a World Cup final?

'So that in that first minute I was well into my stride. I wasn't going to be distracted by something I should have dealt with already. All I was aware of was an orange shirt going through and being whacked down blatantly by a white shirt.'

Hoeness had brought down Cruyff . . . and Neeskens scored from the penalty. But the German equaliser was not long in coming . . . and it came from a penalty. This time Bernd Holzenbein went sprawling in the area after a wild tackle by Wim Jansen.

'People have always said that Holzenbein dived,' Jack recalls. 'In fact Holzenbein himself has suggested that he made it look worse than it was—though he said it much later, he didn't say it at the time.

'My answer to that is that the law doesn't just say "tripping" . . . the law says "tripping or intending to trip".

Jack Taylor and the man who scored from the first penalty, Johan Neeskens.

And I've seen that film so many times that for a player as skilful as the Dutch defender to be tackling a player like Holzenbein with the ball five yards in front of him, then even if he wasn't blatantly tripping, he was *attempting* to trip. And the fact that Holzenbein was doing a bit of play-acting had nothing to do with it.'

Syndication International

Founded: 1894 (as Pine Villa)
Address: Boundary Park, Oldham, Lancs
Ground: Capacity 30,000; Playing area 100.6 x 67.7 m
Record attendance: 47,671 v Sheffield Wednesday, FA Cup 4th round, 25.1.30
Record victory: 11-0 v Southport, Div. 4, 26.12.62
Record defeat: 4-13 v Tranmere Rovers, Div. 3(N), 26.12.35
Most League points: 62, Div. 3, 1973-74
Most League goals: 95, Div. 4, 1962-63
League scoring record: 33, Tommy Davis, Div. 3, 1936-37
Record League aggregate: 110, Eric Gemmill, 1947-54
Most League appearances: 452, Ian Wood, 1966-78
Most capped player: 9 (24 in all), Albert Gray, Wales, 1924-27
League career: 1908-1910 Div. 2; 1910-23 Div. 1; 1923-35 Div. 2; 1935-53 Div. 3(N); 1953-54 Div. 2; 1954-58 Div. 3(N); 1958-63 Div. 4; 1963-69 Div. 3; 1969-71 Div. 4; 1971-74 Div. 3; 1974- Div. 2
Honours: Div. 3(N) Champions 1953; Div. 3 Champions 1974

OLDHAM ATHLETIC

Ford sporting gesture
Oldham were the big winners in the season (1970-71) history of the Ford Sporting League. Their total winnings from the sponsored competition, which rewarded teams for scoring goals and good disciplinary records, were £68,000—all of which had to be spent on ground improvements. The result is the new Ford stand.

John Hurst, an England squad member in his days with Everton, throws Bolton's Roy Greaves off balance in an early season Anglo-Scottish Cup clash.

Boxing Day knockouts
Oldham's record win and record defeat both occured on a Boxing Day. Their record win (11-0 over Southport in 1962) is also a record for the Fourth Division and their record defeat (4-13 v Tranmere in 1935) is the highest scoring game ever in the Third Division (North).

Can Oldham Athletic come out from under the shadow of the big Manchester clubs and prosper in the First Division?

It seems impossible. On gates of 10,000 they can't compete in the transfer market for big name players. And without big name players they can't attract attendances to rival Old Trafford and Maine Road.

But Boundary Park has some of the best facilities in the country . . . it's easily reached by road . . . and Oldham's record in recent months has been good enough to suggest they are among the Second Division promotion candidates.

In his eight years in charge, Jimmy Frizzell has already guided the club from the lower reaches of the Fourth Division to safe waters in the Second.

Part of his success is due to shrewd dealing on the transfer

Ray Green

231

market. Hardened veterans Mike Bernard and John Hurst were signed cheaply from Everton, Vic Halom cost only £25,000 from Sunderland and young Steve Gardner was picked up from Ipswich for a mere £10,000.

But his biggest bargain of all may turn out to be Steve Taylor, who cost £38,000 from Bolton last October.

In his first game for his new club, the strong-running striker scored both goals in a 2-1 win over Notts County. In his first seven games he scored all seven of Oldham's goals, launching the Latics on a 13-game unbeaten League run that carried them from 20th to 6th in the division. In 32 games for the club last season Taylor scored 20 goals.

'That's my job,' says Frizzell. 'To pick up bargains . . . to find players here and there who will do a job for us.'

Jimmy Frizzell believes his most important signing is a man who has never kicked a ball for the club—former England goalkeeper Colin McDonald.

McDonald, the man who discovered Colin Bell and a whole crop of talent for Bury, has already had some success signing youngsters for Oldham.

Most highly rated of their home-produced players are Graham Bell and Carl Valentine. Midfielder Bell has been compared with the young Alan Ball, while winger Valentine has the kind of speed and control that big clubs will always pay for.

Right now though, Oldham are looking to join the big clubs . . . not to sell to them.

Jimmy Frizzell has been with Oldham for 18 years—the last 8 as manager—joining them as a young inside-forward from his local club in Scotland, Morton.

Boundary Park has a new stand, unequalled behind-the-scenes facilities and a convenient location alongside a motorway . . . but it last saw First Division football over 55 years ago.

Colorsport

ABOVE *Oldham's best-ever side . . . ? In 1915 the Latics finished as runners-up in the League after Everton overtook them in the very last match. Their skipper was Charlie Roberts—in the middle of the front row—who had earlier captained Manchester United to their first ever League and Cup triumphs. Roberts later became Oldham's manager.* BELOW *Oldham today: a shrewd mixture of hard-bitten veterans—Halom, Bernard and Hurst—and skilful youngsters—Taylor, Bell and Valentine—of bargain buys and home-grown talent. Can Jimmy Frizzell and coach Andy Lochhead take them into the First Division?*

Ray Green

233

France open fire in the first minute

'It's almost as if the French expected to score in the first minute. They thought quicker and acted faster . . . while the Italians were really caught cold. It certainly looks like the key factor is mental preparation.' GRAHAM TAYLOR

The first shock of the World Cup is always worth looking at again.

But what would be even more valuable would be a look at what went on in France's and Italy's changing-rooms just before the game—one in which France scored after just 31 seconds.

Why were the Italians caught cold? What led up to the French going out and getting such a splendidly conceived and clinically ex-

ecuted goal so early on?

It seems incredible that after months of build-up a team could be so unprepared for the big day. It could have been the old Italian problem of temperament: they seemed to suffer badly from nerves and 'froze', while the French seemed alert and confident.

The move started with French keeper Bertrand-Demanes rolling the ball out to full-back Bossis. His pass up the left touch-line found

Didier Six, who pushed it inside to Jean-Marc Guillou. He flicked on to Michel Platini, whose pass sent Six away on that devastating run. One touch and he was past Gentile . . . and the second touch was a long, sweeping cross into the Italian penalty area, where Bernard Lacombe, untended by the transfixed Italian defence, headed past Zoff.

The Italians didn't lose—but they learnt a lesson.

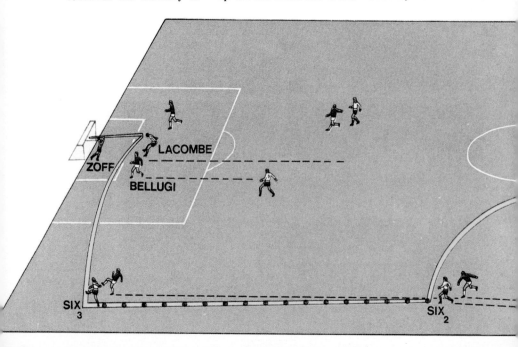

Colorsport

We could point to the way the French built the move from the back—both Bertrand-Demanes and Bossis resisted the temptation of the long boot upfield—or we could mention that the Italian centre-back Bellugi was guilty of 'losing' Lacombe. We could talk about the way Six turned and ran for the return ball the moment he played it inside.

But because it all happened in the first half-minute of the game—because, as Graham Taylor points out, 'the French thought quicker and acted faster' than the Italians—it all seems to come down to being mentally as well as physically prepared. All the things the Italians are renowned for—giving nothing away at the back, good cover and so on—went by the board. It's unlikely that such a goal could have been scored 10 or 15 minutes into the game, after the Italians settled down.

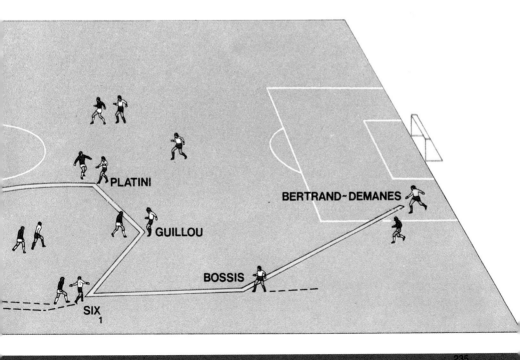

Sportapics

RIƧING ƧTAR BOBBY RUSSELL

It took the sting of rejection to make Bobby Russell realise that his great talents would waste away if he didn't do something about it.

He was freed as a raw 17-year-old by Sunderland with the criticisms ringing in his ears . . . 'not enough enthusiasm—wouldn't work hard enough.'

The blow brought midfield player Russell back to earth. He signed for Glencairn Juveniles and quickly re-emerged as a youngster with marvellous potential—enough to have Rangers' scouts on his trail.

The giant Glasgow club signed him on a provisional basis and completed the deal a year later as Dundee United cast envious glances in Russell's direction.

And so, as he prepared for Rangers' bid to win the European Cup, Bobby looks back on the Roker experience as the turning point in his career.

He says: 'Perhaps I was too young at 16 to go south. I never felt really content at Sunderland and my game probably suffered as a result. But being released by them brought home the harsh realities of football.'

Certainly, the experience enables the 21-year-old to deal with praise like 'He's the new Jim Baxter.'

He says: 'It's nice to be compared with a player like Baxter, but I don't think it's

Russell skips past keeper Jim Blyth during a game against a Scottish Select team. 'It's nice to be compared with a player like Jim Baxter,' says Bobby, 'but I don't think it's accurate. I never try to model myself on anyone.'

Sportapics

'Things have happened a lot quicker than I anticipated ... I never dreamed I'd finish the season with League Championship, Cup and League Cup medals'

Honours: Scottish League Championship medal 1977-78; Scottish Cup Winners medal 1977-78; Scottish League Cup winners medal 1977-78

Club	Season	League		Cup		Lge Cup	
		Ms	Gs	Ms	Gs	Ms	Gs
Rangers	1977-78	33	3	4	–	7	–

accurate. I never try to model myself on anyone, although there are obviously players I admire.'

John Greig, Bobby's team-mate last season and now his boss at Ibrox, says: 'Bobby had a tremendous first season with the club and I'm sure he will go on improving.

'With the club winning the treble last season Bobby has tasted success and now he'll be out to win even more.

'He's got a great football brain, always making himself available to pick up the ball and use it constructively.'

Bobby never doubted his ability but confesses: 'Things have happened a lot quicker than I anticipated. I thought I might get a few first team games but not hold down a regular place.

'And I never dreamed I'd finish the season with League Championship, Scottish Cup and League Cup medals.'

Success brings its pressures, however.

Bobby says: 'Anything less than the treble

The new, hard-working Russell gets in a cross—despite the lunging left leg of Partick Thistle defender Brian Whittaker.

Sportapics

this season will be seen as failure. The European Cup is the obvious target, but we're not kidding ourselves about how hard it is to win that trophy.

'But the prospect of playing against the best doesn't bother me. I'll try to carry on playing my own game and improve it in any way I can.

'My biggest assets are going forward and moving into space well—and I like to think I'm good at reading situations.

'Passing the ball accurately is vital for a midfield player because you've got to hit your man with the ball when the marking is so tight.

'But I must improve my defensive play. I've been caught ball-watching and my tackling isn't up to scratch.'

During the close season Bobby trained on Tuesday and Thursday afternoons at Ibrox to make sure he was extra fit for the new session.

This contrast with the Russell of old doesn't surprise Jock Wallace, Rangers' boss last season and now in charge at Leicester.

'This boy is a natural footballer,' reckons Jock, 'and he's eager to be involved in everything and do the work that often goes unnoticed—off the ball.

'I never hesitated in bringing him into the first team because I knew he could play. He played a key part in winning the treble because he does the unexpected so well.'

Already the owner of an Under-21 cap, Russell must have higher honours on the horizon ... not bad prospects for a reject.

237

'One in a million'

The disappointing World Cup finals had one saving grace—the array of goals scored from long range. But even Cubillas, Luque and Nelinho couldn't match the sheer nerve of Holland's Arie Haan . . .

'You can't legislate against that,' claimed Brian Clough after Arie Haan's 30-yard equaliser against West Germany. 'One in a million.'

But just three days later the Forest manager was forced to repeat himself as the Dutchman hit the winner against Italy to put Holland through to the World Cup final—from even further out.

The 76th minute masterstroke came with a free-kick just inside the Italian half. Rudi Krol nonchalantly rolled a quick, short pass to Haan, who took a few paces,

lined up his shot and threaded it between two unsuspecting defenders.

The ball flew—with an ever-increasing curve—to Dino Zoff's left. The keeper got his fingers to it but could only watch it rocket in.

BELOW *Arie Haan lets fly from nearly 40 yards following Krol's quick free-kick. Zoff's late despairing dive can only flick it on to the inside of the post—and Holland are in the World Cup final.*
OPPOSITE *Haan (9) about to be buried by Dutch team-mates.*

Graham Taylor's analysis
'The Dutch "shoot on sight" policy really worked out for them again—but there's a lot more to it than that.

'Too often players dither about indecisively at free-kicks, allowing the opposition to reorganise. But Krol saw the possibility early, slipping the ball to Haan.

'Zoff should have had it. Whereas Maier had been beaten by sheer pace in the previous goal, from closer in, Zoff had time to take a couple of steps and get to the ball. He saw it very late—and didn't read it.'

ROOBA
R.F.ALEMANIT

ZOFF

HAAN 2

KROL

HAAN 1

Fotosports International

Ray Green

CRIME
& PUNISHMENT

'This is the fairest system we've ever had. It has cut out a lot of the abuse of the old system—the hopeless, time-wasting appeals against suspensions, for instance . . . It ideally serves the best interests of all concerned.' Norwich City manager JOHN BOND

Ray Green

Arsenal's Bob McNab began his 1972 Cup final with this spectacular foul on Peter Lorimer.

A forward breaks clear and looks sure to score . . . until a defender clobbers him from behind on the edge of the box.

The crowd roars. The referee tugs out a yellow card to caution the offender.

And that, as far as the crowd is concerned, is that—apart from the excitement of the free-kick.

But for the people involved in football's code of conduct, it's only the beginning.

So what happens when the wheels of soccer justice grind into action?

Heartfelt warning

Until a few years ago the referee was able to put his hand to his heart—where he kept his notebook—and warn players that way. But not any more. Under the new points system, if he goes for his gun he's got to use it.

What happens is this: Joe Cloggs is asked for his name and asked to turn round for a note of his number. The referee then tells Cloggs he is being cautioned or sent off—and why—and that the facts will be reported to the Football Association.

Anything Cloggs has to say is noted by the ref, who also makes a mental note of where the offence took place. Then, after showing the yellow or red card to Cloggs, the linesman and spectators, the referee restarts the game.

Men only

Linesmen also have to take notes on the incident and most have a sketch of a football pitch to help them. At half-time or the end of the match, the three officials check each other's notes to confirm the basic facts.

Within two days of the match—not including Sundays—the officials have to send their reports to the FA in London.

The ref's report would go something like this: 'I have to report that after 44 minutes of the above match, an Addington Academicals player was in possession of the ball just outside the penalty area when he was deliberately tripped from behind by Joe Cloggs, wearing number six.'

If the offence is of using foul language, the exact words *must* be reported but sent in a separate envelope from any other disciplinary report and clearly marked 'report contains foul and abusive language . . . not to be opened by females'.

Syndication International

The yellow card, first introduced in international matches. Kevin Keegan's booking followed retaliation after several crude Italian tackles— but the ref has to play it by the book.

So the scene shifts—through the post—to football's 'corridors of power', the FA headquarters at 16 Lancaster Gate.

There, in charge of the FA's disciplinary department, is Mr H. N. 'Dickie' Bird, the man who walks out ahead of all FA Cup final and international teams at Wembley.

His department has a card index system for all English club players in the Football League and top non-League clubs; Cardiff City, Wrexham, Swansea and Newport County are dealt with by the Welsh FA.

So when a report arrives, the details will be filled in on the players' cards, together with the number of penalty points recorded against him (see box on page 244). The points also go on club cards, so that any club with 150 points in one season will face the music—a warning or a fine.

Details of the offence are then sent to the player's club. He has no right of appeal but can make his views known. Any player who reaches the dreaded 20-point mark is liable to suspension by an FA commission, which

Owen Barnes

ABOVE *Joey Jones of Wales is the victim of some ungentlemanly shirt-tugging by Scotland striker Derek Parlane in the frustrating 0-0 draw at Wrexham in 1977.*

BELOW *Joe Jordan seems determined to leave a tattoo on Emlyn Hughes' kidney in the game at Hampden last season . . .*

Bob Thomas

. . . with inevitable results. Hughes is down—and soon out of the match. French referee Konrath calls on the trainer. Jordan was later booked.

will listen to pleas for leniency.

There are three offences which can earn instant dismissal from the pitch. For violent conduct, serious foul play or abusive language, a player is automatically suspended from his club's next approved match—so there's no point in a hastily-arranged friendly to save him for a vital game.

He also collects 12 penalty points, but if a player is sent off for two bookable offences, he gets no points—only the ban.

A player with 20 points might get off with a warning, but it's more realistic for him to fear a suspension—from one to three games. If he wants to, he can ask for a personal hearing to have his say.

Until two years ago, when players were free to appeal against cautions and sendings off, the system was abused. Players or clubs could appeal just to delay the sentence until after a particular match—and they often did, even though they knew they didn't have much of a case.

Club action

Fines were abolished when players gave up the right of appeal but several clubs—notably new champions Nottingham Forest—take their own action against players who fall foul of refs, particularly for dissent.

Players may complain bitterly about referees—but they have few complaints about the FA's system.

So, all in all the points system is generally accepted. It saves time and a collosal amount of money for the FA; refs no longer have

Ray Green

Ray Green

ABOVE *Referee Castle going in where it can hurt . . . the players are Trevor Hockey and Eddie McCreadie.* BELOW *Rodney Marsh tries to keep Asa Hartford from putting his foot in it.*

Sportapics

North of the border
John Gordon, Scotland's World Cup ref, about to book John Cushley, then of Dunfermline. This season the Scottish FA have adopted a points scale similar to the English system.

those eyeball-to-eyeball confrontations with players at appeals; and players feel that it acknowledges the physical side of football.

But is it working? Figures are a jealously guarded secret but cautions in the First Division have risen sharply—from 433 in the last season of the old system to 603 last season.

But that could be because referees were reluctant to use their power under the old, time-wasting system. And the number of sendings off remained about the same, just over 100 in the Football League last season.

Conclusion: fair enough!

Fair or foul . . . ? The split-second in which the referee has to make up his mind. Did Wilkins foul Johnston even though he played the ball?

Suspended . . . ? Players are allowed to state their case, as Villa's Andy Gray did on this occasion.

Sporting Pictures UK

Ray Green

SCHEDULE OF PENALTY POINTS

Sending off offences

Violent conduct	12
Serious foul play	12
Foul or abusive language	12
(all plus one match suspension)	

Caution offences

Law 1: Illegal marking of pitch	1
Law 12: Deliberate handling of the ball	2
Deliberate obstruction	3
Deliberate tripping	4
Entering or re-entering field of play without referee's permission	1
Persistent infringement of the laws of the game	3
Showing dissent—interference by other players when the referee is speaking to player(s) after an offence and continued comment to the referee concerning his decisions in an effort to intimidate him	4

Wasting time	2
Shirt-pulling etc.	3
Player using shoulders of team-mate to assist him in heading the ball	1
Moving arms about to obstruct opponents	2
Dangerous or foul play	4
Foul tackle from behind	4
Law 13: Encroachment within 10 yards of the ball at free-kicks	3
Gesticulating in front of player taking free-kick	2
Law 14: Encroachment by defender or attacker at a penalty kick	2
Gesticulating by penalty kicker	2
Law 15: Gesticulating in front of a throw-in	2
Any other offence not listed above deemed by the referee to be ungentlemanly conduct	2

A player is liable for suspension once his total has reached 20 points.

A Matter of Fact

The 'old man' of Wimbledon, full-back Dave Donaldson, didn't make his League debut until he was almost 36, but that didn't stop him from winning the club's 'Player of the Year' award last season.

What a way to go! Cardiff trainer Ron Durban quit football after being accused of pouring a bucket of water over a York fan's head in 1974.

In Liverpool's 11-0 win over Stromgodset of Norway in 1974, 9 players scored. Only Hall and Clemence missed out.

Terry Venables (seen here in his QPR days) is a man of many talents. Last year the Palace manager's novels about private detective 'Hazell', became a TV series and he once sang with a leading dance band, the Joe Loss Orchestra.

When Billy Bremner retired last summer he was just two goals short of a ton in League soccer. Johnny Giles, his old Leeds team-mate, had 99 to his name when he left West Bromwich in 1977.

Paolo Rossi's club Lanerossi Vicenza made it into the UEFA Cup this season. Yet in 1972 they crashed 10-0 to Blackpool, now in the Third Division, in an Anglo-Italian Tournament match.

Accrington Stanley, one of the League's 12 founder members, had to drop out of the competition midway through the 1961-62 season. The club was re-formed in 1968, and are now proud champions of the Lancashire Combination.

Billy McNeill is only the fifth manager in Celtic's 90-year history. When he took over from Jock Stein last summer, he joined an elite comprising Willie Maley, Jimmy McStay, Jimmy McGrory and the current Leeds boss.

Ex-Italian international Giorgio Chinaglia is now banging 'em in for New York Cosmos. But before he rose to fame with the Rome club Lazio, he'd failed to get established in Swansea Town's first team . . . and was finally given a free transfer.

Homecoming time for the Sunderland players at Roker Park after their 1-0 victory over Leeds United at Wembley in 1973. Sunderland were the first Second Division side to win the FA Cup since WBA back in 1931.

PRO FILE

CYRILLE REGIS

'There's no doubt he's one of the most exciting players around. He's big, powerful, thrusting and brave—the sort of fellow who could succeed at almost any sport he chose.' RON ATKINSON

Monte Carlo or . . . the Baggies ? French champions Monaco are interested in big Cyrille.

Almost overnight Cyrille Regis became a soccer star.

He was an electrician in London playing part-time football for Isthmian League Hayes when West Bromwich Albion signed him for £5,000. He was to be a long-term prospect . . . and a bit of a long shot.

But he paid off despite the odds . . . and he paid off straight away. He came into the Albion side for the injured David Cross and caused an immediate sensation. He had speed, power, control . . . and he scored goals.

'He's big, powerful, thrusting and brave,' said Albion manager Ron Atkinson. 'And it's up to us to encourage him to use these assets to the full.'

Cyrille made his first team debut in a

Kenny Clements steels himself at Maine Road . . . when Regis scored in a 3-1 League win.

Colorsport

Alcoholic Hayes . . . ? Cyrille's first television appearance was in this lager commercial. He and some of his Hayes team-mates were employed as extras—for the team that was happy to lose.

Up for the Cup . . . Regis tests the Forest defence. A superb goal—his sixth in the competition—helped Albion into the semi-finals.

League Cup win over Rotherham—and scored twice in a 4-0 win. He made his League debut three days later against Middlesbrough—and scored again. He finished the season with 18 goals from 41 games.

Can he live up to the promise of such a start? 'Last season I was a surprise packet,' reckons Cyrille. 'But now everybody knows about me. I've got to prove that I'm not just a one-season wonder.'

But then the 20-year-old Regis must be learning fast about the demands of full-time football.

'I'm confident I can improve,' he told *Handbook*. 'Obviously I'm still learning and this time I'll be aiming at a higher standard of consistency. I was very pleased with my performance last season, but there were games that I didn't play well in. It could be lack of concentration . . .

'But last summer we had a fairly light pre-season build-up, while under new boss Ron Atkinson we did a lot more work this summer. I feel it'll help me.

'I knew how tough it would be in the First Division . . . against players who had been there for years and who had also had the benefit of training with a top professional club since they left school.'

But there was one area where Regis wasn't

at any disadvantage to his professionally trained opponents—his strength and power were already massively impressive. Teammates called him 'Smokin' Joe' after former world heavyweight champion Joe Frazier.

'Perhaps if I hadn't been lucky enough to have my build I wouldn't have been able to survive last season. I might have tired and faded out of the picture.'

Instead Regis's strength helped him score some great goals: one of them was against Manchester City when he powered through the centre from inside his own half.

'When I played non-League I was always faster than my opponents,' says Cyrille. 'But I was surprised that I've still been able to get away from players even in the First Division.'

Another of his goals made the televiewing public sit up in their armchairs one Saturday night—his spectacularly struck shot that helped put Nottingham Forest out of the one competition they failed to win last season. Even Brian Clough was moved to call it 'a superbly taken goal'.

But that win set the scene for Albion's biggest disappointment of the season . . . With only Ipswich between them and their fourth Wembley appearance in 12 years,

they went out of the Cup 3-1 at Highbury.

At least Albion qualified for European competition, as Regis rediscovered his explosive form right at the end of the season

'The other players helped me,' say Cyrille. 'When things were going wrong they'd take me to one side and help put me right.'

And the development of his partnership with Ally Brown must have helped.

'We really hit it off,' admits Cyrille, 'but I've got to give credit to the whole team.'

Already Regis has attracted the attention of big clubs abroad. Although he figured in the England Under-21 squad for the match against Italy last March, he has still qualified to play for France through his French Guianan birth.

Until recently he didn't sound sure which country he would choose if an international call-up came. 'I've got to be chosen first,' he told one interviewer. 'It's something I'd have to talk over . . .'

But he was firm when he spoke to Handbook. 'English football is what I want to play,' he said, 'and if I'm lucky enough to be selected in the future, I want to play for England.' His wish came true a few days later with a call-up against Denmark.

Quite an achievement, going past the England centre-half in your first year as a professional . . . Regis proved a lively handful for Dave Watson at Maine Road last April.

Ray Green

Club	Season	Div	Pos	League		FA Cup		L Cup	
				Ms	Gs	Ms	Gs	Ms	Gs
WBA	1977-78	1	6	34	10	5	6	2	2

ROKER'S RIGHT-HAND WOMAN

'I couldn't do another job after being here. It's so different. You get involved. If the players are up, so are we. If they're down, we're miserable as well.' Jimmy Adamson's
secretary KAREN BRIEN

League football may be a man's world, but if all the women behind the scenes suddenly deserted many a club would be on its knees.

Take Karen Brien's role at Roker Park.

She's manager Jimmy Adamson's secretary—but don't think she spends the day painting her nails and typing the odd letter.

For a kick-off, Karen is the person who plots the route to away matches, a vital job if the team wants to eat at the right place at the right time—not to mention turning up at the right ground.

She sorts out passports for foreign trips and is mum to the players every time any small thing goes wrong. 'I suppose I do namby-pamby them a bit,' says Karen, 'but that's what football clubs are like.'

Then there's Adamson's 'hot line', a red phone without a number used by managers on the transfer grapevine.

'It's quite exciting when there's a big transfer in the air,' says Karen, who didn't know where the ground was when she applied for the job ten years ago.

Now, as players and managers come and go, Karen's displays have made her a permanent fixture. 'It's like having a new job every time there's a new manager,' she says. 'My first boss, Allan Brown, was rather strict and efficient, while Bob Stokoe was very easy-going. Mr. Adamson? I think he's a little more in the Brown mould, although I

don't think he likes to be thought of like that. But they've all been great to me.'

And she's been a great secretary. Even while she was having her two kids—Ghislaine (a Welsh/French name) and Kieran—she worked part-time to keep Roker rolling.

'I used to be a secretary in a business but I couldn't do that again after being here,' says Karen. 'It's so different. You get involved. If the players are up, so are we. If they're down, we're all miserable as well.

'When we won the Cup in 1973 it was just great . . . a party atmosphere all the time. We were rushed off our feet but no one minded.

'Now we're waiting for the next time!'

On the hot line . . . Karen Brien answers the red phone. And (below) with the other women who help make Roker tick—Marilyn McAndrew, Dawn Wilkinson, Jean Johnston, Carol Raphael, Hazel Gordon, Ethel Hedley, Moira Withmore, Brenda Harlend and Margaret Richardson.

Mike Cowling

Mike Cowling

COMPETITION

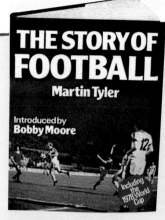

THE STORY OF FOOTBALL
Martin Tyler

Introduced by
Bobby Moore

Including the 1978 World Cup

30 copies of the second edition of the best-selling 'STORY OF FOOTBALL' to be won in this week's free-to-enter quiz

Bob Thomas

1. Only one club has played in all *six* divisions of the Football League: 1, 2, 3, 4, 3(S) and 3(N). Which one?

2. Which two of these Aberdeen stars have never played in the Football League: Harper, Jarvie, Ritchie, Scanlon, Clark?

3. George Best once played in the Fourth Division. Was it for Bury, Rochdale, Stockport or Oldham?

4. Which club represented Wales in the Cup Winners' Cup in 1963-64?

5. LEFT Cruyff's last competitive game in Britain: which ground is it?

6. In which European capital are these clubs all based: Rapid, Steaua, Dinamo?

7. Name the top scorer in the 1974 World Cup.

8. Match the club to the country:
(1) Beveren-Wass, (2) NK Rijeka,
(3) Marek Dimitrov, (4)
Lillestroem, (5) IFC Norkoping;
(a) Norway, (b) Belgium,
(c) Sweden, (d) Bulgaria,
(e) Yugoslavia.

9. RIGHT Name these two players.

10. Who scored the goal which won the FA Cup in 1973, and where is he now?

Ray Green

HOW TO ENTER
List your answers to the questions on a postcard, add your name and address, cut the 'Part 9' flash from the cover and attach it to the postcard (entries that do not bear the flash will be ineligible), then mail to Football Handbook, 600 A Commercial Road, London E14 7HS. Entries must arrive by November 9, 1978, the closing date. The sender of the first 30 correct answers scrutinised after that date will each be awarded a copy of THE STORY OF FOOTBALL (256 pages). The Editor's decision on all matters relating to the competition is final and binding. All winners will be notified as soon as possible and a full list of prize winners to date will be available from *Football Handbook* on request.

Joe Gallagher

Ray Green

A man who relishes responsibility . . . Birmingham captain Joe Gallagher.

By example . . . Joe fights for the ball in the 1975 FA Cup semi-final against Fulham.

'Being captain is about using your personality, but it's no good a quiet bloke like me trying to be like Billy Bremner . . . I try to lead just by example.'

Most players are too busy improving their own game to want the added pressure of being captain.

But when Birmingham City were looking for a new skipper, big Joe Gallagher jumped at the chance.

'I must admit I really wanted to be captain,' says Joe, City's 23-year-old centre-half. 'I liked the idea of having authority on the pitch. It also gives me more understanding of players' problems and those of the managers.'

So what makes a good captain? 'It's a question of using your personality,' explains Joe, 'but it's no good a quiet bloke like me trying to be like Bremner or Hughes.

'My model would be Bobby Moore, someone who leads by example. He was an inspiration to his colleagues, and far from overawing youngsters who came into the side, he made them feel secure.'

What about the inevitable shadow that Trevor Francis casts over everyone at St Andrew's?

'It's not something that we're aware of all the time, but it's a fact that Trevor is an extraordinary player and he's bound to be in the spotlight more than others. We're just glad to have him around . . .'

Ray Green

'Tucking them in': Alan Buckley

'Scoring regularly is ninety per cent confidence. You've got to go out there believing you're bound to score—that it's just hard luck on the goalkeeper.' Walsall striker ALAN BUCKLEY

Bob Thomas

Syndication International

Ray Green

Cool and confident: Alan about to tuck another one in without fuss . . .

. . . eye on the ball, arms for balance, left leg as an anchor, side-foot shot . . .

. . . away it goes—a short, sharp shot that brings Alan 20 goals a season.

Some fans see Alan Buckley, Walsall's phenomenal goal-scorer, as a cocky little so-and-so. And so does someone else—Alan Buckley himself.

'Well, cocky's a bit strong, but you could say I'm very extrovert. You've got to be to score goals regularly,' says the 5′ 5″ forward who has found the net 137 times in five seasons at Fellows Park.

'It's a state of mind', says Alan, 'I always go out there and believe I'm going to tuck them in—one or more.

'When I watch football I

Tucked past Pat Jennings . . . Buckley scores the goal for Walsall in last season's 4-1 FA Cup defeat at Arsenal.

don't look for the great shots from 35 yards. I'm more interested in the bloke who puts them away from five or ten yards.

'Jimmy Greaves and Joe Baker—they were my heroes. Scoring was a job well done. Tucking them in; no bother; no sweat.

'When you get a chance in a match it's usually a split second thing. You've got one touch, two if you're lucky. So it's a question of seeing an unguarded part of the net and striking the ball hard enough to find it.

'If that sounds too easy, I can't help it. That's the way it is. If you miss a simple chance it's usually because you make too much of it,

make it too complicated.'

As most of Alan's goals come fairly close in, he often uses the side of the foot.

'That's all you need most of the time,' he says. 'You can hit it hard enough with the side of the foot and you'll nearly always be more accurate than if you blast it.

'Try not to panic. You've nearly always got more time than you think you have—especially in junior football.

'My approach is simple: slot it where the keeper isn't, *then* feel sorry for him.'

Alan says it's good to get in the habit of 'tucking them in' during training matches.

But he adds: 'There's no substitute for scoring when it matters—in matches.'

Net's-eye view of the Buckley method ... Alan is ready for the ball pulled back from the by-line.

Close up shows the 'wide side-foot area.'

Pop ... Alan slots the ball towards the inviting gap between the post and goalkeeper.

At impact there's little chance of a miss-kick.

Ray Green

The ball is buried and the keeper left for dead as the ball is tucked inside the post.

Away it goes ... straight and firm—'tucked in'.

Even if the ball goes near the keeper . . .

. . . it should still find the net if it's struck low and hard.

Perfect finish . . . Alan meets the ball . . .

. . . and, as the keeper advances . . .

. . . tucks it into the corner—'no sweat'.

Ray Green

'I like the way Alan puts it, slotting the ball where the keeper isn't', says Graham Taylor. 'Someone like Stan Bowles can bend the ball round two or three defenders, but that's not what's wanted here. This is not so spectacular, but every manager loves players who have the knack of popping them in, week in week out. That's what it is—a knack, a habit—and the best practice is one for three players—one serving, one shooting and the third in goal. See how many each of you can slot home out of 10 or 20.'

RISING STEVE
STAR WILLIAMS

When Alan Ball was the idol of the Arsenal crowd, among the worshippers on the Highbury terraces was a soccer-mad youngster named Steve Williams.

Now Ball has moved on to Southampton, where he is again the midfield conductor in another success story. And the young lad who admired him from afar at Arsenal still watches him every week—but now from a much closer view.

For Steve Williams has grown up to realise his dream of making it to the top in professional football, and he plays alongside Ball as the Saints compete among the First Division big-shots.

'Ballie's had a tremendous influence on

'The player I admire most in this country? It's Steve Williams.' ALAN BALL

Club	Season	League		FA Cup		Lge Cup	
		Ms	Gs	Ms	Gs	Ms	Gs
Southampton	1975-76	1	–	–	–	–	–
	1976-77	33	–	4	1	2	–
	1977-78	39	5	4	–	3	–
		73	5	8	1	5	–

me—and still has,' admits Steve, now 20. 'He's always having a go at me on the pitch . . . but it's not for his benefit—it's for mine.

'He says that his dad always taught him to do something better each year . . . and I want to improve with each season too.

'We're different types of players, though. He's one-touch, quick and precise. I like going at men and beating them. I like to think I'm good on the ball.'

Manager Lawrie McMenemy has emphasised to Williams that he is expecting him to develop his game further. He wants the midfield man to take up more scoring positions and, away from home, to show more defensive discipline by covering space and sacrificing a little of his free-running.

Steve appreciates the challenge. 'I'd like to score more goals,' he told *Handbook*. 'I get into the box a lot, but somehow I always seem to be too early or too late!

'I think a midfield player should have eight to ten goals a season to his credit. Last year I got only five—and that's not really good enough.'

McMenemy's influence has made itself felt in other ways, too.

'Lawrie McMenemy settled me down at an early age when I was a bit hot-headed,' admits Steve. 'And I've also benefitted from playing and training alongside some really quality people—like Ballie, Peter Osgood, Mike Channon and Jim McCalliog.

'Ballie, for instance, is very quick to see openings, and Ossie was good at turning people . . . I like to think their strong points have rubbed off on me.'

Southampton—not to mention Ron Greenwood— is impressed at the all-round ability Steve has shown. The young Londoner defends strongly (left, tackling Manchester United's Sammy McIlroy), looks good on the ball and (right) loves to join the attack . . . quite a discovery for Southampton's London scout Bob Higgins.

Steve was still an apprentice when he made his first team debut. He was called up at the last moment to face local rivals Portsmouth in front of 24,000 fans at Fratton Park.

A month later Saints, without Steve, marched on to Cup glory against Manchester United at Wembley.

The following season Williams made the breakthrough to regular first team football. He played a key role in last season's promotion drive . . . and he's now a regular in England's Under-21 side.

The one blemish on a highly promising career came on a bleak November day at Blackburn last year, when Steve was sent off.

'It was for a late tackle,' he admits. 'But I've learned my lesson.'

Bob Thomas

259

JUVENTUS

The money involved in Italian football is enough to make your head spin.

A player with one of the crack Italian clubs can earn as much in two successful seasons as an English player can in his entire career. For big league games a place on the terraces can cost as much as £6 . . . while the price of the best seats can go above £30.

European ties can bring in as much as £250,000 in gate receipts . . . and more from television.

And transfer fees are gigantic. One million pound deals are common and the record—for Roberto Pruzzo, a player

Founded: 1897
Ground: Stadio Comunale, Turin
Capacity: 71,000
Record attendance: 79,245 v AC Milan, Serie A, 1950
Record victory: 9-1 v Inter-Milan, 1961
League scoring record: 32, Felice Borel, 1933-34
Honours: League Champions 1905, 1926, 1931, 1932, 1933, 1934, 1935, 1950, 1952, 1958, 1960, 1961, 1967, 1972, 1973, 1975, 1977, 1978; Cup Winners 1938, 1942, 1959, 1960, 1965; UEFA Cup Winners 1977; Fairs Cup runners-up 1965, 1971

Exit in Glasgow
Rangers put Juventus out of this season's European Cup 2-1 on aggregate.

'The gentle giant'
For five seasons, from 1957 to 1962, John Charles starred for Juventus. A great player, powerfully athletic and versatile, Swansea-born Charles was idolised in Turin, who paid £65,000 to Leeds for his services.

With the newly-signed Argentinian, Omar Sivori, he formed a lethal goal-scoring partnership for the Italian club —who were transformed from a team that had struggled against relegation the season before they arrived to a side that finished top of the league.

During his five prolific seasons with the club, Juventus were Italian League champions three times.

Known as 'il buon gigante', Charles (right, playing against Genoa) never resorted to dirty play and rarely retaliated in the face of it. He once said: 'If I have to knock them down to play well, I don't want to play the game.'

Popperfoto

Big money, small return
Although Juventus don't often pay out big money for players, it wasn't so long ago that they paid the world record transfer fee— £440,000 for Varese centre - forward Pietro Anastasi — back in 1968. Anastasi never lived up to his fee. He moved to Inter-Milan, but failed to gain a regular place, and now plays for newly-promoted Ascoli.

Chairman superstar
Juventus chairman Giampiero Boniperti once scored two goals for a FIFA XI . . . against England at Wembley in 1953. An Italian inter-national, he also holds two Juventus records as a player: most League ap-pearances (440) and most goals (177).

who didn't even make the Italian World Cup 22—is £2,100,000.

Even the clubs' debts are enormous . . . though champions Juventus don't have that problem. They're backed by the huge Fiat Motor Corporation and its bosses, the Agnelli family.

Yet Juventus have never paid more than £500,000 in cash

ABOVE *Roberto Bettega, major scoring threat for Juventus and Italy, gets in on the end of another pass.*

BELOW *Juventus's 1977 championship winning side— their fourth title in six years.*

for a player. Most of the fees they pay are reduced by offering players in part exchange.

For instance, the most expensive player in the current squad is Pietro Virdis, a 21-year-old the 'Zebras' obtained from Cagliari. His £1,200,000 fee was made up of cash and players. Virdis was injured for much of last season, but Juventus are hoping that he will form an effective goal-scoring partnership with World Cup star Roberto Bettega.

At the age of 27, Bettega looks the complete striker: good in the air, deadly on the ground and with that special Italian elusiveness developed by playing against packed *catennacio* defences.

But at one stage it looked as though Roberto wasn't wanted at Juventus: he was loaned out to Second Division Varese for a whole season. When he scored 13 goals in helping Varese to promotion, however, Juventus recalled him to their first team squad.

Bettega is one of nine Juventus players who played in Argentina. Up front there's the endlessly versatile Franco Causio; in goal there's the majestic Dino Zoff; there's the talented sweeper, Gaetano Scirea; there are *three* full-backs, Claudio Gentile, Antonello Cuccureddu and 21-year-old Antonio Cabrini.

Then in midfield there are two men who had World Cup watchers wincing in pain more often than gasping in admiration: Marco Tardelli ('one of the best markers in the world today,' says Kevin Keegan) and Romeo Benetti ('we went to a social do the other week and it's the only time I've been within ten yards of him and he hasn't kicked me,' said Kevin).

Believe it or not they aren't the players that normally do the specialist marking jobs for Juventus. The real hit-man is Sicilian Giussepe Furino, the 32-year-old club captain.

Yet Juventus are still affectionately known throughout Italy as *La Vecchia Signora* . . . 'The Old Lady'!

Six million dollar man
Juventus supplied 9 of Italy's World Cup squad . . . $9\frac{1}{2}$ if you count Paolo Rossi. 'Juve' had a half share of him even though he plays for Lanerossi Vicenza. After the World Cup they wanted to buy out Vicenza's interest . . . while the wooltowners understandably wanted to hold on to their star player.

Italian League rules called for one sealed bid from each side. Juventus bid £700,000 for the half they didn't own . . . which was easily topped by Vicenza's bid — of £1,500,000! Rossi therefore can claim to be the world's most valuable player — his £3,000,000 price tag is six times as much as SV Hamburg paid for Kevin Keegan.

So while the rest of the Italian League breathe private sighs of relief, modest Lanerossi are left with a star-sized headache: how to raise the £1,500,000 they have to pay to Juventus?

Juve v Leeds in the 1971 UEFA Cup final. On Jack Charlton's shoulder is record buy Pietro Anastasi.

Ray Green

A Matter of Fact

Ray Green

Denis Law (*above*) won only one FA Cup winners medal (in 1963), but his total of 41 goals in the competition is still a postwar record.

The League's oldest club, Notts County, became the first to reach 3,000 League matches on 25 March 1975 when they entertained their Forest neighbours in a 2-2 draw at Meadow Lane.

While Dixie Dean was amassing 60 goals in 39 League matches for Everton in 1927-28, Ayr United's Jim Smith was outscoring him with a staggering 66 in 38 Scottish Second Division games.

Argentina's River Plate club propose to run two 'first teams' in future—one to play in domestic competitions, the other to make foreign tours to bring in extra revenue for buying players.

The first £100,000 teenager in Britain was Alun Evans, then 19, who moved from Wolves to Liverpool in September 1968.

How times change! In 1962-63 Cologne, who carry West German hopes in this year's European Cup, crashed 8-1 in that competition to Dundee, who again failed to climb out of the Scottish First Division last season.

Last season Everton striker Bob Latchford scored more League goals (30) than Leicester City managed to produce in all three major competitions (27).

Peterborough United centre-forward Terry Bly scored 52 of the club's staggering 134 goals in 1960-61, their first season in as a League club—the highest postwar total by any player.

In August Alan Cork hit the first-ever League hat-trick for Wimbledon, against Northampton. The club also suffered their record defeat —8-0 at Everton.

263

PRO FILE

KENNY DALGLISH

'He's a golden player, so brave, so committed, the kind who'd play for nothing.' TOMMY DOCHERTY
'What's Kenny Dalglish's best position? Och, just let him on the park.' JOCK STEIN

One of the Kop's banners says it as well as anyone . . . 'Kenny's From Heaven'.

Kenny Dalglish did come from 'up there' —Scotland—and the gain is not only Liverpool's.

The No. 8 with the cheeks that flame in a game is adding a whole new dimension to the weekly grind of League football.

He's no six-footer. He's up front but he's not just a target man. The lad can play!

And, with another Scot who relies more on skill and subtlety than sweat—Graeme Souness—Dalglish has added something else to Liverpool's consistency and character.

It's called class.

So is he one of the greats? There'll be

LEFT *The man who took more class to the Kop— Kenny Dalglish.* RIGHT *Doing it for Celtic— Dalglish shows the style that helped the Glasgow hoops run rings round the opposition for successive championships.* BELOW *Which way will he go? A Rangers defender gets the treatment from a player who's now causing problems down south. Kenny won nine winners medals in Scotland, including four League Championship titles.*

265

Dalglish is often at his best under pressure: here he holds off a Chelsea defender with a combination of skill and determination . . .

Seconds later the ball is still his—proving how important it is to have a player who can hold the ball in tight situations.

The familiar puffing cheeks as Dalglish skips past big Larry Lloyd in last season's League Cup final between Liverpool and Nottingham Forest.

Colorsport

All-Sport

arguments. During the World Cup in Argentina many a pundit was saying that Kenny had never really turned it on for Scotland.

They forget to point out that 'pulling on a Scottish jersey' was supposed to win matches —not high-quality football. And that once Souness took his rightful place on the pitch, against Holland, Scotland and Dalglish began to boil.

Still, forget about all that for the moment. It's enough to concentrate on Kenny's contribution at places like Bolton and Birmingham.

His presence might just mean thousands of people wondering whether 'big and brave' are the only qualities needed up front.

Which can't be bad, can it . . . ?

Kenny's from Glasgow. Brilliance in boots showed itself in the Glasgow United side that ruled amateur football in that part of the world.

Being a Protestant and within chipping distance from Rangers' Ibrox Park, it was always assumed he'd play in blue, not green and white hoops.

But Celtic signed him. He was at Parkhead at the time of the European Cup winning side but soon showed qualities they couldn't refuse—including the art of scoring.

He could also hold the ball under pressure; escape from tight situations; use one-touch whenever he wanted to; think fast; keep cool

The moment that began to raise Scotland's World Cup hopes after their disastrous start against Peru and Iran . . . Dalglish blasts the ball past Dutch keeper Jongbloed for a goal that showed he can also 'turn it on' at international level.

Always concentrating, always looking to get involved . . . Dalglish in the colours of Liverpool, the club he joined for a record between British clubs of £440,000.

when it gets exciting. He looked pretty useful.

In eight seasons with Celtic the lowest League position he knew was third—how disappointing! Celtic won the title six times and one player hankered for new horizons, forward K. Dalglish.

That could be the key to Kenny. It's always been football first—new goals, new challenges. Of course he's made money opening fetes worse than death, but what he's got in his feet has never gone madly to his head.

The men you can rely on to come up with

Not bad in the air, either . . . Dalglish gets above two England defenders in an 'auld enemies' international at Wembley.

gems about really good players have had their succinct say about Dalglish.

Listen to Tommy Docherty (when he was Scotland's manager): 'A golden player, so brave, so committed, the kind who'd play for nothing. Never talks about what he's going to do but just goes and does it.'

To Jock Stein (when asked what Dalglish's best position was): 'Och, just let him on the park!'

Left for dead ... Dalglish gets past a Bruges defender in last season's European Cup final—a match in which Kenny scored a winner with a cool mastery only the greats possess.

Finally, fittingly, to Bob Paisley: 'From the off, Dalglish read my team better than they understood him. That's the hallmark of a great player.'

Another hallmark is a goal that sticks in the memory. Dalglish got one that won the European Cup for the second successive year for Liverpool—the chip that dribbled into the far corner after Dalglish had waited for the Bruges keeper to commit himself . . . a goal so subtle the TV commentators kept relatively quiet about it.

Kenny is a quiet person, too—unlike many of his passionate compatriots. He lets his skill—and his record—do the talking.

Bob Thomas

Honours: Scottish League Championship medal 1972, 1973, 1974, 1977; Scottish FA Cup Winners medal 1972, 1974, 1975, 1977, Runners-up medal 1973; Scottish League Cup Winners medal 1975, Runners-up medal 1972, 1973, 1974, 1976, 1977: European Cup Winners medal 1978

Club	Season	Div.	Pos.	League		FA Cup		Lge Cup		Int'nls	
Coltic	1969-70	1	1	2	–	–	–	2	–	–	–
	1970-71	1	1	3	–	1	–	–	–	–	–
	1971-72	1	1	31	17	4	1	8	5	2	–
	1972-73	1	1	32	23	6	5	11	10	8	2
	1973-74	1	1	33	18	5	1	10	3	12	3
	1974-75	1	3	33	16	5	2	8	2	9	2
	1975-76	P	2	35	24	1	1	10	4	6	3
	1976-77	P	1	35	14	5	1	10	10	10	5
Liverpool	1977-78	1	2	42	20	1	1	9	6	10	4
				246	132	28	12	68	40	57	19

Brady

It looks like Britain's professional footballers took more than a passing interest in the World Cup.

The message didn't take long to sink in . . . Cubillas, Nelinho and Haan proved that top-class goalkeepers should be beaten more often from long range.

And the opening day of the season over here brought a whole volley of spectacular goals.

At Highbury there were two. Tony Currie smashed in one . . . immediately after hinting to the press that they could expect something special.

'During the summer I went to Elland Road at least three times a week to practise shooting,' he told *Handbook*. 'Probably I was inspired by

Colorsport

MADELEY

BRADY

BRADY 1

HARRIS

70

pens up for the Gunners

'Chippy's started with two goals and I expect double figures from him this season . . . without counting penalties.' DON HOWE

that breathtaking shooting in the World Cup.'

And then Liam Brady answered him with a long-range effort for Arsenal.

It stemmed from a mistake by Paul Hart, still settling into the heart of the Leeds defence, who lost the ball to Frank Stapleton.

Stapleton's long cross-field pass found Brady in acres of space on the left.

Paul Madeley moved across to cover Brady, then backed off as the Irish international advanced to the edge of the area.

Brady didn't seem to be looking for a shooting position: he didn't appear to want to take Madeley on the inside or the outside.

Instead he looked up and gestured to Stapleton, who made a run across the face of goal.

A cross to Stapleton's head seemed the likeliest course of action, until Brady let fly . . . and found the back of the net behind Harvey's groping left hand.

The whole Leeds defence had been surprised by Brady's shot . . . and, in addition, Harvey had been unsighted by Stapleton's intelligent run.

But all credit to Brady for seeing the possibility of a goal . . . and producing it.

Graham Taylor's analysis
'I don't really believe Madeley did anything wrong. He couldn't dive in and risk leaving Brady with a clear run at goal. All he could do was jockey him, offering him the chance to go inside on his weaker right foot, while waiting for a loss of control.

There comes a point, though, when a defender has to stop retreating. As a guideline for young defenders, the edge of the penalty area is usually considered to be that point.

But at the top level that idea is beginning to look old-fashioned, with so many goals, it seems, being scored from outside the area.'

'I'm prepared to come off the park having made a mistake about a goal, but I don't like the thought of a nasty foul that could have been avoided.'

One of the biggest headaches for a referee is caused by a single word . . . 'intentional'.

He can only blow for a foul if he decides that a player did it on purpose. But Tom Reynolds, a common sense ref, dodges the dilemma.

'The player making the tackle has the responsibility for getting the ball and not breaking the other fella's leg,' he explains.

'If a player clobbers an opponent and turns to me and says: "Ref, I went for the ball," my answer is always the same. I tell him: "But you didn't get it, did you?" '

Tom uses the same approach with 'smilers', players who try to get away with a foul by smiling at the ref.

Tom says: 'I make up my mind about the foul play and it makes little difference to me if they smile, pick up the opponent, pat him on the head and dust him down.'

So does Tom think the word 'intentional' should be removed from the law on fouls and misconduct, and that players should be penalised if they simply miss the ball and get the man?

'No, not really,' says Tom. 'This game's all about controversy—but I do think we've got to make protection from bad fouls a top priority.'

'Football at the highest level is a tough, competitive business. But there's nothing clever about putting some bloke in hospital—perhaps wrecking his career for good—when it could easily have been avoided.'

'What's he doing down there then—resting !' Tom makes his point at an early season League Cup tie between Bournemouth and Exeter City.

Running a pub in Wiltshire means Tom is always open to jibes from regulars after games, especially when there's been some controversy. 'They pin match reports up in the bar if I've had a poor game,' says Tom. 'One bloke came in and said: "It was a penalty—it says so in the paper." 'They're jokers, but you have to be a joker to be a ref.'

Founded: 1897
Address: County Ground, Abingdon Avenue, Northampton NN1 4PS
Ground: Capacity 20,000; Playing area 109.7 x 68.6 m
Record attendance: 24,523 v Fulham, Div. 1, 23.4.66
Record victory: 10-0 v Walsall, Div. 3(S), 5.11.27
Record defeat: 0-10 v Bournemouth, Div. 3(S), 2.9.39
Most League points: 62, Div. 3(S), 1952-53 & Div. 3, 1962-63
Most League goals: 109, Div. 3(S), 1952-53 & Div. 3, 1962-63
League scoring record: 36, Cliff Holton, Div. 3, 1961-62
Record League aggregate: 135, Jack English, 1947-60
Most League appearances: 521, Tommy Fowler, 1946-61
Most capped player: 12 (16 in all), E. Lloyd Davies, Wales, 1908-14
Honours: Div. 3 Champions 1962-63
League career: 1920-21 Div. 3; 1921-58 Div. 3(S); 1958-61 Div. 4;
1961-63 Div. 3; 1963-65 Div. 2; 1965-66 Div. 1; 1966-67 Div. 2;
1967-69 Div. 3; 1969-76 Div. 4; 1976-77 Div. 3; 1977- Div. 4.

NORTHAMPTON TOWN

Manager Mike Keen supervises five-a-sides. Keen, who played in midfield for Queen's Park Rangers and Luton Town, is in his second season with a club that has had a total of eight managers in the last ten seasons.

Northampton's County Ground has been a graveyard for managerial hopes.

Since Dave Bowen, who led the club in a miraculous rise from the Fourth to the First Division, moved aside to become club secretary ten years ago, there has been a succession of young men hoping to establish the basis of a managerial career.

The most successful was Bill Dodgin Jr, a manager with a

Bob Thomas

273

Aristocratic cobbler
One of Northampton's newest directors is Lord Hesketh, whose previous sporting connections were with the Hesketh Racing team in the high speed world of Formula One . . . the team that propelled James Hunt to fame.

Midas touch for lower division clubs. In his first season he took a club that had been forced to apply for re-election the previous two seasons to the very brink of promotion.

He inherited what proved to be an excellent crop of young players. Phil Neal, now England's right-back, endured the two re-election seasons at Northampton and was at such a low ebb before Dodgin arrived that he nearly signed for non-League Kettering Town.

John Gregory, now with Villa, was also there, but the hottest property was thought to be striker Paul Stratford, whose career was tragically ended by knee injury last season at the age of 22.

All of these players came up through Northampton's youth scheme . . . Dave Bowen's lasting legacy to the club.

Having led the club to promotion in 1976, Bill Dodgin shocked supporters by resigning.

After an unhappy 18 months—during which the club saw off two more managers (Pat Crerand and John Petts) and were relegated again—the board appointed a more experienced man . . . Mike Keen, who had had four seasons as manager of Watford.

Northampton finished that season with an attractive flourish as the newly-formed goal-scoring partnership of

Gypsy Johnny . . . ? John Farrington played for Wolves, Leicester and Cardiff before settling with Northampton in October 1974. He was a regular in Leicester's Second Division championship side of 1970-71.

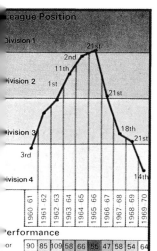

Division 1

21st

2nd

11th

Division 2   1st

21st

Division 3

18th
21st

3rd

Division 4

14th

	1960 61	1961 62	1962 63	1963 64	1964 65	1965 66	1966 67	1967 68	1968 69	1969 70

Performance

For	90	85	109	58	66	55	47	58	54	64
Against	62	57	60	60	50	92	84	72	61	55
Points	60	51	62	41	56	33	30	41	40	44

Average Attendances

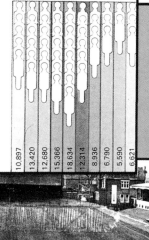

10,897 | 13,420 | 12,680 | 15,366 | 18,634 | 12,314 | 8,936 | 6,790 | 5,590 | 6,621

George Reilly and Andy McGowan blossomed.

Complications after a simple cartilage operation have put McGowan out for a long spell, but Reilly remains Northampton's key player: a striker with immense talent who scored 22 League goals last season. Surprisingly for a player of 6′ 4″, his strength is on the ground . . . but Keen and coach Clive Walker have been working on developing his aerial power.

Now he has £8,000 John Froggatt from Port Vale as his partner, with black winger Derrick Christie, another youth product, making up the front line.

In midfield, veteran John Farrington is partnered by the fiercely competitive Steve Bryant and Keith Williams, signed for small fees from Birmingham and Aston Villa respectively.

Another veteran, Alan Woollett, has brought a wise head into defence, while yet another former Leicester player at the County Ground is Carl Jayes, considered by some pundits to be a First Division goalkeeper in exile.

The collection of small money buys and high-priced potential is a good bet for promotion . . . and perhaps this time they can take up more permanent residence in the Third Division.

Northampton's rise and fall

Dave Bowen has known good days and bad at the County Ground. When he was appointed manager in 1960 the team was in the Fourth Division. By 1965 they rose to the First —miraculously it seemed—a cut above the likes of Wolves, Derby and Manchester City.

They lasted only one season . . . before plunging back to the Fourth by 1969. 'The maximum wage came off as soon as we got out of the Fourth Division,' recalls Bowen. 'That was our great undoing. But it was a great experience, mind.'

Syndication International

Outside his old school—Aveley Comprehensive
—with its Manchester United graffiti !

The skinny kid in midfield caught the eye of the West Ham scout.

He liked the way he buzzed about, always in the game. Plenty of skill, too.

So a quick chat to the lad's dad on the line and the first step in another promising career had been taken.

Paul Allen was 14 at the time and playing for Thurrock District against Havering—only a Saturday morning friendly.

'We lost 3-2 but I suppose I had a pretty good match,' grins Paul, a chirpy character who's obviously chuffed at being an apprentice professional.

After the initial approach, Paul was invited to train at Upton Park two evenings a week and play friendlies during the school holidays.

He did well and soon signed schoolboy forms, which are designed to stop other clubs poaching him.

Then, after going the right way in the

A penny for his thoughts . . . a quiet moment for Paul with a ball.

...the boy spotted

APPRENTICE 2

The second apprentice pro whose progress will be followed by *Football Handbook* is 16-year-old Paul Allen, who signed for West Ham United in the summer. Cheerful and keen,

Paul was snapped up in the way that supports the advice given to youngsters over the years: 'Play as well as you can in every match—you never know who is watching on the line . . .'

South East Counties League for the colts' team, the offer was made.

'Ronnie Boyce, our coach, asked me to join the club on the coach ride to a game against Charlton colts,' recalls Paul. 'I didn't have a bad game that day!'

Now just turned 16, Paul lives in the Essex countryside, at Aveley, a small town with no railway station—but five pubs.

He went to Aveley Comprehensive—'I didn't realise how much I liked it until I left' —and biology was his best subject.

His is a footballing family. Dad—Ron— played in the army and Paul's brother, Peter,

Attitude is everything in a young pro, and Ronnie Boyce says Paul has got what it takes.

'He gets a bit het up at times but that's because he wants to do so well.'

Boyce himself didn't do so badly as a pro. The 'engine room' of the 1960s team, he dived to head the winner in the 1964 Cup final.

Duncan Raban

a Saturday morning friendly

277

was at Charlton Athletic before losing interest and becoming a bricklayer.

Cousin Clive, son of Tottenham's 'double side' star Les Allen, is a colt at QPR.

'Clive and me were always over the park with our dads,' says Paul. 'We both wanted to be footballers from when we were about eight.'

Paul has settled down well at Upton Park because he knew some of the other apprentices from their district days.

Pre-season training was a knock-out . . . literally. 'I used to get home, fall asleep, get up, have a bath, have a bite to eat, then go back to bed,' says Paul.

Odd jobs on top of the football include pumping up the balls, sorting out the kit in the laundry room at the Chadwell Heath training ground, sweeping up and getting the weights out.

'I don't mind all that,' says Paul. 'It's not bad when there's eight of you.

Chore bore . . . 'actually, it's not bad when there's eight of you,' says Paul.

'What I like is being out in the open air most of the time. I can't help thinking that a lot of my mates are in factories. I'm not having a go at that, but I've got to think I'm lucky, haven't I?'

Despite his happy-go-lucky exterior, Paul admits he's a worrier.

He says: 'If I take on someone and fail, or if I mess up a pass, I start worrying.'

Nerves attack him in the dressing-room just before matches. 'Once I'm out on the pitch it's okay,' he says, 'and if I knock a couple of good balls about early on I feel fine.'

Most days Paul goes straight to Chadwell Heath—by bus. 'I have to catch a couple and it costs me thirty bob a day,' says Paul, but I get it back on expenses.'

Hammers' manager John Lyall sees Paul as an Alan Ball type, a player who loves to get involved.

'That's what we look for in a young player—enthusiasm and a willingness to learn,' says John. 'The first year of the apprenticeship is taken up with basic skills—all the different kinds of passing, volleying, chipping, shooting.

'We never tell young players not to do something. Everything has a place. It's up to them, with a little help from us, to make decisions, make choices in different situations.

'A player in a match has to make choices. How good he becomes depends on how many correct choices he makes.'

'It's the weights that get me' . . . Paul tucks in at West Ham's training ground at Chadwell Heath.

12 professional training bags from

Gola

to be won in this week's free-to-enter competition

1. Which current First Division club began life as St Domingo Church Sunday School in 1878?

2. He left Arsenal to play for a Third Division club. Now he turns out for a club managed by a former England centre-half. Who is he?

3. Which club, currently in the Second Division, has been in 4 FA Cup finals since the war and never won?

4. RIGHT Kevin Keegan's return to Anfield. Who is the Liverpool player and what was the score?

5. One of the Berwick Rangers team which knocked Glasgow Rangers out of the Scottish Cup in 1967 is now at Leicester City. Who is he?

6. Who was Scotland's top scorer in the 1974 World Cup finals?

7. He plays for a Midlands club and spent summer in the USA. Who is he?

8. These clubs are all playing in European competition this year: AEK, VfB, PSV, CSKA, AZ 67, WBA. Which towns or cities do they come from?

Ian Wallace

'After the car crash I thought I would lose the sight of an eye and that my career was finished ... when something like that happens to you it makes you realise just how lucky you are to be alive—to be a pro footballer.'

An icy road almost ended Ian Wallace's brilliant career before it had really begun.

Soon after his £50,000 transfer to Coventry from Dumbarton, Ian smashed his car into a tree and badly damaged an eye.

That was 18 months ago and Ian recalls: 'It was a terrible time. I was just about to get the chance of a first team place. For a while I thought I would lose the sight of the eye and that my career was finished.'

Ian was lucky—but there was another scare ahead. 'In my comeback game at Norwich the ball hit me in the same eye and I got blurred vision. I had to go to hospital but it was only bruising and it cleared up in a matter of days.'

And the 22-year-old Scot was one of the main reasons why Coventry came so close to a place in Europe last season.

The razor-sharp reflexes that keep defenders constantly on their toes were produced on Dumbarton's right wing.

'When I came to Coventry the boss, Gordon Milne, moved me into the middle and I've found that sharp play is even more successful there because central defenders don't usually recover as quickly as full-backs.'

Still there after a scare ... Coventry's Ian Wallace.

Being small can help ... Wallace gets in an acrobatic effort during one of Coventry's pre-season friendlies.

Razor sharp ... Wallace is now using his speed in the middle for Coventry—'it's even more successful because central defenders don't usually recover quickly.'

Bob Thomas

Andy Gray on the attacking header

'I don't think there's such a thing as a perfect footballer—especially me. There's always something I should be working on, whether it's my shooting, my control—or my heading.'

You don't have to be big to be good in the air. Take Andy 'I'm just a wee fella' Gray. At 5′ 10½″ he's smaller than almost all of the centre-halves he comes up against; but he still wins—and puts away—more than his fair share of balls in the air.

'It's not really a disadvantage,' Andy told *Handbook*. 'I find that most of the leggy guys I come up against can't jump as well as I can.

'The most important thing is to give yourself plenty of space and really attack the ball.

'I try to start off on about the 18-yard line—the edge of the area—and attack the goal on a diagonal.

'Start out wide—beyond the far post—and you'll tend to find a defender coming with you, so you'll get that little bit of extra space as well.

'You should try and pick up the flight of the ball as early as possible . . . anticipate where it's going to come down.

'Then really go for the ball. The point where to take off for the header and the point where you land after the header should be anything from three feet to six feet apart.

'And, of course, try and get as much power into the actual header as you can . . . use your neck muscles as much as possible.'

It might prove difficult to get that much power in your heading at first. 'To begin with,' recommends Graham Taylor, 'aim towards the far corner of the goal. That's the sure way to get accuracy.'

And Andy makes another point about heading for the far corner. 'It means the goalkeeper has to change direction,' he points out.

'First of all he's got to face in the direction the ball is coming from, then he's got to turn and face the header, then he's got to dive back across the goal.'

Andy recommends regular practice. 'I used to practice every afternoon at Dundee United,' he recalls. 'Manager Jim McLean used to have me out working—especially on far-post heading, because I'm a bit small for a striker—without a goalkeeper. And it's amazing how many I used to miss . . .'

Andy then put on an awesome display for our photo-

Ray Green

Ray Green

dy goes up with Frank McLintock, then of QPR. 'You can't ways get in a perfect header under pressure,' he says.

Heading for the top corner ... the top half of the body should be a hammer, with the forehead the hammer-head.

Taking off ... with three points to remember: give yourself plenty of room, pick up the flight early, and attack the ball.

Andy says: 'The point where you take off for the header and the point where you land should be anything from three to six feet apart' ... and, as this sequence shows, his jump is about that length.

But don't concentrate on getting a long jump ... it should follow naturally from attacking the ball.

Ray Green

session at Villa's training ground. Using the whole of his upper body, he repeatedly hammered the ball with his forehead . . . sending it ripping into the net.

'I don't agree with those people who say that you have to head the ball downwards,' Andy explained. 'I believe in taking the shortest route to goal.

'If you're six yards out and you head the ball straight in, then it only has to travel six yards. If you head it downwards it has to travel further . . . there's more chance of the goalkeeper or a defender getting to it.

'If you're that close, then I believe in going straight for goal.'

Although Andy was a keen Rangers supporter and a Glasgow Schools player, he signed for Dundee United. 'I don't think Rangers fancied me at the time,' says Andy.

Once you've mastered the timing of your run and jump, concentrate on developing power.

'Practise regularly,' advises Andy, who really worked hard on his heading when he was a young player at Dundee United.

'Get a friend to throw the ball up to you from no more than the width of a goal away.' Then you can work on getting the kind of power Andy shows in these shots. Eye on the ball ... then deliver the hammer blow.

Most of the power comes from the arched back and the neck muscles, but note how the outstretched arms (bottom left) help with balance.

'It's always worth taking your time improving your heading ability,' says Graham Taylor. 'Building up your confidence, timing and power.

'Start off by getting a friend to throw the ball up to you. Concentrate on hitting the ball with the right part of the forehead at first, heading the ball straight back at him. Then try for more power.

'Then get your friend to chip the ball up to you. You really need more than one ball for this, otherwise you'll be spending a lot of time just retrieving it.

'Your mate should chip the ball in from both sides of the goal and from anywhere between the by-line and the 18-yard line or beyond.

'Aim mostly at the far corner of the goal, at least to begin with. That's the surest way to develop power and accuracy.'

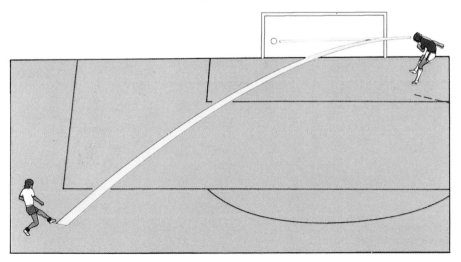

Founded: 1905
Address: Selhurst Park, London SE25 6PU
Ground: Capacity 51,000; Playing area 100.6 x 68.6 m
Record attendance: 49,498 v Chelsea, Div. 1, 27.12.69
Record victory: 9-0 v Barrow, Div. 4, 10.10.59
Record defeat: 4-11 v Manchester City, FA Cup 5th rd, 20.2.26
Most League points: 64, Div. 4, 1960-61
Most League goals: 110, Div. 4, 1960-61
League scoring record: 46, Peter Simpson, Div. 3(S), 1930-31
Record League aggregate: 154, Peter Simpson, 1930-36
Most League appearances: 432, Terry Long, 1956-69
Most capped player: 13, Ian Evans, Wales, 1975-77
League career: 1921 Div. 3; 1922-25 Div. 2; 1926-58 Div. 3(S);
1958-61 Div. 4; 1961-64 Div. 3; 1964-69 Div. 2; 1969-73 Div. 1;
1973-74 Div. 2; 1974-77 Div. 3; 1977- Div. 2
Honours: Div. 3(S) Champions 1921

CRYSTAL PALACE

Colorsport

Soccer for sinkers
Malcolm Allison took Palace from the First to the Third Division—and his most successful season with the club ended in disappointment . . . and his resignation. But Big Mal built the basis of a more soundly run club and his flair for publicity left them with a more positive image and outlook. At the end of his three years chairman Ray Bloye could say: 'He's done a fine job for us and I can't thank him enough.

Jerry Murphy, just one of many immensely promising Palace youngsters, has two Youth Cup winners medals.

Terry Venables is sick of hearing the word 'potential', especially when applied to Crystal Palace FC. Since extrovert manager Malcolm Allison left Selhurst Park in 1976, Venables has stopped the South London public day-dreaming about Palace running away with the First Division title and got on with the job of running a football team.

With the club a million pounds in the red, that should be

Duncan Raban

The spring of '69 . . . and Palace are on the verge of promotion to the First Division for the first time in their history. Here midfielder Steve Kember scores in a vital 3-1 win over Portsmouth at Selhurst Park.

enough of a job for anyone. But Palace have never been a side for the faint-hearted or easily depressed. In the past, success has given away all too easily to failure.

Ninth in the Second Division was a respectable place to finish last season—the first after promotion—although it *was* five rungs below arch-rivals Brighton. Even without Peter Taylor, the England winger Venables sold to Tottenham for £200,000 in September 1976, Palace played some slick, tidy football that was a lot more positive than their record of 15 draws and only 13 wins suggests.

In a roundabout way, being short of cash has had its advantages. Transfer dealings have been almost at a stand-still, guaranteeing a settled side, while Venables has continued Allison's policy of giving good young players an early chance to establish themselves in the first team.

Kenny Sansom at left-back and Vince Hilaire on the flanks are only the two most publicised prospects to emerge from what is currently the most productive youth scheme in the country.

Other youngsters whose progress has excited Palace supporters include the midfield partnership of Welsh youth international Peter Nicholas, Irish youth international Jerry Murphy and central defender Billy Gilbert—an English youth international. On the edge of the first team are others like forward Ian Walsh, midfielder Terry Fenwick and defender Kevin Dare—all of whom are youth internationals.

Another new face in the line-up is £200,000 striker Mike Elwiss, Palace's first major signing for some years.

Budgie's brief song
Johnny Byrne played for England while still a Third Division player with Palace. He had four seasons at West Ham, before returning, his skills blunted, for a brief and disappointing spell.

In 11 full internationals, Byrne, known as 'Budgie', scored eight goals. Former Palace manager Arthur Rowe rated him 'in the top four centre-forwards I ever saw. For two or three seasons he was fantastic.'

287

Colorsport

Don Rogers teases United during Palace's classic 5-0 win in December 1972 ... but the season still ended with relegation. BELOW *Nick Chatterton in action against Sunderland in September.*

But problems remain. Ian Evans, whose command in the air was crucial to Palace's defence, broke his leg in a clash with George Best at Fulham last year and he has still not fully recovered. The loss of Welsh international Evans is especially damaging since he was one of the few really experienced players in the Palace squad.

Venables and coaches Allan Harris, John Cartwright

Duncan Raban

Colorsport

Malcolm Allison once said:
'Until now I've never met a
coach who has made me think:
"You might be better than me."
Well, Terry Venables has
made me think that.'

TV repairman
Current manager Terry Venables was brought to Selhurst Park by Malcolm Allison to run the side on the field. A former Chelsea, Spurs and QPR midfielder, and the first player to represent England at five levels—schoolboy, amateur, youth, under-23, and full international—Terry was appointed club coach after one season. Venables took over as manager after Allison resigned and led the club to promotion the same season. He also helps coach the England Under-21 side—where he continues the policy of pursuing skill which has made Palace so entertaining in recent years.

and Ernie Walley put emphasis on skill, which can mean that the younger players have trouble holding their own when first introduced to League football.

Yet the team should only get better. 'I firmly believe that we can do well with the squad I've got,' explains Venables, 'but there could just be an age factor. The team averages 21.

'I have more ball-winners now and players prepared to tackle, while the youngsters are gaining experience all the time. But they're still young . . . it's in my mind that the season after this one could be our big one.'

Mally's Pally
Malcolm Allison arrived at Selhurst Park in 1973 . . . Palace needed just three points from their last seven games to ensure survival in the First Division, but despite the general manager Bert Head's pleading, the team was immediately reshuffled—and Palace sank like a stone . . . right through the Second.

Then in 1976 it seemed as if the Allison formula was paying off: seven points clear at the top of the table and heading towards the Cup semi-finals —with Big Mal taunting the opposition at every tie. But promotion was missed . . . and Allison resigned.

Duncan Raban

Vince Hilaire, the subject of a TV documentary when an apprentice, now looks set to earn fame on the field.

Krankl buries the Germans

West Germany's faint hopes of reaching the World Cup final finally blew up in Cordoba with one moment of explosive magic from Austria's Hans Krankl.

The holders fell 2-1 behind to one of the finest pieces of skill in the tournament.

The cross from Hickersberger in the 66th minute seemed harmless enough: there were five Germans in the box. But they failed to make it and it fell to Krankl, lurking a few yards out from the far post.

He cushioned the ball, at knee height, with the inside of his left foot, and volleyed it into the top far corner.

Krankl (on the ground) sees his volley flash past Maier.

Graham Taylor's analysis

'A brilliantly taken goal—even though the ball should never have reached Krankl. One of the German defenders was ball-watching only a yard away.

'Most players would either have swung at it or, if they did decide to try and control it, use their thigh or let it fall.

'It was that combination—the idea *and* the execution.

Presse—Foto—Baumann

'If we're not in the right frame of mind things can go terribly wrong. It's up to the ref and his linesmen to keep mistakes to a minimum.'

Ray Green

It's not only the players who have to prepare mentally for matches—referees have to gee themselves up as well.

'Everyone knows about the pressures on players,' says World Cup ref Pat Partridge, 'but it's almost as bad for referees and linesmen. If we're not in the right frame of mind things can go terribly wrong.'

Pat's priorities include a good night's sleep before every game, followed by a giant breakfast.

'I usually have a mixed grill, with plenty of everything,' says Pat. 'Enough to get me through the day, because I'll have nothing immediately before the game.'

Nothing, that is, except tea—buckets of it.

'I don't know why it is—perhaps it's the tension and needing something to do,' he says. 'I don't drink tea during the week but on match days I drink it all the time, cup after cup.'

Getting on the same wavelength as your linesmen is essential, says Pat. 'The way I see it, there are three teams out there—the two football teams and the officials—and it's up to all three to provide a good game. So we have to get it together and make sure mistakes are kept to a minimum.'

Refs are only human

There was a time when Pat's preparation for a match fell below his normal high standard.

It was in 1975, just after Pat heard he would take charge of the FA Cup final.

'I was on cloud nine,' he recalls. 'The phone didn't stop ringing and, all in all, I just wasn't my normal self.

'The trouble was, I had a game that evening, the West Riding Cup final in Bradford.

'I never get changed earlier than 15 minutes before the kick off, so it was quite late to find I'd left my kit at home, on the bed!

'I said to my linesmen: "Okay where is it?"—thinking they were having a laugh at the Cup Final referee's expense. Then panic set in as I realised they had done nothing—they must have thought I'd cracked up after getting the big news!'

Luckily, Pat found a local referee in the tea room and borrowed his kit—still sweaty from the previous Sunday.

Two of a kind

'It always gets on my nerves you know, that people say I've lived in his shadow. I never have . . . The only shadow I've lived in is my own.' RON FUTCHER

When the Futchers were each scoring 50 goals a season—four or five goals a game—for their primary school in Chester, or when the van der Kerkhofs were bemusing opponents of their junior team in Helmond, no prospect can have seemed more pleasant than to play the game they loved together in the First Division—inseparable, twin terrors.

But reality tends to be harsher . . . even if both brothers make it to the top—as the

Colorsport

Roger (left) and Ian Morgan (above) were twins who played together—one on each wing—for QPR. The twins were separated when Roger, an England Under-23 international, moved on to Spurs in February 1969, where he spent what he considers his 'worst four years in football'. Both players were plagued by injuries: Roger was forced to retire at 26 and Ian at 28—after only 16 games for his new club, Watford.

Colorsport

Club	Div	Pos	Season	League		FA Cup		Lge Cup	
				Ms	Gs	Ms	Gs	Ms	Gs
Chester	IV	15	1972-73	2	–	–	–	–	–
	IV	7	1973-74	18	–	1	–	–	–
Luton	I	20	1974-75	19	–	1	–	—	
Town	II	7	1975-76	41	–	2	–	1	–
	II	6	1976-77	40	1	2	–	1	–
	II	13	1977-78	31	–	1	–	2	–
				151	1	7	–	4	–

Futchers and the van der Kerkhofs did.

Willy and Rene van der Kerkhof began playing together for one of the junior teams of FC Mulo of Helmond, aged eight. At 18 they were signed by Twente Enschede and at 21 they moved together to PSV Eindhoven —for a fee variously reported as anything between £60,000 and £600,000!

Soon after signing for PSV, the brothers made their international debut—together again—against Austria.

RIGHT *Ron* (left) *and Paul* (right) *Futcher . . . together again at a First Division club.*
BELOW *Paul Futcher playing against Liverpool in an early season match at Maine Road.*

Bob Thomas

Ray Green

Club	Div	Pos	Season	League		FA Cup		Lge Cup	
				Ms	Gs	Ms	Gs	Ms	Gs
Chester	IV	7	1973-74	4	–	–	–	–	–
Luton	I	20	1974-75	17	7	1	–	–	–
Town	II	7	1975-76	31	10	2	1	1	1
	II	6	1976-77	33	13	2	–	–	–
	II	13	1977-78	39	10	3	–	5	–
				124	40	8	1	6	1

Ron has also played for Minnesota Kicks (USA) 1976-78

Bob Thomes

Their boyhood dream was coming true. Even the pressures and demands of the professional game could not separate them. Willy, the midfielder, was acknowledged to be the more thoughtful, but Rene's speed and skills were also highly rated.

Willy can still say: 'Our relationship is perfect. Not just as twin brothers and team-mates, but as close friends.'

As Willy explained to *Handbook*: 'We have a very good understanding. We can find each

BELOW *Ron completes his hat-trick against Chelsea. He scored his three goals in a 15-minute spell either side of half-time, scored in the next game . . . and was then dropped.*

Press Association

295

REINER (RENE) VAN DER KERKHOF
born Helmond, 16 September 1951

		Matches	Goals
Twente Enschede	1970-73	92	29
PSV Eindhoven	1973-78	152	57
HOLLAND	1973-78	26	4

he's the best midfielder in Holland!'

The first cracks in their togetherness could appear at the end of this season, when their contracts with PSV run out. And both van der Kerkhofs seem determined to move.

'I want to play in English football,' said Willy. 'It's marvellous to play every Saturday before 50,000 people. We go tomorrow to Venlo where we will be playing in front of five or six thousand.'

Rene agrees. 'I see English League games on television every week and they're very fast, very exciting. I would like very much to other almost blind. After all, we have been playing together for 19 years now. When he has the ball I know what he's going to do. So it is easy for me to find positions—in front of goal, deep on the right side or wherever.'

We asked Rene if there were any disadvantages to playing alongside his twin. 'No,' he said without hesitation. 'After all,

WILHELMUS (WILLY) VAN DER KERKHOF
born Helmond, 16 September 1951

		Matches	Goals
Twente Enschede	1970-73	101	14
PSV Eindhoven	1973-78	160	29
HOLLAND	1973-78	24	3

play in English football.'

But given the choice, Willy would choose Spain. 'In Spain the pay is much better than in England. If the pay was the same then I

ABOVE *The fast and elusive Rene takes on a St Etienne defender in a European Cup tie.*

LEFT *The Holland line-up as we have been used to seeing it over the last four years . . . including Rene (left) and Willy (right) van der Kerkhof— separated on this occasion by Wim Jansen.*

BELOW LEFT *Willy and Kempes in the World Cup final.*

BELOW *Rene (left) and Willy (right) . . . leaving Eindhoven soon and leaving together, says Willy.*

would certainly prefer to go to England.'

And whereas Rene doesn't rule out the possibility of them going to separate clubs, Willy is adamant: 'We will go together.'

The Futcher twins have been together for most of their career as well. From school they went to local club Chester . . . as virtually the only apprentices on the staff. Soon after signing as full professionals for Chester, the twins moved on to Luton.

'It was a shock, sure, especially at that age,' says Paul. 'But there was no pressure on us. We just thought we'd go out and enjoy it in the First Division.'

Like Paul, Ron talks—with absolute confidence—for both brothers. He told *Handbook*: 'We enjoyed it at Luton, except possibly the last six months of last season when things started to go wrong a bit.

'Harry Haslam left and David Pleat took over. He had his own ideas and he wanted his own players in there.'

So the Futchers moved on again—this time to Manchester City. Once again Paul moved first . . . and Ron followed soon after.

For a short while the Futcher partnership flourished at the top end of the First Division. In his second League game for City Ron scored a well-taken hat-trick.

'When I make a run he knows where I'm going . . . and the ball goes there—instinctively. So there's a good understanding.'

Is it anything to do with . . . telepathy?

'No, I don't believe that. I think it's just something you get from playing together for so long.'

But there are signs that their on-field partnership is under strain. In each of the moves the twins have made, Paul has gone first for a big fee, followed shortly by Ron for much less. In their latest move, Paul's

Sporting Pictures UK

fee of £350,000 dwarfed Ron's £80,000 . . . and there were snide suggestions that Ron had been bought as a make-weight—to keep his brother happy.

Ron is angry at such talk: 'It's just the press. They jump to conclusions all the time. I can't get away from it. You score a hat-trick and the next day you get terrible reviews in the press. About being in his shadow—things like this.

'Wherever I go until we're separated we'll always have that. Until I get away I'll always have that.

'I feel that I've done enough in the short time I've been in the game to warrant people talking about me on my own. I've done well on my own. I know I'm here on merit.'

Ron's record backs him up. He was Luton's top scorer in each of the last two seasons, and he was equal top scorer for City until he was dropped for the local derby game at Old Trafford.

'When I came in against Chelsea people were saying I was third choice. But the fact is I played and scored a hat-trick. I played against Tottenham the following week and scored again. What more can you do? You come in and score goals and then you get left out.'

Twins are something of a mystery to the rest of us. Even when we've sorted out which twin is which, distinctions blur in the middle. Sometimes it seems they're overlapping, not separate, personalities. There's a tendency to take them together, as two of a kind . . .

And this can cause problems. There comes a time when everyone, even twins, must seek out their own character and ambition.

A Matter of Fact

When Moscow Dynamo became the first team from the Soviet Union ever to play in Britain in November 1945, gates were broken down and fans perched on the stand roof as an estimated 100,000 saw them draw 3-3 with Chelsea at Stamford Bridge.

Brian Clark's goal which put Cardiff ahead of Dinamo Berlin in September 1971 took their Cup Winners' Cup tally to 71, past Atletico Madrid's record.

Forest's Steve Elliott won a League Cup winners' tankard last season as non-playing sub in the replay with Liverpool before he'd ever played in the first team.

The original F.A. Cup

The original FA Cup was stolen from a shop window in Birmingham in 1895, where it was on display after Aston Villa's final win over West Bromwich Albion. A replica was used until 1910, and the FA commissioned a new trophy from Fattorini & Sons of Bradford in 1911. The first winners? None other than Bradford City!

Dutch champions PSV Eindhoven went the first 31 games of last season without defeat—and then lost 1-0 to Haarlem and 3-2 to Ajax in successive matches.

In Bill Nicholson's first game as Spurs manager in October 1958, his team celebrated by crushing Everton 10-4 at White Hart Lane!

In 1973 the volcano on the Vestmann Islands off Iceland erupted, and the local IVB club had to flee their ground. Two years later they dug out the pitch, and last September sent the 5,800 inhabitants wild by knocking Glentoran out of the UEFA Cup.

During Orient's remarkable run to the FA Cup semi-finals last season just two players accounted for all 9 of their goals—Peter Kitchen (7) and Joe Mayo (2).

In 1972-73 all four divisions of the Football League were won by teams from Lancashire: Liverpool took the First Division title, Burnley and Bolton the Second and Third Divisions respectively, while Southport won the Fourth. Southport's place in the League has now gone to another Lancashire club, Wigan Athletic.

Sportapics Ltd

RI*S*ING PAUL
*S*TAR HEGARTY

Nothing is more frustrating for a manager than an obviously gifted player who is failing to produce the goods.

Dundee United's young star Paul Hegarty was in that worrying category until manager Jim McLean tried him in a different position.

It worked. Hegarty, whose talents had been wasted in midfield and attack, was an instant hit at centre-half.

And now, less than a year after the experiment in a challenge match against Everton at Goodison Park, Hegarty is that underrated football asset—an inspiring captain at the heart of the defence.

'The switch worked out fine for me,' says Paul. 'I now see my future as a defender. Mind you, I haven't given up the idea of scoring goals. I got nine last season, five with my head.'

And that was only one less than his tally for the previous season, when he played further forward.

McLean is not normally quick to praise, but he says of Hegarty: 'He's probably the best centre-half in Britain. I wouldn't swap him and David Narey for Manchester United's Gordon McQueen and Martin Buchan.'

Such was Hegarty's improvement last season that he made Ally MacLeod's squad of 40 for the World Cup—it's ironic that the man who kept him out of the final party of 22 was McQueen, who never kicked a ball in Argentina.

A front player with two Edinburgh boys'

club sides, Hegarty joined Hamilton as an 18-year-old in 1972. Then he was bought by McLean for £40,000 in November 1974.

Tremendous heading ability is his strong point in defence, but he knows there's a lot more to defensive play than that.

He says: 'You have to read situations

Sportapics Ltd

For a player who cost £40,000 to score goals, Paul Hegarty has done remarkably well . . . as a defender. He says: 'I never felt I was quite sharp enough to be a really successful scorer. I was only getting 13 or 14 goals a season and that's not enough. Now that I've moved back I reckon I'm here to stay.'

'He's probably the best centre-half in Britain. I wouldn't swap him and David Narey for Manchester United's Gordon McQueen and Martin Buchan.'

JIM MCLEAN

Club	Div	Pos	Season	League		FA Cup		Lge Cup	
Hamilton	II	8	1972-73	36	7	4	1	4	–
Academicals	II	3	1973-74	31	6	2	–	4	–
	II	4	1974-75	12	5	–	–	8	7
Dundee	I	4	1974-75	17	4	2	–	–	–
United	P	8	1975-76	33	8	3	1	4	–
	P	4	1976-77	36	6	1	–	6	1
	P	3	1977-78	36	4	4	2	8	3
				201	40	16	4	34	11

quickly and mark your man tight. Give him too much space and he'll murder you.

'I suppose I'm a fairly hard player, too, but I like to think I play fair. I was booked three times last season, but I don't think that's a bad record in my position.'

It seems inevitable that Hegarty, 24, will move south. But for the moment he believes a lot can be achieved at Tannadice.

He says: 'I think we showed last season by finishing third in the League and reaching the Scottish Cup semi-finals that we're capable of greater things.

The imposing figure of McQueen stands between Hegarty and international honours,

but he's not downhearted.

He says: 'Four years ago in West Germany, Jim Holton was one of the stars of Scotland's World Cup side, but then an injury kept him out of the picture.

'Football's like that. One minute everything's great, the next all wrong. All I can do is keep on improving and make people sit up and take notice.'

They're taking notice, that's for sure.

Happier at the back . . . Hegarty gets up higher than anyone else to end a Partick Thistle attack. 'I now see my future as a defender,' says young Paul.

Sportapics Ltd

Down but not out: the art of recovery

Lots of what was good in the World Cup was also obvious —there for everyone to see and appreciate.

But other things may have gone unnoticed—the kind of commitment top players show as well as their skills.

Here, in a sequence of four pictures, Wim Jansen makes the unglamourous effort of 'getting back' . . .

The World Cup final: Mario Kempes skips past Wim Jansen and leaves him on his back. A lesser player might have taken little further interest in the proceedings, but Jansen keeps thinking, keeps alert. Quick to his feet, he makes a bee-line for another defensive position. Perhaps he'll make it; perhaps he won't. But one thing's clear: he's still out there having a go . . .

'Recovery is not only about being fit,' says Graham Taylor. 'It's an attitude of mind. It's your way of saying that you're not finished, that you'll make another contribution if given half the chance. Look at Jansen: "Left for dead" is the phrase, but there's plenty of life left in him! So the lesson is: never give up—always try to get back. Often, another player will slow the progress of someone who has gone past you and that will give you the chance to cover, to get back behind the ball. One tip—try to use the pitch markings as an extra aid to your positioning. I always ask my players to familiarise themselves with the grounds we play on so they can get this extra help. You can do the same—knowing, for example, that something near the touchline is 25 yards from goal can help you make a better decision when you are on the ball in that area.'

Peter Robinson

PRO FILE

TONY WOODCOCK

'He's an exciting player with many of the qualities of Kevin Keegan and Trevor Francis. He's a quiet, modest lad, but he expresses himself where it matters—on the field.' RON GREENWOOD

Forest burst on the First Division last season like a herd of rogue comets. Names like Clough, Shilton, Gemmill and Burns lit up the scene. But the shooting star that caught Ron Greenwood's eye was Tony Woodcock . . . possibly the least known and certainly the quietest member of the team.

Greenwood noted Woodcock's skill and pace, his exciting running with the ball and

Said Tony: 'I went there hoping someone would spot me . . . and to escape reserve team football. When I got back to Forest I gained a first team place only because Barry Butlin was injured.'

The change in Tony Woodcock's fortunes was sudden. At the beginning of Forest's promotion year he was playing in the Fourth Division. Less than two years later he had

Ray Green

One of Tony Woodcock's five goals in two games at Under 21-level . . . and one of two he scored against Italy in a 2-1 win at Maine Road last March.

intelligent running without it, and capped him at Under-21 level. Woodcock responded with five goals in two games—three against Finland, two against Italy.

So Greenwood selected him to play against Northern Ireland in the Home Internationals at the end of last season . . . and the press beat a path to his door.

'Turning people is the strongest part of my game,' Woodcock explained. 'A lot of players get the ball and lay it off. Not many turn with it.'

But inevitably there were questions about Brian Clough and Peter Taylor.

'They haven't made me a better player, but they have given me more confidence,' Woodcock replied.

But what they were most interested in was the reason why he had gone on loan to Doncaster only 18 months before.

won League and League Cup winners medals, he had gained a full England cap and he had been voted Young Player of the Year by his fellow professionals.

One moment, it seemed, Brian Clough was ready to sell him for £15,000 . . . the next, he was scoring regularly—and playing brilliantly—in Forest's first team.

So what happened?

Some people have suggested that Woodcock's month-long spells on loan—to Lincoln and Doncaster—somehow turned him into a much better player . . . that two months away from the City Ground changed him from a player being lined up by a couple of Fourth Division clubs to a player showing international form . . .

But it was a positional switch that made the big difference . . . to his confidence, his happiness and his form.

Tony's favoured position is striker—alongside the centre-forward. But a whole series of managers and coaches seemed to have different ideas for him. He was played mainly as a left-winger, Clough even played him at left-back.

Tony joined Forest straight from school in 1972. Within two years he had made his first team debut—in a Second Division game at Villa Park. He played in his favourite number 10 shirt, but with the job of providing some width for the main strikers—big John Galley and Duncan McKenzie.

He made occasional first team appearances the following season, during which manager Allan Brown was sacked. The new man was

Tony won Championship and League Cup winners medals, an England cap and was PFA Young Player of the Year last season.

Colorsport

Honours: League Championship medal 1978; Football League Cup winners medal 1978; PFA Young Player of the Year 1978

Club	Div	Pos	Season	League Ms	League Gs	FA Cup Ms	FA Cup Gs	L. Cup Ms	L. Cup Gs
Nottingham	II	7	1973-74	2	–	–	–	–	–
Forest	II	16	1974-75	9	–	–	–	–	–
	II	8	1975-76	–	–	–	–	–	–
Lincoln C. (on loan)	IV	1	1975-76	4	1	–	–	–	–
Doncaster R. (on loan)	IV	8	1976-77	6	2	–	–	–	–
Nottingham	II	3	1976-77	30	11	5	5	–	–
Forest	I	1	1977-78	36	11	6	4	8	4
				87	25	11	9	8	4

Tony has won 1 England cap, against N. Ireland last May

Tony Woodcock proving the England team manager right . . . said Ron Greenwood after picking him against Northern Ireland last May: 'He's quick and unflappable, he scores goals.' He added: 'I've asked him to do just what he does for Forest . . . and he'll give us width at the right time.'

Brian Clough . . . and for a while Woodcock's career was stalled.

He didn't make one single appearance for Forest in 1975-76. After spending most of a miserable season in the reserves, he went on loan to Lincoln, who were on course for the Fourth Division championship.

'We brought him in as cover for our left-winger, Alan Harding, who'd had injury problems,' recalls Graham Taylor, Lincoln's manager at the time. 'At first we thought his best position was left side of midfield, but when we asked the lad, he said he wanted to play up front—feeding off the centre-forward.'

Taylor used him there in a practice match . . . and was impressed.

'So we played him alongside John Ward in the first team against Brentford. He played brilliantly for half an hour, then another injury meant he had to move back to the wing.

'I think his first game when he went back to Forest was at Burnley Reserves . . . as a left-back.'

Help was at hand, though, in the shape of Peter Taylor. Taylor, Clough's right-hand man at Derby and Brighton, had resigned as manager of Brighton and rejoined Clough at Forest during the close season. Graham Taylor's attempts to sign Woodcock for Lincoln were thwarted and, after a month's loan to Doncaster—who used him as a left-winger—he broke into the Forest first team . . . as a goalscoring inside-forward.

His first game was an Anglo-Scottish semi-final second leg at Ayr. Tony played along-side Peter Withe . . . and scored in a 2-0 win.

He stayed in the side for the rest of the season, scoring 11 goals in 30 League games as Forest surged to promotion.

Peter Robinson

TO BE WON!

30 COPIES OF THE NEW 'SOCCER—THE WORLD GAME' TO BE WON IN THIS WEEK'S COMPETITION

1. Who were the only team not to lose a match during the 1978 World Cup finals?

2. Which club was once demoted, rather than relegated, to the Fourth Division?

3. Two present Second Division managers have scored in a League Cup final. Terry Venables is one, but who is the other?

4. Since the war, only one FA Cup final has gone to a replay. Where, and who won?

Presse—Foto—Baumann

5. Before last season Brian Clough had only led one team to Wembley as manager. Name the club and their opponents?

6. RIGHT Leopoldo Luque volleys his second goal of the World Cup—against whom?

7. On which Mediterranean islands are Bastia of France and Cagliari of Italy based?

8. Everton's Gordon Lee and Brian Horton of Brighton were once together as manager and captain of the same club. Which club?

9. With which League of Ireland clubs did the following players begin their careers: Paddy Mulligan, Gerry Ryan, Paul McGee?

10. Which current Fourth Division club played in a Wembley final in 1973?

Ron Greenwood

'Football is a simple game made complex by all the talk of systems and numbers. But that's not to say you haven't got to work very hard at all the simple things.'

The man and his men . . . Ron Greenwood spreads the word at an England training session, passing on his belief that 'good habits'—started ideally at an early age—are the secret to success in football. It's not just a matter of having skills . . . it's knowing how to use them.

'Good habits' is the phrase England manager Ron Greenwood has given to the football vocabulary. But what exactly does he mean by it?

'I mean mastering the basics of control, then using them for the various selections you have to make in matches.

'Every time you receive a pass you have to decide whether to kill the ball, lay it off first time or—and this is not done nearly enough—simply let it go and follow it, really let the ball do the work!

'You don't need opposition to get into these habits, just the ball and the wall I've seen in *Football Handbook*.

'But when you've got both, think about your feet positions. Never receive the ball standing square. Always try to be sideways on because that way all the alternatives are open to you. If you're square you're closed in—you blinker yourself from what's happening on the pitch. Try it and see what I mean.

'It sounds easy but you have to work very hard to perfect something so simple. Ask any pro.'

Graeme Souness: the swerving pass

'I reckon to achieve about 90% accuracy with passes curled with the inside of the foot ... I rarely try to hit them with the outside of the foot because the success rate is more like 50%—and that's just not good enough.'

Much of the credit for the 'new' Liverpool—as committed as ever but with more variety in their play—must go to Graeme Souness.

The midfield man was worth every penny of the £350,000 Liverpool paid

Middlesbrough for him last season.

And one of the subtleties that has made Liverpool an even sharper proposition is the Souness 'bender', his swerving pass.

'I curl the ball with the

inside of my right foot,' says Graeme. 'I reckon to achieve about 90% accuracy with it.'

The swerving pass can be seen as the brother of the chip—which was demonstrated by Graeme's teammate Terry McDermott in Part 7 of *Handbook*.

As with the chip, the swerving pass is used to 'avoid' defenders. The chip goes over the top: the 'bender' goes round.

And the great thing about both skills is that they are easily disguised.

Not until the actual moment of impact is it certain what kind of kick is being used because the approach and techniques are very similar.

As you can see in the diagrams, Graeme's approach to the ball could be for a shot, a chip—almost anything. It's only when he makes contact that you can see his intentions.

'I lean away from the ball slightly,' says Graeme, 'and hit right through it to make sure it goes where I want.

'I strike the outside of the ball with the inside of the foot to make it curl.'

The real thing ... Graeme sends off one of his benders in a match for the 'new' goal-scoring Liverpool.

Peter Robinson

The approach to the ball is similar to most other kinds of kick and helps to disguise Graeme's intentions.

Just before impact you can see that Graeme is going to curl the ball by using the inside of his right foot.

'I lean away from the ball slightly,' says Graeme, 'but make sure I hit through it for the right distance.'

Away it goes . . . the pass, because it's curled, will 'bite' as it hits the ground and not run away from the receiver.

What about passes swerved with the outside of the foot, as used a lot by some of the top continental players?

'I rarely use it,' says Graeme. 'For me, it reduces the accuracy of the pass to, say, 50%.'

Another asset of the swerving is that—again like the chip—the ball will 'bite' as it hits the ground . . . which means the pass will rarely run away from the teammate who receives it.

It's not surprising that Graeme is keen on the skill.

Last season's BBC 'Goal of the Season' started from a swerving pass from the Souness right boot.

And the scorer—with a perfect left-foot volley against Manchester United at Anfield—was G. Souness.

From the side you can see how Graeme's body turns slightly to help the curl of the ball.

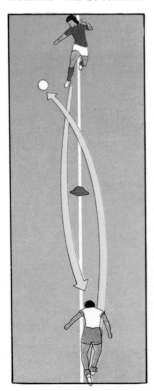

Graeme reckons he can achieve about 90% accuracy with the inside of his right foot.

He rarely uses the outside of his foot because the 50% accuracy 'just isn't good enough'.

A close up shows how Graeme hits the outside of the ball.

'It's important to hit through the ball to get distance,' says Graeme.

'And the natural spin on the ball will help keep it in play.'

'The swerving pass is a good one to practise because it also helps you get the "feel" of the ball,' says Graham Taylor. 'Two of you [*diagram, facing page*] can simply curl the ball across a straight line between you. Don't try to bend it miles—a good arc is all that's required.

This is one skill that's probably best to leave to your stronger foot because it's not that easy. Graeme rarely tries with the outside of the foot for the same reason—though many good players do. For an element of competition you can use posts [*right*] and score points for swerving the ball through the various "gates" —with higher points for the more difficult passes. All good practice and enjoyable, too.'

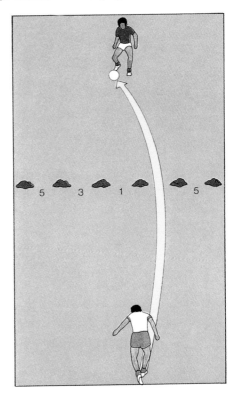

Balance in the follow through is essential.

Throwing

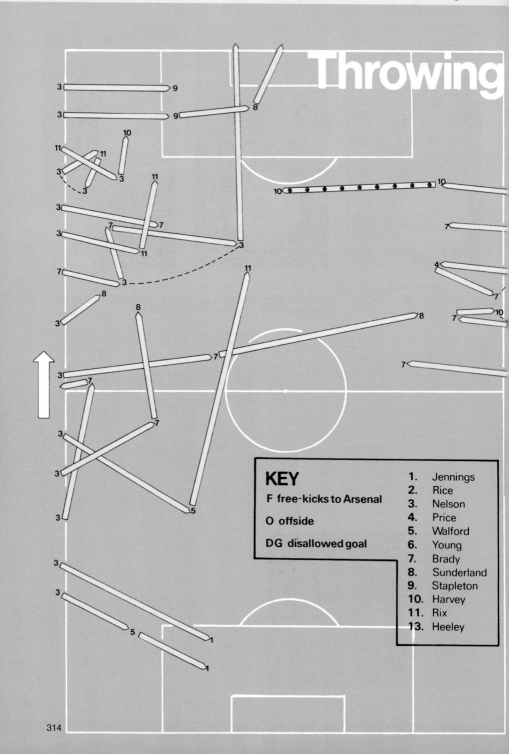

KEY

F free-kicks to Arsenal

O offside

DG disallowed goal

1. Jennings
2. Rice
3. Nelson
4. Price
5. Walford
6. Young
7. Brady
8. Sunderland
9. Stapleton
10. Harvey
11. Rix
13. Heeley

light on Arsenal's play

Many aspects of top-class football go unnoticed, and *Handbook* will be putting them under the microscope in **Match Point.**

We went to Arsenal's UEFA Cup game against Lokomotiv Leipzig just to study the throw-in.

Firstly, it showed that Arsenal are a very left-sided team (24 throws on the left, 7 on the right), with Liam Brady (7) always looking to get involved on that flank.

Sammy Nelson (3) takes

nearly all the throws and near goal he uses his long throw to find Frank Stapleton (9). One in the first half (*left*) led to a headed goal by Alan Sunderland (8) which was disallowed. Sunderland eventually scored in the second half (*below*)—in a move begun from a throw-in.

It also illustrates how throw-ins are generally 'wasted': 18 of the 31 broke down after two passes.

Manager Terry Neill found the diagram 'very

interesting. I'll discuss it with my players. We had Malcolm Macdonald missing that day, so we would have had an even greater bias.

'It shows clearly why I bought Alan Sunderland—to balance the side by having someone wide on the right.

'The lesson for my players, I think, is to keep their heads up for people making runs down the right. Otherwise we could get very predictable—especially with the teams who see your diagram!'

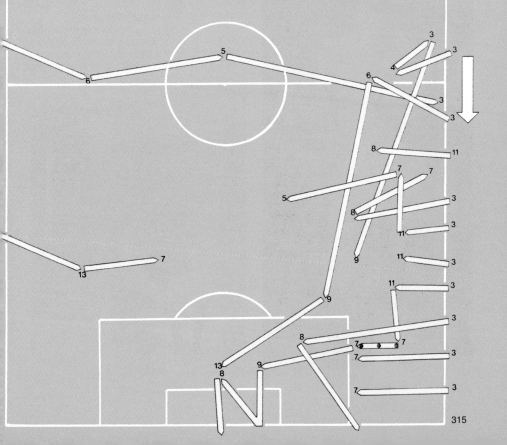

RISING VIV STAR ANDERSON

It'll surprise no one that Viv Anderson puts his success down to the well-known double act of Clough and Taylor.

But Forest's dashing black defender is at a loss to explain their secret.

'They just concentrate on getting the best out of every individual,' says Viv. 'If I could explain how they do it I'd probably be a football manager myself!

'When I first came across the boss he just told me to go out and enjoy myself and not be frightened of trying different things.'

Clough's blunt way was to tell Anderson he had the ability to be in the side: otherwise he wouldn't be there.

'The boss and Peter really work at building your confidence. There are times when you've had a bad game and wonder if you'll be dropped. At some clubs you would be, but here you get a fair crack of the whip.'

But a run of poor performances means the chop—'and that goes for the experienced players as well as the younger lads.'

At 22, Viv finds himself a regular in the side that won the First Division Championship and League Cup. And selection for the England Under-21 side last season was

'If I could explain how the boss and Peter Taylor do it I'd probably be a manager myself ... the boss just told me to go out and enjoy myself and not be frightened of trying things.'

further proof of his remarkable progress.

But, just as he has to keep on top of his game to keep Clough in clover, Viv knows he's got to keep getting better if he wants to make the full England side.

'There's still a lot for me to work on. Although I haven't done badly, I wasn't all that happy with my early season form.

'I'm always trying to improve my defensive game because that's the biggest part of my job, but I also want to make better use of the forward positions I often get into.

'There are lots of occasions when I hit the by-line, but it's not much good doing that if goals don't come from them.'

Heading used to be an Anderson weakness —'I used to be coming down when I should have been going up!'—but Bert Johnson, youth coach when Viv was an apprentice at Forest, helped him get his timing right.

'Bert was terrific. He did a lot to improve both Tony Woodcock and myself.'

Bob Thomas

ABOVE *Anderson surges past Coventry City's Alan Green on one of his attacking runs.*

LEFT *Attack and defence: on the overlap at Old Trafford ... and battling with new Spurs signing Ricardo Villa at the City Ground in the 1-1 draw in the first League game of the season.*

Viv's surging runs upfield helped to get him in the first team when he was only 18, then an injury kept him on the sidelines up to the time of Clough's arrival.

But he was soon back in the side and, in his own words: 'My career has just kept going up and up since then.'

Founded: 1927
Address: Recreation Ground, High St, Aldershot GU31 1TW
Ground: Capacity 20,000; Playing area 107 x 69.5 m
Record attendance: 19,138 v Carlisle United, FA Cup 4th round replay, 28.1.70
Record victory: 8-1 v Gateshead, Div. 4, 13.9.58
Record defeat: 0-9 v Bristol City, Div. 3 (S), 28.12.46
Most League points: 56, Div. 4, 1972-73
Most League goals: 83, Div. 4, 1963-64
League scoring record: 25, Jack Howarth, Div. 3, 1973-74
Record League aggregate: 172, Jack Howarth, 1965-71 & 1972-77
Most League appearances: 450, Len Walker, 1964-76
Most capped player: None
League career: 1932-58 Div. 3 (S); 1958-73 Div. 4; 1973-76 Div. 3; 1976- Div. 4

ALDERSHOT

One of the Football League's longest serving managers, Aldershot's Tommy McAnearney, strolled contentedly in the sunshine, joking and organising seating arrangements for a photo session.

The scene at the council-owned Recreation Ground, set in a public park, was a lively one, all light-hearted and

Aldershot action against Portsmouth in September's 2-0 home defeat by Portsmouth. The crowd was a respectable 8,967.

Praying for promotion
Aldershot are among the few League clubs with an official chaplain. 'I'm a servant to the staff and the players,' says the Rev. Mike Pusey. 'It doesn't win matches.'

Duncan Raban

laughter, and for the players a welcome respite from the punishment of sprints and 'doggies'.

Seven seasons in charge and looking natty in his new England-type Admiral kit, McAnearney faced a familiar routine. Only Alan Dicks at Bristol City, Bobby Robson at Ipswich and Jimmy Frizzell at Oldham have served longer.

For in the hazardous profession of football management, McAnearney can hold his head high. It hasn't been chopped off. And an understanding board of a financially sound little club had given him cash to spend on strengthening his squad further.

'There's a challenge here at Aldershot. Some think we're not concerned about our image but that's wrong. We've

Only 12 years after their formation Aldershot found they had an array of internationals in their wartime side. 'Guest' players stationed there included [1] Tommy Lawton and [2] Joe Mercer (both Everton & England), [3] Matt Busby (Manchester City and Scotland), [4] Frank Swift (Manchester City and later England) and [5] Stan Cullis (Wolves & England).

tried to put the promotions side on a much more professional basis and it's paid off.

'We're working on a new administration block and new dressing-rooms. We've added to the coaching staff, increased the squad and organised a small scouting network to attract youngsters. And we're not in the red, either!'

In the line up out on the park there was no Ardiles or Tarantini on show. But 'Mac' enthusiastically identified his new recruits—three of them snapped up on free transfers.

'I'll tell you something,' said Mac: 'they're the best crowd I've worked for.'

Outside, the Army presence is evident. Helicopters hover, jeeps and trucks convoy about and short-haired soldiers mingle with the shoppers in this garrison town.

It's against this unique regimented background that McAnearney, a knowledgeable and likeable Scot, together with his coach Dave Turner and loyal trainer, John Anderson, conducts the affairs of The Shots.

A solid squad includes an experienced goalkeeper in Glen Johnson, a skilful and reliable player in the all-rounder Murray Brodie and a real trump card in forward John Dungworth. He came on a 'free' in 1977, rattled in 23 goals and lifted the club's player of the year award.

Back in the cramped office under the stand Mac is still talking about football. 'I love the game. It's a way of life for me. And I'm happy here. It's a friendly club.'

Leaving the little office you may just catch a clue. On a laden shelf nearby, the reference books and annuals constantly reassure Tommy McAnearney that Aldershot always come first in the League—if only alphabetically!

Long-serving boss Tom McAnearney arrived at Aldershot as player-coach back in 1966. He soon left to be assistant manager of his old club, Sheffield Wednesday. After brief spells in charge at Bury and Crewe he took over at Aldershot in 1972.

Ups and downs
Aldershot have been promoted once in their 51-year history, when Tom McAnearney led them into Division 3 in 1973.

Unlike most small clubs, Aldershot can boast no giant-killing acts. Their best year in the FA Cup was 1933, when they reached the last 16, but they've never been past the second round of the League Cup.

Public property
Aldershot FC are hardly geared for the big-time. Their council-owned ground is situated in a public park, and has one landmark which captures the character of the club—a large 'trawler net' supported by scaffolding strung up behind the open-ended goal. This insures that preciously donated match-balls don't end up in the High Street.

Duncan Raban

Joe Jopling is in his second spell with Aldershot. 'It's a friendly club players like to come back to,' he says.

PRO FILE
LIAM BRADY

'That left foot . . . he can do almost anything with it . . . and his right's not just for standing on. He's got superb control, his vision's excellent and he keeps hitting those long, accurate first-time passes—and great shots.' RAY CLEMENCE

Liam had his moments in the Cup final, though he went off with a leg injury . . . Here he keeps control and balance despite a challenge from Ipswich's surprise star David Geddis during a game Arsenal were expected to win.

England's toughest opponents in their European Championship qualifying round might well turn out to be the Republic of Ireland.

The Irishmen have an astute, ambitious, young manager in Johnny Giles and a team brimming with skill and experience. Two years ago they gained a well-merited 1-1 draw with England at Wembley.

And they have in Arsenal's Liam Brady one of the best midfielders in Europe.

That claim—for a young man who has yet to establish any kind of reputation on the Continent—is not as wildly extravagant as it might seem. Of the players of his type seen in the World Cup finals, for instance, Germany's Rainer Bonhof and Italy's Giancarlo Antognoni both disappointed. Perhaps only Poland's Deyna or France's Platini could honestly keep him out of a European XI.

Brady has the deadly accurate pass, the vision and the deft change of pace of a great player. All he lacks is the experience.

Yet in his brief career he has already gained 16 caps for Eire.

'It was an enormous thrill to play for my country,' Brady recalls. 'My first cap was a great occasion. It was against Russia in the previous European Championship back in October 1974. Don Givens scored a hat-trick

and we won convincingly 3-0.'

For Eire, Brady has come under the expert eye of Johnny Giles, himself one of the finest midfield players of modern times.

'Giles has taught me an awful lot by his example on the field and in talks before and after matches,' explains Liam. 'We've talked over things like positional play, releasing the ball at the right moment and covering counter-attacks by opponents.

'Training is always so enjoyable with him. He makes you want to do things you didn't even know about. You don't get the same feeling at club level, where training is more like a job, a daily routine.

'My style has often been compared with his . . . I admire his play tremendously, but I haven't modelled myself on him.'

At Arsenal there was the experience of playing alongside another seasoned international. When Brady first broke into the Arsenal first team five years ago his midfield partner was that outspoken perfectionist, Alan Ball.

'Chippy' made his debut against Birmingham City, coming on as substitute for the injured Jeff Blockley. In that first season his name appeared on the scoring lists twice—once for his own club against QPR . . . and

Honours: FA Cup runners-up medal 1978

Club	Div	Pos	Season	League Ms	League Gs	FA Cup Ms	FA Cup Gs	Lge Cup Ms	Lge Cup Gs	Int'nls Ms	Int'nls Gs
Arsenal	I	10	1973-74	13	1	1	–	–	–	–	–
	I	16	1974-75	32	3	5	–	2	1	5	–
	I	17	1975-76	42	5	1	–	1	–	3	1
	I	8	1976-77	38	5	3	–	6	–	6	1
	I	5	1977-78	39	9	5	–	6	4	2	–
				164	23	15	–	15	5	16	2

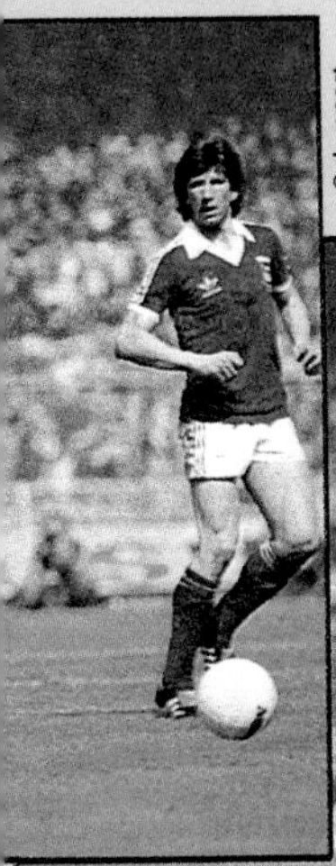

Colorsport

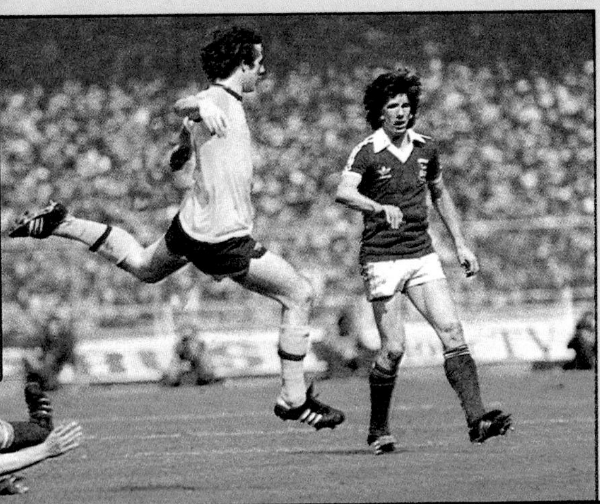

Colorsport

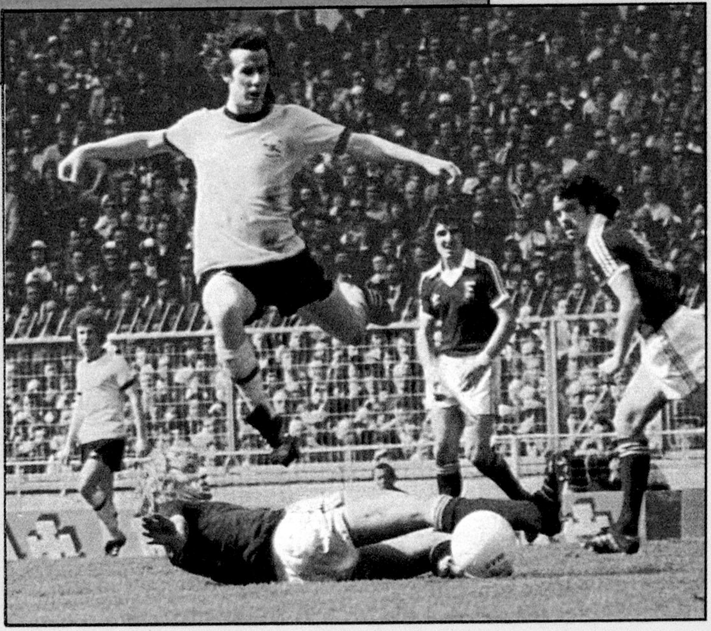

Owen Barnes

once for the opposition. Burnley was the club that benefitted from a Brady own goal.

Liam has since improved his goal total yearly. In the first League game of this season he hit two against Leeds, one from the penalty spot and the other a cunningly disguised shot from the edge of the area.

Said Arsenal coach Don Howe: 'Chippy's started with two goals and I want a lot more from him. I'll expect double figures . . . without counting penalties.'

Brady immediately obliged—with further goals against QPR and Forest.

'I've never been what you might call a defensive midfielder,' says Brady in a frank assessment of his game. 'Don Howe and Terry Neill are always getting on to me to drop back and help out in defence . . . and I think they're right.

'But I like going forward. I'm prepared to take people on anywhere, especially in the last quarter of the field.'

Brady's connection with Arsenal actually goes back more than nine years—to when he

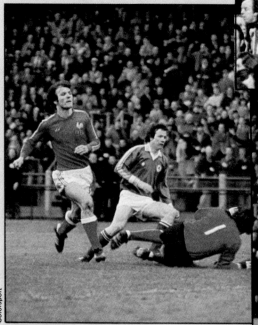

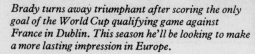

Brady turns away triumphant after scoring the only goal of the World Cup qualifying game against France in Dublin. This season he'll be looking to make a more lasting impression in Europe.

LEFT *Heresy at Wembley, 1978.*
ABOVE *Control at Highbury on a happier occasion against Bolton.*

Duncan Raban

was a 13-year-old. He'd been spotted by a scout called Melvyn Roberts, who fixed him up with a trial at Highbury during the summer holidays.

It wasn't quite a journey into the unknown for the Dublin schoolkid. Two elder brothers, Pat and Ray, had both settled in London after playing careers with QPR and Millwall.

Liam eventually signed for Arsenal as an apprentice two years later. Two other Highbury imports, David O'Leary and Frank Stapleton, followed soon after. All three are from the Whitehall district of North Dublin.

'I joined as a 15-year-old in July 1971,' Liam recalls, 'only two months after Arsenal had clinched the League and Cup double.

'Since then we've won nothing . . . a long time for a club like Arsenal. We've not even had success in the Youth Cup, though we twice reached the semi-finals when I was in the team.'

Since then, of course, Arsenal have had the major disappointment of losing a Cup

final they were hot favourites to win.

It isn't a match Brady cares to remember. He was limping from early on in the game and was substituted by Graham Rix. Said his midfielder partner Alan Hudson after the game: 'We didn't shout about it, but we had men out there who weren't strong enough to play in a Cup final after injury. The whole business was a nightmare.'

At least Arsenal gained the consolation of a UEFA Cup place—their first venture into Europe since their European Cup quarter-final in 1971-72.

It will be Liam's first European club tournament—another opportunity to impress the continentals with his ability.

But his best chance may turn out to be the European Championships. If Eire can put out their powerful neighbours and fellow countrymen—plus Denmark and Bulgaria—then Europe will have to sit up and take note of names like Gerry Daly and David O'Leary.

And especially one **Liam Brady.**

325

Two-touch play:
Martin Dobson

'When I first went to Everton it was all long balls and I felt like the net in a game of tennis. Now we're knocking it about, keeping possession—and playing real football.'

'Get it, give it and go' has always been one of the simplest—and best—pieces of advice to anyone who wants to play football well.

Because if you're doing just that—getting the ball, giving it and taking up a fresh position—you're half-way towards having a fine match.

And if you want a good example of such a player in the First Division, look no further than Everton's Martin Dobson.

The whole of Martin's role is based on this kind of two-touch play.

'It's especially important for midfield players,' says Martin, 'but you can do it all over the pitch.

'What you're doing, if you think about it, is playing in lots of triangles. If you turn with the ball in midfield, play it forward to a front man and go to support him, you've created a triangle.'

The point about giving and going, he says, is that the pass forward must be a good one—'not too hard but not slow and bobbling, either.

'This kind of play means that everyone sees more of the ball and the confidence spreads through the side.

'Also, it makes it easier if you want to take on someone when you've got alternatives. The defender knows it, too, so you've got the initiative.'

Martin says the way for youngsters to appreciate this kind of play is in lots of three-, four- or five-a-side practice matches.

'Play in a small area and use the two-touch rule—so that no one hogs the ball!'

About to give and go . . . Martin Dobson in action for Everton against Manchester United in September.

'There's an old saying in football that you make the ball do the work,' says Graham Taylor, 'and this diagram shows how Martin does exactly that.

He receives the ball from a team-mate, controls it, plays it forward and goes looking for the return—then he's looking to do the same thing further forward. If you do it as well as Martin does, you'll take defenders out of the game—it's much easier to play the ball and run past them than it is to dribble past them.

And the beauty of it is that if you've knocked the ball past a defender a few times, he's likely to start anticipating the pass and you can then take the ball past him. It's the old rule of giving yourself alternatives.'

DOBSON 1

Ray Green

'This kind of two-touch play is best practised by three players,' says Graham. 'The first player (X in the diagram) plays the ball to the second (Y), who returns it as X comes up in support. X then finds the third player (Z), who makes a run behind Y's back. It may look a little complicated but you should soon get the hang of it.

Just remember these things: when you get the ball, give it and go looking for the return, then find the third player. For example, when Z passes to Y in the diagram, he follows the pass, gets the ball back and gives it to X, who makes a run behind Y. Give yourselves plenty of room and speed it up only as you improve. You soon will if you keep at it.'

Whistle Test

'There's only one change I'd like to make in the laws: I really don't see why you should be in danger of being ruled off-side from a free-kick.'

Jack Taylor doesn't think there's much wrong with the rules of the game as they are. Calls for bigger goals, the abolition of the indirect free-kick and the North American experiment with the off-side law all leave him unmoved.

'The whole framework of the laws is very, very good,' claims Jack, who still referees regularly in the Belgian League. 'There's only one thing I've ever advocated—the only change in the laws I'd like to see—and it's got as far as the FIFA International Board for review . . .

'I've never felt it right and just that a player can be off-side from a free-kick.

'You can't be off-side from a drop ball, a throw-in, a corner or a goal-kick; so why from a free-kick?

'Of course the goalkeeper would often be crowded, but you've always had this at corners anyway.

'And if you did away with that then the traditional wall of defenders that forms up at free-kicks—a thing which has given referees so many problems—wouldn't be much good. Attacking teams could simply put as many players as they liked behind the wall.'

Jack knocks the Yanks

Talk of changes in the laws naturally led us to ask Jack what he thought of soccer in the United States . . . and the answer is: not a lot.

'I think football's a joke,' said Jack. 'To say their soccer is the football of the future is ludicrous. You've got to see football in the black townships of South Africa or in Rio before you can talk about the football of the future. That's what it's all about.

'I read a lot about American soccer and I still can't name five top American players.'

A Matter of Fact

Presse—Foto—Baumann

Bobby Charlton may be joining Spurs! But this particular Charlton is not the one who became a legend with Manchester United and England: he's a 17-year old striker from the North-East who's been recommended to Tottenham boss Keith Burkinshaw.

Swansea's exciting young striker Jeremy Charles comes from a great Welsh soccer family. Dad is ex-Arsenal star Mel Charles, while uncle John became a favourite with crowds all over Europe after leaving Leeds for Juventus in August 1957.

LEFT The man getting an uncomfortable close-up of Austrian striker Willy Kreuz's boot during a World Cup clash in Argentina is West Germany's Bernd Holzenbein. The word 'Holzenbein', incidentally, means 'wooden leg' in German!

Keeping tradition

There must be something in the water in Chesterfield that helps to produce top-class goalkeepers. Gordon Banks began his career there before moving on to glory with Leicester, Stoke and England. Arsenal double-winning hero Bob Wilson was born in the town, although he went on to represent Scotland. That great character John Osborne (right) started at Saltergate; now, having been freed by West Bromwich, he's a member of Shamrock Rovers' squad in the European Cup Winners' Cup. Burnley's Alan Stevenson also learned his trade there, going on to win 11 England Under-23 caps. The latest discoveries from the Chesterfield goldmine are Steve Hardwick and Steve Ogrizovic, sold to Newcastle and Liverpool respectively. Manager Arthur Cox now reckons he's found another gem in giant Welshman Glan Letheran, signed last season from Leeds for £10,000 and now attracting six-figure offers. When Glan left Elland Road his place was quickly filled by John Lukic . . . from Chesterfield!

Sheffield Wednesday drew 4-4 with Manchester United in December 1974, but hit only 5 more goals in the next 21 games, and plunged into Division 3.

In 1946 Newcastle beat Newport 13-0 in a Second Division game. Only a penalty miss prevented the Magpies from bettering the League record, established when Stockport beat Halifax by the same score in 1934.

Keegan headers put

Sporting Pictures UK

The Trevor Brooking-Kevin Keegan production line was in full flight against Denmark at Copenhagen in September.

The first two goals in England's 4-3 win came from Keegan. Both were headers, both were from Brooking free-kicks.

The first, from the right, was a curling ball to the near

One up . . . Jensen is beaten as Keegan loses his markers to convert Brooking's free-kick.

KEEGAN

10

BROOKING

England on course

post; Keegan's speed off the mark and finishing did the rest.

The second, from the left, had Dave Watson out-jumping the Danish defence to head across for Keegan to score with a diving header.

'With players like these,' said European Footballer of the Year Allan Simonsen after the game, 'England are playing the kind of football that wins prizes—even the biggest prize of all.'

Graham Taylor's analysis

'Kevin must be the best tonic in the world to those youngsters who want to be strikers. At only 5' 8" he heads goals from every angle.

They're a great combination, these two—Brooking's beautiful free-kicks and, in both cases, Keegan beating close marking by several defenders.'

Two-up ... Congratulations for Kevin after diving to head home Watson's headed pass.

Sporting Pictures UK

Founded: 1882
Address: St James' Park, Newcastle-upon-Tyne NE1 4ST
Ground: Capacity 54,000; Playing area 105.2 x 68.6 m
Record attendance: 68,386 v Chelsea, Div. 1, 3.9.30
Record victory: 13-0 v Newport County, Div. 2, 5.10.46
Record defeat: 0-9 v Burton Wanderers, Div. 2, 15.4.1895
Most League points: 57, Div. 2, 1964-65
Most League goals: 98, Div. 1, 1951-52
League scoring record: 36, Hughie Gallacher, Div. 1, 1926-27
Record League aggregate: 178, Jackie Milburn, 1946-57
Most League appearances: 432, Jim Lawrence, 1904-22
Most capped player: 40, Alf McMichael, Northern Ireland, 1950-60
League career: 1893-98 Div. 2; 1898-1934 Div. 1; 1934-48 Div 2;
1948-61 Div. 1; 1961-65 Div 2; 1965-78 Div. 1; 1978- Div. 2
Honours: Football League Champions 1905, 1907, 1909, 1927; Div. 2
Champions 1965; FA Cup Winners 1910, 1924, 1932, 1951, 1952, 1955,
Runners-up 1905, 1906, 1908, 1911, 1974; Fairs Cup Winners 1969;
League Cup runners-up 1976; Texaco Cup Winners 1973, 1974

NEWCASTLE UNITED

If Newcastle United don't have a side capable of winning promotion back into the First Division, it isn't as a result of lack of effort by manager Bill McGarry.

The former Wolves boss has dealt frantically in the transfer market in an attempt to find the right blend of players—players prepared for a promotion fight.

So many players changed hands that fans of the famous Magpies were having difficulty sorting out which faces were which. The first team used 35 different players last season: and then only five of them played in the club's first ever League visit to Cambridge early this season. Most of the others have gone: there have been 16 transfer deals of £50,000 or more in the nine months to the end of September.

Naturally enough, McGarry has not pleased all the fans with his buying and selling. Some have dubbed his new side

Magpies Cup hoard

Only Aston Villa have won the FA Cup more often than Newcastle, who have six wins to their credit. Of the five finals they played at the old Crystal Palace ground (*not* Selhurst Park), they failed to win one, while up to 1974 they never lost an FA Cup final at Wembley. Their Crystal Palace games all fell in a seven-year spell from 1905 to 1911, in which they lost three times (to Villa in 1905, Everton in 1906 and Wolves in 1908) and drew twice, losing one replay (to Bradford City at Old Trafford in 1911) and winning one (against Barnsley at Goodison Park in 1910). They won their next five finals, which were all at Wembley—including three triumphs in five years in the 1950s—before coming up against Liverpool in the 1974 final . . . when they fell apart in the second half against the Keegan-inspired Reds and lost 3-0 —and their great record.

Ray Green

Micky Burns (now Boro'), last season's top scorer with 16 goals but one of the many players Bill McGarry has recently sold, up against Manchester United.

Colorsport

Associated Press

a 'Dad's Army', who, even if they do blend together successfully and win promotion, wouldn't survive in the First Division.

McGarry is upset by claims he has invested in a bunch of ageing players. He told *Handbook:* 'I don't know why people say we wouldn't be able to play in the First Division. Most of my players have got First Division experience.

'I've got a better squad than when I took over last November. If we can win promotion there's every reason to believe we can do well again at the top.'

McGarry started his spree shortly after joining the club, when Newcastle were a struggling First Division side and among the favourites for relegation.

Just after Christmas he completed a double deal with Scottish clubs, investing £150,000 in Morton's Mark McGhee and £100,000 in Clydebank's Mike Larnach. He immediately balanced the books by selling former skipper Tommy Craig to Aston Villa for £275,000.

By the end of the season, Alan Gowling had joined Bolton for £120,000, Dennis Martin had moved to Mansfield for £40,000 and Carlisle came in for David

TOP *In the early 1950s Newcastle won the Cup three times and went close in the League. The 1955 Cup winning side* (above) *beat Manchester City, handicapped by injury to Jim Meadows, 3-1.* Left to right, back row: *Bob Cowell, Bob Stokoe, Ronnie Simpson, Ron Batty, Tommy Casey.* Front: *Bob Mitchell, George Hannah, Vic Keeble, Jimmy Scoular, Jackie Milburn.* Insert: *Reg Davies (who did not play).* ABOVE *Jackie Milburn (pictured scoring against Arsenal in a League match in November 1953) scored both goals in the 1951 FA Cup final and added another in 1955.*

McLean at a rock-bottom £10,000.

During the close season McGarry swapped winger Stewart Barrowclough for Birmingham's John Connolly and Terry Hibbitt in a deal valued at £150,000, with Hibbitt, in his second stint at St James' Park, being made captain. Jim Pearson was signed from Everton for £80,000 and Colin Suggett from Norwich for £60,000.

Meanwhile, McGarry was also off-loading. He sold Alan Kennedy to Liverpool (£300,000), Geoff Nulty to Everton (£80,000), Micky Burns to Cardiff (£70,000), Aidan McCaffery to Derby (£60,000) and one of his first buys—Larnach—to Motherwell for £80,000 after an eight-month stay which failed to produce a first-team goal. Paul Cannell, Graham Oates and Ray Hudson were transferred to American clubs.

Then came McGarry's biggest buy. Peter Withe, centre-forward with all-conquering League Champions Nottingham Forest, agreed to step down a division in a £200,000 deal.

'I wouldn't have come unless I didn't believe Newcastle were going straight up again,' he claimed.

McGarry followed up by signing his first defender, despatching Ralph Callachan and £40,000 to Hibernian for international right-back John Brownlie.

'Money is available,' McGarry explained to *Handbook*. 'At the moment I'm concentrating on finding a top-class midfield player. But that doesn't mean I'll stop there. If the right men become available, I'll show interest . . . You can never get enough good players.

'There's no way of knowing when the right men will come on the market. I tried all summer to sign players—without success—and then suddenly, at the start of the season, I was

Howay the lads . . . Newcastle fans set a League record when an average of 56,351 turned up to home games in 1947-48, a season when United gained promotion. Could they cheer them up again in 1978-79?

Ray Green

Bill Shankly and Joe Harvey lead their teams out at Wembley in 1974. Harvey led the club to successes in the Fairs, Texaco and Anglo-Italian Cups . . . but his one FA Cup final ended in a 3-0 defeat against Liverpool. Harvey became general manager in 1976.

Malcolm Macdonald came for a record £180,000, went for a record £333,333. In between: 95 goals in 187 League games.

Magpies over Europe
Newcastle's first venture into Europe was their most successful: they won the old Fairs Cup in 1969. They qualified by finishing 10th in the League the previous season—thanks to the old one club-one city rule—and then won through on away goals against Real Zaragoza, survived a pitch invasion by Rangers fans in the semi-finals, and beat Ujpest Dozsa 6-2 on aggregate in the final, with the help of three goals by defender Bobby Moncur.

They played in the next two Fairs Cup campaigns, but didn't qualify again until last season, when two second leg goals from Dutch star Johnny Rep, playing for the Corsican club Bastia, sunk them at home after they'd beaten Bohemians in round one.

Peter Robinson

Wembley 1974 . . . Clark, Howard, Moncur and Tudor against Liverpool's Toshack.

Ray Green

335

St James' Park is Council owned . . . In the past that has caused talk of moves to Gosforth, but the new stand implies permanent residence.

Already out of date: the early season line-up. Left to right, back row: *Ralph Callachan (now Hibs), Mike Barker, Andy Parkinson, Mick Mahoney, John Bird, Kevin Carr, David Barker, John Blackley, John Connolly.* Middle: *Alan Kennedy (now Liverpool), Ken Mitchell, Mark McGhee, Tommy Cassidy, Bill McGarry, Mike Larnach (now Motherwell), Irving Nattrass, Peter Kelly, Terry Hibbitt, Peter Morris (coach).* Front: *Alan Guy, Nigel Walker, Jaime Scott, Ray Blackall (now S. Wed.).*

able to conclude several satisfying deals.'

The changes have at least revived interest in the club on Tyneside—early season home gates were above 20,000.

But they haven't stopped the criticism of the way the club is run. Newcastle United have one of the largest and most passionate sets of supporters in the world. Their loyalty to a team that has mounted all too rare challenges for major honours since the 1950s has produced good profits for the club—profits which have too often been squandered.

In an unprecedented move, the Newcastle Supporters Association is taking the club to the high courts. United's directors, including president of the Football League Lord Westwood, face accusations of 'ill-administration'.

Said Malcolm Dix, head of the association: 'We've been forced to do things this way to achieve our aim of making the club a success.'

The association have launched a 'Stay with Newcastle' campaign . . . and they've started up their own newspaper—'The Supporter'.

The directors have remained united in the face of repeated attempts to get businessman Dix a place on the board. And the majority of the shareholders support them.

Whether or not they can hold on to that support depends mainly on the success of one **Bill McGarry.**

Alfie Conn

'Other people seemed more concerned about me joining Celtic than I was. I'm a professional paid to do a job, not someone who went over to the other side.'

These are the words of Celtic midfield star Alfie Conn, whose transfer from Spurs to Celtic in March last year rekindled a bonfire of controversy in Scottish football.

It was only natural that fans should find Conn's decision to sign for Celtic such a surprising one. He is only the third player to play for both Old Firm clubs.

'Perhaps I was a shade apprehensive when I played against Rangers for the first time,' Alfie admitted to *Handbook*. 'Obviously, certain players tend to be singled out for extra stick, but that happens all the time. I expected a few boos on my first appearance for Celtic against Rangers . . . and I wasn't disappointed.'

Conn has had a lot more to worry about than the reaction of Rangers fans. Injuries of one sort or another have plagued him for the past year or so, limiting his first team appearances. Alfie's toughest break came last season when he was laid up for a long time with a knee injury that threatened to end his career.

Now that has been overcome he says: 'You've got to accept the knocks, put them out of your mind completely . . . If you start worrying about what might happen there's no point in being involved.'

An Old Firm clash from the other side . . . Alfie Conn gets in a shot for Celtic against Rangers in the 1977 Scottish Cup final . . . Celtic won 1-0 to complete a League and Cup double.

337

Neil Whatmore on shielding the ball

Ray Green

Bolton forward Neil Whatmore ... 'football's so fast these days that you shield the ball to give you a breathing space.'

'The difference in the First Division is that everything is so much sharper ... if you give the ball away you can't expect to get it back quickly.'

Shielding the ball—'screening it'—used to be seen as very much a Continental skill.

Some people even thought it was unfair, that 'the foreigners' weren't brave enough to face a tackle.

But, fortunately, that point of view is buried in the past and now the skill is used at all levels of the game in this country.

One player who sees it as a vital skill is Bolton forward Neil Whatmore.

'Football's so fast these days that you need something that will give you a breathing space,' says Neil, 'and often the answer is to shield the ball.'

Neil has played both in midfield and up front.

He says: 'When you receive the ball in midfield you

Neil, seen here under pressure from Bolton team-mate Peter Nicholson, uses a 'flapping arm' behind him to feel for defenders.

Once he's got the ball under control he tries to get as much of his body and as much distance between himself and the defender as he can.

can usually lay it off first time to someone. But up front you're more likely to find yourself isolated without any easy options.

'Also, playing up front you're likely to receive balls that are more difficult to control—like chipped passes —and the need to shield the ball and gain time is obvious in those kind of situations.'

Defenders, of course, are expecting forwards to shield more and try even harder to get to the ball first.

Neil says: 'The danger for forwards under pressure is that you'll rush to meet the ball and lose control—trip over it or do something hasty.

'It's best to keep reasonably calm and approach the ball not too fast—or too slow —and just make it difficult for the defender to get at the ball.

In close up you can see how Neil transfers the ball to the outside of his left foot to make it as difficult as possible for the defender to get at it . . . keeping the ball as far away from the defender as possible.

Ray Green

'They're not supposed to tackle from behind,' says Neil, 'but a quick touch between the legs is O.K . . . and no defender is going to waste that opportunity.

'So I try to get the ball on the outside of the foot with my body sideways on, which makes it virtually impossible for the ball to be nicked.'

Ray Green

Here you can see how Neil can 'turn' a defender . . .

If the defender commits himself on one side . . .

A sharp turn and Neil is heading for goal!

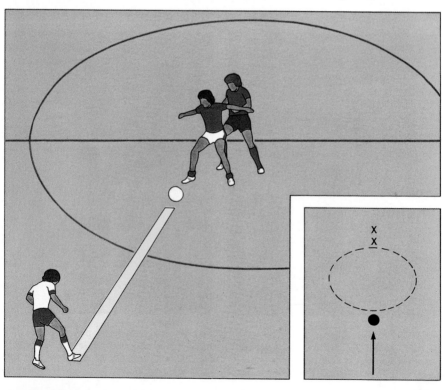

These three pictures show how you can shield the ball 'side-on' to win time for a team-mate to come up in support. Neil holds the ball and keeps Peter at bay until it's time to lay it off and go looking for space behind the defender.

'You have one obvious advantage as a forward: the defender has to keep goalside or he's asking for trouble, and you should get to the ball first.

'What I do is use a "flapping" arm behind me, which feels for the defender without breaking the laws. Normally there'll be no one so close that you're unable to control the ball and shield it.

'Once you've controlled the ball, the defender will get close and try to pressurise you into making a mistake.

'That's when you've got to keep calm and look up for support, not knock the ball hastily and hope it does to a team-mate.'

'The best practice for shielding the ball is simply to play the ball to someone marked in a confined space—say, the centre circle,' says Graham Taylor. 'It's important for the receiver to get his body in line with the ball so that it can't be nicked. We say the ball should "stick" in the space in front of the receiver. Try and shield the ball for about 30 seconds—just for the practice. If the marker commits himself, then turn him and shield in another part of the circle. Another thing: the server should give the receiver plenty of awkward balls—bouncing or spinning—because that's how it often happens in a match and that's when the shielding skill is most needed.'

A Matter of Fact

Craig Johnston was born in Johannesburg, South Africa, played his early soccer in Newcastle, New South Wales in Australia and now turns out in the First Division for Middlesbrough. But 12 years ago Craig suffered from a rare bone disease and only a top American specialist saved his leg from amputation.

RIGHT *Sounding out a warning to defences for the 1990 World Cup . . . that's Edson Arantes do Nascimento junior, son of the immortal Pele.*

Scotland boss Jock Stein's early playing career took in a spell at centre-half with Welsh League club Llanelli.

It hasn't always been one-way traffic between England and South America. In 1950 Stoke City's Neil Franklin, the lynchpin of England's World Cup hopes, joined Santa Fe of Colombia. Within two months he returned disillusioned, but never played for his country again. He now runs a pub in the Potteries, and still plays in a local league.

The first match ever to be played on a full-size pitch completely under cover was between Real Madrid and West Ham. A crowd of 33,351 in the Houston Astrodome in Texas saw the Spanish side win 3-2 in April 1967.

Willie Johnston 'banned' his wife from watching him when he was with Rangers. In over 200 games she saw only one—the Cup Winners' Cup final triumph in 1972. 'I didn't think it was right for a girl to hear her husband being shouted and sworn at,' the Albion winger says, 'but now she watches me every week.'

Bob Thomas

Celtic have appeared in 14 successive Scottish League Cup finals since 1964-65, when Rangers defeated them 2-1. They took the trophy on each of their next five trips to Hampden Park, but since then have managed just one victory—a 6-3 win over Hibernian in 1974-75—in their last eight finals.

Ever hear the one about the referee who was suspended? John Yates of Redditch was banned for three matches for allowing a newspaper to photograph his note-book after he'd booked several Chelsea players at Everton on 26 October 1974.

On 12 October 1957 Tony McNamara played his last game for Everton in the First Division. Within 11 months he'd played for Liverpool in the Second, Bury in the Third and Crewe Alexandra in the Fourth.

342

Founded: 1876
Address: Vale Park, Hamil Road, Burslem, Stoke-on-Trent
Ground: Capacity 35,000; Playing area 106 x 69.5 m
Record attendance: 50,000 v Villa, FA Cup 5th rd, 20.2.60
Record victory: 9-1 v Chesterfield, Div. 2, 24.9.32
Record defeat: 0-10 v Sheffield United, Div. 2, 10.12.1892 &
v Notts County, Div. 2, 26.2.1895
Most League points: 69, Div. 3(N), 1953-54
Most League goals: 110, Div. 4, 1958-59
League scoring record: 38, Wilf Kirkham, Div. 2, 1926-27
Record aggregate: 154, Wilf Kirkham, 1923-29 & 1931-33
Most League appearances: 761, Roy Sproson, 1950-72
Most capped player: 7, Sammy Morgan, N. Ireland, 1972-73
League career: 1892 Original members of Div. 2; failed to gain
re-election 1896; re-elected 1898, resigned 1907; returned Oct.
1919; 1929-30 Div. 3(N); 1930-36 Div. 2; 1936-38 Div. 3(N);
1938-52 Div. 3(S); 1952-54 Div. 3(N); 1954-57 Div. 2; 1957-
58 Div. 3(S); 1958-59 Div. 4; 1959-65 Div. 3; 1965-70 Div. 4;
1970-78 Div. 3; 1978- Div. 4

Port Vale

A crushing 3-0 home defeat by Colchester last April meant that Port Vale had to win their last game at Plymouth to send Malcolm Allison's team down to the Fourth Division in their place.

Vale scored inside two minutes, but Argyle eventually won 3-2 . . . and the Potteries club were relegated after a season of behind-the-scenes turmoil.

It had begun amid quiet optimism with former player Roy Sproson at the helm. But when early results went against the Valiants he lost his job.

Player-coach Colin Harper, the former Ipswich defender, took over on a caretaker basis before he too was dismissed in November.

Meanwhile, up at Bury, Bob Smith and his assistant Dennis Butler were also sacked . . . and within 24 hours they had moved in at Vale Park.

Smith recruited strikers Mick Moore from Wigan and John Froggatt from Colchester, and introduced a young winger with a famous name, Neville Chamberlain.

Froggatt made a sensational start with a goal after just 15 seconds against Exeter; and Chamberlain marked his home debut with an injury-time winner against Swindon.

For a while Vale looked capable of saving themselves.

But, a terrible run of six successive away defeats and a plague of home draws (11 in all) meant that the damage was done long before that nail-biting finale down at Plymouth.

In the summer Smith stunned the club's dwindling band of followers by accepting a lucrative offer to manage Swindon.

Into the hot seat stepped Butler, a former winger who played in all four divisions with Bolton and Rochdale—but who readily conceded that he was very much an unknown quantity in the managerial game.

Lowered to half-mast by a fan who shinned up the flagpole, the Vale flag tells its own sad story after that April defeat by Colchester.

Vale Park, the club's sixth home, was opened in 1950 when Vale moved north to Burslem from their Old Recreation Ground in Hanley. Its 50,000 capacity was only tested twice before ground improvements cut it to 35,000 last season—when the average was 3,946.

One-club man Roy Sproson served Vale for 27 years as player, coach and manager. Between 1950 and 1972 he made 761 League appearances and 83 in cup competitions, including the famous 1954 FA Cup semi-final. He was booked only twice.

Valeites see his appointment as an omen. In 1968 Vale were expelled from the League for making illegal payments to young players. and Sir Stanley Matthews quit as manager.

Although the club were immediately re-elected, nobody envied the little known coach from Shrewsbury who took the job.

His name was Gordon Lee. In 1969-70 he steered Port Vale into the Third Division. Soon his cheaply assembled squad, led by current Brighton skipper Brian Horton (a Walsall reject) and including Northern Ireland star Sammy Morgan (picked up from non-League Gorleston) were pushing for Second Division status.

It wasn't to be. Lee finally moved on to Blackburn on a path which eventually led him to Everton. And while Vale flickered briefly to life in 1976-77 with a splendid run in the FA Cup, the old will-to-win was a fading memory by the time Dennis Butler took charge.

Like Lee, his first task was to restore his players' shattered confidence.

'The atmosphere was terrible when we took the drop,' he says. 'But we really didn't deserve to stay up.

'At least relegation has forced us to re-organise the way a League club *should* be organised . . . something that was badly needed at Vale.

'When I first came here I asked who did the scouting. We hadn't got one; now I've got two full-timers.

'We also have two fine player-coaches in Graham Hawkins from Blackburn Rovers and Alan Bloor, who gave Stoke such great service.'

Butler's philosophy is one of 'if they're good enough, they're old enough.' Teenagers like Chamberlain, centre-back Phil Sproson (Roy's nephew), midfielders Russell Bromage and Ged Stenson, along with 21-year old Ken Todd, form the nucleus of the new Port Vale.

Todd cost a record £37,000 from Wolves. Butler is sure it's money well spent: 'Ken is a class player—he ought to have been in Wolves' first team.'

The Vale boss underlined his ambitions by paying £15,000 for Bury defender Gerry Keenan, and £10,000 for striker Felix Healy from Finn Harps after he'd impressed in the Irish club's UEFA Cup games with Everton.

'We're not well off. But if a player leaves it won't be because we're scraping around for money. It'll be because they're not good enough or because they don't want to be part of the future we're building here.'

Top scorer Ken Beamish, a £12,000 Sproson signing, fell into the second category: he wasn't happy with Fourth Division soccer so Butler sold him to Bury for £35,000.

'We've had 20 years of relative failure here,' he points out. 'Pessimism has become a way of life. It's hard to ask our fans to be patient, but I honestly believe this club has a very bright future.'

Roy Sproson once complained that 'people still ask where Port Vale is.' If determination counts for anything, it won't be too long before Dennis Butler puts Stoke-on-Trent's 'other' club firmly on the soccer map.

Sammy Morgan, the Vale discovery who became an Irish international, takes on Bobby Moore.

Wembley beckons
In 1953-54 Vale won the Third Division (North) by 11 points. Among their FA Cup victims were the holders Blackpool, complete with Stanley Matthews—seen here firing in a shot which Vale's famous defence kept out. In the semi-final a 68,221 crowd saw Vale score first against First Division leaders West Bromwich at Villa Park. Wembley beckoned, but Albion netted twice in the last 24 minutes. The winner was a hotly disputed penalty, slotted home by centre-forward Ronnie Allen who, ironically, began his career with Port Vale.

Positional play:

Colorsport

'We complement each other. I usually attack the ball, while Alistair does most of the covering. If we both went for the same ball we'd be in trouble.' JOHN WILE

A nod is as good as a wink— or a shout—in one of football's long-lasting partnerships.

John Wile (*left*) and Alistair Robertson (*opposite page*) have played more than 250 times together at the heart of the West Bromwich Albion defence . . . and their

play is almost telepathic.

'We can tell what we're going to do just by glancing at each other,' says John. 'It's a great advantage—we know what we're doing but the opposition doesn't.

'It's useful when we want to play the off-side trap. By glancing, and not shouting,

Fotosports International

'That's my job' . . . John Wile takes responsibility for a high ball and beats Liverpool's Kenny Dalglish. Who's covering ? Centre-back partner Alistair Robertson.

centre-backs

Duncan Raban

we can move out without warning our opponents.'

The players complement each other neatly as well. It's usually down to John to attack the ball, while Alistair does most of the covering.

'Alistair picks up the pieces,' says John. 'If we both went for the ball we'd be in trouble—and the same if we both stood off.'

What target man does John prefer to play against?

'Well, they're all good players in the First Division and there are no easy games, but usually I like to be given the chance to compete for the ball—in the air or on the ground.'

John makes the point that midfield players, even attackers, can make his and Alistair's job a lot easier.

'If they are putting opponents under pressure it often means that we get easy balls to deal with—hurried crosses, for example. So defending is not only about defenders!'

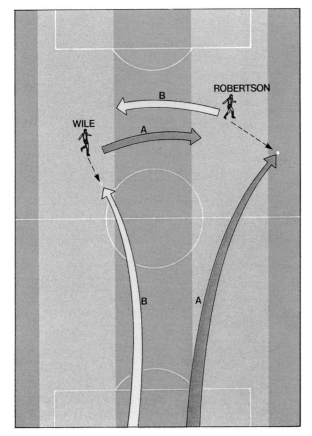

Our diagram shows the 'channels' that John and Alistair play in for Albion.

John is looking to attack the ball anywhere in his channel or in the centre of the pitch.

Alistair usually filters across to give John cover and generally 'pick up the pieces'.

These are the positions they take up from their opponents' goal-kicks and keeper's clearances—but every arrangement needs to be flexible and their's is no exception.

John says: 'If the opposing keeper kicks or throws down their right, it wouldn't make much sense for me to go right across to that side of the pitch if Alistair is already halfway there—so he'd be ready to compete and I'd do the covering.

Does this mean that other teams should try to attack Albion down the right as much as possible? 'In theory, I suppose they should. But it doesn't work like that. Teams play to all kinds of strengths and weaknesses . . . And this is just one.'

Bob Thomas

RISING GORDON STAR COWANS

A young Durham lad with matchstick legs is making life difficult for seasoned stars in Aston Villa's midfield.

Gordon Cowans, 19 and frail of frame, can thank injuries to others for his chance at Villa Park.

But the luck stops there. Cowan's talent and tenacity is real competition for the likes of Frank Carrodus, Alex Cropley, Dennis Mortimer and Tommy Craig.

Five into three won't go. Cowans might have been expected to wait his turn, but his form last season makes him a live candidate.

'I was on stand-by until Alex tragically broke his leg. Then when Tommy arrived I thought I'd have to stand down, but after four games he was out for a cartilage operation.'

And all the while young Cowans was playing brilliantly. His spindly legs, like dynamite, exploded at the ends. He tackled like the proverbial tiger. He was more than worth his place.

'When we got to Wembley for the League Cup final I was substitute, but in the replay

Looking for the action . . . but Gordon Cowans had to wait again after he broke a bone in his right foot against Forest on September 30.

we won at Old Trafford I played throughout. But even then I didn't think I'd be a regular by now.'

Cowans has respect for forwards and defenders but insists that 'midfield is really where it happens. If they have the ball I have to hustle and compete. And if we're pinned back I've got to be there helping out in the area.

'But if we've got it, it's a different story. It's my job to be available, make runs, create angles. In modern football, with only two forwards up, the midfield player has to get into good forward positions and always be on the look-out to score himself.'

That's Gordon's main responsibility in Villa's 4-4-2 set-up—and finding the net has not presented him with any great problems so far.

He got seven last season and really enjoyed one he got against Newcastle.

'There was a free-kick on the edge of the box. Dennis Mortimer touched the ball to me

Bob Thomas

348

'When we got to Wembley for the League Cup final I was substitute, but in the replay we won I played throughout. Even then I didn't realise I'd be a regular so soon.'

Honours: League Cup winners medal 1977

Club	Div	Pos	Season	League Ms	Gs	FA Cup Ms	Gs	Lge Cup Ms	Gs
Aston	I	16	1975-76	1	–	–	–	–	–
Villa	I	4	1976-77	18	3	3	–	5	–
	I	8	1977-78	35	7	1	–	2	–
				54	10	4	–	7	–

and I bent it into the top corner.'

Yet another stroke of luck for Cowans was his opportunity to play against Johan Cruyff when Villa met Barcelona in the UEFA Cup.

'He stood out a mile but, funnily enough, it wasn't something that bothered me. It's marvellous to have played against him.'

He also played when the two Argentinians made their home debut for Spurs. But they were humbled 4-1 and most observers put it down to the contribution of one player . . young Cowans.

Even Saunders, usually slow to praise, said: 'Gordon had a great game. In fact, this is the best I've seen him play.'

Not surprisingly, Saunders added: 'But he can do better.'

Someone else who had gone along mainly to marvel at Ardiles and Villa (Ricardo) was England manager Ron Greenwood. who pencilled Cowans in for his Under-21 squad.

That luck again!

The tigerish tackle . . . Cowans may have matchstick legs but that doesn't stop him taming that other tiger, Alan Ball.

TONIGHT'S ATTENDANCE: 74·901 SOCCER FEVER!

The big day for the ne

Peter Robinson

Bob Thomas

ER BOWL

American ball game...

New Jersey, August 25 ... the fans gather in the car park ... have a slap-up meal ... move inside Giants Stadium for the pre-match entertainment ...

'No way, Tampa Bay' said the sign . . . and the lady was right. Cosmos had little trouble holding on to their NASL title, winning 3-1 with two goals from Dennis Tueart and one from Giorgio Chinaglia. *Below* Giuseppe Wilson gets in a tackle on Peter Anderson, now back in England with Sheffield United.
Bottom Rowdies' Davie Robb (now with Norwich) missed the injured Rodney Marsh up front. Here he is thwarted by Cosmos Jack Brand and Werner Roth. *Right* A shot from Dennis Tueart (corner of picture) wraps it up at 3-1.
Bottom right Werner Roth receives the trophy from former FIFA president Sir Stanley Rous . . . but has very different company in the dressing-room.

Peter Robinson

Sporting Pictures

PETER WARD

'It doesn't matter who we're playing against—I still get clobbered all the time. And they hit you hard. The only way to get back at them is to play well or, even better, just score.'

Now and again 'Match of the Day' deserts the First Division for highlights of the action from football's 'lower reaches'.

Sometimes it's dreary but often it's a delight—and the producer who took his cameras to Hove on 18 September 1976 could hardly believe his luck.

Not only did the Third Division match produce the amazing scoreline of 7-2. It also made a star out of an unknown . . . a lad named Peter Ward.

One goal in Brighton's crushing of York City made Saturday night viewers take note for the chat in the pub at Sunday lunchtime . . . a goal scored by Ward.

Smoothly, effortlessly, Ward cut inside and danced past several defenders before slamming a right-foot shot high into the corner of the net.

It was clear to everyone that here was someone special—his control at speed, his ability to turn defenders and, above all, his precision finishing.

And there was expression in his play that made a mockery of the 'fear element' that had spread through every level of the game.

Yet there was a time when Ward himself was in danger of being a victim of the 'too small' syndrome.

'I got no encouragement at all at school,' says Peter. 'Just

I get clobbered every game,' says Brighton's star striker Peter Ward. And here's one time it was worth it—Ward wins a penalty from Blackpool last season.

before I left they came round asking everyone what they wanted to be.

'When I said a footballer they laughingly said, "Oh no, you're too small". I believed them and ended up in a factory as an apprentice fitter.'

His football was played in local parks until Burton Albion took his talent into the Premier Division of the Southern League. Little over a season later Brighton made the offer of full-time football.

'After knowing what it's like to clock in and out, I'd have signed for tuppence.'

A quiet start to his pro career might have been expected—certainly not the 36 goals he scored as Brighton scorched into the Second Division.

Almost inevitably the goals dried up a bit the following season and Brighton paid out over £200,000 for Teddy Maybank to take some of the load off Ward.

Success was not immediate.

Brave as well as skilful . . . Ward keeps close control despite the attentions of a defender who dwarfs him.

355

Ward says: 'I'd played alongside Ian Mellor for a season and a half and we'd built up an understanding. When they bought Ted to replace him we didn't start off too well. I was going through a bad patch and he was trying to justify his fee.

'But, all of a sudden, it just clicked, and we played really well together for four or five games. Then he was injured and had to have a cartilage operation.'

Brighton went straight back into the transfer market and Malcolm Poskett became Ward's next striking partner.

These upheavals did not help Peter's play and he finished the season with 17 goals — plenty for most players but well below the standard he had set himself.

Peter doesn't mind the pressure. 'I'm glad the fans expect more of me. It's a challenge when they want you to do something out of the ordinary.'

He accepts the stick he takes every week, too.

'It doesn't matter who we're playing—I still get

A sequence that shows it all . . . Ward on one of his long-striding, uninhibited runs between opponents: 'All I want to do is beat defenders until the goal is big enough to shoot at'.

A dog's best friend . . . Peter Ward with his pet Great Dane 'Sumi'.

Club	Div	Pos	Season	League		FA Cup		Lge Cup	
				Ms	Gs	Ms	Gs	Ms	Gs
Brighton	3	4	1975-76	8	6	—	—	—	—
	3	2	1976-77	46	32	3	1	7	3
	2	4	1977-78	39	14	2	1	5	2
				93	52	5	2	12	5

be too good. I'm always trying to improve, always sharpening up.'

After training you'll see him practising shots on the turn with an apprentice marking him.

Last season's lean spell helped in terms of attitude. 'It helped me get my head down a bit.'

All the Brighton heads went down a bit when Spurs pipped them for promotion on goal difference last season.

'When the whistle went at the end of our final match against Blackpool we thought we'd done it.'

But they hadn't. Disappointment was acute.

'I've never played in the First Division, so it's something I've got to do. It's no good looking back when I'm 35 and saying, Oh well, I was good, I made a bit of money.'

Amazing to think that Burton Albion got £4,500 for the player that Brighton manager Alan Mullery considers 'priceless'. Peter himself concedes: 'They'll make a profit if they sell me, won't they?'

clobbered all the time. They all hit you hard. The only way to get back at them is to play well or score.'

Peter remembers in detail the goals he scores, but he has no set plan for finding the net.

'I like the ball played to my chest or feet, in and around the box. It's pointless me trying to turn a defender on the half-way line—I can't shoot from there!

'I don't know what goes through my mind when the ball's coming to me. I'm just aware of the defence and the goal behind them. All I want to do is beat defenders until the goal is big enough to shoot at.'

Indefinable instinct gets him into scoring positions in crowded areas, but control counts just as much.

'I'm always working on my close control. You can never

Peter was one of the first to join football's 'perm set' last January. 'I was a bit self-conscious, sitting next to girls in my rollers,' says Peter, 'but nobody recognised me. My wife just laughed when she saw it.'

The goal that shattered

Every now and again a player bursts into the spotlight from nowhere—like Nottingham Forest's Gary Birtles.

Millions of viewers saw him destroy mighty Liverpool in the first round of the European Cup, scoring the first goal and playing a major part in the second goal in the 2-0 first leg victory.

No. 2 was the knock-out blow three minutes from the end. Full-back Colin Barrett's rebound sent the long-striding Birtles away on the left and he did well to skip over a tackle from Phil Thompson.

From there it was the pro's route to the by-line and the deep pull-back beyond the keeper.

Woodcock was where he was supposed to be but, with Alan Kennedy in the way to goal, he decided to head-pass to someone in a better position—Barrett!

The full-back had run half the length of the pitch. And he got his reward, a ball perfectly teed-up to smash on the volley past Ray Clemence.

The two goals, despite Brian Clough's much-publicised doubts, were enough to knock out the double European champions.

Birtles? Clough's reaction to the display by the 22-year-old he bought for £2,000 was typically dry.

He said: 'Birtles did well. Two years ago he was laying tiles, and if he doesn't score again on Saturday he could be back there.'

He didn't ... but got three in the following three weeks.

Birtles in full stride ...

Woodcock, coolness itself ..

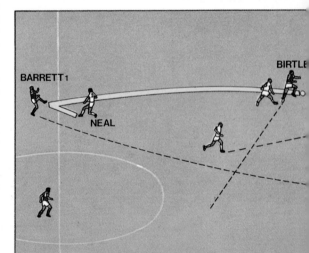

Graham Taylor's analysis
Normally you'd say that the contributions from Barrett and Woodcock were crucial—and of course they were. But I can't help concentrating on the things Birtles did.

Here he was, slung in to face Liverpool on a giant occasion, and he plays with all the confidence we've come to expect from Forest. Okay, he scored from an open goal —but they can be fluffed, especially in a match like that, and Birtles' overall

performance was really impressive. Not many players leave Phil Thompson for dead, but Birtles did—and at a time when a reserve could have been feeling the pace and the pressure.

Some people said he didn't look up to make the cross, but he didn't have to—you hit areas from the by-line, not players. It's up to your team-mates to be there.

Woodcock was, of course, and how cool can you get! Nine players out of ten would

a dream

Barrett's sweet volley . . . *. . . a dream is shattered.*

Bob Thomas

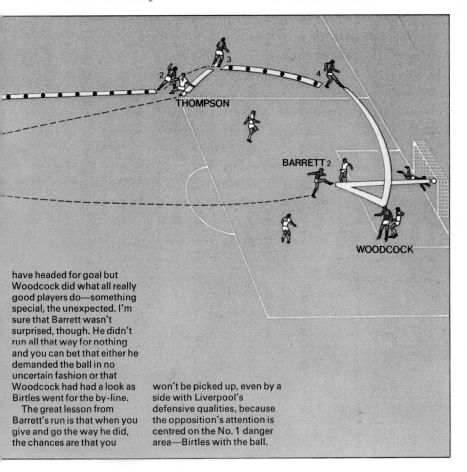

have headed for goal but Woodcock did what all really good players do—something special, the unexpected. I'm sure that Barrett wasn't surprised, though. He didn't run all that way for nothing and you can bet that either he demanded the ball in no uncertain fashion or that Woodcock had had a look as Birtles went for the by-line.

The great lesson from Barrett's run is that when you give and go the way he did, the chances are that you won't be picked up, even by a side with Liverpool's defensive qualities, because the opposition's attention is centred on the No. 1 danger area—Birtles with the ball.

WORLD MASTERS

ROBERTO BETTEGA

Born at the end of the Christmas festivities in 1950 (December 27), the baby Bettega was fated for a tough ride to the top in the harsh world of Italian football.

He had all the skill in the world, but doctors discovered he had something else, too . . . a touch of tuberculosis.

The young Bettega, having scored 13 goals in his first full season with Juventus in the First Division in 1970-71, had to forget about football for the longest eighteen months of his life.

Would he ever kick a ball for cash again? Everyone close to him said, Of course he would, and he was confident himself. but what young man could live through such a trial without even a lingering doubt?

The old one-two

Certainly, the illness delayed the start of an international career that reached some kind of pinnacle with the marvellous goal he scored against Argentina before the host country became world champions.

In a competition which, in retrospect, produced few magical moments, the one-two

LEFT *Bettega, one of the best headers of a ball in the world, in action during Italy's 2-1 opener against France in Argentina.*
BELOW *Holland's Ernie Brandts brings down Bettega in a game the Italians had to win if they were to reach the final . . . Italy took the lead when Brandts was harried into putting past his own keeper . . . but bowed out to two second-half Dutch goals.*

he played with Paolo Rossi before scoring will stick in the memory of all who saw it. And the Argentinians.

Before the TB became a turning point, Roberto Bettega's career had seemed to be taking a steady, unspectacular course.

He was the product of the Juventus youth scheme and, because Italian clubs have no reserve sides, it was only natural—and no slur on his abilities—that he be loaned out to a Second Division side to get some valuable experience.

On loan to Varese!

That's what happened. He went to Varese for the 1969-70 season and in 30 League games scored the respectable total of 13 goals.

Brought back to Juventus for the following season—much to Varese's disappointment—he scored the unlucky number of goals again . . . just before TB struck.

So his chances of making the Italian squad for the 1974 World Cup were virtually non-existent.

After the competition in Munich, the Bettega luck changed. The Italian disaster—

Fotosports International

361

County Press Photos

Bettega shoots past Manchester United's Lou Macari and Stewart Houston in a UEFA Cup game in 1976. Juventus lost 1-0, but went on to win the trophy after taking the second leg 3-0.

an early and ignominious return to their own country—meant that new faces would soon be seen in Italian blue.

One of them was that of Roberto Bettega.

But still the path wasn't easy. He played in the 1-0 win away to Finland in June 1975 —the only goal scored by Giorgio Chinaglia, now with Cosmos—and was then dropped.

Several games after that were spent among that anonymous and despairing band on the bench, the substitutes.

Substitute to superstar

Bettega had still to break through. A couple of star performances would do it. They came within two months, late in 1976.

In September he made his comeback against Yugoslavia and scored one of the goals in a handsome 3-0 victory.

And in October he scored twice in the easy—but vital—World Cup match away to Luxembourg.

If manager Enzo Bearzot needed a little more evidence to put Bettega in the 'regular' class, it came triumphantly against England, a magnificent diving header from Romeo Benetti's cross in Rome putting a sturdy nail in England's World Cup coffin. Four goals in the 6-1 thrashing of Finland were, perhaps, Roberto's way of making up for lost time.

Ahead, of course, was the World Cup itself —after helping Juventus to their fifth League

Championship in seven seasons. And early in the competition lots of people thought that— at last—the Italians had shed their defensive shell and had a real chance of becoming champions.

If that had happened, Roberto Bettega would have been sitting at No. 1 instead of Mario Kempes. As it is, we can only recall the flicks and feints, the power in the air and the deadly finishing that make Bettega such a wonderful player to watch.

Sporting Pictures UK

Already the conquerors
Bettega and Giacinto Facchetti arrive for the qualifier against England last year. They lost 2-0 but then needed only to beat Luxembourg 1-0 to make Argentina. Bettega scored in that match, taking his tally to nine in six games . . . And England went out on goal difference.

Colorsport

ABOVE *Despair and joy for Bettega in the World Cup finals: turning away believing he'd scored against West Germany, only to find out (insert) that Manny Kaltz has got back to clear.*
BELOW *The superb goal that beat Argentina in an earlier group match.*

Peter Robinson

363

Whistle Test

'A ref can be wrong . . . just like anybody else. He's got to be big enough to admit it, that's all—and that's not easy for any of us' TOM REYNOLDS

Wessex Press Agency

Is all the swearing we can lip-read on television a good indication of the relationship between players and referee? Or is there another side we never hear about?

Luckily there is—as top ref Tom Reynolds is able to prove, with the help of West Ham's Pat Holland.

Twice Tom has been in charge of matches where there has been controversy involving Pat.

'First, there was a televised game between West Ham and Derby,' says Tom. 'Not for the first time, the Hammers were desperate for points and when Pat was clobbered just outside the area he made sure he finished up inside.

'He turned to me and said: "Look, ref, that had to be inside." But I said: "Look, Pat, you left your boot outside!" It had come off as he was tackled.

'Brian Moore shouted "penalty" on 'The Big Match' . . . but agreed with me after seeing the slow-motion replay. And, knowing Pat, I bet he did as well in his living-room.

'The second time, with West Ham playing Everton, Tom booked Mick Lyons for a foul on Holland. 'Pat entered into a discussion with Lyons about the incident and, when I went over to sort it out, he started doing the same with me—so I booked him.

'But at home after the match I thought I'd over-reacted and that Pat had every right to protest about the foul. I said as much in my report to the FA and they took no further action. About a year later Pat thanked me for getting him off.'

Tommy Craig

Bob Thomas

*£250,000-worth of left foot
... Aston Villa's midfield ace
Tommy Craig: 'I try to adjust
my body positions to use my
left.' Below: Tommy's lethal
left grabs a goal against
Everton at Villa Park
earlier this year.*

**'I used to practise all day with my right
foot, then my coach at Aberdeen told me to
forget all about it and concentrate on
making my left even better.'**

One-footed? Well, don't worry too much about it. Tommy
Craig, Aston Villa's midfield ace, is one player who doesn't.

'When I was a kid at Aberdeen I was always worrying
about having only one good foot, the left, and I suppose it
must bother youngsters all over the country, too.

'I used to practise all day with my right foot, just knocking it against a wall, until one day Eddie Turnbull, the
Aberdeen coach, asked me what on earth I was doing. I told
him—and he told me to forget about my right and concentrate on making my left even better.'

Eddie's advice, as well as making Tommy feel a whole lot
better, was the encouragement needed to develop one of the
sweetest left foots in the League.

'My right is still the same—I can't do a thing with it,'
says Tommy. 'I try to adjust my body positions so that I'm
always able to use my left and not keep dragging the ball
over from the right.'

Tommy's left foot is the best example for the argument
that one really good foot is better than two average ones.
Another is the £250,000 Aston Villa paid for it!

Peter Robinson

Dave Thomas on crossing the ball

'There's no doubt that the main reason I reached 30 League goals last season was the service I received from Dave. He's the best crosser of a ball in the game.' BOB LATCHFORD

They've always been a major part of the English game—the crosses from the wings. Shouts of 'Sling it over' or 'Get it across' have been heard at grounds for years.

But there's a lot more to a good cross than just getting the ball into the middle.

Everton's Dave Thomas, one of the best crossers in the business, puts a lot of thought into a skill that's central to his role as a provider on the wing.

'Basically, a winger tries to get to the dead-ball line to cross the ball, pulling it back for forwards coming in.

'Nearly always it's best to cross the ball deep from that position because it gets behind defenders rushing back to cover and gives your players coming in a definite advantage.'

One thing that makes Dave special is his ability to cross so well on the run. He can cross balls that other players do well to stop going for goal-kicks.

He does it by being able to clip the ball with the inside of his foot while being very square with the ball—a curious kind of hooked cross.

'I don't know when I started doing it,' says Dave. 'I think it must be one of

One of the best crossers in the business . . . Everton's Dave Thomas provides the kind of service that strikers looking for goals love.

No ties
Socks round the ankles is the Dave Thomas trademark. They slip down soon after the start of every game he plays in.

Dave says: 'It's because I never wear tie-ups. I don't wear shinguards either.

'I know it may be asking for trouble but I just can't wear anything round my legs. I like to feel loose. You have to feel comfortable to play football.'

Ray Green

366

Sporting Pictures UK

Three stages of a perfect cross . . . Dave approaches the ball with his eye on it and his right arm out for balance. He's aiming to pull the ball back almost square, so he'll hit the ball about the area of his big toe. At impact you'll notice he leans back slightly—that's to make sure he gets under the ball and gives it height. Even after the ball is on its way, Dave is still looking down —like a golfer who's determined to keep his shots accurate.

If Dave lifts his head as he makes the cross he's liable to miscue it in some way.

those habits you develop at an early age without really knowing it.'

This ability means that Dave is able to cross the ball accurately under pressure as well as at speed, whereas another player will need that vital second of time or yard of space.

But he adds: 'Very often you'll have space and time to cross and at those times you should look up and use the ball as well as you can.

'It's important to concentrate, yet feel relaxed. If you're tense you'll tighten up and put over a bad ball.

'Near-post crosses are used more these days and, as a general rule, I play these type of crosses from deeper positions because there's more space and a better angle for the forwards getting on the end of them.

'These crosses are usually

'It's important to concentrate yet feel relaxed,' says Dave. 'If you're tense you'll tighten up and put over a bad ball. It's not enough just to get it across—it's the quality that matters. Ask any centre-forward in the country!'

From the front you can see the extraordinary angle Dave gets on his crosses.

A close up shows how Dave clips the ball from about the area of his big toe. He clips the ball on the outside and gets well underneath it for height.

Ray Green

Dave plays mainly on the left but the right foot is his strongest—so he can switch wings to good effect.

hit with more pace and bend on them—the so-called early balls.

'So, as a general rule, the nearer you get to the dead ball line the deeper the cross should be, the further it should be pulled back. The deeper you are the better it is to look for the near post.'

Bob and Dave
One player who's glad that Dave Thomas does his crossing in an Everton shirt is their centre-forward Bob Latchford.

'There's no doubt that the main reason I reached 30 goals in League last season was the service I received from Dave,' says Bob.

'One of the problems with playing for England is that it takes time to build up the kind of understanding that Dave and I have at Goodison. 'As soon as Dave goes on a run I've a good idea where he'll cross it—it's just up to me to get there!'

Dave can cross on the run and under pressure by using his own special kind of hooked cross: 'I don't know when I started doing it. I think it must be one of those things you develop at an early age without really knowing it.

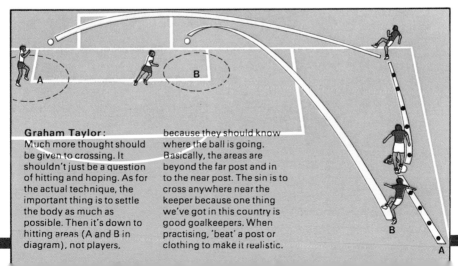

Graham Taylor:
Much more thought should be given to crossing. It shouldn't just be a question of hitting and hoping. As for the actual technique, the important thing is to settle the body as much as possible. Then it's down to hitting areas (A and B in diagram), not players, because they should know where the ball is going. Basically, the areas are beyond the far post and in to the near post. The sin is to cross anywhere near the keeper because one thing we've got in this country is good goalkeepers. When practising, 'beat' a post or clothing to make it realistic.

RIƧING KENNY
ƧTAR SANSOM

Kenny Sansom is sure that Crystal Palace can help him achieve his two main ambitions: to play in the First Division . . . and to win a full England cap.

'We have a young side, full of potential,' says Sansom. 'Terry Venables has tremendous confidence in us.

'He allows us to play to our strengths. For instance, I'm given the chance to push forward, knowing that the midfield players will cover my runs upfield.

'We played some good football but lacked consistency last season. We were guilty of thinking about more than the next game.

'But we gained in experience last season. A settled side could see us in line for promotion—even the championship.

'And the fact that we're doing well should mean I've got a better chance of being seen by the England selectors.'

Kenny has already won youth and Under-21 honours for England. He has skill and determination and he is a clever and accurate user of the ball.

He joined Palace after brief spells with a number of other London clubs, and was introduced to the Selhurst Park outfit by chief scout Arnie Warren.

Sansom made his debut at Tranmere on 7 May 1975—the last match of the season.

He didn't wear the number three shirt in his six games for the first team the following season, but made it his own the next—Palace's promotion year—and didn't miss a League match.

That season he also received an FA Youth Cup winners medal, captaining the side that beat Everton in the final. He was also captain of the England youth side . . . and, at the age of 18, was voted the 'Palace Player of the Year'.

Only 5′ 6″ but full of tackling and running . . . Palace ace Kenny Sansom.

The flair that's taken Kenny to the edge of the full England squad . . . beating the tackle from Sunderland's Jack Ashurst at Selhurst Park in September, then lining up a telling cross. His obvious rival is WBA's Derek Statham.

Club	Season	League		FA Cup		Lge Cup	
		Ms	Gs	Ms	Gs	Ms	G:
Crystal	1974-75	1	–	–	–	–	–
Palace	1975-76	6	–	–	–	–	–
	1976-77	46	–	6	–	3	–
	1977-78	41	2	1	–	4	–
		94	2	7	–	7	–

Duncan Raban

Last season he missed only one game . . .
when he was late for the train to Bristol.

But Kenny has consistently shone in one
of the youngest back fours in the League.
When Ian Evans broke his leg against
Fulham last season, his fellow central defender, Jimmy Cannon, took over as captain
and yet another youngster, Billy Gilbert,
filled in alongside him.

Sansom believes that Cannon deserves
more credit than he's given.

'Jimmy's a great influence on the lads,'
says Kenny. 'He's done a great job since
Ian's unfortunate injury.'

But all of Palace's young eagles have
earned praise this season—and none more
than Ken Sansom. His performance for the
England Under-21 side in Copenhagen
earned extravagant raves from sportswriters
whose assignments don't usually take in the
Second Division grounds where Sansom
shines every week.

It's a fair bet that all that will have changed
by next season.

Duncan Raban

Frank Stapleton: 'never say die'

'Every defence that faces Frank knows they can't let up once in 90 minutes. He has determination, perseverance. It's not just about fitness . . . it's about enthusiasm for the job.' TERRY NEILL

Nobody is more important to a side than a player who treats every minute as if it's the very last.

The one who chases the bad pass that is nearer to the corner flag than the goal . . .

The one who always be-

lieves that a back pass to the keeper might be mishit—and therefore intercepted . . .

The one who never gives a

Duncan Raban

Bob Thomas

defender a moment's rest.

Such a player is Arsenal's Irish international front runner Frank Stapleton.

'Front runner' sounds like some kind of workhorse, a good honest pro who keeps going but hasn't got that much between his ears and even less in his feet.

But everyone knows that's not the case with Frank. He can play. But, at the same time, he's not past chasing what another player might consider a hopeless ball.

Frank's boss, Arsenal manager Terry Neill, knows his worth.

He says: 'Every defence that faces Frank knows they can't relax once in 90 minutes.

'That's some kind of pressure on them, isn't it? Everyone likes to think that a match is over if, say, you're leading 2-0 with five minutes to go. With Frank about, you can't make such generalisations.

'But what do you call such a quality—determination, perseverance? They're all such grim words. Everyone can think of words to describe great ball-players—who might only turn it on when it

Frank battles with another wholehearted player—Allan Hunter of Ipswich—in last season's FA Cup final.

1-0 . . . after 85 minutes of frustrated hard work (left, with Paul Jones) Stapleton gets his reward with the winner against Bolton at Highbury last September.

suits them—but players who have skill *and* show such qualities are never showered with the superlatives.

'But all the truly great players had it on top of their artistry.

'Frank is always looking to make himself available to the midfield players. He'll make a double run and then, if it's necessary, do it again.

'And that's not just about fitness—it's about enthusiasm for the job. It can be a thankless task sometimes if you're not getting much of the ball, if the service is poor.

'But the attitude of players like Frank is that the next one might be the one that leads to a goal.

'A word for it? Well, it's unselfish, isn't it? It's understanding fully the importance of a team attitude—using your skill and energy not for yourself but for the team.'

Duncan Raban

xit Southport

David Obree

Friday, 2 June 1978 . . . the end of Southport's 57 years in the League . . . the beginning of a new era for Wigan Athletic, elected to the League at their 35th attempt.

When the League clubs first cast their votes Wigan and Southport were deadlocked with 26 votes each . . . but the second ballot separated them, with Wigan triumphant by 29 to 20.

For Wigan it was the just result of their persistence and energy, as well as their success in non-League football and in the FA Cup. For Southport it meant that they were doomed to the obscurity of non-League football.

Last season, though, Southport's fortunes had seemed to change for the better. The board was shuffled, debts were paid and more people came to watch . . . though the total attendance was still the lowest in the League. But the team remained basically unchanged, so did the results, and for the third year running Southport sank into the bottom four.

Meanwhile only 20 miles away Wigan were finishing as runners-up in the Northern Premier League—and were nominated to stand for election to the League. Immediately the chairman Arthur Horrocks and manager Ian McNeill arranged to visit all the First and Second Division clubs, who have most of the votes at League meetings.

In contrast, chairman Walter Giller and his Southport directors contented themselves with sending each of the clubs a letter asking for support at the summer meeting.

No wonder supporters were infuriated when the club failed to gain re-election. 'The directors were ridiculously over-confident for no real reason,' says Southport regular Debbie Pennington. 'What did they expect when no effort had been made to strengthen the team?'

Although Southport's record has been poor recently, during the ten years prior to 1975, when their troubles began, the club had enjoyed some of its most successful years ever.

Out of all the 92 clubs in the League, only the two giants Liverpool and Leeds scored more home points than Southport during this period.

It began with the arrival of Billy Bingham in 1965, at a time when Wigan were dominating the Cheshire League.

In the following season Southport finished as runners-up in the Fourth Division— gaining promotion for the first time in their history.

Bad luck in 1970 brought them back to the Fourth Division, then three years later Jimmy Meadows led them to their greatest honour to date . . . they won the Fourth Division championship.

It was the year all four championships went to Lancashire clubs. Bill Shankly remarked that, in view of Southport's limited resources, it was a greater achievement for them to win the Fourth Division than for Liverpool to win the First.

That championship was Southport's last taste of success. They went straight back into

. as the Football League casts votes to decide their fate

...Enter Wigan

Wigan's Springfield Park, hosting League football again after a 47-year break.

Southport's Haig Avenue ... memories of nearly 60 years of League soccer.

Changing places ... Southport (top left) play in the NPL, while Wigan say hello to League football.

Sandgrounders' sorrows
Southport, founded in 1881, were original members—along with Wigan Borough—of the Third Division North in 1921 ... They gained promotion only twice in their history, in 1967 and 1973, for a total of four seasons outside the bottom division ... In 1931 they reached the sixth round of the Cup, three rounds further than Wigan have ever gone ...

Wigan's second chance
Formed by 11 local business men in 1932, Wigan Athletic took over as soccer standard bearers in the Rugby League stronghold from Wigan Borough, who had gone into liquidation early in the 1931-2 season in the Third Division North ... On election to the League at their 35th attempt in 46 years, chairman Arthur Horrocks then pledged: 'League football must never be allowed to leave this town again.'

the Fourth Division while neighbours Wigan were notching up their second Northern Premier League championship.

At Springfield Park they were enjoying the best overall record of NPL clubs, having finished in the top three eight times in the League's ten-year existence.

'We have run a non-League club as a League club . . . and it has paid off,' says chairman Arthur Horrocks.

'We're not a rich club, so there'll be no panic buyings. But given time to acclimatise ourselves to League football, I think our chances of becoming a fair First or Second Division club are quite good.'

Nine of last year's players have thrown up their jobs and turned full professional.

Ian McNeill thinks there is little difference between Northern Premier League football and Fourth Division football. 'The lads are enjoying themselves in the League . . . only one or two are finding it a wee bit difficult. There's no more skill or pace in the Fourth Division, just that wee bit more aggression.

So far McNeill, who himself gave up a job as a representative of an industrial chemical company, is enthusiastic about full-time professionalism.

'The only player on the staff who's still a part-timer is Micky Worswick, certainly one of the best non-League players around these parts in the last 10 years or so. He's 31 now and he's got a very good job, so there was no

Rav Green

Fotosports International

Wigan chairman Arthur Horrocks and manager Ian McNeill.

way he was going to give that up.'

Meanwhile, at Southport, the team has changed almost beyond recognition. Only a couple of players remain from last season, most of the rest have signed on with other League clubs. A few of the playing staff have even joined Wigan.

There are cautious hopes expressed that one day soon Wigan and Southport will be staging passionate derby matches for Football League points . . . but others see the gap between them is more likely to widen.

Ian McNeill sees Wigan on the way up. 'We have the potential to build a first class ground, we have the potential support as this season's gates have shown, and we have the potential to build a good side.'

Former Southport captain Tom O'Neil, now at Tranmere, sees Southport on the slide. He says: 'This has really put the lid on Southport's coffin. I think they'll really struggle now.'

So far, though, there's no sign of either prediction coming true. Southport are comfortably placed in mid-table a third of the way through their first Northern Premier League season, while Wigan started promis-

Wigan keeper John Brown playing for Stockport County . . . against Southport. John was given a free transfer by Stockport in 1976 and dropped out of League, but now he's a full-time professional again. The Southport attacker is John Hughes . . . Both Hughes and Brown were on loan from Preston at the time.

Rav Green

Springfield Park's popular end watch Wigan's Alan Crompton take on Welsh international Malcolm Page in a pre-season friendly against Birmingham City.

ingly enough in their League Cup tie with Third Division Tranmere Rovers. At Tranmere they drew 1-1, their first goal as a League club coming with nine seconds of the match left to play from a 40 yard shot by former Tranmere reserve Tommy Gore. Ian McNeill described it as 'one of the finest goals you will see anywhere.' 'Our goalkeeper should have swallowed it,' observed Tranmere manager Johnny King, a former Wigan player.

Wigan won the second leg at home, 2-1, Tom O'Neil scoring for Tranmere . . . and 8,512 spectators saw the game.

But Wigan's start to their League campaign was not successful. Injuries to key players, including their main striker, John Wilkie, left them short of goals, but the newly-formed left-sided partnership between Frank Corrigan and former Scotland Under 23 international Ian Purdie looked promising. Results have improved . . . and Wigan have begun to climb again.

COSMOS super move

Giorgio Chinaglia finds himself with only Chelsea's debut keeper Bob Iles to beat . . .

In a game full of memorable moments, one of the best was created by Cruyff for Giorgio Chinaglia, the Italian international centre-forward.

Cruyff started the move, controlling the ball with his instep just outside his own penalty area, then playing a one-two with Franz Beckenbauer. The Dutch master controlled the ball, then hit a long pass into the path of the charging Chinaglia.

Chinaglia took the ball inside young David Stride . . . was then foiled by the rush of another Chelsea youngster—Bob Iles—and lost it.

To be fair to the Cosmos striker, he was unlucky not

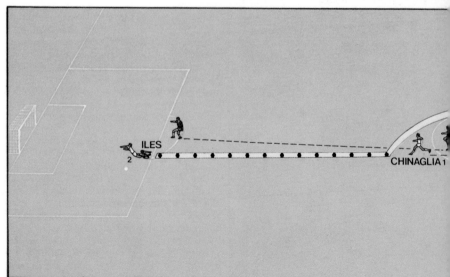

It was the night the stars came out at Chelsea. Stamford Bridge was fuller than it has been for some time to see the London team take on Tueart, Beckenbauer, Cruyff and their Cosmos team-mates—New York's finest . . .

. . . Iles comes out quickly to save the day . . .   *But should it have been a penalty . . . ?*

to win a penalty. The ball screwed away across the penalty area, but from the replay it looks as though it was Chinaglia's left foot that changed its direction . . . not Iles's brave dive.

Graham Taylor's analysis:
'Cruyff still has a great deal to offer: the control he showed, the confidence to play that one-two deep in his own half—and don't let anyone talk you out of wanting to play football in your own half —the vision to see that the move was on, and the ability to set up the move . . . perfectly. That pass with the outside of the foot was superbly struck and beautifully weighted.'

A Matter of Fact

County Press Photos

Dad's Army (1) ... Norwich stars Kevin Keelan, Martin Peters and Martin Chivers have an aggregate age of 105 and a total of 52 years in the League between them. Keelan, 37, began in 1959-60 with Villa; Peters, 35, with West Ham in 1961-62; and Chivers, 34, with Southampton in 1962-63.

Dad's Army (2) ... Shamrock Rovers' team often includes no fewer than six players over 30.

ABOVE *Superstars together ... Elton John and Kevin Keegan. The Watford chairman is no stranger to the charts, but did you know that Keegan once released a single, '5 Years', which flopped?*

Last season no fewer than *ten* Sheffield Wednesday players missed penalties! Now Jack Charlton, hoping to break the Owls' spot-kick jinx, has given the job to ex-Arsenal man Brian Hornsby.

Former Sunderland, Newcastle and England inside-forward Len Shackleton's autobiography 'Clown Prince of Soccer', had one page blank—apart from the heading : 'The average director's knowledge of football I' Talented 'Shack' played just 5 times for England.

A local paper offered goalless Wolves £50 a goal at the start of the season. Bristol City's David Rodgers promptly obliged with an own goal—and then repeated the feat at Spurs two weeks later.

Derek Johnstone is the youngest player ever to appear in a Scottish FA Cup final. He was 16 years 11 months old when he played for Rangers against Celtic at Hampden Park in 1971.

Bobby Stokes, goalscoring hero of Southampton's F A Cup triumph at Wembley in 1976, is now turning out for Southern League strugglers Dartford after spells with Portsmouth and Washington Diplomats in the USA.

Ex-Stirling striker Hugh Maxwell never really settled in England with the now defunct Bradford Park Avenue. But on returning to his native Scotland he hit all of Falkirk's goals in a 7-3 defeat of Clyde at Brockville in December 1962.

Queen's Park Rangers chairman Jim Gregory claims that the club's controversial forward Stan Bowles has made 34 transfer requests since joining them for £110,000 from Carlisle United in September 1972.

Oh, those strips! Isthmian Leaguers Corinthian Casuals' traditional strip is chocolate and pink, while neighbouring Dulwich Hamlet's colours are pink and blue.

Notts County's Eric McManus saved penalties in the League and FA Cup at Charlton last season, and earned his team a point at The Valley this September with another spot-kick save from Dick Tydeman.

Billy Wright won 105 England caps between 1947-59. Now the Everton defender with the same name could be on the verge of an international career, having played for England Under-21s against Denmark recently.

Whistle Test

'It was one of those moments when a player just forgot about hard professionalism and was genuinely concerned for two fellow pros.' PAT PARTRIDGE

Syndication International

English football is known as the toughest in the world—but there is a softer side to it, as Pat Partridge can testify.

'It was during a Manchester United game against Everton last season. Bob Latchford and Terry Darracott went for the same ball in the United area and there was a clash of heads.'

It didn't seem much at the time. Indeed, the crowd thought it was hilarious. But then United defender Gordon McQueen said: 'Quick ref, stop the game!'

Pat went to the spot and saw 'blood pouring all over the place.

'Here was a situation where McQueen could have ignored what had happened. Both the players hurt were in the opposing team— and Gordon's not known as the softest player in the world, is he?

'But at that moment he forgot all about hard professionalism and was genuinely concerned for two fellow pros.

'I can remember Everton's manager, Gordon Lee, making a point of shaking McQueen's hand at the end of the game.

'This is not the sort of stuff that makes the headlines but it's certainly an example of the small things that keep my faith in football.

'This *is* the most professional league in the world. The will to win is always there in every game . . . but to win fairly.'

Staying neutral

Pat is on first name terms with most players . . . and on one occasion it almost landed him in trouble.

During a Norwich-Tottenham game a few years ago Martin Peters —then playing for Spurs—made a bad pass and Pat said: 'Come on Martin, you can do better than that.'

Doug Livermore heard him and said: 'What's all this then, ref—is he a personal friend of yours or something?'

Pat replied: 'Okay, Doug, what's your problem, then?'

Now Pat says: 'I think it's alright to be on first name terms as long as it's not seen as favouritism. I'm glad I knew Livermore's first name!'

Ice cool Pat

Pat Partridge is not one of those refs who thinks there should be lots of changes to the laws of the game.

Even the tactic of 'freezing' the ball by the corner flag doesn't bother him too much.

'It can lead to aggro, but so can many things. If you remove these areas of conflict, it'll only water the game down.

'Also, I think that particular tactic is on the decline. Players feel the crowd's annoyance and take notice of it.'

381

GLASGOW'S

Last summer Jock Wallace quit as manager of treble-winning Rangers and Jock Stein stepped out of the Celtic hot seat . . . so the Old Firm turned to a new firm . . .

It was a gamble. When Celtic appointed Billy McNeill and Rangers appointed John Greig, both clubs were signing men who were familiar with their policies and personalities . . . but whose managerial experience was in one case limited and in the other non-existent.

McNeill, 37, had 15 months experience at Clyde and Aberdeen behind him; Greig, 35, had only just retired from playing.

But both men had spent nearly two decades playing for the famous clubs they now manage. And both know what is expected of them.

Unlike fans of smaller clubs, the followers of Celtic and Rangers demand unbroken success. One season with an empty trophy cabinet is a lifetime to them.

So that while Greig took charge at a time when Rangers were holders of all three major trophies his task is no less demanding than that of McNeill . . . who inherited a Celtic team which failed to win anything last

A familiar sight at Old Firm clashes . . .

season . . . and to qualify for Europe for the first time for more than a decade and a half.

After years of Old Firm tussles and handshakes at the centre-circle, McNeill has lost none of his respect for his great rival.

He told *Handbook:* 'I have every reason to respect John Greig as a player, a person, and now in his capacity as a manager. 'His enthusiasm and dedication demands the respect of his colleagues. He's the kind of straightforward individual who influences others with his forthright manner.

'He knows the players and their personalities through playing alongside them. He knows which ones need to be encouraged and those whose feet must be kept on the ground.

John Greig in his playing days with Rangers. A classy half-back—later full-back—he won 44 caps for Scotland in a career spanning nearly 20 years. He retired this year, taking over as manager when Jock Wallace joined Leicester.

NEW FIRM'

. . captains Greig and McNeill on the spot.

hat's a very important aspect of football
management.

'Although he has no previous experience
f managing a club I don't think it'll hamper
is progress. He has the advantage of having
ade the move up without a break away from
e club.'

Greig is equally respectful of McNeill's
apabilities. 'As a player Billy McNeill had
emendous dedication to his profession,' he
xplains. 'The fact that Celtic won so much
nder his leadership on the pitch illustrates
is ability to lead.

'And it's that same quality which could
rove most decisive in his career as a
anager.'

After just four weeks of this season, the
vo clubs met in the first Old Firm clash of
e two men's managerial careers.

'Yes, these games are a bit special,' said
AcNeill, whose side triumphed 3-1. 'The
tmosphere and great rivalry between the

clubs sees to that. But, all said and done, you
still only get two points for winning, the same
as any League game.

'As a player I looked forward to meeting
Rangers. You always knew it would be tough
and no quarter would be asked for or given
by either side. But, contrary to what some
people seem to think, Celtic and Rangers
players don't go out with the express purpose
of intimidating one another.

'Certainly, I was always on speaking terms
with the Rangers players when I was captain
of Celtic and the position is no different now.'

Greig shares these views. 'Of course
there's great competition between the clubs,'
he said. 'But the preparation for an Old Firm
game is no different from what it is for a
match against say, Dundee United or Hibs.
They all count, and it's how you perform on
the day that matters.'

Apart from the obvious pressures and the
different approach to managing instead of
playing, Greig has experienced a new feeling
—a sense of helplessness.

He explained: 'Before there was always

*Billy McNeill is chaired off by his team-mates
after yet another triumph for the Celts. During
his time at Parkhead, Celtic won 23 major
trophies, including nine successive League
Championships—from 1966 to 1974—and the
European Cup in 1967.*

Syndication International

383

the chance to do something on the park . . . change the pattern of play or have a word with another player.

'I suppose I feel slightly helpless at times now because I've got to rely on having laid down the correct tactics and hope that the players are in the right frame of mind.'

Greig's sense of fair play and willingness to give everyone a good crack of the whip has been evident early in his managerial career.

Even though Rangers mustered only one League victory in the first quarter of the Premier League programme, he resisted the temptation to make repeated changes and stood by his players.

That faith was repaid when Rangers caused a massive European upset by knocking red-hot favourites Juventus out of the Champions Cup in the first round.

Instead of bemoaning his luck at the draw Greig convinced his players that they could beat the Italian masters, and gave them a helping hand to complete the job when he produced a blue-print for victory which proved correct in every detail.

But there's nothing pretentious or big-time about Greig as an individual. A family man who paved the way for a career in management by selling business interests, he never made any secret of the fact that his one big remaining ambition in football was to manage the club he had served for so long.

It was an ambition shared by McNeill. Yet when the chance to succeed Jock Stein

Billy McNeill is by no means new to football management. He started with Clyde when they were struggling in Division 1, then joined Aberdeen and took them to runners-up spots in both the League Championship and Cup last season.

Honours: Championship medal '66, '67, '68, '69, '70, '71, '72, '73, '74; Cup winners medal '67, '69, '71, '72, '74, '75; Cup losers medal '61, '63, '65, '66, '70, '73; League Cup winners medal '66, '67, '68, '69, '70, '75; League Cup losers medal '71, '73, '74; European Cup winners medal '67; European Cup losers medal '70; Scottish Footballer of the Year '67

Club	Season	Pos	League Ms	Gs	SFA Cup Ms	Gs	Lge Cup Ms	Gs	Int'nls Ms	Gs
Celtic	1958-59	6	17	–	–	–	3	–		
	1959-60	9	19	–	5	–	6	–		
	1960-61	4	31	1	7	–	5	–	4	–
	1961-62	3	29	1	4	–	5	–	4	–
	1962-63	4	28	1	6	–	6	–	2	–
	1963-64	3	28	–	4	–	6	–	3	–
	1964-65	8	22	–	6	1	6	–	4	–
	1965-66	1	25	–	6	–	8	–	2	1
	1966-67	1	33	–	6	–	9	2	1	–
	1967-68	1	34	5	1	–	10	–	1	–
	1968-69	1	34	3	5	2	8	–	4	2
	1969-70	1	31	5	4	–	10	2	1	–
	1970-71	1	31	1	7	–	11	–		
	1971-72	1	34	3	6	1	8	–	3	–
	1972-73	1	30	–	7	1	10	–		
	1973-74	1	30	–	5	–	11	–		
	1974-75	3	30	1	4	–	9	–		
			486	21	83	5	131	4	29	3

VISITORS

Peter Robinson

First encounter of its kind
Four weeks into the season . . . and the two men are thrown into their first Old Firm clash as managers . . .

At the end of 90 minutes, it was first blood to McNeill. Celtic had won 3-1, watched by 60,000 fans at Celtic Park. The game was a personal triumph for Celtic centre-forward Tom McAdam, who opened the scoring in the very first minute, then added a clincher midway through the second half.

George McCluskey (Celtic) and Derek Parlane (Rangers) scored the other goals.

John Greig's managerial career did not start very promisingly this season ... Rangers didn't win a League game until their seventh match—against Motherwell.

Sporting Pictures UK

Sportapics

Good old boys

Greig and McNeill have a lot more in common than the responsibility for Scotland's two richest clubs. They both spent their playing careers with the clubs they're now managing, they were both club captains and they both have a total of six Scottish Cup winners medals. Both men have been awarded the MBE . . . and both share a belief in attack.

Says McNeill: 'You don't win honours playing defensively. That's why Celtic will continue to play open attacking football.' Explains Greig: 'It's my policy to play attacking football and entertain. There's no way we will change that approach.'

Honours: Championship medal '63, '64, '75, '76, '78; Cup winners medal '63, '64, '66, '73, '76, '78; Cup losers medal '69, '71, '77; League Cup winners medal '64, '65, '76, '78; League Cup losers medal '66, '67; European Cup Winners Cup winners medal '72, losers medal '67; Footballer of the Year '66, '76

Club	Season	Pos	League		SFA Cup		Lge Cup		Int'nls	
			Ms	Gs	Ms	Gs	Ms	Gs	Ms	Gs
Rangers	1961-62	2	11	6	1	–	2	1		
	1962-63	1	27	5	5	–	4	5		
	1963-64	1	34	4	6	2	7	–	2	–
	1964-65	5	34	4	3	–	7	–	7	1
	1965-66	2	32	7	7	–	9	1	9	2
	1966-67	2	33	2	1	–	6	–	3	–
	1967-68	2	32	11	4	2	6	–	4	–
	1968-69	2	33	6	4	–	6	–	8	–
	1969-70	2	33	7	3	2	6	–	5	–
	1970-71	4	26	8	6	–	9	–	5	–
	1971-72	3	28	8	6	1	6	–		
	1972-73	2	30	7	6	–	10	3		
	1973-74	3	32	6	1	–	10	2		
	1974-75	1	22	1	–	–	1	–		
	1975-76	1	36	2	5	–	10	1	1	–
	1976-77	2	30	–	5	–	11	1		
	1977-78	1	29	2	5	1	5	1		
			502	86	68	8	115	14	44	3

presented itself McNeill still hesitated. 'I asked for time to think the move over because I was happy at Aberdeen. My wife and family were happy living in the north-east and the club had just finished a great season as runners-up to Rangers in the League and the Cup.

'But in the end I knew I couldn't turn down the chance. Celtic was my life as a player for 17 years and I was flattered that they should want me as their manager. Frankly, few other jobs would have tempted me away from Pittodrie.'

It hasn't taken McNeill long to make his presence felt at Parkhead, establishing a new internal Scottish transfer record with the £120,000 signing of winger Dave Provan

from First Division Kilmarnock.

And the spending is unlikely to stop there. 'It's my job to be interested in good players whenever they become available,' says McNeill. 'But they must be better than the ones I've got. I would never buy for the sake of providing the fans with a new face.'

Neither is McNeill prepared to make rash predictions. 'I'm confident that we can start winning trophies again,' he says. 'But it takes time to create the right kind of team.

'The important thing is that the players have regained their pride and their belief in themselves. There will be set-backs—like the 4-1 defeat at Aberdeen—but the important thing is to ensure that there are far more winning days.'

KEEPERS

Giving it the boot ... Bristol City's John Shaw aims for Ritchie and Royle.

Duncan Raban

'We haven't got big men up front so we ask our full-backs to look for the throw from Phil Parkes and build up from the back.'
QPR manager STEVE BURTENSHAW

Although it may be taken for granted by spectators, the keeper's distribution is just as important as the other aspects of his play.

Every time he has the ball safely in his possession, he has to make the decision: to kick or to throw.

Handbook went to the Queen's Park Rangers game against Bristol City last month just to study the distribution of Phil Parkes and John Shaw.

And the results show that even this simple part of the game is given the pro treatment.

Shaw, with two big target forwards to aim for—John Ritchie and Joe Royle—used the long kick much more than Parkes, who found his defenders with short throws whenever possible, often going very wide to find them.

Shaw's tactics are obvious —if you've got big men up front it makes sense to use them often.

Both Ritchie (5′ 11″) and Royle (6′ 1″) got their fair share of the high balls and were a constant menace to the Rangers defence, even though the home side finished winners 1-0 through

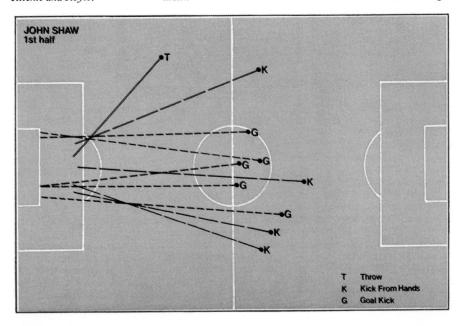

JOHN SHAW
1st half

T   Throw
K   Kick From Hands
G   Goal Kick

kick or throw?

a late goal from substitute Martyn Busby.

Parkes threw the ball no fewer than 22 times during the game, mostly to full-backs Don Shanks and Ian Gillard, while Shaw used the throw only 8 times.

And he was playing, of course, to orders—those of Steve Burtenshaw.

'I found the diagram very interesting,' says Steve. 'In fact, we've been intending to carry out a similar analysis ourselves.

'It's pointless belting the ball upfield because we haven't got big men up there and we don't want to be in the position of continually having to fight for the ball around the centre circle.

'So we ask our full-backs to look short and build up

from the back, and if our central defenders or midfield players can get into good positions we ask the same of them.

'Usually the positions they take up are slightly out wide, so that if they are caught in possession the danger is not quite so great.'

Does Steve prefer this type of football anyway? 'Well, I do as a general rule but I'm not in favour of possession for possession's sake. I've seen teams play 15 passes and then give it back to the keeper—that's not for me.

'No, I think you play the game according to your strengths and try to remain flexible. For example, if a team closes our full-backs down quickly, Phil would soon start kicking!'

Duncan Raban

Looking to keep possession . . . Phil Parkes throws to one of his defenders.

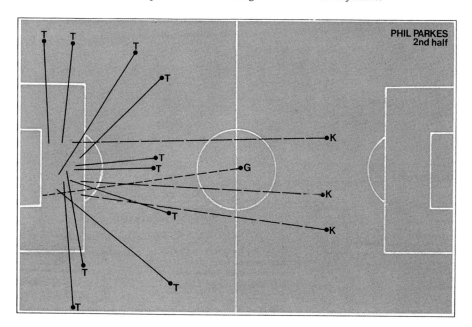

PHIL PARKES
2nd half

387

'If there's a lesson from my career it's don't join your favourite club ... I'm sorry that certain things happened at Arsenal and I was branded the villain. That was never really the case.'

Some saw him as the morons' Messiah, 'Jack the Lad' who came down from Arsenal's North Bank to take his place in a side that went on to do the 'double'.

And the sendings off, the scowls and scuffles, and the infamous V-sign to the Derby crowd he now plays for, did nothing to restrain the reputation he came with.

Even the name, Charlie George, seemed to fit into the image of menace and rebellion.

So how does Charlie, now a milder, more mature man at the Baseball Ground, look back on all that?

'The trouble at Arsenal was that I was too closely identified. I was the Londoner who stood on the North Bank and then fulfilled the dream of actually playing for my team.

'I even went to Wembley and scored the winning goal in a Cup final. There was a lot of pressure. I admit I found it hard to cope. Arsenal had just done the double and I was in demand. But I'm older now ... and more experienced.'

'If there's a lesson from my career it's don't join your favourite club. Just imagine growing up and going to school with a crowd of lads who are Arsenal daft and being there on the terraces with them on match days, then suddenly you're in that side as a teenager.

'I was at the centre of everything in football and it became increasingly difficult to remember the right things from the

Bob Thomas

ABOVE *Charlie gets close attention from Chris Nicholl, then with Villa.* BELOW *Charlie long-legs ... George competes for the ball with Leeds' Jack Charlton in the 1972 Cup final, which Arsenal lost 1-0. The previous season Arsenal beat Liverpool 2-1.*

Ray Green

389

The moment that made George a legend . . . a stunning right-foot shot gives Arsenal an extra-time winner in the 1971 FA Cup final against Liverpool—and the League and Cup double. His reaction: to lay flat out on the turf!

Honours: League Championship medal 1971 ; FA Cup winners medal 1971, runners-up medal 1972 ; UEFA Cup winners medal 1970

Club	Season	Div	Pos	League		FA Cup		Lge Cup		Int'nls	
Arsenal	1969-70	1	12	28	6	1	–	2	–		
	1970-71	1	1	17	5	7	5	–	–		
	1971-72	1	5	23	7	8	3	2	–		
	1972-73	1	2	27	6	4	3	3	2		
	1973-74	1	10	28	5	–	–	–	–		
	1974-75	1	16	10	2	1	–	1	–		
Derby County	1975-76	1	4	35	16	4	3	2	1		
	1976-77	1	15	29	5	4	3	5	3	1	–
	1977-78	1	12	34	11	3	–	1	–		
				231	53	32	17	16	6	1	–

Sporting Pictures

Charlie's style . . . Dave Mackay says : 'I'll never forget the night we beat Real Madrid in the European Cup. Netzer and Breitner were in their side but Charlie slaughtered them.

RIGHT *A familiar sight . . . Charlie has to be restrained by a team-mate during a flare-up against Aston Villa. But when he was sent off against Bolton this season Docherty stoutly defended him.*

wrong. I don't regret playing for Arsenal but I'm sorry that certain things happened there.'

One man who has no complaints about the new George is his Derby boss Tommy Docherty. He says: 'There are two different Charlies. The first is the one everyone knows—the second is Charlie George the model professional.

'I've known players who project a good guy image to the public but in private they're a real handful. Charlie's a joy, one of the easiest players I've ever had to handle.

'There are few players who spot things as quickly as he does . . . and fewer still who can knock the ball about like he can.

'Just watch the way he leaves an opponent beaten—you seldom see a defender get a second chance once Charlie's past. He has great control and a wonderful body swerve.'

It was another straight-talking Scot, Dave Mackay, who took Charlie to Derby—and his praise is stunning. 'Quite simply, Charlie won Derby the League Championship. The club was in turmoil when I took over from Brian Clough.

'Players were threatening to strike and there was a battle for power in the boardroom. I had to give Derby something, so I gave them Charlie George. He got a barrow-load of goals and we took the title.'

The tragedy, of course, is his England career—which lasted for exactly an hour against Eire two years ago. Last season Charlie refused to play for the England 'B' team . . . and seemingly committed soccer suicide.

About that he says: 'I know I have no real chance of making the England team and I've resigned myself to that.

Ray Green

Bob Thomas

'What does disturb me is all those wasted years. I used to wince at some of the names that made the England line-up. At least Ron Greenwood is looking for people who can play the game a bit.'

Whether Charlie will ever find himself back in the England fold is anyone's guess.

But, as usual, the Doc's diagnosis gets right to the sore spot: 'If he were a Scot he'd be in any team I chose. But he can't get a look in because he's English.'

Lifted to greatness . . . Charlie is helped back to his feet by Arsenal colleagues (*top*). The double has been done and the name Charlie George will take its place in soccer's history books. If only he'd done it for England as well . . .

from
DiXONS

5 PRINZTRONIC VIDEO SPORT 800 GAMES

Play squash, football, tennis, even target practise! Simply plug it into your T.V. and the rest is up to you.

Ray Green

1. LEFT Madrid, 1968: Manchester United have made it at last . . . they're in the European Cup final. But who is the man seen here celebrating with Bobby Charlton and Sir Matt Busby? A clue: he took over as temporary manager after the Munich disaster in 1958.

2. He scored 41 League goals for Liverpool in 1961-62, won a World Cup winners' medal in 1966 and finished his career in the Second Division. Who is he?

3. Name three Argentinian cities that staged World Cup games in 1978, other than Buenos Aires.

4. The leading scorer in the First Division in 1973-74 played for a club who were relegated: was it Ted Macdougall, Mike Channon or George Best?

5. By what name were Oxford United known until 1960?

6. Former Everton keeper Gordon West made just one Third Division appearance last season. Who for?

7. Both Sheffield clubs had a change of manager during the 1977-78 season. Name the men who lost their jobs and the two who replaced them.

8. By what name were Meadowbank Thistle known prior to their election to the Scottish League in 1974?

9. Who was Barnsley's manager before Allan Clarke took over at Oakwell?

10. Which of these clubs has Bobby Gould never played for: Bristol City, Arsenal, Coventry, Swindon, Hereford?

11. Which First Division side drew with a Saudi Arabia XI in September.

HOW TO ENTER
List your answers to the questions on a postcard, add your name and address, cut the 'Part 14' flash from the cover and attach it to the postcard (entries that do not bear the flash will be ineligible), then mail to: Football Handbook, 600A Commercial Road, London E14 7HS. Entries must arrive by 11 December, 1978, the closing date. The senders of the first 10 correct answers scrutinised after that date will be awarded a DIXON'S TV SPORTS GAME. The Editor's decision on all matters relating to the competition is final and binding. All winners will be notified as soon as possible and a full list of prize winners to date will be available from *Football Handbook* on request.

Phil Dwyer

'The man is simply one of the great competitors. He doesn't go out to play games, he goes out to win them. His ambition is fuelled by this desire always to come first.' JIMMY ANDREWS

Phil Dwyer's reign as successor to John Toshack in the Wales team has now ended by mutual consent.

He responded to the challenge of playing up front in typically positive fashion, scoring the only goal of the game in his debut in Iran and repeating the treatment in his next appearance against England on his home ground last May.

Ex-Cardiff manager Jimmy Andrews regards him as a potential top-class centre-half and has also used him as a centre-forward this season . . . but Phil says he feels most comfortable at right-back.

He explains: 'Wales manager Mike Smith and Jimmy Andrews at Cardiff both asked me if I would mind playing up front for a while and I agreed to give it a go.

'But the novelty soon wore off. Now I've said I want to be considered only as a right-back.

'I appreciated the chance to switch to right-back against Scotland when Malcolm Page was injured. It was a chance to show what I could do best.'

Now Phil has to convince Mike Smith. The Cardiff skipper says: 'I reckon I've made a start, that's all.'

What's Phil Dwyer's best position? He thinks it's right-back . . . but his managers sometimes disagree.

Jimmy Rimmer on

Suddenly, a forward breaks clear and, in the words of every football reporter in the country, 'has only the keeper to beat'.

Only? Countless TV replays have shown that very often the keeper is more than equal to the task.

And that's because of the extraordinary high standard of League goalkeepers—a fact recognised all over the world.

Stopping the opponent who breaks clear is largely a question of the keeper 'spreading himself'—getting out to narrow the forward's angle for a shot and using the whole of the body to smother the shot or force the forward wide.

'First and foremost you've got to get your angles right,' says Aston Villa's experienced keeper Jimmy Rimmer.

The strong arm of the keeper ... Aston Villa's Jimmy Rimmer gives his orders to defenders during a period of pressure.

As the forward approaches him, Jimmy comes at an angle—inviting him right.

It's cat-and-mouse as Jimmy tries to shut down the angle to the goal behind him.

'Spreading Yourself'

'That's the starting point.

'Of course you leave your line to narrow the angle—but not too quickly. If you rush out you leave yourself open for the chip.

'Usually, the forward will be coming at you from some sort of angle, either left or right, and the keeper's job is to force him wide. If he gets past you, at least his angle for a shot is more acute and there's a split second for a defender to get behind you.

Jimmy moves in: eye on the ball, not the man.

Harry's help . . .
Jimmy puts his success down to one person—Harry Gregg, the great Manchester United goalkeeper who survived Munich and played in the 1958 FA Cup final.

Their paths crossed at United and Swansea, and Jimmy says: 'Harry made me believe in myself. Even now he rings me up and we talk for ages. I owe it all to him.'

Now the 'spread' as Jimmy has to commit himself at the forward's feet.

He smothers the ball, but even if he hadn't he would have narrowed the angle.

From behind Jimmy you can see how he leaves his goal at an angle which invites the forward to take the ball wide.

If the forward tries an early shot, it's likely to go towards the near post, the one Jimmy has covered.

Graham Taylor:
The important thing is to be able to spread yourself both ways. Everyone has their favourite way but you'll be a better keeper, certainly in terms of confidence, if you can go down equally well on both sides. As Jimmy says, it's cat-and-mouse as you leave your line—you shouldn't come out to quickly or too slowly. Alan Hodgkinson, the former England keeper and now coach at Gillingham, had a good tip: make your positive move when the forward takes that split second to glance down.

So, generally speaking, it's a case of coming out cagily, then covering the final five yards or so very quickly. That gives you the chance, as the forward glances down, to smother the ball as Jimmy demonstrates or make him lose that vital bit of control. Also remember that he'll be a bit nervous because the pressure's on with only the keeper to beat!

his time the forward manages to get past Jimmy but, s well as making the angle more difficult, he's earned recious time for a defender to cover.

rave keeping . . . if the ball's for the taking, then you've got to take it.

If you want to get a photographer's job, get a hat ! This snappy dresser was ready for every eventuality during the World Cup finals in Argentina.

'We've got to stop meeting like this' —Terry Conroy drops in on photographers during a Stoke game.

The Photographers

They're always there, rain or shine, good game or bad . . . the photographers.

Some from Fleet Street, some from 'local rags'. All with a 90-minute mission. To get the great goal, the punch-up. If it happens, their editors want—demand—a picture of it.

Ray Green, one of the country's top freelances, got his large frame behind a typewriter to record an afternoon spent at Old Trafford . . .

'Out on to the pitch to grab a place by the goal, dodging the skilfully-thrown lighted fag-ends on the way . . . two frantic little arm-waving men shout something about having to move from my position because the TV cameras are here. I manage to convince the two messengers (why two) that I'm staying put . . . It's a boring and goalless first half. The half-time whistle arrives like the end of a prison sentence . . . As the second half starts concentration is broken by a large police sergeant yanking a protesting cherub out of the crowd and insisting that the lad wipe the spittle from the back of the quiet photographer from the *Daily Mail* . . . Still no score, which means I'm going to have to stay to the end in case there's a last-minute goal . . .

Anybody seen a photographer? Aston Villa players take up a new trade. What you can't see are 11 photographers kneeling in a neat group.

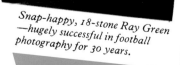

Snap-happy, 18-stone Ray Green —hugely successful in football photography for 30 years.

On Cup final day there are more photographers than players. This bunch looks bored as the play is centred at the other end—it's not all glamour, photography.

399

RISING STAR TOMMY LANGLEY

Tommy Langley's been a first-team regular at Stamford Bridge for about 18 months. For all but the first month the side have struggled.

But no one is blaming Langley, Chelsea's top scorer last season. His pace, enthusiasm and, above all, his effort have not wavered. Even if he does feel that Chelsea haven't been making the best use of him.

'I enjoy playing as a central striker, but not as target man,' he says. 'I prefer to be able to get out to the wing occasionally and put some crosses in. I don't like all this facing up business, that's not my game. My game's trying to use a bit of pace to get crosses in and get shots in.'

That's why he likes playing alongside big front men like Bill Garner.

'Bill's assets are in the air. He's no slouch on the floor, but he's really good in the air. He gives us an extra option. With him in the side we can hang balls up and we know we've got a good chance of winning them. Players are looking for knock-downs in and around the box.

'Without him our backs look up and see me facing up and they think: "Oh God, I can't hit a high ball because there's a chance he won't win it in the air."

'That's one of the reasons things haven't gone as well as they perhaps should have done. We've not been able to hit long balls

Tommy (left) *playing against West Bromwich Albion, whose skipper John Wile he rates very highly. 'John always gives me a hard game,' he says. 'He's a very experienced player.'*

with any confidence.'

That confidence seems to be in short supply at Stamford Bridge. As Tommy told *Handbook*: 'We've been playing very well away and terrible at home. Of course, we started against four good sides: Everton, Manchester City, Leeds and West Brom, They'll all be up there at the end.

It will surely work just as soon as Tommy's partnership with Duncan Mc-

'I don't like all this facing up business, that's not my game. My game's trying to use a bit of pace to get crosses and shots in.'

Club	Div	Pos	Season	Lge		FA Cp		Lge Cp	
				Ms	Gs	Ms	Gs	Ms	Gs
Chelsea	I	21	1974-75	8	1	–	–	–	–
	II	11	1975-76	10	1	–	–	–	–
	II	2	1976-77	6	2	–	–	–	–
	I	16	1977-78	41	11	4	2	–	–
				65	15	4	2	–	–

Tommy shows his pace and control against Coventry City's centre-back Gary Gillespie.

Kenzie develops fully. It's a partnership that promises a lot. Two quick-thinking, skilful and very mobile strikers zipping around your defence is a chilling prospect for First Division central defenders.

'It'll obviously take some time for us to get used to each other,' says Tommy. 'Duncan's a bit unpredictable . . . which is really one of his strong points. And it's probably one of the reasons we signed him. Because we were too predictable, you know.

'But we've had all the teething problems . . . and we should hit it off quite well.

'But there's a bit of competition there. We've got Gary Johnson now. He'll be there or thereabouts. There's Bill Garner. And big Trevor—Trevor Aylott. He'll be fighting for a place.'

They'll have to fight hard to displace Tommy, who made his League debut as a raw 16-year-old and who scored his first ever

League goal on his 17th birthday just under four years ago, and who is now an England Under-21 squad regular.

The Under-21s are run by those coaching priests, Dave Sexton and Terry Venables.

Says Tommy: 'Obviously I knew David when he was at Chelsea and I've known Terry for a while.

'Dave's coaching methods are a bit intricate . . . they're very intricate in fact. Obviously they do you good, because they make you think about the game. Then Terry's got so many ideas on free-kicks it's unbelievable. Terry does all the set pieces and he makes it really interesting. You have a laugh and do the work as well.'

There's no danger of Tommy Langley shirking the work. The prospects are bright for the 20-year-old from Basingstoke with the pace, the finish . . . and the right attitude.

DERBY LATE FOR RYAN'S EXPRESS!

'Too many players pass the buck on the edge of the area.' JOHN BOND

PETERS

Graham Taylor's analysis

Every manager wants midfield players who score goals, and it's amazing how few of them are about.

The secret, I think, is that if you play in midfield you've got to see yourself as a finisher, get into that frame of mind.

Nobody can doubt that John Ryan thinks exactly that way. He hits the ball with the confidence of any striker you care to mention. And he took up that position because he wasn't frightened of finishing. He has a real striker's appetite for goals.

Kevin Bond looked for Martin Peters from the free-

Midfielder John Ryan's goal-scoring exploits have been a major factor in Norwich City's encouraging form of recent months. Other factors include young Kevin Reeves's development and Martin Peters's mature authority.

All three players were involved in a spectacular goal against Derby at Carrow Road in September.

It stemmed from a free-kick taken by Kevin Bond inside the centre circle. Young Kevin's kick was directed towards Peters, who got up

well and headed on to Reeves just inside the Derby area . . . Reeves rode Steve Buckley's strong challenge to head down into the path of John Ryan, who was steaming in.

Ryan took it in his stride, blasting the ball past John Middleton from 25 yards.

REEVES

kick and Martin, as ever, got there first because of his marvellous gift—timing.

Reeves proved, if it needed proving, that the ball played back can be far superior to ones played forward. With defenders intent on getting goalside, as from Bond's free-kick, the space in front of them—behind the strikers—is the one to be used by midfield players, or defenders, following up.

And if it's someone like John Ryan, watch out !

RYAN

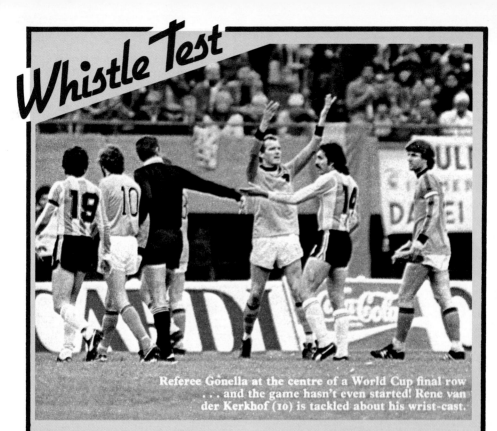

Whistle Test

Referee Gonella at the centre of a World Cup final row
... and the game hasn't even started! Rene van
der Kerkhof (10) is tackled about his wrist-cast.

What went wrong with the World Cup final? A lot of people said that the refereeing of Sergio Gonella was at least partly to blame . . . and former World Cup referee Jack Taylor couldn't agree more.

'If we're going to accept what I said last time about refereeing being about concentration, then the referee should be involved in the match before he gets out on the pitch,' Jack told *Handbook*.

'I would come out and say that the referee in this World Cup final did not do his job off the pitch . . . and that gave him problems from then onwards.

'He should have started refereeing long before he got out there. He had to go to the dressing-rooms to look at studs; he must have been aware that Rene van der Kerkhof had a plaster on his wrist.

'And should have made sure he brought both teams out together. It's the oldest trick in the book to keep the opposition waiting—Jack Johnson used to do that when he was fighting 70 years ago.

'The Argentinians systematically and deliberately came out late. Then they argued about the plaster. Hadn't they now done exactly what they set out to do? The Dutch were upset. Krol was so incensed that he was going to fetch the team off.

'For the first time in the World Cup—because their behaviour had been exemplary even in the Hungary match, when the Hungarians were really meaty—the Argentinians had resorted to extreme gamemanship. And the referee was not aware of the things he should have been ready for.

'And because he hadn't done his homework he faced the awful problems he had later. Neither side had respect for him.'

Gentleman Krol

'Rudi Krol's a super bloke,' reckons Jack Taylor. 'He came and played in my testimonial at Molineux without being asked. Cruyff was injured and couldn't come . . . so Krol phoned up and offered to play. He's a gentleman. So for him to be as incensed as he was in the World Cup final is really out of character.'

GRAEME SOUNESS

'Graeme is running things on the left ... giving us depth, width and a hell of a lot of great thinking.' EMLYN HUGHES

Every knife-edge pass, every deft incision into the opposition that Graeme Souness makes this season is like a cutting reproach for Argentina.

Not that this quietly-spoken young man is complaining publicly about being left out of Scotland's first two World Cup games, when the side was crying out for his vision and control.

'The whole trip was a disaster,' he says flatly. 'But it's history now. Yes, I was frustrated at being left out ... But I didn't feel resentment towards anybody.

'In a way I was lucky. I came out of it well.'

His single but impressive World Cup appearance—in the 3-2 win over Holland—and his brilliant displays this season have left his pride and his ambition undented.

'It's all about getting into the side regularly and winning regularly ... and winning something at the end of it,' he says. 'And for me, it's about establishing myself in the national team with good performances for both club and country.'

405

After lying low in Majorca during the summer, Graeme returned refreshed to a new season ... scoring twice in a 4-1 win at Maine Road. Tommy Booth and Ged Keegan (right) *and Paul Futcher* (below right) *get a close look at his impressive skills.*

Honours: European Cup winners medal 1978

Club	Div.	Pos.	Season	League		FA Cup		Lge Cup		Int'nls	
				Ms	Gs	Ms	Gs	Ms	Gs	Ms	Gs
Spurs				–	–	–	–	–	–	–	–
Middles-	II	4	1972-73	11	–	1	–	–	–		
brough	II	1	1973-74	35	7	2	–	2	–		
	I	7	1974-75	38	7	5	–	4	–	3	–
	I	13	1975-76	35	3	–	–	5	–	–	–
	I	12	1976-77	38	2	5	1	1	–	–	–
	I	14	1977-78	19	3	–	–	3	–	–	–
Liverpool	I	2	1977-78	15	2	–	–	–	–	4	–
				191	24	13	1	15	–	7	–

One thing he will say about Argentina—he learnt lessons from it. 'I think I've learnt how to handle different situations if ever I'm in them again,' Graeme told *Handbook*. 'It was also interesting to see how other people reacted under pressure.'

Souness was born in Edinburgh and went to the same school—Carickvale—as Dave Mackay. He doesn't come from a footballing family ... but it didn't take him long to make his mark in the game.

He was in the Scotland schoolboy (under 15) side that beat England boys 2-0 at White Hart Lane—where he was later to begin his career.

Team-mates in the Scotland schoolboy side of that time included John Robertson, the Forest winger who was also in Argentina, and Alistair Robertson, the West Bromwich Albion central defender.

Graeme first met Kenny Dalglish, who was later to become his Liverpool colleague and close friend, when he trained twice a week at Celtic during his last year at school. Kenny was two years ahead of him and on the way to fame and glory ... Graeme took some time to catch him up.

It wasn't Celtic who came for his signature but Spurs ... and he joined the London club when he left school at 15.

His four and a half years there were not particularly happy. 'I felt, as many young lads do, that I wasn't making enough progress with Spurs. I played in only one first team game ... in Iceland in a UEFA Cup tie.'

At one stage it seemed Hearts were prepared to take him back to Edinburgh. Souness, impatient and occasionally home-

sick, would have welcomed the move.

But he didn't think twice when Middlesbrough came in for him with a £35,000 fee in 1972 . . . and when Jack Charlton took over as manager from Stan Anderson, the Teesside club won the Second Division championship by a record 15 points.

After a fairly successful start to their latest spell in the First Division, however, Boro seemed to be slipping back. Charlton left, and new boss John Neal inherited a team that has had a persistent problem scoring goals.

Souness was growing in stature faster than the club. He had won youth caps while at Spurs . . . and he followed those up with two Under-23 and three full caps while at Middlesbrough.

'I enjoyed my years at Boro, but I realised I was never going to get anywhere with

Souness thoughtful (above) and skilful (right) against Wales last season . . . when he re-established himself in the Scottish squad.

The Souness story

Graeme was a Scotland schoolboy international when he was signed for Spurs by Bill Nicholson, but in four and a half years at White Hart Lane he made only one first team appearance—in a 6-1 UEFA Cup win in Keflavik in 1971 . . . He once walked out on the club and returned to Scotland, though he was persuaded to return . . . He was sold to Middlesbrough and made his League debut on 6 January 1973 at Fulham—Boro lost 2-1 . . . He played the first of his two Under-23 internationals against England on 13 March 1974, his second in Holland nearly two years later—both games were lost 2-0 . . . He made his full international debut against East Germany on 30 October 1974 at Hampden—Scotland won 3-0 . . . He joined Liverpool in January of this year.

them,' he explains. So he was delighted to join Liverpool just under a year ago.

The fee was £352,000—then a record cash deal between English clubs.

'Any player, anywhere, would give his right arm to come here. They're the best club in the world and any player would love to play for them. I couldn't get here quickly enough.

'I'm hungry for success . . . and Liverpool are a club where everything is geared to success.

'Quite honestly I'm really ambitious. And I knew I couldn't use that ambition at Middlesbrough. The set-up at Anfield is altogether different . . . and I'm thrilled at the chance of being part of it.

'I wanted a club where I could win something. All I had when I came here was a Second Division championship medal that I won in my second season at Middlesbrough.'

In less than a year at Liverpool he has won a European Cup winners medal . . . and in May he celebrated his 25th birthday . . . and his selection for Scotland's World Cup squad.

'It's fantastic when you think back to how things were last Christmas for me,' Graeme recalls. 'Everything seemed so black. It was the worst Christmas and New Year I've ever had.

'Then Liverpool came in and bought me—and everything has been roses since.'

The first sign of blight was in the European Cup defeat by Nottingham Forest. But Liverpool's start to the season has been impressive enough to suggest that they could well be back in Europe's top competition next year.

Souness also believes Liverpool have helped his game. 'The lads here knock the ball around more quickly than I had been used to . . . and that suits my style of play.'

'It's absolutely marvellous to play with world-class players around you, players who aren't just good on the ball, but who work for the good of the team all the time.'

Those players appreciate having him around as well. Such is his coolness and control in the centre of the pitch that the other midfielders—Ray Kennedy, McDermott and Case—can constantly get forward into attacking positions.

And Souness himself is no slouch when it comes to finding the net . . . as he proved when scoring twice in Liverpool's 4-1 win over Manchester City at Maine Road in August.

Souness against Bruges at Wembley in May . . . when he laid on the winning goal for Dalglish.

'We've been very good at getting people forward,' agrees Emlyn Hughes, 'especially from the right, with Terry McDermott and Jimmy Case. But it all stems from the other side . . .

'Graeme is running things on the left, giving us depth, width . . . and a hell of a lot of great thinking.

'Don't get me wrong, he was a hell of a player last season.'

But now, since Argentina, he's extra special.

'He's not come back shouting the odds or anything, but I think we all knew how steamed up he was to play out there. And there's no one in Liverpool who doesn't think it's criminal that he didn't get a real chance.'

But while others might admire his control, the way he always seems able to make time and space for himself and the quality of imagination he has brought to what has in the past looked to be a rather unexciting Liverpool side, Souness remains self-critical.

'I've always thought I could play better,' he told us. 'I reckoned it would take a season to settle down with Liverpool. What I'm looking for is consistency. It's no good having a good game now and again . . . You've got to do it week in and week out.'

A Matter of Fact

Messrs Villa, Ardiles, Sabella and Tarantini aren't the first South Americans to make an impact in English soccer. Newcastle United's FA Cup winning team of 1951 contained two Chileans, the brothers George and Ted Robledo.

Southampton's former England star Alan Ball emulated his father, Alan Ball Senior, when he succeeded Richard Dinnis as manager of Philadelphia Fury during the summer. Dad was formerly in charge at Preston North End, Halifax Town and Southport.

ABOVE Happier days for Ally MacLeod, now back with Ayr United. His full record as national team manager (won 7, drawn 5, lost 5) began with a bang, gradually evened off, and ended with a whimper...

1977:
28 May	Wales 0 Scotland 0 (HI)
1 Jun	Scotland 3 Northern Ireland 0 (HI)
4 Jun	England 1 Scotland 2 (HI)
15 Jun	Chile 2 Scotland 4
18 Jun	Argentina 1 Scotland 1
23 Jun	Brazil 2 Scotland 0
7 Sep	East Germany 1 Scotland 0
21 Sep	Scotland 3 Czechoslovakia 0 (WC-QR)
12 Oct	Wales 0 Scotland 2 (WC-QR).

1978:
22 Feb	Scotland 2 Bulgaria 1
13 May	Scotland 1 Northern Ireland 1 (HI)
17 May	Scotland 1 Wales 1 (HI)
20 May	Scotland 0 England 1 (HI)
3 Jun	Peru 3 Scotland 1 (WC-F)
7 Jun	Iran 1 Scotland 1 (WC-F)
11 Jun	Holland 2 Scotland 3 (WC-F)
20 Sep	Austria 3 Scotland 2 (EC).

[HI—Home International Championship; WC-QR—World Cup Qualifying Rounds; WC-F—World Cup finals; EC—European Championship].

In 1977 George Best played in all four home countries within just 10 days. His whirlwind tour began on 21 September when he helped Northern Ireland to a 2-0 win over Iceland in his native Belfast. On 24 September he turned out for Fulham in their 3-1 reverse at Cardiff; two days later he hit Fulham's third goal in a 5-3 defeat at St Mirren in the Anglo-Scottish Cup. Then, on 1 October, it was back to London for Best as Fulham won 3-2 in a stormy 'derby' match at Crystal Palace in the Second Division.

The pluckiest team in Wales ... that's Llandudno Swifts. For the past three seasons they've been propping up the entire Welsh League (North). In 1975-76 they lost all 20 games; the following season they actually gained two wins and a draw. But it was back to normal in 1977-78—no wins, two draws and 20 defeats, with the staggering goal difference of minus 107!

Former Mansfield striker Ray Clarke, once rejected by Spurs, found himself in the UEFA Cup this season with Ajax following his move from Sparta Rotterdam.

The One-Club Man

Bulging neck muscles shows Keith's effort in training.

'I made Keith club captain because he's a great influence on the youngsters here. He still trains like an apprentice.' Charlton manager ANDY NELSON.

The young Peacock didn't seem an obvious recruit to the brash world of pro football.

He was a small, rather quiet grammar schoolboy . . . 550 first team games ago—give or take the odd 90 minutes.

'I'd got six "O" levels and was halfway through my "A" level course when I turned pro,' recalls Keith. 'My teachers weren't too pleased. They thought it was a waste of a good education.'

Sixteen 'wasted' years later, Keith is still doing the job he loves for Charlton Athletic.

He has a nice house for his family down in picturesque Kent and a testimonial a few years ago will keep him in shin-pads for life.

'I suppose I've missed out on transfer money but there's a lot to be said for staying at one club. You put your roots down in one area and there's no upheaval for your family. Also I've coached in local schools for years—and the testimonial helped.'

Only the legendary Sam Bartram has played more times for the Valley side—and Keith's career hasn't

411

Morning in the life of one-club man Keith Peacock at Charlton Athletic's training ground

Brazil . . . nuts!

Brazil had a lot to answer for in the early part of Keith's career at Charlton.

'They'd won the World Cup in Sweden, then in Chile in 1962, and their 4-2-4 style caught on.

'I was playing as an inside-forward and either had to be one of the two midfield players or one of the four up front.

'I went up front but had problems with my height. I was in and out of the side for a couple of seasons, a very troubling period.'

exactly coincided with seasons of stirring success.

'No, they haven't been all that hot, have they. At the start of each season every pro says: This is the one, but for 95 per cent of us it never is.

'All I've ever won—apart from promotion to the Second Division—are the Wembley Five-a-Sides, not much to tell the grandchildren really.

'But that's not what it's all about as far as I'm concerned. It's about being

involved in all that football— and I've got a lot of satisfaction from doing my bit for Charlton.

Keith, 33, has been at The Valley since he was a 14-year-old Newcastle supporter.

'My dad fixed me up with a trial and I had to show what I could do in 20 minutes. I must have shown something.'

He signed pro in 1962— 'July 19th it was'—and made his debut in front of a 40,000 crowd at Roker Park.

412

Still working on the skills . . . still listening to the 'boss' until it's time to go.

'We lost 1-0 and I decided, that's it, pack it in. Actually, I didn't have a bad game.'

Countless clubmates have come and gone since then—'must be hundreds'—and Keith has turned it on for five different managers.

'The best team I played with was probably the one with Alan Campbell, Graham Moore and Paul Went. In fact, the only time I came close to leaving was after Alan was transferred.

'We had this great understanding on the pitch. I was out on the wing in Alan's day and how you play as a winger depends a lot on the service you get. Alan could find me with his eyes closed.'

How much life is left in the Peacock legs?

'It's all in the head, this age business. Reaching 30 is a terrible psychological blow to some people, but you don't change overnight from an athlete to an ageing wreck.

'I still look forward to Monday morning training!'

Sub standard

Keith's name will always be in the record books.

On 12 August 1965, he was the first player in the League to jog down the touchline, stretch his muscles, take off his tracksuit and join the action from the dug-out.

Yes, he was the very first substitute to be used in a Football League match.

That Saturday was the first in the new season and Charlton were up against Bolton at Burnden Park. An early injury sent on Peacock.

Steve Hunt turned down super stardom to send himself to Coventry—and no hint of regret.

'England is the place to prove yourself a top-class player. After the disappointment of not getting the chance to break through at Aston Villa, I intend to make it here now.'

Make no mistake, Mr Hunt could have made it big in Manhattan. He admits himself: 'I would have been set up for life there.'

The kid who went for £30,000 from Aston Villa reserves became the pin-up boy of the star-studded New York Cosmos.

Owned by the movie moguls Warner Brothers, the Cosmos were mad-keen to put Hunt in the penthouse league alongside Franz Beckenbauer and Dennis Tueart—just to get him to sign another contract.

'I can't really explain how I did so well. I just seemed to catch on with the fans—perhaps because I was English.

'At the start we were only getting small crowds but then, as we won matches, the people started turning up.

'Out there you're a winner or nothing. We were winners and pretty soon there were 50,000 crowds.'

With Hunt the hero, Cosmos took the title . . . and the American dream began.

'It was just unbelievable. The club gave me a car worth £4,000 to drive around in and they also paid for the flat where my wife Sue and I lived. It was a luxury place in New Jersey—£500 a month —and Miss Universe had a flat in the same block.'

But even that was nothing compared with mixing with Franz and the boys in Manhattan. The Cosmos were virtually asking Hunt to name his own price.

But the lure of the English First Division—with its slush and fog—was too great.

'I always knew I would come back. Last winter I kept in shape at Coventry. I liked the set-up there and when Gordon Milne asked me to join the club I didn't hesitate for a moment.

'The American trip was a great experience but I always looked upon it as just that.'

Part of that experience was playing with a bloke called Pele. 'Here was this great man, the most famous footballer in the world, but there was no big-headedness about him. He had time for everyone and I learned a great deal from him.'

Yet Hunt doesn't rate Pele as the greatest in terms of ball skills. The person he puts on that particular pedestal is another player who went west in more ways than one . . . a lad by the name of George Best.

HUNT FOR A CAP

Hunting for goals—Steve gets past Tampa Bay Rowdie Frantz St Lot in a Cosmos raid. Now he's after an England cap...

From East Coast to West Midlands... Steve Hunt opts for the harsh reality of a nine-month English season instead of the marvels of Manhattan. He's here to prove himself in the toughest league in the world... and here he's proving himself against Chelsea's Gary Locke at Highfield Road. 'The American trip was a great experience,' says Steve, 'but I always looked upon it as just that—a great experience.'

Socks round his ankles, flowing blond locks, Steve Hunt was a natural for the image-making Americans ... 'I can't really explain how I did so well,' says Steve. 'I just seemed to catch on with the fans.'

STEVE'S AMERICAN DREAM

ABOVE **Hunt in the forefront ... Steve waits with the other Cosmos— including Dennis Tueart and Franz Beckenbauer— before the game against Tampa Bay Rowdies. As part of the American way of selling their football, each player is introduced individually to the crowd. And number one pin-up among the star-studded Cosmos was an ex-Villa reserve ... Steve Hunt.**

Founded: 1883
Address: Edgeley Park, Stockport, Cheshire SK3 9DD
Ground: Capacity 24,900; Playing area: 100.6 x 68.6 m
Record att'd'ce: 27,883 v Liverpool, FA Cup 5th round, 11.2.50
Record victory: 13-0 v Halifax Town, Div. 3(N), 6.1.34
Record defeat: 1-8 v Chesterfield, Div. 2, 19.4.02
Most League points: 64, Div. 4, 1966-67
Most League goals: 115, Div. 3(N), 1933-34
League scoring record: 46, Alf Lythgoe, Div. 3(N), 1933-34
Record League aggregate: 132, Jack Connor, 1951-56
Most League appearances: 465, Robert Murray, 1952-63
Most capped player: 1, Harry Hardy, England, 1924
Honours: Div. 3(N) Champions 1922, 1937; Div. 4 Champions 1967
League career: 1900-04 Div. 2; *1905-21 Div. 2; 1921-22 Div. 3(N); 1922-26 Div. 2; 1926-37 Div. 3(N (; 1937-38 Div. 2; 1938-58 Div. 3(N); 1958-59 Div. 3; 1959-67 Div. 4; 1967-70 Div. 3; 1970- Div. 4
[*failed to gain re-election 1904. Rejoined when Div. 2 increased from 19 to 20 clubs in 1905.]

STOCKPORT COUNTY

The trouble with being in the Fourth Division is that it seems such a long, long way from the First.

Lower gates, lower wages . . . the whole scene encourages players to think of themselves as fourth-rate.

One way out of this vicious circle is self-confidence . . . but that doesn't come out of thin air.

Watford walked away with the Fourth Division title last season, and there's no doubting the talent in their team—just ask Manchester United. But who would deny that those three 'winners' Graham Taylor, Elton John and Bertie Mee have had a fantastic psychological effect on the Watford players?

And so to Stockport County.

The team from 'somewhere near Manchester' have spent 17 of the last 20 seasons in the League's bottom grade.

Then Mike Summerbee came along. By his own admission, he's not the world's greatest coach.

Stockport line up for the 1978-79 promotion assault under new player-manager Mike Summerbee.

Nor is he everyone's cup of tea—as the many refs who have had to ask him about the number of m's in his name will testify.

But Mike Summerbee, like Watford's big three, is a born winner. He won a League Championship medal with Manchester City in 1968 and followed that with FA Cup, League Cup and European Cup Winners' Cup medals, as well as eight England caps.

Suddenly, with Summerbee's appointment as player-manager, Stockport County were back on the soccer map. Confirmation came at Old Trafford in front of 42,384 fans at the end of August.

It looked like an easy League Cup opener for Manchester United against the team from down the road. But with less than two minutes left, Stockport led 2-1. With Gordon McQueen already taking an early shower, Sexton's men looked down and out.

Then . . . disaster for County. Two last-gasp goals, the first a deflected free-kick and the winner a hotly-disputed Ashley Grimes penalty, turned their glory into despair.

In the past, Stockport have had to look forward to giant-killing jam to improve on the weekly bread and butter.

In 1965 County travelled to Anfield for a

Mike Summerbee's side almost brought off a shock win at Old Trafford in August.

Mike on Mike

Mike Summerbee talking: 'I've met a million people who say they're FA coaches and I'm not interested.

'I've played for 20 years and I know it's about getting players to work for you. You've got to be a motivator and if I couldn't do it I'd jack it all in tomorrow.

(He gets a phone call about a player he wants to watch: 'I don't want to go in a great big car, a Yankee 26-footer. I want to be inconspicuous!')

'I've got First Division experience and a Fourth Division club. It's not hard to make Fourth Division players feel like First Division ones—that's my job.

Hard man with a tough task . . . Mike Summerbee with the job of getting Stockport promoted.

'I've got no ambition to be a First Division manager. I want to do it at Stockport.

'It's a nice little club and there's plenty of crowd potential with Manchester United on our doorstep.

'We play home games on Friday nights and we can all watch other games on the Saturday or have a long, relaxing weekend.

'Malcolm Allison was the biggest influence on me. He made me believe in myself. Everyone needs to be told: "You did well today". It means everything.

'I've never been a popular player in the public eye, but if you asked the opposition they'd all want me in their team.'

Eddie Prudham fires one past Hartlepool defender Dick Malone in September's League game.

fourth round FA Cup tie, and held mighty Liverpool to a 1-1 draw. They put up a fierce fight in the replay too, before losing 2-0.

In 1972 they ended the League Cup hopes of West Ham and Crystal Palace, both in the First Division, before losing to eventual finalists Norwich City.

Cup runs are always welcome, but Summerbee's top priority is success in the League—something Edgeley Park hasn't tasted for more than a decade.

The last time County won promotion from the Fourth was in 1967, two years after finishing in 92nd place in the League.

Backed by an ambitious board, they stormed to the Fourth Division title by a five point margin. Crowds regularly topped 10,000 as 'Go Go County' prepared to 'do a Coventry' and climb into the Second.

The Stockport bubble burst dramatically as the ageing stars signed to draw the crowds failed to produce the goods on the pitch.

By 1970 they had slipped back into the Fourth. The fans deserted the club in droves —with gates often below the 2,000 mark.

Now, slowly but surely, Summerbee is breathing life into Stockport again.

He's building a team to match the best in the lower divisions. Les Bradd, who hit 125 goals in Notts County's rise from the depths of the Fourth to Second Division respectability, arrived for a £15,000 fee, which equalled County's record buy.

His partnership with Stuart Lee, snapped up on a 'free' from Wrexham—for whom he once scored in a Cup Winners Cup tie with Anderlecht—is already terrorising defences.

The team and the town are geared for a higher grade of football in the near future... and with Mike Summerbee at the helm, it would be a real gamble to bet against it.

Stockport's Friday Best
In 1975, with County struggling at the wrong end of the Fourth Division, manager Roy Chapman persuaded the one and only George Best to turn out for the club; 9,220 fans braved the weather on Friday 28 November to see the former idol of Old Trafford score in a 3-2 win over Swansea—nearly four times the crowd at their previous home game. Best notched another in a 2-2 home draw with Watford, but appeared only once more in Stockport colours, in the 1-0 victory over Southport.

Spot the spectator
In May 1921 Edgeley Park was under suspension, so County were forced to play their Second Division fixture with Leicester at Old Trafford. The Manchester public weren't very interested—only 13 fans turned up! That fixture is still the smallest ever recorded at a League game.

Like father, like son
Alec Herd and his son David played together for Stockport against Hartlepools United in the last Third Division North match of the 1950-51 season —the only instance of father and son appearing together in League history. David later played for Arsenal, Manchester United and Scotland.

Franz Beckenbauer

Franz Beckenbauer would have loved to have played in the English First Division!

'It is the home of football, isn't it, and every top player thinks about playing there. But the door was never open for me and, now that it is, it is too late. Even if I had the chance I have an Achilles problem which makes things very difficult for me.'

'Kaiser Franz' was talking during a break in training before the Cosmos game against Chelsea in September.

Why, apart from the money, did he go to America?

'What else can I do? I have been with the German, European and World champions. Now I like to help in a country where the game is beginning. But of course I miss the big football atmosphere. I like the English style. It is still one of the best in the world, and English football is coming up again for sure.

'You are as strong as ever but now you are thinking more about skill, it seems. You have always had big players at centre-forward and of course it is important to use their strength in the air, but you never had enough variety. Now, with players like Kevin Keegan, you are more dangerous.'

His advice to youngsters echoes most of what's been said in *Handbook*: 'Practice and more practice—and listen to the coach. If you have a weak left foot, work to make it stronger. Or, like me, see if you can use the outside of the right!'

ABOVE *Kaiser of the world . . . Franz Beckenbauer holds aloft the World Cup won by West Germany in 1974.* BELOW *Franz during training at Stamford Bridge for the Chelsea game.*

Alan Woodward on taking corners

'You've got to vary your corners, as with anything else you attempt . . . what you don't do is float over the type of corner that goalkeepers love to gobble up—that's being sloppy, unprofessional.'

Crowds love corners—they invariably bring the kind of goalmouth excitement that's so much a part of the British game.

And they shouldn't be put down as just another excuse for players to fight for the ball. Much thought and no small amount of skill goes into taking corners at the highest level of the game.

Alan Woodward has taken them on both sides for Sheffield United and, during a session at Bramall Lane, only one out of 20 inswingers failed to find the back of the net!

'It's largely common sense, taking corners,' says Alan. 'If your centre-half comes up and gets beyond the far post you should at least bear him in mind!

The Woodward outswinger . . . usually for the big men beyond the far post or for someone to glance on from the near post.

Alan gets his foot slightly under the ball and, at the same, 'punches' through it for the pace that's needed.

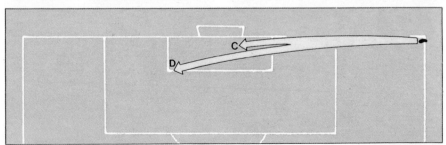

The strength that Alan Woodward can put into his corners has also been known to shock goalkeepers when he lets loose from 25 or 30 yards. By the end of last season he had notched up no fewer than 158 League goals in more than 431 appearances for Sheffield United, his only club before joining the Tulsa Roughnecks.

From this angle you can see how Alan balances —helped by both arms.

These are the two basic areas Alan aims for from the right— near post, for glances on into the danger area, or beyond the far post for the big men looking for headers. 'Don't float over the kind of corner that goalkeepers love to gobble up —if you give it to him you're asking to be dropped,' warns corner king Woodwood.

'But there's got to be variation, as with anything else you attempt. Being predictable is one of the biggest sins in top-class football.

'I'm right-footed, so from the right I'll generally be aiming to hit them deep to the big men or find someone by the near post to head for goal or flick the ball on into the danger area.

'What you don't do is float over the type of corner that goalkeepers love to gobble up —that's being sloppy, unprofessional'.

From the left Alan will often look to get in one of his many dangerous inswingers— which have earned him a few 'direct from a corner' goals during his long career.

'Opponents always stick someone on the near post but if you give the ball a bit of air and curl it in, it can still cause a lot of trouble.

'Again it's important to vary them—unless the inswingers cause panic every time—and you can do it by hitting the far corner of the six-yard box. If you can hit it even further you might find an attacking full-back who's unlikely to be marked and can cause a real surprise.

'Whatever you do, keep it away from that keeper—if you give the ball to him you're asking to be dropped!'

Graham Taylor:

The point about a corner is that you've got possession and it's a crime not to make positive use of it. So the general rule is, keep it simple. Don't try inswingers with the outside of the foot—unless your name is Cruyff! And, as with crosses, it's largely a question of hitting areas, not aiming for players— near-post and beyond the far post—and you use inswingers or outswingers. The high inswinger always causes problems to keepers and defenders. The outswingers are usually for the big men, often defenders.

Always make sure there's good pace on the ball—

Alan's inswinger . . . 'I make up my mind beforehand where I'm aiming for and then it's concentration on the ball.'

'Opponents always stick someone on the near post but if you curl it in, it can still cause a lot of trouble.'

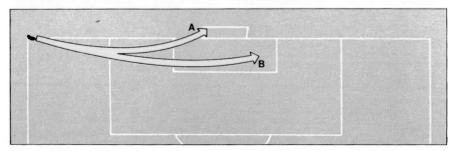

remember Latchford's goal from Brooking's corner against the Republic of Ireland, which beat Givens at the near post?—because it gives your forwards something to attack and only a touch can lead to a goal.

Balls that hang about in the air give defenders more of a chance—especially goalkeepers who are prepared to leave their line to win the ball.

One more aspect—I tell whoever takes Watford's corners not to stand and admire them but to get back into play. If your recovery line is to the corner of the area, you can pick up clearances or be ready to get back and defend.

Alan gets the distance by using a long follow-through after his kicks.

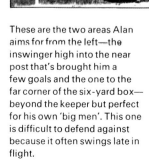

A corner made popular by Manchester United's Steve Coppell is the hard, low one—like a shot. Here (above and below) **Alan shows how it's done. You get over the ball more and drive it into the area —a corner that depends very much on the element of surprise.**

These are the two areas Alan aims for from the left—the inswinger high into the near post that's brought him a few goals and the one to the far corner of the six-yard box—beyond the keeper but perfect for his own 'big men'. This one is difficult to defend against because it often swings late in flight.

RISING ROY STAR AITKEN

With seven 'O' levels and two 'A's, Roy Aitken could have opted for a secure career in commerce. Instead, he chose football.

And if the last two seasons are anything to go by, he made the right choice.

For the 19-year-old Celtic midfielder is fast emerging as one of the most exciting talents in Scottish football.

Listen to what the experts say about him.

Jock Stein: 'Aitken is a player of tremendous potential. He'll go all the way.'

Billy McNeill, who succeeded Stein as Celtic's boss: 'Roy is perhaps the biggest Celtic success of the last year. He came into the side as a stop-gap and has grown in stature and confidence.'

Aerobatic Aitken . . . Celtic's young midfield player/defender on his way down after trying to relieve pressure on his defence.

'Naturally it's my desire to play for my country, but you've got to produce the goods at club level first ... One thing I'm not is a ball player. I make no bones about the fact that I go in hard.'

Honours: League Championship medal 1977; FA Cup Winners medal 1977; League Cup runners-up medal 1976-77, 1977-78						
Club	Season	League		FA Cup		LgeCup
Celtic	1975-76	12	–	–	–	2	–
	1976-77	33	5	7	1	6	–
	1977-78	33	2	3	–	5	1
		78	7	10	1	13	1

Yet Aitken's development has been during —for Celtic—a sticky period.

With the break-up of the 'Lisbon Lions', the European Cup winners of 1967, Aitken and other talented youngsters at Parkhead have had to accept the kind of responsibility normally shouldered by seasoned players.

'I've probably grown up a lot quicker as a result,' Roy told *Handbook*. 'Frankly, I've enjoyed the responsibility.'

Aitken was still at school when he made his Premier League debut against Aberdeen at Pittodrie on 21 February 1976.

A few weeks later he sampled European football for the first time in a Cup Winners' game against East Germany's Sachsenring Zwickau.

He quickly grabbed the public's imagination as the piano-playing schoolboy with the sting in the tackle.

A short time later Roy swapped his schoolbooks for the boots of a pro.

'I wasn't taking an enormous gamble because I already had academic qualifications.'

His versatility is almost a problem—he has yet to find a settled position. 'I'm happy in the middle of the park or as a central defender. I suppose I have a preference for a deep-lying role because you're more involved.'

'One thing I'm not is a ball player. I'm a ball winner. I make no bones about the fact that I go in hard for the ball, although I always try to get it cleanly.'

With a crop of Under-21 games under his belt, he must be thinking about a full international career.

But he says: 'You've got to produce the goods at club level first. Naturally it's my desire to play for my country, but consistency in the domestic game comes first.'

Already with three Cup finals and two championship seasons behind him, Roy is more like a 'Young Veteran' than a 'Rising Star'. But honest Aitken would be the first to say: 'Still a long way to go.'

Aggressive Aitken ... all the honesty and commitment in Roy's play shows on his face as he plays the ball forward for Celtic.

Paul Taylor (left) **and Jim Hinch flank a group of soccer-mad American youngsters.**

Sowing the seeds of US soccer

The Americans know their soccer boom can't survive for ever on expensive imports. They must develop their own potential—and the kids must be caught early . . .

Beverly Hills is known for its stars. Most of the big names from the Hollywood movie world live there. But that same plush California city could produce a different style of big names in future . . . the new American soccer stars. That's if two ex-Football League pros have their way.

Beverly Hills is just one of many venues in the Los Angeles area where Paul Taylor and Jim Hinch run soccer camps. Both are fully qualified FA coaches who served their apprenticeships in the League.

Hinch, a tall striker who never quite fulfilled his undoubted potential, finished last season at Barnsley after spells with Tranmere, Plymouth, Hereford, Southport, York and Sheffield Wednesday. Taylor, who played for Wednesday in the Second Division, also turned out for Colchester, Southport and York and Hereford.

Now they are sowing the seeds of soccer for the young Americans of the West Coast. Girls as well as boys from five to 15 attend week-long sessions which would be the envy of any youngster in Britain.

The week is packaged in true US style. On arrival

each youngster is presented with the camp T-shirt to wear. At the end of the course everyone leaves with their own soccer ball. Food and soft drinks are liberally supplied during breaks in the sessions, and there is a photographer on hand to capture a permanent reminder of a course that is both fun and functional. All for just over £20 for the week ... including of course the guaranteed supply of California sunshine.

Spreading the gospel
Jim and Paul's 'Pro-Soccer Coaching' enterprise does not ignore the competitive elements. During the week the youngsters are split into teams, and the Friday inter-camp tournament is one of the highspots of the course.

Bobby McAlinden is another Englishman spreading the gospel on the West Coast. Once with Manchester City, he resumed his professional career with the Los Angeles Aztecs, where his duties also include supervision of coaching.

His task was made more difficult last summer by the horrendous experience of the club on the field, where they lost 13 out of 16 home matches. Every youngster loves to identify with a successful professional club, and Californians are no exception. Though the California Surf of the NASL and three Los Angeles clubs in the professional American Soccer League offered alternatives.

Soccer breakthrough
Gordon Jago, now manager of the Tampa Bay Rowdies, reckons that it will still be 20 years before the NASL is dominated by United States players, but acknowledges that the ultimate survival of

Spreading the word ... former Manchester City player Bobby McAlinden's duties with Los Angeles Aztecs include the supervision of coaching sessions for groups of all ages—and both sexes.

soccer as a major sport depends on that break-through being made.

So the pioneer work done by the likes of Hinch, Taylor and McAlinden is crucial.

They do work with some basic advantages. Soccer is now a much-approved family sport by parents, who in recent years have been frightened by the alarming injury rate in American 'grid-iron' football. And equipment is relatively inexpensive compared to the traditional American games.

Guys and gals
The kids themselves particularly appreciate participating in a game which at the moment is relatively free of the blight of the continual substitutions

afflicting so much of their sport. And of course girls are also encouraged to play; indeed girls leagues are a regular feature of the organisation of youth soccer.

'Biting the hand'
In the end this extensive missionary work will surely produce an end product. The very competitive streak in Americans will ensure that they won't settle for second best. And one day the United States, like so many other nations in the past, will 'bite the hand' that fed it on the international scene.

Then the likes of John Travolta and Paul Newman might have to share some of that Hollywood limelight—with the soccer stars from Beverly Hills ...

A Matter of Fact

ABOVE Villa's John Robson, who won a Championship medal with Derby, enjoyed a testimonial recently after being forced to retire due to multiple sclerosis.

Who's a pretty boy then? Female readers of an Italian paper have voted Mario Kempes of Valencia Europe's most beautiful player, with Hans Krankl, Paolo Rossi and Kevin Keegan close behind.

What's in a name? Orient keep changing theirs: from 1881 until 1946 they were known as Clapton Orient; then they became Leyton Orient until 1967, when the club decided on plain simple Orient.

Mexico's squad for the 1978 World Cup finals contained only two keepers, Pedro Soto and Jose Pilar-Reyes, whereas every other country took three. Perhaps they should have used them both at once . . . Mexico lost all three games, conceding 12 goals.

Going for the Golden Boot award for Europe's top First Division scorer . . . that's Rudi Geels. Signed by Anderlecht from Ajax in the summer for £200,000, Geels smashed nine goals for his new club in his first four matches in the league.

Whistle Test

'A big game can be a hard time for some linesmen—50,000 people telling you which way to point your flag can be a persuasive source of argument.' TOM REYNOLDS

Top ref Tom Reynolds is under no illusions about the importance of getting on the same wavelength as his linesmen before a big match.

'It's absolutely vital,' he says. 'That's why the two hours or so before the kick are so useful. It's all about soaking up the atmosphere—refs need to as much as players—and, even more important, getting to know your linesmen.

'As far as that's concerned, it's not only a question of telling them about anything special you want them to look out for. It's also about getting to know them as people, what makes them tick and anything else that might be relevant.

'Let's face it, there are personality clashes in all walks of life and there's no reason why that shouldn't be the case on the football pitch.

'Also, it's true that a big game can be a hard time for some linesmen without much experience. When there're 50,000 people telling you which way to point your flag it can be a pretty persuasive source of argument!'

Getting to know you . . . Tom's linesmen introduce themselves.

LEFT Berlin 1938: The England team give the Nazi salute—on the advice of the British ambassador Sir Nevile Henderson, who felt it would 'appease the crowd'—before thrashing Germany 6-3 in the Olympic Stadium. The players are (from left to right): Bastin, Robinson, Goulden, Sproston, Matthews, Welsh, Willingham, Young, Broome, Woodley and Hapgood. The following year the two nations were at war with each other. It was 1954 before they met again on the football field.

The crowd of 1,711 for the Cardiff City-Torquay United League Cup tie in 1977 was the Welsh club's worst ever at Ninian Park.

Frank Haffey was in goal for Scotland when England beat them 9-3 at Wembley in 1963— their worst ever defeat by 'the auld enemy'. A few years later, with Celtic leading Airdrie 9-0, he took a penalty . . . and missed !

There is a club called Derby in the Swedish League; Chile has an Everton and a Rangers; while Uruguay have a Liverpool in their championship !

The present Lord Grosvenor, now one of Britain's richest men, was a fine schoolboy player at Harrow and was offered a trial by Fulham.

Stay with it, linesman
One time a linesman dropped Tom in it came during a Luton-Stoke game a few seasons ago.

'It was a glaring example of a linesman wilting under pressure. A ball was played into the Stoke target man just past the halfway line.

'Unknown to me he was off-side and the linesman flagged. But the ball was played first time through to Alan Hudson, who made a run from his own half.

'The linesman should have stopped where he was with his flag raised, but he followed the play.

'Hudson, with only the keeper to beat, was a bit flash and his shot trickled towards the line.

'All the controversy— it made the Sunday headlines—would have been avoided if the linesman had kept calm . . . and kept his flag up.'

'BRILLIANT,

A North London school teaches Sout

If you watched the television coverage of the World Cup you'll surely remember the piece Bobby Charlton did on those boys in Argentina showing off their skills. Remember the breathtaking control, the absolute dominance they had over those footballs?

Those youngsters displayed a kind of skill we have come to associate with South American players. The great Brazilian teams, Uruguay, Argentina—all World Cup winners—and even the lesser foot-

balling nations like Chile and Peru all have a tradition of outstanding ball skills.

Whatever their other strengths and weaknesses, such national sides always seem to comprise players who can, with almost disdainful ease, kill a travelling ball stone dead on any part of their bodies and, once it has dropped to their feet, can dribble, swerve and bend that ball to their will.

But don't believe the argument that says it's a matter of birthright—that the South Americans have the sun and the Samba and

VITAS'
American skills

the skill in their blood—whereas we're from a different and colder part of the world. We play faster and harder. That's the way we are and it's pointless trying to acquire techniques that are alien to us.

Don't believe it. British kids are just as skilful as South Americans . . . if they're given the right encouragement and the right coaching. Just look at Holloway Comprehensive School in North London.

There you can see young British boys performing skills similar to those produced by South American kids. Furthermore the coach in charge, Alan Wright, has been developing young footballers along these lines ever since he came to the school—20 years ago.

When *Handbook* went to see them, the boys, all second years, were kicking a few practice balls around while they waited for their coach. The first thing he did when he arrived was to ask them to put the balls away.

As we had come to watch them work on their ball skills, this seemed a little strange, but Alan promptly upended a sack which he had brought with him and out tumbled balls which were only one-third the normal size—and much more difficult to control.

The boys were on to them in a flash. Each boy with his own ball. There was a constant patter of plastic on parquet flooring as they dribbled their way around the gym, tip-tapping the ball from one foot to the other and paying just enough attention to their feet to retain control but looking up all the time so as to avoid an almighty pile-up.

Alan Wright jockeyed them around, talking all the time . . . ordering changes of direction, changes of pace . . . getting them to flick the ball up with one foot and then pat it down with the other . . .

He kept the boys involved and on the move with constant encouragement.

'Well done, Stevie son.'

'That's the way, Tony lad.'

'*Brilliant*, Vitas.'

He explained the reasoning behind these exercises: 'We're all born physically illiterate. We have to learn how to express ourselves with our bodies.

'These exercises smooth out the rough edges of our body movements. I emphasise lightness and fluency. It's at this stage in their development that they could start to form bad habits which they'll end up stuck with for the rest of their playing careers. So rather than see them contorting themselves to keep hold of a ball I would prefer them to lose possession of it and learn how to control it properly.

'Performing seals'

'People often say to me that the best place for these sorts of skills is the London Palladium, not the football field. They tell me I'm turning these youngsters into performing seals . . .

'But I'm opening up alternatives for them. In England most passes are played along the ground. That's fine as far as it goes . . . But there is only one level of ground, there are endless levels of air. If you pass a ball through the air you have more space to work in and more options.

'You know, teachers from other schools are always remarking on how small Holloway footballers are. But we don't need to pick big lads. Because of these sessions our players can use skill instead of muscle.

'When people see a player execute a delicate skill they think that it's instinctive. In a way they're right . . . but that instinct has to be learned. The South Americans are no more naturally gifted than we are; it's just that they place greater stress on learning ball skills.'

Even the great Pele used to practise for hours on end. And he used a small ball because he couldn't afford the real thing. Once he'd mastered that small ball actual footballs were almost a doddle.

The boys were now sitting on the gym floor juggling the small balls from foot to foot. Alan Wright could scarcely contain his delight. 'Look at them now. They're learning by instinct. Adjusting their bodies all the time. Learning without thinking about it—and that's the best way. They use exercises just like a young musician practises scales on an instrument.

'Once they reach a certain level of ability they start yawning. That's when they'll need to get out and compete . . . to move on and test their skills against players from other schools.'

Practice makes perfect

Alan doesn't bother with these skills sessions once the boys reach 13, but he relies on them to keep up with their 'scales' on their own—just as Pele used to continue to practise with a small ball right up to the end of his career.

Nearly an hour had passed since the session had begun and the exercises had become increasingly difficult. Just before we left Alan Wright offered to show us some volleying technique. He picked a boy to demonstrate.

'Which foot do you kick with son?'

'Both, sir.'

'But which one do you prefer?'

'Either one, sir.'

When Alan Wright gets that sort of reply he knows he's well on the way . . .

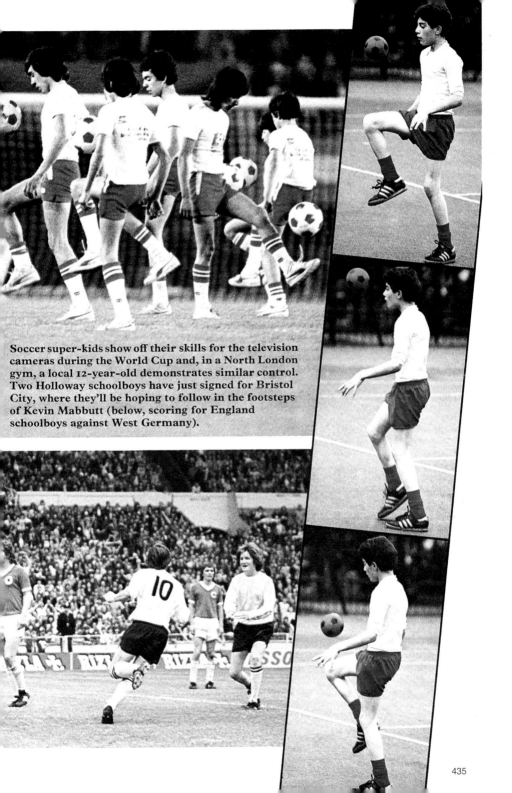

Soccer super-kids show off their skills for the television cameras during the World Cup and, in a North London gym, a local 12-year-old demonstrates similar control. Two Holloway schoolboys have just signed for Bristol City, where they'll be hoping to follow in the footsteps of Kevin Mabbutt (below, scoring for England schoolboys against West Germany).

The Wembley myth

Football's most famous arena seems to hold an enormous pitch—but the facts and figures tell a different story.

Alan Durban—now manager of Stoke City—was football's man for all pitches. Before Wimbledon and Wigan came along, he had played at all 92 Football League grounds in a four-division career with Cardiff City, Derby County and Shrewsbury Town, the last as player-manager.

The evening before every Cup Final you can bet there'll be talk of Wembley's 'wide open spaces'.

But how much space is there really across the once-hallowed turf? Is it even the widest pitch in Britain?

Not by a five-yard pass, it's not. No fewer than 26 Football League pitches are as wide or wider—and have a bigger area—than the famous international arena.

It would be more accurate to talk of the 'wide open spaces' of Edgar Street— Hereford United's pitch— which is 80 yards wide, five more than Wembley's.

Other places to be a winger are Manchester City (79 yards) and Doncaster (79), while it's hardly claustrophobic at Cardiff,

Carlisle, Charlton, Everton, Nottingham Forest, Oxford, Preston and Scunthorpe— which are all 78 yards across.

You've got to be really fit to turn it on at Maine Road, which has the biggest playing surface in Britain—a lung-bursting area of 9,401 square yards.

By coincidence, Scottish clubs Rangers, Celtic and Kilmarnock have exactly the same vital statistics as Wembley (115 yards by 75).

Overlapping is no joke for full-backs at Hampden Park, which is a staggering 125 yards long (area 9,375 square yards), puff-a-minute for the Queen's Park amateurs!

If you've got a long throw the place to do the most damage is Eastville. The Bristol Rovers ground is Britain's smallest (110 by 70).

WEMBLEY   115 × 75 yds (8625 sq. yds)

There are 26 Football League grounds bigger than Wembley, *all* of which are as wide or wider; and 15 are longer than Wembley:

Manchester City	119 × 79 yds	(9410)
Doncaster Rovers	118 × 79 yds	(9322)
Carlisle United	117 × 78 yds	(9126)
*Northampton Town	120 × 75 yds	(9000)
Nottingham Forest	115 × 78 yds	(8970)
Aldershot	117 × 76 yds	(8892)
Cardiff City	114 × 78 yds	(8892)
Charlton Athletic	114 × 78 yds	(8892)
Leeds United	117 × 76 yds	(8892)
Notts County	117 × 76 yds	(8892)
†Hereford United	111 × 80 yds	(8880)
Manchester United	116 × 76 yds	(8816)
Port Vale	116 × 76 yds	(8816)
Shrewsbury Town	116 × 76 yds	(8816)
Bournemouth	117 × 75 yds	(8775)
Sheffield United	117 × 75 yds	(8775)
Wrexham	117 × 75 yds	(8775)
Rotherham United	115 × 76 yds	(8740)
Everton	112 × 78 yds	(8736)
Oxford United	112 × 78 yds	(8736)
Preston North End	112 × 78 yds	(8736)
Scunthorpe United	112 × 78 yds	(8736)
West Bromwich Alb.	115.5 × 75.5	(8720.5)
Hartlepool United	113 × 77 yds	(8701)
Stoke City	116 × 75 yds	(8700)
Chester	114 × 76 yds	(8664)

*longest in Football League   †widest in Football League

Hampden Park, the home of Queen's Park, is the biggest ground in Scotland ($125 \times 75 = 9375$ sq. yds) and only Maine Road in the Football League is larger. Hampden's closest rivals in the Scottish League are at Celtic, Kilmarnock and Rangers (all $115 \times 75 = 8625$ sq. yds, the same as Wembley).

Bristol Rovers ($110 \times 70 = 7700$ sq. yds) is the smallest pitch in the Football League.

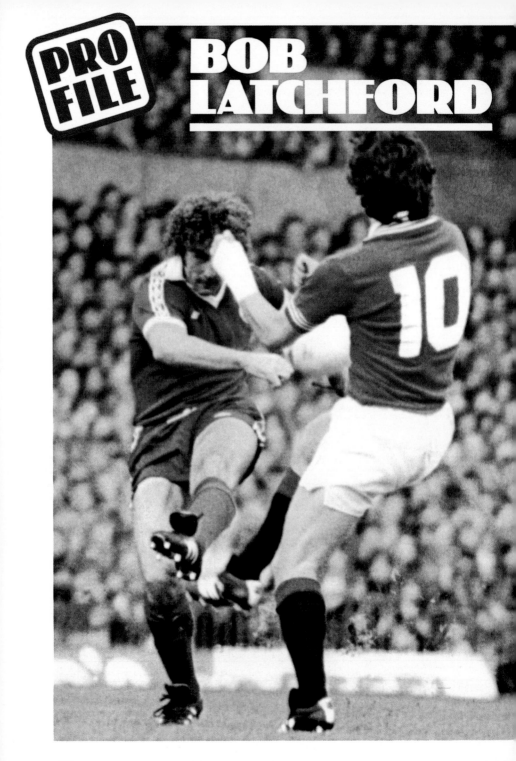

PRO FILE

BOB LATCHFORD

Bob Latchford is normally a nervous observer every time Everton are awarded a penalty.

But one sunny afternoon last April big Bob was put on the spot. Everton were already leading Chelsea 5-0, so another goal would make little difference to the result.

But £10,000-worth of difference to Latchford. He scored. The crowd went mad, as if Everton had won the Cup.

The cash—half to Latchford, half to charity—was the 'Daily Express' prize for scoring 30 League goals last season.

The goal means that the star striker will be marked even more closely this season—if that's possible.

Bob says: 'Defenders can't wait to say: "Bob Latchford didn't score against us." It's only natural.'

There was an amazing incident in a game against Coventry last season when the publicity about his £10,000 target was growing.

'Big Jim Holton refused to leave me even though Andy King was bursting through the middle,' says Bob. 'It seemed he was more interested in stopping me scoring than preventing a goal by Andy. Only when Andy was well inside the box did he do anything

about it. I was hoping we'd win the League this season without me scoring!'

Bob believes that several strikers will follow him through the 30-goal barrier.

He says: 'It happens in all sports, doesn't it? Once someone hits a target, others soon get there as well. It's still difficult but less frightening.'

And anyone who thinks that Bob himself will start having difficulties finding the net would be dismissed by Everton manager Gordon Lee's reaction—'once a goalscorer, always a goalscorer'.

Like most top scorers, Bob has that uncanny knack of losing his marker in crowded areas.

Near post is another place where Latchford is lethal. It was no coincidence that his first goal for his country—against Wales at Ninian Park last season—came from Peter Barnes' near-post cross.

Latchford v United—powering a shot past Lou Macari, holding off a challenge from Arthur Albiston, and saluting Everton fans after one of his two goals at Old Trafford last March as he edged nearer his target of 30 in the League for a £10,000 prize.

Big Bob in action against Brazil at Wembley last April, having made his England debut in the World Cup qualifier with Italy. In May he notched his first England goal—a header against Wales.

Honours: League Cup runners-up medal 1977

Club	Div	Pos	Season	League		FA Cup		Lge Cup		Int'nls	
				Ms	Gs	Ms	Gs	Ms	Gs	Ms	Gs
Birmingham	II	7	1968-69	4	2	–	–	–	–	–	–
City	II	18	1969-70	10	1	–	–	1	–	–	–
	II	9	1970-71	36	13	2	–	4	–	–	–
	II	2	1971-72	42	23	5	4	1	–	–	–
	I	10	1972-73	42	19	1	–	5	1	–	–
	I	19	1973-74	26	10	2	2	5	5	–	–
Everton	I	7	1973-74	13	7	–	–	–	–	–	–
	I	4	1974-75	36	17	3	1	2	1	–	–
	I	11	1975-76	31	12	1	–	4	1	–	–
	I	9	1976-77	36	17	5	3	9	5	–	–
	I	3	1977-78	39	30	2	1	5	1	3	1
				315	151	21	11	36	14	3	1

And it can't be coincidence that Bob got 30 goals after Everton had splashed out £200,000 to QPR for the best crosser in the country, Dave Thomas.

While Latchford was out on his own as leading scorer, Thomas was streets ahead in the 'assists' department.

Bob says: 'The majority of my goals last season came from Dave's crosses. He has the ability to pick you out with his crosses. Eight times out of ten he'll put the ball into the space where I want it.'

Getting an understanding with players is one of the problems of playing for England. 'People come from different clubs, you only meet for two or three days and it's not easy to work out patterns of play,' says Bob.

'I know how Dave Thomas will react in a given situation but at international level it might be different. It takes quite a few games

to get it anywhere near right.'

Five goals against Wimbledon in the League Cup early in the season equalled the individual record for the competition.

But he knows that other defences won't be quite so obliging. 'Hughes and Thompson of Liverpool are two of the best defenders around. They never used to trouble me when I was at Birmingham, but now they do. Arsenal's David O'Leary is another good player and I'm sure Russell Osman, of Ipswich, is going places.'

As for the physical side of the game, Bob says: 'You get the odd centre-half who wants to have a kick at you, but most of them just want to play football.'

Bob went to St Andrews after being spotted playing for Brandwood School—in the King's Heath area of Birmingham—and representing Birmingham Schools.

LEFT *Target man's control . . . with Sammy McIlroy, Martin Dobson and Steve Coppell among the spectators.*
BELOW *Bob's at his most lethal in the air—in the tradition of great English centre-forwards. Here he takes on Ipswich's Allan Hunter.*

'I enjoyed my apprenticeship,' he says, 'but my career didn't seem to be going anywhere until Freddie Goodwin took over as manager.

'He didn't have much money to spend, so he had to make the best of what he had. He used to have me back in the afternoons working on things he thought needed improving.

'In 1971-72, with Trevor Francis playing brilliantly, we won promotion and I scored 23 League goals.

'I haven't really looked back since and it's all down to Freddie Goodwin. His efforts and encouragement made all the difference.'

Now Bob is hoping this season will bring real success for the Merseyside 'second team'. He says: 'I'd gladly settle for ten goals fewer this season and a trophy of some description.'

Luther lights the way for Watford

'Blissett's goal showed that if you go out and do good things it doesn't matter who you're playing against.' GRAHAM TAYLOR

If ever a team made nonsense of their status it was Watford when they beat Manchester United 2-1 in the League Cup game at Old Trafford.

It was not only the fact that they defeated a First Division club on their own ground. It was the *way* Watford did it.

They played skilful, controlled football that wouldn't have looked out of place in any grade of the game.

There was little of the hustle and bustle that's normally used to unsettle higher division sides.

And the goal that put them through was full of class—

intelligently created and ruthlessly finished.

Ross Jenkins chased a Brian Pollard pass towards the corner flag and got the ball back to full-back John Stirk; Stirk to Dennis Booth, also supporting, and a floated cross that Luther Blissett flashed past Paddy Roche.

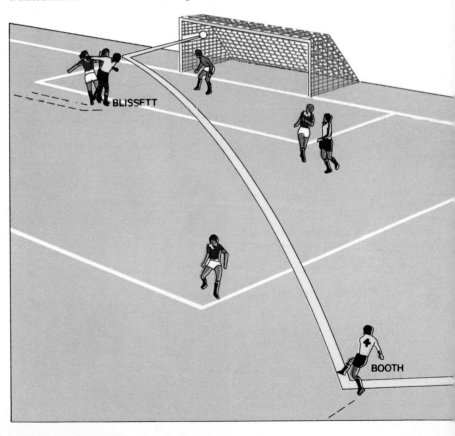

BLISSETT

BOOTH

The moment Watford came of age . . . Luther Blissett's stunning header that knocked Manchester United out of the League Cup—and proved that it's not only hustle and bustle that unsettles top sides.

Graham Taylor's analysis

We knew Stewart Houston was very left-footed, so we asked Brian Pollard to take him on on the inside—and that's how the goal started.

Brian went inside and his pass to Ross Jenkins was a little too strong, but it had the effect we wanted—to stretch United's two world-class central defenders, Martin Buchan and Gordon McQueen.

Perhaps McQueen, having committed himself to following Jenkins, should have got a lot tighter, but that takes nothing away from the effort Stirk made to support Jenkins. And Stirk's ball to Booth gave him the comfort to get in a good cross.

A lot is said in favour of near-post crosses, but I'm a great believer in the far-post cross—if it's properly delivered in front of players, not at them.

Booth did it perfectly, a deep curling cross that was always going to leave Roche and get beyond Buchan.

All this time Blissett had been holding his run, and when he went he was really positive to get there before Arthur Albiston.

So—it was a goal that certainly pleased us ! Getting McQueen wide ; good support for a player in a difficult situation ; a fine cross and a punishing header.

The lesson, if there is one, is that you can do good things against any opposition if you play the right way.

Founded: 1879
Address: The Hawthorns, West Bromwich B71 4LF
Ground: Capacity 44,000; Playing area 105.5 x 68.9 m
Record attendance: 64,815 v Arsenal, FA Cup q-f, 6.3.37
Record victory: 12-0 v Darwen, Div. 1, 4.3.1892
Record defeat: 3-10 v Stoke City, Div. 1, 4.2.37
Most League points: 60, Div. 1, 1919-20
Most League goals: 105, Div. 2, 1929-30
League scoring record: 39, W. Richardson, Div. 1, 1935-36
Record League aggregate: 209, Tony Brown, 1963-78*
Most League appearances: 533, Tony Brown, 1963-78*
Most capped player: 33, Stuart Williams, Wales, 1954-63
Honours: FA Cup Winners 1888, 1892, 1931, 1954, 1968, Runners-up 1886, 1887, 1895, 1912, 1935; League Cup Winners 1966, Runners-up 1967, 1970; Div. 2 Champions 1902, 1911
League career: Original members of the League 1888; Div. 1 1888-1901; Div. 2 1901-02; Div. 1 1902-04; Div. 2 1904-11; Div. 1 1911-27; Div. 2 1927-31; Div. 1 1931-38; Div. 2 1938-49; Div. 1 1949-73; Div. 2 1973-76; Div. 1 1976-
[*as at October 15]

West Bromwich Albion

Derek Statham looks on as Tony Godden resists a challenge from Liverpool's Phil Thompson in September's draw at The Hawthorns. Caught in the middle is skipper John Wile, who has made over 300 League appearances for the Baggies since joining them from Peterborough. He now leads a side which is a solid blend of experience— Robertson, Cantello, Johnston, Tony and Ally Brown—and exciting young players—including Statham, Cunningham, Robson and Regis.

Teams that do well on the pitch but not at the turnstiles are waiting for some bright spark to come up with the answers.

But in the meantime they can only bemoan their lot—or, rather, their little!

One such side is West Bromwich Albion.

Last season they finished high enough in the First Division to earn a coveted place in this season's UEFA Cup, not to mention reaching the semi-final of the FA Cup.

Clearly a club with an immediate future, they must have expected a big crowd on the first day of the new season. But how many turned up? Just 21,700.

Once again they have put themselves among the pace-setters, and once again their home gates are only around the 25,000 mark —respectable but nothing to phone the bank manager about.

Two top-class and successful managers, Johnny Giles and Ronnie Allen, have quit the club in the last 14 months. Both had good reasons for going—Giles to his native Ireland and Allen to Saudi Arabian currency.

But who's to say that neither of them would have been encouraged to stay if 40,000 people were turning up on every other Saturday?

Still, conjecture counts for nothing in this game. And Albion, however many are watching them, are doing well under a third and equally excellent manager—Ron Atkinson, who graduated from Third Division Cambridge United to The Hawthorns.

His words on West Brom's way forward are worth listening to:

ABOVE *The Albion side which beat Villa 3-0 to take the FA Cup in 1892.* BELOW *Today's WBA.*
Top: *George Wright (physio), Mulligan, Godden, Hughes, Brian Whitehouse (coach);* Middle:
Regis, Martin, Tony Brown, Cunningham, Robson, Ally Brown; Front: *Statham, Trewick,*
Robertson, Wile, Ron Atkinson (manager), Colin Addison (asst. manager), Batson, Johnston.

Cyrille Regis beats Gary Locke—and then Peter Bonetti—to score against Chelsea in September. A £5,000 snip from Hayes, Regis is one of three black players in Albion's first-choice side.

'Of course it would be nice to be in the position where I could go out and spend big money for players. But, even if I could, that's not always the way.

'At Albion I have to think long and carefully about the transfer market. I'm not saying we haven't got any money—just that we can't be considered one of the richest clubs in the land.

'But we're a happy club and that goes a long way. We don't have stars in this team. Everyone works together and that's the way I like it.

'We started the season well, and with a fair squad I think we can make some kind of breakthrough.'

Strength in depth has been the key to Liverpool's continued success and this is what Atkinson is aiming for.

Albion lack experienced striker cover but he has players like Tony Brown, Len Cantello, John Trewick and Bryan Robson fighting for midfield places.

It pleases Atkinson. 'If you've got different players with different styles you can make changes for tactical reasons—which is a nice position to be in.'

Not surprisingly, Cyrille Regis gets most of the glory that's going. A £5,000 present from non-League Hayes, he's a marvellous black athlete who'll score goals for seasons.

Atkinson says: 'There's nothing this lad

Tony Brown, Albion's double record-holder . . .

can't achieve, but with Cyrille around people tend to forget about the others—Ally Brown, for instance. When I came here he was almost heading for Stockport.

Brown cost Albion £65,000 from Leicester six years ago but has spent more time in the reserves than the first team.

Ally explains how Ron revitalized him. 'Every manager I've played for says my strength is to keep running and worrying defences, but somehow I always allowed myself to fade. Ron finally got the message through to me and now I work for 90 minutes and really enjoy it.'

With Laurie Cunningham, Albion's other black star, now beginning to realise his special potential—and Willie Johnston still a match-winner on his day—Albion are never short of attacking ideas.

But, even so, it's their defence that real success will spring from.

At its heart is skipper John Wile, who shot to prominence with the televised clash of heads with Brian Talbot in last season's FA Cup semi-final. His courage unquestioned, Wile also has that calm authority that spreads confidence throughout a side.

With Wile is Ally Robertson, former Arsenal and Cambridge defender Brendan Batson and one of the game's emerging stars, left-back Derek Statham.

Atkinson is the first to point out that Giles and Allen (who signed Regis) bequeathed him a stirling squad.

'When I arrived here the quality of these players made working with them easy.

'Of course I've got my own ideas about how the game should be played and how the team should play. I've made alterations in style but it's a gradual process.'

Whatever the changes, Albion's attacking policy will remain the same.

Wile says: 'Johnny Giles really got us to use the ball—before him we were too concerned with method.'

It was Giles' belief in the short ball and building up from the back that lifted Albion out of the Second Division three years ago after a three-year exile.

Smack in the middle of the industrial Black Country, Albion are not short of population. But not enough of them visit The Hawthorns.

Atkinson's reaction is what it has to be—philosophical. 'All I can do is pick the players and plan the games to make them as attractive as possible to spectators. If people still won't come, I don't see what else I can reasonably do.'

It's a problem that plagued Albion even after they won the FA Cup in 1968. Their first game the next season attracted a paltry 22,000 crowd. As that team broke up, Albion struggled and eventually dropped a division.

The good days came again with Giles, then Allen, now Atkinson.

And there's little chance of Atkinson departing. What other offer would he accept after turning down £1,000 a week to manage Philadelphia Fury? His reason was simple: 'There's a lot happening at Albion and I don't want to miss it.'

ABOVE *Alistair Robertson gets a header in against Liverpool at The Hawthorns in September.*
BELOW LEFT *Ron Atkinson was Bell's First Division 'Manager of the Month' for September.*

Johnny Giles laid the foundations for Albion's present success, taking the side up from the Second Division in 1976, as player-manager. After returning to Ireland, his work was continued by former Hawthorns idol Ronnie Allen and now Ron Atkinson, who has taken them into Europe.

Stuart Boam

'I get annoyed with people who knock coaching because they think it's too complex. It's nothing of the sort. Good coaching is all about the basic skills.'

Stuart Boam, the man guarding the central line to the Boro goal. BELOW *Boam battles with Joe Jordan.*

When a youngster is asked to sign as an apprentice professional, there's a great temptation for him to think that he's 'made it'. But he soon realises—or is made to realise—that there's.an awful long way to go.

Stuart Boam, king-pin of the Middlesbrough defence, found out this fact of football life the hard way.

'My dad wouldn't let me sign pro until I had a trade—tool-making—behind me. I was annoyed at the time because I was already in Mansfield's first team. But now I know he was right because I've seen what a shock it is for some boys to leave school and join a club.

'Let's face it, lots of schoolboy players think they know it all and some teachers encourage them to kick the ball as far as they can or hold on to it all the time—both bad faults.

'Then, when they join a club, they find they can't roll a good five-yard pass. That's why I get annoyed with the people who knock coaching and say it's too complex.

'It's nothing of the sort. Good coaching is all about the basic skills, constantly practising how to control the ball, how to pass it and shoot—the opposite of the criticism.'

Dennis Tueart on the volley

'Volleys go wrong because players think only about striking the ball and not about how their body should be positioned.'

Volleying is one of the most spectacular—and so therefore satisfying—soccer skills.

But it follows, inevitably, that it's also one of the most difficult to get right.

Even in the Football League a high percentage of volleys have embarrassing results—the ball being more of a danger to spectators than the back of the net.

And the further down you go in the football world, the worse it gets. Very many players prefer to ignore the skill altogether.

Dennis Tueart has always been a good volleyer—for Sunderland, for Manchester City and now for the Cosmos.

'Timing is everything,' says Dennis. 'If you get that right, the power will take care of itself. If you're volleying a knee-high cross, all the momentum you need is there. What you've got to do is make good contact.

'You must have a swivel movement, rather like a discus thrower, and you can practise this without a ball.

'The swivel is all to do with the hips and the shoulders. If you're volleying with your left foot the secret is to duck your right shoulder into the path of the ball, stand firmly on your right foot and strike the ball as part of the whole movement.

'Volleys go wrong because players think only of striking the ball and not about how

Dennis prepares to volley—eye on the ball, right shoulder ready to start the 'swivel'.

Just before impact Dennis is perfectly positioned and balanced.

their body should be positioned. That's why so many volleys are snatched at and why so many go miles over the bar.'

If Dennis has any regrets about going to America it's that he's missing out on the Greenwood era of attacking football.

'It was all work-rate in my day and skill came second. But with skills like volleying you've got to spend time on them.

'I've always been a pretty good volleyer but I still give five or ten minutes to it in training.'

The old Tueart ... Dennis in a Manchester City shirt before joining the New York Cosmos. If he has any regrets about going to America it's that he's missing out on the Greenwood attacking era.

Away it goes ... with Dennis like a corkscrew.

'Start square on and as the ball comes to you . . .

duck your right shoulder into the path of the ball.

The shoulder will take the rest of your body with it ...

Training for the volley

It's best to practise the volley with three players—one serving, the second volleying, the third catching. 10 or 15 yards is a big enough distance between the volleyer and the catcher because mastering the skill is much more important than thoughts of power. If there is a key to success, it's definitely in the left shoulder (for a right-foot volley). Duck the shoulder into the path of the ball and you should find that it creates the swivel movement you need for a good volley. If you're fluffing it, try the movement without the ball— get the rhythm right and the rest should follow. And don't try to 'take the leather off the ball'.

and then back again to complete the swivel.

Do this without the ball to get the rhythm of it.'

Graham Taylor:
Dennis's point about seeing the volley as part of a whole movement seems to me to be the crucial one. With a pass or shot, the preparation—the backlift and body positions—comes naturally to almost everyone, certainly to anyone with ball sense.

But the volley is different. Apart from a minority of people, it's not a natural skill—it's one that's got to be worked on very hard.

The rhythm of the skill, from start to finish, is vital. Players tend to panic more with a volley —and therefore snatch at it— than any other part of the game. But it should be the opposite. You should wait for the ball as long as possible—hold your shape, I call it— then get your shoulder—right for left foot and vice versa—in line with the ball.

What you shouldn't do is leave your body 'open' to the ball because there's bound to be the fear that the ball will hit you in a painful region. On top of that you won't be able to complete the swivel movement from a square stance—you'll just have a leg flapping awkwardly about in the air.

The more you think about power the more you're likely to make a hash of it—as Dennis says, the pace is already in the ball as it's coming to you.

One final thing, it's better to top the ball than get under it. One of the most miserable moments in football is seeing the ball disappear high into the terraces—it's an insult to all the training you've put in. At least if you top the ball it's likely to go in the right direction.

Volleying is a difficult skill but if you practise to get it right it's the sort of skill that makes you feel good—and does wonders for your confidence.

Whistle Test

PAT PARTRIDGE, England's ref at the World Cup finals in Argentina, tells of the day he and Nobby Stiles—former Manchester United and England star who now manages Preston North End—were in the same jail . . .

'We were in Yorkshire's North Allerton Prison—for a sports panel, I hasten to add.

'The inmates seemed very amused by a story I told them about Nobby's antics in a particular match which could have landed him inside.

'It was a floodlit League game between United and Burnley at Old Trafford, and Burnley's centre-forward Andy Lochhead was giving Nobby the runaround.

'Nobby kept snapping at Andy's heels and in the first half I whispered to him to cut it out. Nobby apologised, then grinned.

'And so it went on, Lochhead buzzing about and Nobby a little terrier at his feet. Then, in the second half, Nobby caught him and I said: "Okay, next time you're cautioned."

'Sure enough, there was a next time. Andy

> Although the Stiles story was told for laughs, Pat believes there's a lesson to be learned from the incident. 'Nobby had to be cautioned— there's no doubt about that—and if he'd done it again he would have gone off. No doubt about that, either. The point is that Nobby, for all his antics, accepted the situation. There was no animosity between us and if you could get on to that level in other situations, half of football's problems would be solved.'

was streaking towards goal when Nobby clipped him from behind.'

Out came Pat's notebook and Stiles was asked his name, but instead of giving it was all apologies, adding: 'It's the floodlights, ref, they shine in my contact lenses and I can't see a thing!'

Nobby's excuse was making little impact on Pat and he didn't exactly improve his case when Pat was writing in his little black book.

Nobby leaned over and said: 'You spell it with an "I", not a "Y".' And Pat, quite rightly, said: 'I thought you were supposed to have bad eyes!'

Founded: 1900
Address: Goldstone Ground, Old Shoreham Road, Hove, Sussex BN3 7DE
Ground: Capacity 33,000; Playing area 102.4 x 68.6 m
Record attendance: 36,747 v Fulham, Div. 2, 27.12.58
Record victory: 10-1 v Wisbech, FA Cup 1st round, 13.11.65
Record defeat: 0-9 Middlesbrough, Div. 2, 23.8.58
Most League points: 65, Div. 3(S), 1955-56 & Div. 3,1971-72
Most League goals: 112, Div. 3(S), 1955-56
League scoring record: 32, Peter Ward, Div. 3, 1976-77
Record League aggregate: 113, Tommy Cook, 1922-29
Most League appearances: 509, Tug Wilson, 1922-36
Most capped player: 8, Jack Jenkins, Wales, 1924-27
Honours: Div. 3(S) Champions 1958; Div. 4 Champions 1965
League career: 1920 Original members of Div. 3; 1921-58 Div. 3(S); 1958-62 Div. 2; 1962-63 Div. 3; 1963-65 Div. 4; 1965-72 Div. 3; 1972-73 Div. 2; 1973-77 Div. 3; 1977- Div. 2

BRIGHTON & HOVE ALBION

Alan Mullery is aiming at the very top . . . at the same rarified summit where Liverpool are now sunning themselves.

He says: 'When you talk about Liverpool now you're not talking about a football club, you're talking about an institution.

'That's what I'm trying to instil here.'

Alan Mullery is the manager of a club which has spent most of its existence in the Third Division. They don't occupy too big a space in the record books, there aren't many trophies in the display cabinet, and their stadium has a distinct Third Division aura about it.

Yet they came within goal difference of the First Division last season and the whole town believes they can make certain of promotion this year. More to the point, when (and most Brightonians now say 'when' and not 'if') they do get among the big names, they plan to adapt their image.

Alterations to the ground are a priority. As Mullery says: 'Most stadiums were built years ago when football was a poor man's game. But now we've become a little bit more sophisticated and you've got to offer the fans comfort to draw them in.

'I don't think there's any need to extend the capacity of our ground. If we can draw 33,000 every home game and seat most of them that's a fair amount of revenue.'

But first things first. Mullery considers super stadiums are secondary to a successful side. 'Liverpool are one of the few sides who can regularly attract crowds of over 40,000 because of their record of success.

Brighton's brightest star . . . ? Peter Ward was picked up for next-to-nothing from Southern League Burton Albion. Just over a year later he was being considered for full England honours.

455

BRIGHTON & HOVE A. F. C. 1955-56

D.Tennant   T.Bisset   E.Gill   J.Langley(Captain)   G.Wilson
D.Gordon   A.Mundy   P.Harburn   D.Foreman   F.Howard   K.Whitfield

This 1955-56 side, runners-up in Division 3 (South), contained Jimmy Langley, who later played for England, and Albert Mundy, scorer of one of football's fastest officially-recorded goals.

Brighton today. Back row: *Mark Elliott, Mike Kerslake, Tony Vessy, Ken Tiler, Mark Andrews, Steve Ward, Mike Ring, Russell Cox.* Second row: *Glen Geard, Teddy Maybank, Graham Winstanley, Chris Cattlin, Eric Steele, Andy Rollings, Graham Moseley, Mark Lawrenson, Gary Williams, Malcolm Poskett, Tony Richardson.* Sitting: *Tony Towner (now Millwall), Paul Clark, Peter Ward, Brian Horton, Peter Sayer, Peter O'Sullivan, John Ruggiero, Eric Potts (now Preston).* Front row: *Richard Holliday, Martin Cox, Ian Liddle.*

'Fulham tried to do it in reverse. They have a super stadium that holds 40,000 but if the side's not too clever and they average about 7,000 a game . . . which leaves them with about 33,000 empty spaces. Not very good is it?

'I'd much rather fill our ground each week than have a big super stadium only partially filled. And there's no reason why we can't achieve this. Brighton averaged 26,000 last season. If we continue to get the playing side. of things right the fans will turn up . . . and the trappings like big stands will come as a result.'

Mullery is very definite about what he is looking for in his players. Despite his ambitions for the big time he categorically states that he would not buy players like George Best, Rodney Marsh and Peter Osgood.

'They're super footballers—but when they're not playing they're a headache.

'I wouldn't have that sort of player. I check that potential Brighton players want to be winners.

'I try and instil in people that there's only one thing in this game and that's winning. There's nothing for losers.

'Everybody at this club has got to be a winner, right down to the tea-lady. I want everyone to be upset if we get beaten, which,' he adds quickly, 'is not very often. Thank goodness and touch wood.'

He 'touched wood' several times as he talked to *Handbook*, but although he is superstitious, he is also a realist. If winning means everything to you, you have to be ruthless . . .

In 1972 Brighton gained promotion to the Second Division. They struggled badly for the first few months and, despite finishing with some respectable results, were relegated after only one season. When Mullery took Brighton out of the Third Division—in 1977 at the end of his first full season as a manager —he was determined that history would not be repeated.

'Really, as a young and inexperienced manager, I should have said "Look, I'm going to give this team half a season to see if they're good enough for the Second Division." But I knew they weren't good enough . . . and I knew if we kept them we would only finish halfway up the table at best.

'It's a very hard business, football. We've got to be hard on the managerial side because we've got no security which says we're going

Peter O'Sullivan pursued by Bob Hatton in April's crucial game. Brighton beat Blackpool 2-1, but Spurs held on at Southampton to get the third promotion slot.

to have a job tomorrow. So you've got to be successful. You can't just poodle along in second gear.'

The team was systematically torn apart. Within a season only five or six of the promotion-winning side (Steele, Tiler, Horton, Rollings, Ward, O'Sullivan) remained. Brighton spent over half a million pounds on replacements (including Lawrenson, Potts, Clark, Poskett, Sayer and Moseley), but despite their success there were still problems.

The most expensive signing, for instance, was Teddy Maybank—who cost nearly £250,000. A big man with a subtle touch, he seemed the right kind of investment for a First Division future. But the crowd, reared on the more down-to-earth football of Brighton's Third and Fourth Division days, didn't take to him.

'I believe crowds need to be educated,' says Mullery. 'You have to win them over.

'I would say that the most educated crowd in the country are Liverpool . . . because they've grown up with the team.

'But all this takes time. It's not going to happen overnight. Obviously I'm hoping for promotion this year. Touch wood. But, there's no guarantee of it . . .

'Besides, there are 21 other clubs in our division who don't want Brighton to go up because we attract big crowds . . . which creates a good atmosphere and lifts them to play better. It's a problem, but it's a nice problem.'

It's a 'nice problem' because it shows that Brighton have the potential to become a really successful club. They have no competitors for a radius of 50 miles. 'People come from Crawley, Redhill, Reigate, places like that, rather than go to London to watch football—because it's an easier drive and there's no hooligan element in Brighton.

'If you go to places like the East End in London, or where I was born in Notting Hill, you've still got the problem of lots of families that are struggling to earn a living. You don't see too many slums in Brighton, so the element of unrest which comes from living in these conditions doesn't exist here. Which is marvellous. I'd have no hesitation in bringing my kids to stand on the terraces in Brighton, but I wouldn't take them to too many other places.'

Despite this statement, Mullery envies the raucous vitality of a big match at a big city ground. He mentions Brighton's League match at White Hart Lane last season.

'I don't think my players have ever experienced an atmosphere like it . . . 48,000 people. A third of them were Brighton supporters—and I don't think they'd ever seen anything like it either.

'I want that atmosphere at Brighton.'

A well-behaved capacity crowd seated in a compact but modernised stadium really

Alan Mullery's two predecessors at the Goldstone Ground—Brian Clough and Peter Taylor—arrived together in 1973, soon after resigning from Derby. Immediate results were disastrous. In the space of three days at home, Brighton lost 4-0 to non-League Walton and Hersham and 8-2 to Bristol Rovers. They just missed relegation before Clough moved on to Leeds and Taylor took over as manager.

Captain and midfield inspiration Brian Horton.

Welshman Peter O'Sullivan, one of four full internationals in the current squad, is the only survivor from the team that won promotion under Pat Saward in 1972.

getting behind a Brighton team riding high in the First Division—that's Mullery's ideal. But there may be a price to pay.

The town's last taste of the big time came last season when Spurs came down to play at Hove. Thousands of Tottenham fans made the journey down without tickets for the match and quite literally gate-crashed—pushing down the doors to invade the ground. As a result, Brighton were ordered by the Football League to carry out un-planned ground modifications and they fenced and barbed the north-east terrace to contain away fans.

Is this an accurate indication of what the First Division can bring? Certainly big name clubs—like Liverpool—know all about over-boisterous fans. One consolation for comfy old Fulham is that they don't have too much of that sort of problem.

It might be possible for Brighton to have the success of Liverpool with the cosiness of Craven Cottage . . . but Alan Mullery knows which he would pick if it came to a choice.

More about Mullers
Mullery started and finished his playing career with Fulham. In between, he played over 300 games for Spurs, who paid £65,000 for him, and represented England 35 times. The high point of his career was the Mexico World Cup in 1970, when he played in every game and scored in the quarter-final against West Germany. He was later awarded the MBE. He became manager of Brighton in July 1976.

RISING STAR JOHN CHIEDOZIE

It's a widely accepted fact that television 'Superstar' Malcolm Macdonald is the fastest footballer over the sprint distance of 100 metres.

But there's one young player a few miles down the road from Arsenal who begs to differ—Orient's exciting young winger John Chiedozie.

'I've seen Malcolm and he's very fast,' John told *Handbook*, 'but I still feel I'm a match for him. If he's ready for a challenge, all he's got to do is name the day.

'I know Malcolm's had a cartilage operation and obviously I'd give him time to get back to his peak!'

A familiar sight of Chiedozie—going past a defender—during the Anglo-Scottish Cup match against Mansfield at Brisbane Road in August. It was against Mansfield that John scored his first goal for the club . . . after just 52 seconds.

But while John's lightning speed is central to his role on the wing, it's his close control that's made him a firm favourite with the Brisbane Road regulars.

Before John stepped into the football big time, his experience was limited to village games in his native Nigeria—and then only one match a fortnight.

It was a shy 13-year-old who left Owerri for London with his family in 1973, but John's obvious footballing skills helped him to settle down quickly to life in an East London school.

Within a few months John was playing for St Bonaventures school in his first cup final.

'It was a special day for me for another reason. There was an Orient scout on the line and he asked me to sign schoolboy forms. He didn't have to ask twice!'

Debut goal—in 52 seconds
In his early days at Orient, John was overshadowed by another black winger, Laurie Cunningham. But Laurie's £110,000 move to West Bromwich Albion last March opened the door for John.

His debut was against fellow Londoners Millwall and Chiedozie proved to be the perfect replacement for Cunningham. But he didn't get his next full game until a month later.

And, following nine successive games on the subs' bench at the end of the 1976-77 season, it wasn't until the arrival of manager Jimmy Bloomfield from Leicester in September that John once again slipped off his tracksuit to operate on the Orient flanks.

Eighteen games without injury saw John through his best patch at Orient, which included his first goal for the club in a remarkable 52 seconds against Mansfield in December.

But the good fortune was short-lived as Orient entertained Sunderland in a match which provided John with his second goal of the season . . . and a broken leg.

With the obvious disappointment of such a severe injury, John had the misfortune to

miss the Orient FA Cup run which did so
much for the reputation of the London side.
'It's really terrible to get injured and miss
games like that,' he says. 'The Arsenal match
would have been the highlight of my career.'

Black success

With John's season already over, the defeat
by Arsenal brought Orient's great run to a
sharp halt—and left them to battle against
relegation.

Still only 18, 'Chidders' is not alone in his
bid to be yet another black success. With
players like Fisher, Banjo and Godfrey
coming up through the ranks, there's no
shortage of good young black talent at
Brisbane Road.

'If you see black players doing well it kind
of urges you on, makes you think you've got
something to live up to,' explains John.

And if John keeps on playing the way he
has been, established players like Cunningham may have to look back over their
shoulder as well as to the future
heralded by Viv Anderson.

ABOVE *Black power ... John
in a shoulder-to-shoulder tussle
with Mansfield's John Miller,
one of the first black players to
break into regular Football
League action. Originally at
Ipswich and then at Norwich,
Miller is now a firm favourite
at Field Mill.*

LEFT *Seasoned campaigner
Steve Kember, then with
Leicester but now back in
London with Crystal Palace,
gives chase to a speedy
'Chidders' at Brisbane Road
earlier this year. Chiedozie
broke a leg last season, but
now he's back turning it on
down Orient's wings,
following in the footsteps of
Laurie Cunningham.*

461

Macari's instinct grabs a point

'Tommy Docherty calls us a boring team—but if it's boring to get results like that one we'll carry on that way.'

To entertain with gay abandon, as everyone expects them to do . . . or tighten things up a bit to get a few more points.

That is the question for Manchester United.

Tommy Docherty, former United boss, says he now finds United boring.

But Lou Macari made the point on 'Match of the Day' that there's nothing boring about fighting second-half recoveries.

And it was a goal by Macari that earned United a point after they had trailed 2-0 at Aston Villa.

After Sammy McIlroy had pulled one of the goals back

five minutes after half-time, Macari levelled the scores in the 71st minute.

And, in tune with United's new grit, the goal was more about effort, agility and instinct than any spectacular qualities.

It came from a throw on the left taken by Ashley Grimes, who aimed for a tightly-marked McIlroy, whose job it was to flick the ball on with his head into the danger area—always a brave header with someone 'up your back'.

Not only did McIlroy get his header in under pressure; he also made good contact and sent the ball further than

the defenders expected.

Certainly further than Macari expected! The ball sailed over his head and must have seemed a cert for Villa keeper Jimmy Rimmer, who'd seen the danger and rushed from his line .

But he was left completely cold by Macari's remarkable turn and the lob volley that floated— agonizingly for Villa—into an empty net.

An unlikely goal in many ways. An unlikely result . . . but just reward for a team that wants to prove it can get its head down and graft as well as anyone when it comes down to it.

Graham Taylor:
Not one to write a poem about, but football's more about the everyday goal than the monthly wonder. It's amazing, actually, how vital it often is to just stick a foot out in football. It robs opponents, it clears off goal-lines and it puts half chances in the back of the net.

This was one of those. Macari stuck a foot out—little more than that. The fact that he also produced a lob volley that would have gone down well at Wimbledon can only be explained by that inadequate word 'instinct.'

It seems strange, but he would have probably found it more difficult to lob Rimmer if he had had a bit more time. If the goal proved anything it's that in some situations it's a question of getting the ball 'in there'—into dangerous areas. It's then up to someone to take it from there—like Macari did.

CLEMENCE & SHILTON -best of enemies

It's no coincidence that last season's most successful sides had England's two best keepers. And the argument goes on over Ron Greenwood's embarrassment of riches. The two men are firm friends, room-mates—and forever rivals...

Back in 1966—the year that England won the World Cup —Peter Shilton established a club record at Leicester as the youngest player ever to turn out for them in a League game. He was just 16 years and 228 days old.

By the following season Leicester had sold England's World Cup keeper, Gordon Banks, to Stoke City, their manager Matt Gillies feeling that Shilton had such outstanding potential that he was a better long-term prospect.

Banks had made way for his understudy at club level and it was generally taken for

granted that Shilton would eventually replace him in the national side.

The predictions proved correct—but by the time Shilton won his first full cap against East Germany in 1970 Leicester were in the Second Division and he was worried about losing his edge. 'I dreaded the prospect of a

Clemence has been almost automatic choice for England since mid-1974, when he replaced Shilton after an absence of 16 games from the national side.

Friends and rivals—the two men share a joke during an England session. They also share a room on trips.

Shilton in full voice. Like Clemence he is much more than a great goalkeeper; he is an integral part of his side, radiating confidence to his team-mates during a game.

long spell in the lower grade,' he said later. Several transfer requests led to an 18-month rift with new manager Frank O'Farrell, but when Jimmy Bloomfield succeeded O'Farrell in the managerial chair Shilton patched up his differences with the club. When he became first choice for the England side, his future at top level seemed well on course again.

Unfortunately, his international standing was badly damaged at Wembley when he was slow to get down to a shot by Domarski which gave Poland a 1-1 draw—and a place in the 1974 World Cup finals at England's expense.

Shilton in typically spectacular form for Leicester. City received a record of £325,000 for him in 1974 from Stoke, who recouped £250,000 from Forest early last season.

Honours: League Championship medal 1978; FA Cup runners-up medal 1969; Second Division Championship medal 1971

Club	Season	Div	Pos	Lge	FA Cup	Lge Cup	Int' nls
Leicester City	1966-67	I	8	4	—	—	—
	1967-68	I	13	35	4	—	—
	1968-69	I	21	42	8	3	—
	1969-70	II	3	39	5	7	—
	1970-71	II	1	40	5	5	2
	1971-72	I	12	37	2	1	2
	1972-73	I	16	41	2	1	9
	1973-74	I	9	42	7	2	7
	1974-75	I	18	5	—	1	—
Stoke City	1974-75	I	5	25	1	—	1
	1975-76	I	12	42	5	1	—
	1976-77	I	20	40	1	2	2
	1977-78	II	7	3	—	1	—
N. Forest	1977-78	I	1	37	6	—	2
				432	46	24	25

When Don Revie of Leeds took over from Alf Ramsey as England manager he decided to replace Shilton with a player who at one time had seemed to pose little threat to his national future. After five more games Ray Clemence took over for the 1974 European summer tour—and he's never looked back.

When Shilton had been a teenage wonder displacing Banks at Leicester, Ray Clemence was beginning a three-year stint in the reserves at Anfield in the shadow of Tommy Lawrence.

Unlike Shilton, his start in League football had been a long way from the headlines. Scunthorpe United are known locally as 'The Iron' and the young Clemence had to perform miracles to keep them out of the Fourth Division. Hardly the sort of thing which gets you noted as a future international.

But manager Bill Shankly was shrewder than most and in the 1970-71 season Clemence was not only established as first choice for Liverpool but had also collected England Under-23 caps and had been called up as substitute to the full England team.

Because he played for a successful side Clemence had become used to games which required him to make only two or three saves. This helped to improve his concentration during long spells of inactivity and many people felt that he would have dealt more sharply with

Clemence with skipper Emlyn Hughes after keeping a clean sheet against Newcastle in the 1974 FA Cup final. Shilton's only final—in 1969—ended in a 1-0 defeat for Leicester.

Honours: European Cup Winners medal 1977, 1978; UEFA Cup Winners medal 1973, 1976; League Championship medals 1973, 1976, 1977; FA Cup winners medal 1974, runners-up medal 1971

Club	Season	Div	Pos	Lge	FA Cup	Lge Cup	Int' nls
Scunthorpe	1965-66	III	4	4	–	–	–
United	1966-67	III	18	44	2	–	–
Liverpool	1967-68	I	3	–	–	–	–
	1968-69	I	2	–	–	1	–
	1969-70	I	5	14	1	–	–
	1970-71	I	5	41	7	3	–
	1971-72	I	3	42	3	3	–
	1972-73	I	1	41	4	7	2
	1973-74	I	2	42	9	6	3
	1974-75	I	2	42	2	4	7
	1975-76	I	1	42	2	3	9
	1976-77	I	1	42	8	2	9
	1977-78	I	2	40	1	9	6
				394	39	38	36

the Polish goal.

The critics turned sour on Shilton; he was accused of being 'top heavy', of 'over-training'. But one man who never lost belief in his ability was Peter Taylor, and even after Shilton had lost his England place to Clemence Taylor told him: 'You're the best keeper in the world.'

Shilton was by now with Stoke; but so highly did Taylor rate him that when he signed him for Forest three years later he stated 'anything is possible at this club now.'

Ray Clemence certainly didn't doubt that Clough and Taylor had spent wisely. 'I've always associated Peter with strength. He's a good strong all-round goalkeeper who really commands his area, especially the six-yard box, and he's very good at organising his defence.'

Shilton had always worked hard on his game, but at Forest he underwent long sessions with Len Heppell, an expert on body rhythm and balance. This improved his ability to get down to low shots and the results were seen in two near-post saves during the second leg European Cup clash with Liverpool.

This increased agility has swung many of his old critics back in his favour, and they feel that he should have his England job back on a permanent basis.

But as far as international selection is concerned 'possession is certainly nine points of the law'. Clemence was in goal when Ron Greenwood took charge; he has never let his country down so he keeps his place.

It would be an unwise man who tried to say that one of these two keepers is better than the other. Because if you ever did manage to decide between the two of them the chances are you'd have to change your mind within a couple of months . . . and change it again a couple of months after that.

The truth is that over a period of time there's agonizingly little between them.

While the fans might argue over who should be first choice, the two best goalkeepers in England accept the situation. They even have a long-standing relationship as room-mates on international trips.

'We know what the England position is,' explains Shilton. 'When the side is announced the one who's missing says 'good luck' to the one that's in and that's that.'

Shilton even says he'd be 'sick' if he had to room with anyone else. 'The secret is that we rarely talk about football—and we never mention goalkeeping.'

Both players have helped to transform the idea of a goalkeeper's function. One of Shilton's early managers,

Clemence in training for his next international. Only Gordon Banks (a remarkable total of 73) among England keepers has won more caps.

Jimmy Bloomfield, described him as 'more of a covering defender' and Clemence, who played at left-back for a spell in his early career in Skegness, is a great believer in anticipation —as his dashes to the edge of the area will sometimes testify.

Though both players deny any deliberate showmanship, they radiate confidence. Clemence looks the taller and leaner of the two but he is in fact half an inch shorter than Shilton and there is little difference in their weight. In terms of ability there is even less to choose between them.

Both men have developed into players who would be automatic first choice for the national side in most other countries, but five years after Gordon Banks' last game for England we seem to be no nearer to knowing who his successor will be.

Having two goalkeepers who could fill the role obviously strengthens the England squad . . . and if one has to suffer the disappoint- ment of not being selected there is always success at club level with Liverpool and Forest.

In the meantime both men remain firm friends but maintain a competive edge with each other which ensures that if they can't both play for England they can certainly share equal respect in the world of international football.

Shilton with his England jersey in a League match—a sight no longer possible because the yellow is not one of the four 'approved' colours.

The 'settled side'

In a game where injuries can —and very often do—cause havoc, most Football League managers try to build their side around a 'hard core' of reliable players.

But there's one manager who seems to take the 'settled side' theory to extremes—Rotherham United's Jimmy McGuigan.

One glance at Rotherham's appearance list for the 1976-77 season (right) shows how Jimmy will, if at all possible, stick to the same names and faces.

It's been very much the same since then, only injuries forcing the manager to make changes.

'It's not entirely because I believe in a settled side—it's also because of financial necessity,' says Jimmy. 'We've got a small staff here and we're therefore bound to rely, if possible, on eight or nine players turning out for the majority of games.'

Jimmy admits: 'It gets a bit hair-raising at times.

Some Fridays are spent looking for bodies to play on Saturday!'

Even so, it's still the way Jimmy prefers.

'The problems of a big pool of players is on a par with a large number of directors—we've only got four on the board here and that's how I like it.

Alongside all this, there's also a conscious effort at the Millmoor Ground to produce home-grown players.

'We're similar to Burnley

theory

The McGuigan way ...
Jimmy with six of his regulars
—Trevor Phillips, John
Green, Richard Finney, Alan
Crawford, John Breckin and
Dave Gwyther.

Courtesy of Rothman's Football Yearbook.

McAllister	Stancliffe	Pugh	Habbin	Spencer	Wagstaff	Finney	Phillips	Gwyther	Goodfellow	Crawford	Breckin	Rhodes	Womble	Green
1	2	3	4	5	6	7	8	9	10	11	12			
1	2*	3	4	5	6	7	8	9	10	11				
1	2	3	4	5	6	7	8	9	10	11	3	12		
1	2		4*	5	6	7	8	9	10	11	3			
1	2		4	5	6	7	8	9	10	11	3			
1	2	12	4	5	6	7	8	9	10*	11	3			
1	2		6	5	4	7	8	9	10	11	3			
1	2		4	5	6		8	9	10	11	3		7	
1	2	12	4*	5	6		8	9		11	3		7	2
1	5		4	6		10	8	9		11	3	4	7*	
1	5	2	12	6		10	8	9		11	3	4		
1	5	2		6		7	8	9	10	11	3	4		
1	5	2		6		7	8	9	10	11	3	4		
1	5	2		6		7	8	9	10	11	3	4		
1	5	2		6		7	8	9	10	11	3	4		
1	5	2		6		7	8	9	10	11	3	4		
1	5	2		6		7	8	9	10	11	3	4		
1	5	2		6		7	8	9	10	11	3	4		
1	5	2		6		7	8	9	10	11	3	4		
1	5	2		6		7	8	9	10	11	3	4		
1	5	2		6		7	8	9	10	11	3	4		
1	5	2		6		7	8	9	10	11	3	4		
1	5	2		6		7	8	9	10	11	3	4		
1	5	2		6		7	8	9	10	11	3		4	
1	5	2		6		7	8	9	10	11	3		4	
1	5	2		6		7	8	9	10	11	3		4	
1	5	2	7	6			8	9	10	11	3		4	
1	5	2	7	6			8	9	10	11	3		4	
1	5	2	7	6			8	9	10	11	3		4	
1	5	2		6		7	8	9	10	11	3		4	
1	5	2	7	6			8	9	10	11	3		4	
1	5	2	7	6			8	9	10	11	3		4	
1	5	2	7	6			8	9	10	11	3		4*	
1	5	2	7	6	12		8	9	10	11	3		4	
1	5	2	7	6			8	9	10*	11	3	4		
1	5	2		6	12	7	8	9		10*11	3		4	
1	5	2		6	10	7	8	9		11	3		4	10
1	5	2		6		7	8	9	10	11	3			4
1	5	2		6		7	8	9	10	11	3			9
1	5	2	12	6		7	8*	4	10	11	3			12
1	5	2	9*	6		7	8	4	10	11	3			
1	5	2	9	6		7	8	4	10	11	3			
1	5	2	9	6		7	8	4	10	11	3			
1	5	2	9	6		7	8	4	10	11	3			
46	**46**	**44**	**17**	**46**	**13**	**34**	**46**	**46**	**42**	**46**	**43**	**18**	**18**	**1**

46 46 44 17 46 13 34 46 46 42 46 43 18 18 1
  +4s   +2s   +1s +1s +1s

A manager who sticks
to a settled side as much
as he can—boss of
Rotherham, Jimmy
McGuigan. He kept
Barrie Wagstaff on the
sub's bench for 23
League games in a row
without giving him a
kick in the 1976-77
season (left). But he
says: 'Barrie wasn't
sick—he knew the
score.'

in this respect,' says Jimmy.
'Six of the present squad
came through the club's
apprentice scheme.

'This is also partly due to
finance, but there's no
denying that heavy industry
areas like this breed a better
kind of competitor.'

ASA HARTFORD

He's alive and well and playing in the First Division!

Of course Asa Hartford is playing in the First Division with Manchester City—he's one of the all-action midfield lynch-pins of Tony Book's team—and favourite to retain a regular place in Scotland's side under new boss Jock Stein.

Asa's status as a top midfielder and Scotland international is predictable enough for a lad who was plucked from Scottish amateur football after being spotted by a WBA scout, and who made his First Division debut as a 17-year-old back in the 1967-68 season.

He was soon thrilling the crowds with his mature skill and vision and it was only a matter of time before the inevitable big-

money offer arrived to tempt Albion, then going through an undistinguished spell.

In the event it was Leeds United, then on the crest of a wave, who stepped in with a £177,000 bid—big money in 1971—to tempt Albion into parting with their star. Don Revie was planning to reinforce his ageing midfield and saw Hartford as the centrepiece of his plans for the next decade.

Revie was waiting in a motel on the East Lancs Road with a set of transfer forms and Hartford's £8,800 share of the transfer fee. 'I didn't think *shall I sign*,' Asa recalls, but 'shall I buy a fountain pen so I can stick my name down as soon as he gets out the forms?'

It was indeed a dream move, and when he drove to Leeds the following day he received the big-name treatment from a host of reporters, photographers and back-slappers who crowded into the Queen's Hotel to welcome him.

There were TV and press interviews, meetings with local celebrities like Eddie Waring. 'I went to bed that night sort of glowing,' he remembers, 'thinking *Asa, son, you're a bit of a celebrity and you love it.*'

The next morning Don Revie arrived bright and early to take his new player to a large house on the outskirts of the town. Asa had been there for medical tests the day before, after his first strenuous training session, and he assumed that the tests were to be continued as part of the thorough Leeds system.

He hardly gave the matter a thought,

ABOVE *Hartford with Trevor Brooking on his debut for Manchester City in August 1974 following a £250,000 move from WBA.*
BELOW *The 'News of the World' headline was typical of press reaction to Asa's abortive move to Leeds in November 1971.*

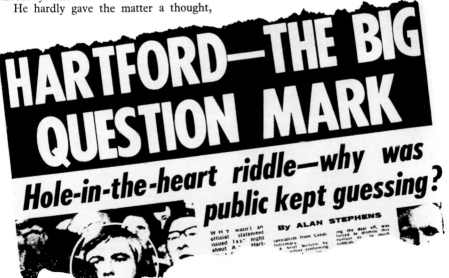

Hartford beats Steve Kember. It seems remarkable now that such a hard-working player was once rejected on medical grounds.

Most referees have learned how to spell 'Hartford' over the years—and Yates was no exception in booking him.

concentrating instead on looking forward to his debut for Leeds against Leicester a few hours later.

After more tests, and questions about his medical history, Revie took Hartford aside for the quiet chat that he has since admitted was one of his hardest ever chores.

'I've got bad news for you, Asa,' he said. 'We can't take you.' He went on to impart the information that could have been a shattering blow to a professional athlete—and particularly one like Asa noted for superb fitness and non-stop effort.

'You've got a medical condition,' Revie continued. 'Don't worry . . . no, that's silly, of course you'll worry . . . it's your heart, there's a slight murmur.' He then told Hartford that Tommy Docherty had picked him for Scotland's team to play Belgium the following week—'one of those *and now for the good news* stories,' Asa recalls wryly.

As they left the hotel Leicester's players arrived for their pre-match meal, but as Revie recited the roads to Birmingham Asa's Leeds career was over . . . before he had kicked a ball in anger. 'Whenever I go back over that morning,' he recalls, 'I feel more sorry for Don Revie than myself.'

The next few days were harrowing—the sensational news bulletins hinting darkly at a mystery medical problem. There was the sympathy of his Albion team-mates and manager Don Howe, who promised: 'It's not the end, Asa. I'll teach you to coach. I'll make you the best coach in the country.'

There was the frantic interest of the press when the truth emerged, and two days spent hiding in a hotel waiting for the verdict of a top Midlands heart specialist. What was that verdict? That Asa did have a hole in his heart, and that Leeds had been quite in order to reject him . . . but that the condi-

Honours: League Cup winners medal 1976, runners-up medal 1970

Club	Season	Div	Pos	League Ms	League Gs	FA Cup Ms	FA Cup Gs	Lge Cup Ms	Lge Cup Gs	Int'nls Ms·	Int'nls Gs
West Bromwich	1967-68	I	8	6	1	—	—	—	—	—	—
Albion	1968-69	I	10	26	7	4	1	—	—	—	—
	1969-70	I	16	35	1	1	—	7	—	—	—
	1970-71	I	17	34	2	4	—	2	1	—	—
	1971-72	I	16	39	1	1	—	1	—	6	—
	1972-73	I	22	41	3	5	1	3	1	—	—
	1973-74	II	8	33	3	4	—	2	—	—	—
Manchester City	1974-75	I	8	30	2	1	—	1	—	—	—
	1975-76	I	8	39	9	2	1	9	2	3	—
	1976-77	I	2	40	4	4	—	1	—	9	2
	1977-78	I	4	37	4	2	—	5	—	9	1
				360	37	28	3	31	4	27	3

tion would not affect or shorten his career.

After a traumatic weekend in which his entire future hung in the balance, it was over—at least as far as Asa was concerned, if not in the eyes of those journalists who instantly dubbed him '*Hole in the Hartford*'.

'I train as hard as any pro,' he says, 'and I must have run thousands of miles by then. I knew there was nothing wrong with me.'

The doubting public couldn't believe that a player could be a desperate heart case one week and fit for First Division action the next. Asa proved them wrong by turning out against Forest the following weekend, and put the icing on the cake with a great display for the Scottish Under-23 side against England, and then against Peru on his debut for the senior side at Hampden.

Lingering doubts were banished when Albion turned down a £220,000 bid for Hartford from Everton in 1972, then sold him to City for £250,000 in 1974.

His international future seems secure and there is every prospect of an honour or two with City—not bad for a lad who must have feared that he was on the soccer scrapheap at the age of 22.

Brian Flynn looks on as Hartford gives a demonstration of perfect balance. He has been a regular in Scotland's midfield since 1976, despite constant changes in its make-up.

Back to school
With the kids at his old school—Clydebank High—in June. There was little to cheer about later in the month—though Hartford held his place throughout the World Cup finals.

A Matter of Fact

On 3 September 1955, Wolves beat poor Cardiff 9-1 at Ninian Park to equal the record First Division away win. But the Welsh club got their revenge, winning the return game 2-0!

Last season six non-League clubs—Wigan (then in the Northern Premier League), Blyth, Enfield, Scarborough, Tilbury and Wealdstone—reached the third round of the FA Cup.

Preston defender Mike Baxter had scored just six goals in nearly 100 League games before the 1977-78 season. In the first three months of the new campaign he scored a further five—four of them own goals!

George Thompson senior, a former York City keeper, was in the stand watching when his sons George (25) and Des (23) kept goal for Scunthorpe United and York in a Third Division (North) game at Scunthorpe in January 1952.

Kuwait's Brazilian manager Mario Zagalo wasn't impressed by Wales when his team drew 0-0 at Wrexham last year: 'Leighton James was their best player. Of the rest, I do not speak', he said.

38-year old Dutch World Cup hero Jan Jongbloed kept a clean sheet in his first five games for Roda JC on joining them from relegated FC Amsterdam this season.

Swansea's capture from Liverpool, Ian Callaghan, played for England against France in the 1966 World Cup. But it was 11 years before he won his next England cap, against Switzerland at Wembley in Sept. 1977.

Tony 'Bomber' Brown of West Bromwich Albion and Leeds United hot-shot Peter Lorimer are the only current players who have scored hat-tricks in the League, League Cup, FA Cup and in European competition.

ABOVE Wyn Davies, one of the best headers of the ball in postwar soccer, left the Football League scene recently to return to his native North Wales with Bangor City of the Northern Premier League, the club for whom former Liverpool and England defender Chris Lawler now plays. Welsh international Davies certainly moved about during a career which began at Wrexham. He went on to Bolton, then played for Newcastle, Manchester City and United, Crystal Palace, Blackpool, Stockport and Crewe, hitting a total of 165 League goals. Wyn played 34 times for Wales from 1964—16 with Bolton, 11 with Newcastle, 3 with Manchester City, 3 with Manchester United and finally one with Blackpool, but never scored!

With over 550 League games behind him, Charlton's Keith Peacock has played against 71 of the 92 League clubs. One of the clubs he's always missed is the one he supported as a boy, Newcastle United. The teams met at The Valley in October but Peacock had to sit it out, having been injured two weeks before. He'll have to wait for the return . . .

All five home nations were in action on 25 October 1978. None of the players who captained their teams that day—Emlyn Hughes (England), Archie Gemmill (Scotland), Leighton Phillips (Wales), Paddy Mulligan (Eire) and Allan Hunter (Northern Ireland)—played for their clubs the previous Saturday. All were either dropped or injured.

KICK OFF WITH...

Gordon Milne

'The game is changing. It used to be full of one-job players, but now there's a greater demand for all-round performances.'

It'll take more than a 7-1 defeat to shake Gordon Milne's belief in open, attacking football.

Coventry City's manager was as upset as his players after the thrashing by Midlands neighbours West Bromwich Albion in October. But he says: 'If anything it made us even more convinced that open football is the way forward. Nobody was laughing at the meeting after the match, but we decided it was nothing to do with attitude but that, on the day, there were poor individual performances.

'We could have gone into a defensive shell after that defeat, but that would have put Coventry back five years. You've got to be big enough to bounce back.'

Gordon is pleased that the game as a whole is getting away from the stifling attitudes of recent years.

'The game was full of one-job players who went out there to do negative things for 90 minutes. Matches were made for them, not for players with expression.

'Now much of that is changing. There's a greater demand for all-round performances from players—which is better for everyone, not least the public. They are entitled to see better football.

'And if it means that a few mediocre players fall by the wayside, well that's hard luck.'

Gordon Milne and his assistant at Highfield Road, former Aston Villa player Ron Wylie. FAR RIGHT *Milne in his playing days with Bill Shankly's Liverpool side of the 1960s. Gordon was a skilful, constructive influence in a hard, fast team that won two League Championships— though he missed the 1965 FA Cup final triumph because of injury. He also played 14 times for England.*

477

'Running at defenders': Mick Channon

'If I get good service—to feet or played in front of me—I still fancy myself to lick anyone.'

One of the most exciting sights in football is Mick Channon in full flight—especially when he's running at defenders.

For Southampton, for England and now for Manchester City, Mick is a fearless and swashbuckling raider.

And there's method to the apparent madness of his flying runs.

'It's about committing defenders,' says Mick. 'They're there to guard the goal, basically, and if you're tearing at them they've got something else to think about, haven't they?

'Also, you find that things open up in front of you. For example, if you run at a defender the chances are that someone will try to give him a bit of cover—which means that one of your team-mates will probably be available for a one-two.'

To make his runs, Mick needs two things: space and decent service from his defenders.

'Sure, you've got to isolate yourself as much as possible when you haven't got the ball,' he says, 'so that when you get it you've got that vital yard or two of space.

'And if you get the ball up round your neck it's not much good to you, is it?

Committing defenders is especially dangerous in the last third of the pitch, says

Mick—'if you can get to the by-line you really get them worried.'

The temptation when running with the ball is to keep your head down. But Mick says it's important to keep glancing up to see how things develop in front of you.

He says: 'You never know, you might even find yourself with a clear run at goal—and to see that you've got to be looking!'

ABOVE *Always a great sight—Channon in full flight.* BELOW *Another defender prepares to follow in Channon's bootprints.*

Channon the cannon
Wiltshire-born Channon began his career with Southampton, where he scored 155 goals in 392 League games before moving on to Manchester City for a £300,000 fee. He has scored 21 goals in 44 internationals for England.

BOBBY GOULD

'I think I got caught up in the work-rate era. My own work-rate improved a lot but I lost my sharpness in the box. Finally Bill

Late trains have been more trouble than late tackles in Bobby Gould's colourful career.

The player who's never been quite sure which shirt he'll be wearing on any given Saturday played for five different clubs from the same house in Bristol.

So Temple Meads, Bristol's central station, had an ever-cheerful pro footballer as its most regular commuter.

'I must have kept the newspaper industry going single-handed all those years. I used to buy the lot and read them all—especially if I'd played a blinder the night before!'

These days Bobby is at Hereford United as player and assistant manager to his old

The ultimate cross-country trek—yet the young Gould who turned out for Coventry City looked a natural one-club player. Born and bred in Coventry, his dad churning out cars for Chrysler . . . but let Bobby tell you all about twists and turns in the life of football's travellin' man:

'I started as an apprentice pro when Jimmy Hill took over at Highfield Road and had five great exciting years there.

Things really buzzed at that place and you've got to hand it to Hill for making the

The face that launched a thousand attacks— Bobby in a Bristol City shirt and (right) *in action for City against Blackpool in 1973.*

Wolves 'mucker' Mike Bailey.

Bobby laughs. 'We had this gentlemen's agreement. Whoever got a job in management first would take on the other as assistant. Nothing like the old pals' act, is there?'

Hereford is club nine for Gould. The others, in order, are Coventry, Arsenal, Wolves, West Bromwich Albion, Bristol City, West Ham, Wolves again and Bristol Rovers.

480

TRAVELLIN' MAN...

McGarry came to take me to Wolves with words that were music to me: "If I see you in our half I'll kick your arse".'

club what it is today.

But then Hill went and Arsenal made a 90-grand bid for me. Well, there was no refusing that, was there, so off I went to the marble halls.

Arsenal is all sophistication. They really look after you there. I was very raw, a proper yokel, but the club looked after all my needs off the pitch.

It was on it that I had problems. Don Howe had taken over as coach and the goals dried up. My average had always been one in

two games, but at Highbury it was about 20 in 80.

Looking back I think I got caught up in the work-rate era. That was a very disciplined Arsenal side and my own work-rate improved a lot—but I lost my sharpness in the box.

Anyway, I was in the reserves and on the list for nine months. I scored 35 goals in 40 reserve games but no-one came for me. The Gould grin wasn't much in evidence those days!

Finally Bill McGarry came to take me to Wolves with words that were music to me: "If I see you in our half I'll kick your arse."

ABOVE *A defensive post in Bristol Rovers' second strip.* LEFT *Using his head for West Bromwich Albion against Manchester City.*

I scored 19 goals in my first season at Molineux. It was a very attacking side, with Derek Dougan, Hughie Curran and David Wagstaffe as well as myself.

Why did I leave Wolves? Well, they had forwards galore, including a youngster by the name of John Richards. Gould packed again ... this time for a move to West Brom.

Albion had been taken over by Don Howe and he invited me to The Hawthorns. He's a brilliant coach but it was obvious Albion

would never become an Arsenal. As for me, I had basically the same problems as before, and with the team on the slide I was on my bike again . . . to Bristol City and Alan Dicks, who had been at Coventry when I was there.

The trouble was, we weren't the same people. We'd gone in different directions over the years. I probably thought I was God's gift to Bristol City, so there were as many problems off the pitch as on it. After 11 months I asked for a move for the first time in my career.

Happy days at West Ham

In came West Ham, looking for a character to get them through one of their famous dodgy periods. Ah, what a club! I'm only sorry I didn't go there earlier in my career. It was the best of the lot for me. You can only improve as a player if you go there. They take away the blinkers. And if you want to be a coach, that's the place to learn.

During the summer I managed Aalesund, a club in the Norwegian Third Division, and you can be sure I took the West Ham ways out there. Well, people are doing it all over the place, aren't they? You can't move for coaches who started at Upton Park.

It's a family club. You're a name, not a number. I can't say enough about it. So why did I move on yet again? Well, there were great young players coming through and Gould was in and out of the side. At the same time Wolves were struggling and McGarry thought I could do a good job there. I went; we got relegated; McGarry was sacked.

Travel sickness

By this time I was sick to death of travelling. I'd been commuting for over four years —and that's a lot of trains.

I got this hamstring injury and had treatment at Bristol Rovers—I wasn't going to commute for that! I liked the scene there and joined them as player-coach with Bobby Campbell.

I scored a hat-trick in my debut then, four or five games later, we lost 9-0 at Tottenham! Still, we kept at it and, with 'Punky' Randall hogging the headlines, we had a great run in the FA Cup.

I'd probably still be at Rovers but for a phone call from Mike Bailey asking me to

With another old-timer . . . Gould for Wolves against Manchester United's Nobby Stiles.

join him at Hereford. I'd also been left ou of a Rovers game half an hour before the kick-off, which didn't please me.

At Hereford I made another good start scoring the equaliser against Huddersfield

Honours: FA Cup winners medal 1975 (as non-playing substitute); Second Division Championship medal 1967, 1977; League Cup runners-up medal 1969.

Club	Div	Pos	Season	League		FA Cup		Lge Cup	
				Ms	Gs	Ms	Gs	Ms	Gs
Coventry City	III	1	1963-64	2	–				
	II	10	1964-65	8	3	–	–	–	–
	II	3	1965-66	19	5	1	–	–	–
	II	1	1966-67	39	24	1	–	3	1
	I	20	1967-68	14	8	–	–	1	–
Arsenal	I	9	1967-68	16	6	3	2	–	–
	I	4	1968-69	38	10	4	1	6	3
	I	12	1969-70	11		–	–	2	–
W. Wanderers	I	4	1970-71	35	17	2	2	1	–
	I	9	1971-72	6	1	–	–	–	–
WBA	I	16	1971-72	31	12	1	–	–	–
	I	22	1972-73	21	6	–	–	3	–
Bristol City	II	5	1972-73	19	8	3	2	–	–
	II	16	1973-74	16	7	–	–	4	2
West Ham United	I	18	1973-74	12	4	1	–	–	–
	I	13	1974-75	34	9	3	1	2	3
	I	18	1975-76	5	2	–	–	–	–
W. Wanderers	I	20	1975-76	17	3	6	1	–	–
	II	1	1976-77	17	10	1	–	1	–
	I	15	1977-78	–		–	–	–	–
Bristol Rovers	II	18	1977-78	32	10	4	1	–	–
				392	145	30	10	23	9

We went on to beat them 3-2.

I really love playing and it'll cut me up when I have to stop. I was never outstanding as a player at school but I kept at it, and I know I've always been a bread-and-butter player in the League, but I think I've given value for money.

I'll tell you something that's kept in my mind all these years. When I was at Coventry there was a young player called Ian Gibson who was out of this world, a really great talent who never really made it big.

I'm not having a go at Ian . . . it's just that it's made me realise that you've got to make the greatest use of any talent you've got. That's all I've ever tried to do.'

Founded: 1905
Address: Carrow Road, Norwich NOR 22
Ground: Capacity 30,000 ; Playing area 104 x 68 m
Record attendance: 43,984 v Leicester City, FA Cup quarter-final, 30.3.63
Record victory: 10-2 v Coventry City, Div. 3(S), 15.3.30
Record defeat: 2-10 v Swindon T., Southern League, 5.9.08
Most League points: 64, Div. 3(S), 1950-51
Most League goals: 99, Div. 3(S), 1952-53
League scoring record: 31, Ralph Hunt, Div. 3(S), 1955-56
Record League aggregate: 122, Johnny Gavin, 1945-54 & 1955-58
Most League appearances: 590, Ron Ashman, 1947-64
Most capped player: 7, Ted MacDougall, Scotland, 1975
Honours: Football League Cup Winners 1962, Runners-up 1973, 1975 ; Div. 2 Champions 1971-72 ; Div. 3(S) Champions 1933-34
League career: 1920 Original members of Div. 3 ; 1921-34 Div. 3(S) ; 1934-39 Div. 2 ; 1939-58 Div. 3(S) ; 1958-60 Div. 3 ; 1960-72 Div. 2 ; 1972-74 Div. 1 ; 1974-75 Div. 2 ; 1975- Div. 1

NORWICH CITY

For all his larger-than-life qualities, John Bond is a realist . . . he accepts that, after five colourful years as manager of Norwich City, his main task is only half complete.

Despite regular attempts to lure him to clubs with bigger resources and brighter reputations, Bond is determined to finish that task—in his own style.

'I have received several tempting and flattering offers, but real satisfaction comes from reaching a target you have set yourself,' he told *Handbook*. 'There are exciting signs of this club taking off after a lot of hard work . . . and I want to be here to savour that success.'

That must be good news for Norwich chairman Sir Arthur South—the man who crossed swords so dramatically with Ron Saunders five years ago. He has vowed: 'We will move heaven and earth to keep John Bond here. He has a job to finish.'

Carrow Road is no longer the cosy, rustic outpost of the First Division, thanks mainly to the man who breezed in from Bournemouth on a wave of outlandish optimism.

Outlandish ? Well, not many people would

Midfielder John Ryan takes on Liverpool's Alan Hansen and Ray Kennedy back in October . . .

ave believed the Canaries could survive happily amid the First Division big guns—especially after relegation in 1974.

'I want players to enjoy themselves and to pass on that sense of fun to the supporters,' said Bond within minutes of joining Norwich. It was a very different attitude from that of the man he replaced—Ron Saunders.

With limited resources, Saunders had worked wonders with his sergeant-major approach. He brought First Division football to the city for the first time in 50 years in the League. And he took the club to Wembley for the first time, though their League Cup final performance against Spurs did nothing to boost their reputation—and City failed to capture the trophy they had won as their only major honour back in 1962.

Saunders resigned in November 1973 . . . and the club signed a young manager—John Bond—and a young coach—Ken Brown—who had been doing great things at Bournemouth.

They had a rough start. Though several of Bournemouth's successful Third Division side were signed immediately, they couldn't save Norwich from relegation.

But the drop did not prove to be a fatal blow. Bond made sweeping changes . . . and the Canaries bounced back at the first attempt, although they once again produced a dismal Wembley display.

The ironic twist was that this League Cup final set-back came against Aston Villa . . .

Canary wing . . . ? Former Spurs flyer Jimmy Neighbour has provided the width in a number of different forward combinations.

The Bournemouth connection
John Bond has signed a total of eight players who have played for Bournemouth in his five years at Carrow Road: Mel Machin, Ted MacDougall, John Benson, Tony Powell, Phil Boyer, David Jones, Kevin Reeves and Mark Nightingale. Benson and MacDougall are now back at Dean Court.

. . . but Norwich still suffered a 4-1 home defeat by the European Cup holders.

ABOVE *The Nest, the Canaries' home ground until 1935.*
LEFT *Terry Bly scores against Cardiff during their famous Cup run of 1959. Norwich, then a modest Third Division side, had already put Manchester United out of the competition and went on to beat Cardiff, Spurs and Sheffield United on the way to the semi-final with Luton.*

Martin Chivers, former England centre-forward, now at Carrow Road after spells with Southampton, Spurs and Swiss aces Servette.

managed by Ron Saunders.

Key figures in the revival of Norwich's fortunes were Ted MacDougall and Phil Boyer—the striking partners who had flourished so effectively under Bond at Bournemouth.

They did so much to help Bond fashion a team capable of returning to the top flight . . . and staying there without being dragged into the danger zone every season.

A winger with the old-fashioned virtues of directness and speed was needed to bring width and flair to Bond's strategy. Jimmy Neighbour moved from Spurs to fill that role.

This season Bond intended that Neighbour's telling service should be aimed towards the newly-forged combination of Martin Chivers and Kevin Reeves . . .

And, at first, the partnership looked good. Chivers, brought back from exile in Switzerland, and Reeves, relishing his selection for the England Under-21 line-up, immediately struck up an understanding that justified Bond's faith in a front-line mixture of experience and youth.

But Chivers' injury—one of several that disrupted the team in the first half of the season—stalled the further development of the partnership.

Other Bond moves have met with more immediate success. John Ryan's conversion from full-back to a midfield man with more freedom than most has paid rich dividends . . . and Ryan was soon up among the First Division top scorers.

Stalwart central defenders Duncan Forbes and Dave Stringer have given way to Tony Powell, another recruit from Bournemouth, and David Jones, the Welsh international. When injury sidelined Jones at the start of the present season, Bond swooped quickly for Orient's Phil Hoadley . . . and that decision again has been fully justified.

Perhaps the most telling coup of all, however, was the signing of Martin Peters for only £40,000 from Spurs back in 1975.

As an international star with 67 caps and a World Cup winners medal, Peters might have felt entitled to play out his days at Carrow Road with the imperious manner of a man who had done it all, watching with disdain while lesser mortals struggled to make ends meet.

In fact, Peters' appetite and skills are as sharp as ever . . . and his influence has been invaluable. At the age of 35, he is playing as well as any stage in his career.

Goalkeeper Kevin Keelan, with over 600 first-team games behind him, is the other character whose long experience and ever-

Kevin Keelan saves under pressure. He played his 500th League game in 1978.

green qualities inspire the kind of confidence so vital to a club aiming to make a lasting impression.

The experience of Peters and Keelan has been especially valuable this season, as Norwich's shallow first team pool was drained by a succession of injuries.

The problem has been made worse by the loss of other senior players. Colin Suggett was sold to Newcastle, Mel Machin has retired and joined the coaching staff and Mick McGuire, Davie Robb and Graham Paddon have been hit by loss of form.

As a result, recent Norwich sides have been full of fresh faces. Clive Baker took over in goal for a few games while Keelan was out and John Bond's son Kevin now has Ian Davies as his full-back partner. By the end of October three youngsters had made their First Division debuts: forwards Greg Downs and Peter Mendham, and Richard Symonds, an 18-year-old who was brought in to do the specialist marking jobs.

Bond's acceptance that Norwich still have

Former World Cup star Martin Peters is enjoying a splendid spell at Carrow Road.

a considerable way to go is based to some degree on a comparison with Ipswich Town up the road. They made a rousing success of their first visit to Wembley by winning the FA Cup last season and they are now well versed in European combat.

'Many fans think we will have arrived when we have won a place in Europe,' explains Bond. 'It's a natural target and an exciting one in itself. But I think we have to win a major trophy—like the League Championship—before we can be classed among the elite. And that's all the harder to achieve when you are a comparatively small club.'

And he continues to stress that the way in which success is earned is just as important as the actual triumph. 'We're not top-bracket material yet, but if we make it, I want everyone to see the smiles on our faces.'

The side haven't always practised what Bond preaches. There have been several verbal lashings for players who have 'let me, the club, the supporters and themselves down'.

Such outbursts have been taken as a sign of managerial weakness. The suggestion is that such criticisms should be made to the players' faces, not to the press.

Bond certainly courts publicity and he is

Kevin Reeves, Norwich's latest Bournemouth signing . . . and possibly the best of the lot.

prone to treat all issues in terms of black and white, rather than a mere cautious shade of grey. He pronounces on every aspect of the game, from the national team to the encouragement of local youngsters at the club's highly successful soccer clinic.

'I say so much because I care passionately about these things. That's why I stay in the game. And if these things strike you as wrong, then you have a duty to say so.'

As a by-product, of course, Bond is drawing attention all the time to Norwich City . . . an outfit not noted in the past for making many headlines.

But in the future . . . ? Bond points out: 'The club has gone through a major shake-up in every department and the proper foundations are there. Our youth policy gives me most cause for optimism . . . and its full value should be realised in the next three or four years.'

Will he make any concessions to those who remain doubtful about his style ? 'I'll try not to talk quite so much.' A broad grin gives the game away.

Bond and Bond
Norwich City have always been known as a family club and now John and son Kevin Bond are proving it. Kevin, like his dad, is a full-back, and made his debut during the 1975-76 season when he appeared briefly as a substitute against Leicester at Filbert Street. He was given a long run in the team last season and now seems to have established himself in the side, usually at right-back but sometimes in midfield. Father played right-back for West Ham in the 1964 FA Cup winning side against Preston.

A Matter of Fact

Left Kenny Dalglish was once described by Danny McGrain as 'the greatest player in the world'. Fans of Cruyff, Kempes, Krol and the man he succeeded at Anfield, Kevin Keegan, might want to dispute that, but they can't take Kenny's international record away from him. He made a modest enough start as sub against Belgium at Aberdeen in 1971. Yet while managers came and went—Docherty, Ormond, MacLeod and now Jock Stein—Dalglish went from strength to strength. He has represented his country in the last two World Cups, and when the Scots drew 1-1 with Iran in Cordoba on 7 June 1978, Dalglish won his 56th full cap, beating the previous record of 55 held by Denis Law. With 21 goals to his name already, he must have every chance of overhauling Lawrie Reilly (22) and Hughie Gallacher (22), and getting within striking distance of Law's record of 30 goals for the national team. Kenny won everything going with Celtic in Scottish football—an in his first English season won a European Cup Winners medal.

Birmingham's Jim Montgomery will always be remembered for his brilliant save in Sunderland's 1973 FA Cup final win over Leeds. His 600th League appearance, made on 30 September 1978, was also against Leeds. But this time Monty was a loser, 3-0.

Kevin Keegan agreed to play in a testimonial match recently in aid of ex-Aston Villa defender John Robson, whose career was ended by illness. When SV Hamburg refused the former Liverpool striker permission to play in the game, he promptly booked a £200 advertisement in the programme that evening ... a fine gesture from a great player.

Ouch! The punch which Milton Viera of AEK Athens threw at Kenny Burns in the Greek club's European Cup tie with Nottingham Forest proved very expensive for the Uruguayan. Not only was he sent off, but he was also fined £2,000 by his manager, the former Real Madrid star Ferenc Puskas.

Huddersfield Town have scaled every height in League soccer since their formation in 1908—including three successive First Division championships in the 1920s. But those days have gone, and before their game against Wimbledon in October they stood 21st in the Fourth, their worst ever position.

Tony Brown's goal at Leeds earlier in the season was his 209th for Albion—a club League record. It was previously held by Ronnie Allen, who promptly sent Brown the gallon bottle of whisky awarded to him as Manager of the Month during his spell as Albion boss.

Billy Walker (Villa) hit a hat-trick of penalties v Bradford City in 1921. Five players have emulated him since: Charlie Mitten (Man. U.) v Villa, 1950; Bobby Collins (Celtic) v Aberdeen, 1953; Ken Barnes (Man. C.) v Everton, 1957; Donald Ford (Hearts) v Morton, 1973, and Gerry Colgan (Queens Pk.) v Brechin, 1976.

Plymouth Argyle created a record for the number of drawn League games in a season 1920-21, exactly half of their 42 Third Division games. Tranmere, in 1970-71, and last season Chester drew no fewer than 22 of their 46 Third Division fixtures.

On 15 October 1977 Bristol Rovers beat Blackburn 4-1 in a Second Division game at Eastville, Bobby Gould notching a debut hat-trick. Exactly a year later, they met on the same ground with the same result—and Paul Randall scored three!

Ex-European champions Ajax drew only 7,000 to their first home game this season.

Everton's 1-0 win over Liverpool recently was their first 'derby' win in seven years.

End to end for Andy

'Often it's not enough just to react to situations. You've got to spot the danger before it develops.' GRAHAM TAYLOR

Great goals are usually hard to come by in derbies. The extra edge in these games means that both sides are determined not to give anything away . . .

So the goal that gave Aston Villa a 1-0 victory over neighbours Birmingham City in their first League encounter this season was extra special . . . a long, sweeping thrust through the heart of the Birmingham defence, a bolt from the claret and blue.

It started with Villa keeper Jimmy Rimmer. He picked himself up after catching a high corner to see that a quick break was on. Dennis Mortimer had already seen the possibilities and was sprinting away from Rimmer's goal into yards of space.

Rimmer's throw was per-fect: right into that open space. Mortimer's first-time pass found Andy Gray deep in Birmingham territory. Gray laid it off to Brian Little, who knocked into the gap between two Blues defenders, then passed back to Gray, who had stolen away into space on the left of the penalty area . . . and Gray's left-foot shot (*right*) beat the despairing advance of City keeper Jim Montgomery.

The move had swept the length of the St Andrews pitch—115 yards—in 13 seconds and just five touches.

Obviously Birmingham were caught out—the speed of the move left them labouring to get back—but could the defenders that stayed back when the corner was taken have done anything

more? Could they conceivably have prevented the goal?

Well . . . possibly. There was a key moment as Little received the ball when the course of events could have been altered. Whether it would have prevented the goal or not is debatable.

When Little knocked the ball into the space between the last two remaining Blues defenders, Alberto Tarantini, struggling to get back goal-side of the Villa forward, gestured to Gary Pendrey to go with Gray . . . and to leave Little to young Mark Dennis.

But Pendrey chose to confront Little . . . and we're not going to say he was wrong.

Pendrey had to choose between the frying pan and the fire . . . and he could have been burned either way.

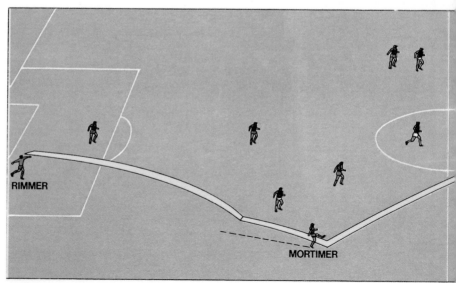

RIMMER

MORTIMER

Graham Taylor's analysis

It was a lack of alertness that let Birmingham down. A team is strangely vulnerable when they are in possession and the Birmingham defenders were guilty of ball-watching at a distance. When Rimmer tumbled over after catching the corner they relaxed a little. Mortimer was thinking ahead; Birmingham weren't. Often it's not enough just to react to situations—you've got to spot the danger before it develops. City's defence did what they could—but quick-moving Villa were too sharp for them.

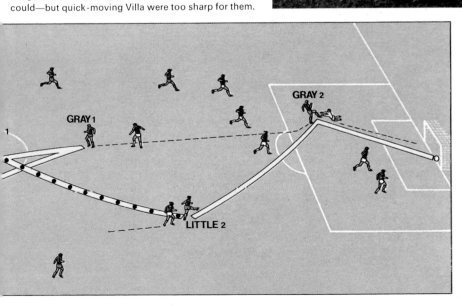

PRO FILE

JOE JORDAN

'Joining United was a great move for me—it's a great club and their style of play will help me become a better footballer. Instead of chasing endless high balls, I find we work attacks up the middle of the park, giving me the chance to show what I can do on the ground. I think this will be my best season ever.'

Big Joe Jordan had something to prove . . . that his contribution to a football match could go deeper than striking terror into the hearts of defenders.

At Leeds he was often used as a target man, but his main function was to 'get in there' when the ball was anywhere near the six-yard box.

At Manchester United he is expected to keep his feet on the ground long enough to play a meaningful part in the build-up.

And Joe loves it. 'I like the freedom it gives me. My role is more flexible and I have to show that I've got something to offer on the ground as well as in the air. My own game is developing as a result.'

But don't get the idea Joe is running down the team that Revie built. He knows he owes much, if not all, to the club that paid £15,000

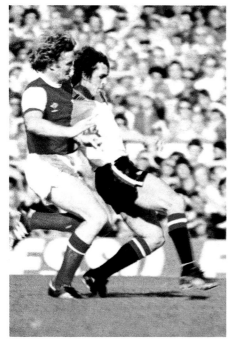

A typical Jordan shot as he puts pressure on fellow Scot Willie Young during United's 1-1 draw with Arsenal at Highbury in September.

for a raw 18-year-old from Morton after he had made only ten appearances for the Scottish club and scored a solitary goal.

After I went to Leeds Bobby Collins carried on where my father left off,' says Jordan. 'Not letting me develop bad habits and encouraging my strengths. I can't speak too highly of the help he gave me under the guidance of Mr Revie. They believed in me from the start, even though I had it all to prove.

The player defenders hate to mark
'I've no thoughts of becoming a manager —I'm 26 years old and my job at the moment is getting out on the pitch and playing to the limit of my ability—but if I ever do go into management the great lesson I learned from Don Revie is that you get the best performance from good players by treating them like men, allowing them to take responsibility, encouraging them to believe that they're an important part of a great set-up.'

But Joe Jordan, for all his competitive aggression and reputation as the one centre-forward every opposing defender hated to mark, attracted criticism from many people who felt that his goals-per-game tally was too low; his 35 from 169 League games with

Leeds leaving him well behind the 125-odd active League players with 75 or more goals to their credit.

Although this seems strange for a man who was consistently chosen to represent his country, his fans countered by pointing out the number of players who benefitted from Jordan's menacing activity in the box, feeding on his knock-downs and cashing in on the confusion caused by the big man's mere presence.

'Give my best, week in week out'

No doubt the likes of Allan Clarke and Peter Lorimer would agree with that view, but the argument leaves Jordan cold. 'As far as I'm concerned, I'm a professional footballer,' he says. 'I live the game and it's up to me to go out there and give of my best, week in, week out. That means fitting in with the team's method of play and making the maximum contribution within it.

'At Leeds I had two main jobs. The first was as a target man for the long ball out of defence, holding and shielding until support arrived. The second was getting into the box and being on the spot when the ball arrived. If the attack broke down that was it.

New freedom

'That was my role at Leeds and it worked ... the club was successful and that was that. If the manager wasn't happy with my contribution, he had the remedy in his own hands.

'But here at United the system of play is very different. We work the ball up through the middle a lot, and that means a much greater involvement for the front men. And I

Power in the air ... beating Dave Watson at Wembley during Scotland's 2-1 success last year and (third from right) scoring against Birmingham in August.

Honours: European Cup Winners Cup runners-up medal 1973; League Championship medal 1974; European Cup runners-up medal 1975.

Club	Div	Pos	Season	League		FA Cup		Lge Cup		Int'nls	
				Ms	Gs	Ms	Gs	Ms	Gs	Ms	Gs
Morton	I	10	1968-69	3	–	–	–	–	–	–	–
	I	10	1969-70	5	1	–	–	–	–	–	–
	I	8	1970-71	2	–	–	–	–	–	–	–
Leeds United	I	2	1970-71	–	–	–	–	–	–	–	–
	I	2	1971-72	12	–	2	–	–	–	–	–
	I	3	1972-73	26	9	1	–	2	–	3	–
	I	1	1973-74	33	7	5	2	–	–	11	5
	I	9	1974-75	29	4	6	–	4	–	3	1
	I	5	1975-76	17	2	–	–	–	–	3	–
	I	10	1976-77	32	10	5	2	1	–	4	–
	I	9	1977-78	20	3	–	–	3	3	3	1
Man. United	I	10	1977-78	14	3	2	–	–	–	6	1
				193	39	21	4	10	3	33	8

love involvement. The more you're in a game, the sharper you get in tight situations, and the better you read the pattern of play. I like the freedom that gives me.

'My role has become much more flexible, depending on the circumstances of the moment, and I find myself taking a fuller part in play and proving that I've got something to offer on the ground as well as in the air. My own game is developing as a result and I'm confident that this is going to be my best season ever.'

Switching styles at Old Trafford
Last season, in the 14 games he played for United, he found the net just three times. But that was at a time when Dave Sexton was evaluating his resources, looking for the best permutations for the future. United persevered with the Docherty-inspired 4-2-4 formation until the end of the season, when a switch to 4-3-3 brought four wins in five games.

This season Sexton—another thinking manager who believes in giving players the credit for knowing their job—has brought success back to Old Trafford. True, it hasn't been without the odd stutter, and in a season where Liverpool streaked clear early on the also-rans attracted less attention; but though United attained a respectable place in the top half of the table, the League Cup shock against Watford increased the pressure.

The Sexton jigsaw
The size of Sexton's problem in breaking up the successful Docherty team and creating one of his own is illustrated by a comparison between the team that opened the 1976-77 campaign (Stepney, Nicholl, Albiston, McIlroy, B. Greenhoff, Buchan, Coppell, McCreery, Pearson, Macari, Hill) and that which defeated Manchester City a little over

a year later in a thrilling local derby watched by 55,317—(Roche, Albiston, Houston, B. Greenhoff, McQueen, Buchan, Coppell, J. Greenhoff, Jordan, Macari, McIlroy).

The changes are only part of the story— United's near £1 million investment in just two players, McQueen and Jordan, underlines Dave Sexton's determination to do things his way, to create his own brand of

Joe screams at referee Konrath during Scotland's disappointing defeat against England at Hampden in May. His commitment often spills over on the wrong side of the law—but most pros prefer playing with him to against him.

ABOVE *Harrassing Ray Clemence at Hampden.*
BELOW RIGHT *Joe was not alone in earning a few
extras with Scotland's qualification for the
World Cup finals, but like the others Heineken's
huge hoarding campaign went a little flat after
two disastrous opening results in Argentina.*

Manchester United magic It is appropriate
that Joe Jordan, the up-front half of the ex-
Leeds duo and a vital piece of the Sexton
jigsaw, should score the dramatic winner in
the dying moments of that derby game.

A comparison between Joe's first 14 games
for Manchester United and his second 14
reveals that he doubled his scoring tally from
three last season to six this, confirming his
optimism about the personal and team
success that lies ahead with United.

Fighting for a Scotland place
But Joe's driving ambition at the highest
level calls for more than success at club
or even European level—it demands that
he should continue to appear for Scotland
as a regular. He had notched 33 caps
to the end of the World Cup—scoring
8 times, including vital goals like the brave
diving header against Czechoslovakia that
allowed Scotland to qualify for the '74 finals.

But the Argentina fiasco has put his
Scotland future on the line. One of the most
persistent criticisms of the unfortunate Ally
MacLeod was his stubborn refusal to include
prolific goalscorer Andy Gray in his squad—

an omission that may have cost Scotland their
chance before they even started. Now Jock
Stein will have to think carefully about which
of the big strikers he prefers. unless he can
find a way of using their combined talents to
feed each other, and the likes of Kenny
Dalglish.

Joe won't talk about Argentina—'nothing
much remains to be said,' he comments
dryly—but like all good pros he looks ahead.

'Quality in depth'
'Now we must prove in the European
Championships that we still have the quality
in depth to be an international force,' he adds,
'and it goes without saying that I would love
to be in the team.' Quality in depth means
real competition for places, and Joe didn't
make Jock Stein's squad for the European
Championship game against Norway—a
game that made Scotland seem hesitant in
defence and lucky in attack.

But you can never accuse Joe of shirking
competition, so he will be trying hard to turn
in performances for United that will force
him back into the reckoning for his country
and confirm that he really has become a
better player since that expensive move
across the Pennines. He himself has no
doubts. 'I really believe we can win something,' he announces firmly, 'and football is
about winners.'

496

Whistle Test

'The biggest cancer in the game at the moment is dissent. I see players everywhere who don't know the difference between appeal and dissent.' JACK TAYLOR

What's the biggest problem in football today? Pundits in this country agonize about violence on the terraces, while our club chairmen assure us that the game is selling itself too cheaply and that many clubs are in danger of going broke. But Jack Taylor, who has had wide experience of football throughout the world in more than 20 years on the international circuit, reckons the biggest problem is dissent.

'I see young players everywhere who don't know the difference between appeal and dissent,' says Jack.

'Modern coaching methods encourage players to call for the ball. If you ever see a team in training the shouting and the noise is unbelievable. It's swallowed up on the Saturday. So the young player is brought up in an atmosphere that encourages him to ask for everything.

'If a player kicks it out and he knows full well it's a corner against him, he will still appeal for a goal-kick—automatically. That is appealing. When the decision is given against him then it becomes dissent.'

ABOVE *Rangers' John Greig and a linesman: appeal or dissent?*

Skipper's perks

The law about dissent says that the dissenting player should be cautioned by the referee and an indirect free-kick should be awarded to the opposition.

'The captain has no special priveleges,' Jack Taylor points out. 'It used to be the thing across the parks, that the captain could dispute the referee's decision. But there's nothing in the rules that makes the captain an exception.'

So just remember, if you're ever tempted to dispute a referee's decision: it's a waste of time. It could cost your team a free-kick and a booking.

David Peach on taking penalties

'I never get nervous. It's just another part of the game for me—like taking a throw-in—except that it's a lot more enjoyable if you get the right result!'

Not everyone fancies taking penalties. The fear of missing, letting your side down and—let's face it—looking foolish can be too much for some players.

But others thrive on it. They love those precious seconds of excitement before the kick and the instant glory afterwards.

They also see it simply as a job to be done—with most of the odds in their favour!

That's how Southampton's penalty king David Peach approaches it.

Typically, he says: 'I just concentrate on hitting the back of the net.'

He's been doing that regularly for Southampton, moving up from left-back

whenever the referee points to the spot.

'I never get nervous,' says David. 'It's just another part of the game to me.'

More often than not he does, but perhaps the secret of his overall success from the spot is that he was speaking with the same confidence after missing a couple.

'I've missed two out of four this season after getting 17 in a row. The keepers moved both times—they always do—but it hasn't put me off. I'll keep banging them in.'

So is David a 'blaster' as opposed to a 'placer'?

'A bit of both really. With so many good goalkeepers about you've got to hit the

ball with some pace, otherwise they'll get to it.'

Although lots of penalty takers use the side of the foot for accuracy, David doesn't go along with that.

'Not enough power for a start—and often you can tell where the ball's going.

'I hit across the ball for power and there's no way the keeper knows which way it's going—sometimes until it's in the net!

'Being left-footed it's natural for me to pull the ball to the left of the goalkeeper [as shown in the pictures] but I'll hit the ball the other side if I have to.

'In the First Division it's very much bluff and double bluff. Goalkeepers get to

Peach of a penalty . . . about to put it away.

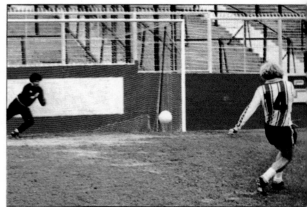

Because he hits across the ball and never side-foots it, David's natural penalty is placed to the keeper's left.

know you and vice versa. They'll remember a penalty you took against them and wonder if you'll put it in the same place or try something different. And I'm placing the ball on the penalty spot thinking the same thing.

'What I do is make up my mind there and then, as I'm placing the ball, and I never change it.

'The corners of the goal are always favourite, so I choose one and that's it. Even if the keeper stands more towards that corner, I'll still put it there.

'The worst thing is to get into two minds. That's why goalkeepers do all that dancing about on the line— their only hope is to put you off and it can work if you watch them and not the ball. So—place the ball, decide where you're going to put it and put it there.'

David thinks keepers should be allowed to move for penalties before the ball is kicked. 'They do move so they might as well be allowed to. It's a silly rule, that one.'

Net's-eye view of the Peach penalty. The keeper doesn't move for the sake of our session but David thinks they should be able to in matches. 'They all do, so they might as well be allowed to. It's a silly rule.'

The keeper dives but the power of the shot puts it past him. 'You can't get the same power with the side-foot.'

'Pick that one out, son' . . . another spot success.

This is the moment (above) **when David decides where he's going to put his penalty—as he places the ball on the spot. 'I choose a corner and put it there even if the keeper stands towards that side. The worst thing is to get into two minds.' He also keeps his eye on ball** (right) **and doesn't get distracted by the keeper.**

What the keeper sees . . . Peach prepares to plant another one past the keeper.

Thump . . . David never side-foots the ball. He hits 'across' the ball.

This time it's a high one—'that's okay if it goes inside the post,' says David.

Graham Taylor:

It's no good being dogmatic about the way penalties should be taken ; if someone can score every time with a back-heel, let him carry on ! Basically, though, it's either a question of blasting them or placing them. I remember Geoff Hurst hammering penalties for West Ham, treating them like a shot but with time and space. He had a lot of success but the one penalty I remember—and probably him, too—is the one Gordon Banks saved for Stoke in the semi-final of the League Cup. The 'placers' include Forest's John Robertson, who tucks them in the corners using the side-foot method David dislikes.

One sound piece of advice to young penalty-takers is to aim for the areas shaded in the diagram. If you hit the ball firmly towards those areas—the lower the better, preferably—it should be a goal every time if the keeper doesn't move early.

Probably more important is that your penalty-taker should be the player who really fancies his chances of regularly hitting the back of the net—however he chooses to do it. He is often the extrovert in the side, the player who thinks it's unfair on the keeper to have a free shot from 12 yards ! And if he misses one early on in a game, it's unlikely to put him off.

How do you find the prospective penalty king in your side ? Just ask. The silence in the dressing-room will tell you that most players are thinking : no thanks ! But one or two, perhaps three, players will want to give it a go.

RISING STAR TONY GALE

When Bobby Moore hands in his shirt, who do you find to wear it? It's a problem that still concerns England . . . but one that Fulham—Moore's last club—seem to have solved.

Tony Gale was only 16 when he made his debut for the Fulham first team—in an Anglo-Scottish Cup defeat at Orient. Three days later he was pitched in for his second game against Norwich and found himself facing that prolific pairing, Ted MacDougall and Phil Boyer.

'I was a bit apprehensive at first,' Tony recalls, 'but the older players in the side like Viv Busby and Alan Slough helped to talk me through it and I learned as the game went on.'

Gale is a strong believer in 'dedication and listening to people', so when Bobby Moore returned from a summer stint in America to reclaim his place in the team, young Tony retired to the sidelines to look and learn.

'He was a model pro,' says Tony now.

'Players like him are bound to have a tremendous influence on you.'

But Moore, Mullery, Best and Marsh were on their way out. Fulham's League position wasn't improving, and so manager Bobby Campbell decided to dispense with the celebrities and put his faith in a squad of virtual unknowns.

'It's a very young side,' Gale points out. 'We've got a few new signings and we're just getting it together.'

Gale warning

Nevertheless, they are already up among the promotion contenders. 'We didn't really expect success so quickly, but after we'd done sides like Palace, Stoke and West Ham we started to realise we were as good as anybody.'

Although he's only just 19, Tony Gale has played a very prominent part in Fulham's rise in the Second Division. He sees himself as a central defender, but he's equally capable of figuring in midfield. For Fulham

Gale down the Fulham Road

Tony is a Londoner, from Victoria. He was a Chelsea supporter who idolised Peter Osgood and as a schoolboy he trained at Stamford Bridge —as well as at Fulham and QPR. When he left school Leeds also offered him a place. But when it came to a choice, 'Fulham won hands down,' Tony told Handbook. 'They might be trying to get rid of their old image but they're still a homely club and that's what attracted me.

'Down at Chelsea there always seemed to be hundreds of kids, but at Fulham everybody knows everybody else . . . and I got my chance much earlier.'

And the highlight of Tony's career so far? 'Beating Chelsea 1-0 in the Anglo-Scottish Cup last season.'

'We didn't really expect success so quickly, but after we'd done sides like Palace, Stoke and West Ham we started to realise we were as good as anybody.'

Club	Season	League Ms Gs	FA Cup Ms Gs	L Cup Ms Gs
Fulham	1977-78	38 8	1 –	2 –
		38 8	1 –	2 –

Policing Palace's Swindlehurst (above) at Selhurst Park and playing against Stoke (left) at Craven Cottage. Both games were won, putting Fulham among Division II's leaders.

he plays alongside Richard Money in the centre of the defence, but he's very much a central defender in the continental style, constantly willing to bring the ball forward

Since he has become established in the first team Tony feels he has grown up far more quickly than he would have done in any other job. He told *Handbook*: 'When I first came into the side and somebody clogged me I'd go all over the field looking for them. But I don't lose my temper now.'

He smiles and adds: 'Then again, the manager wants me to be a bit more aggressive. He thinks I'm too nice. He likes us to play entertaining football but he also wants us to show a bit of steel.

Fulham tea party
'Fulham have always been known as a lovely little club where you could come down for a couple of points and a cup of tea afterwards. But now we've hardened up. We're not a soft touch anymore.'

Not that anyone is likely to mistake Tony Gale for a soft touch. In fact, at 6′ 2″, he prefers to play against bigger men. 'You might not win everything in the air, but they're not as likely to expose you for pace. Whereas the little buzzers like Peter Ward can be electric . . . and I'm not as quick as I could be.'

More like Moore
Bobby Moore wasn't the fastest player around, but his anticipation made him one of the game's greatest defenders. If Tony lacks a bit of pace it seldom shows because he reads the game so well.

He has already captained the England youth team in the European Championship and he is obviously known to Ron Greenwood. If in a few years time the England manager is still trying to fill the gap left by Moore's retirement then it's a safe bet that he'll be looking closely at the man who is wearing the number six shirt with such distinction at Fulham.

10 PRIZES OF 6 GREAT K-TEL ALBUMS

114 TERRIFIC TRACKS...

● 'The Amazing Darts' ● 16 hits on 'Midnight Hustle' ● 'Both Sides of Dolly Parton' ● 18 soul smashes on 'Ecstasy' ● 'Brotherhood of Man's Greatest' ● 20 knockout numbers on 'Emotions'

1. Which Southern League club is Geoff Hurst now managing?

2. Which club knocked Celtic out of this season's Anglo-Scottish Cup?

3. Who was Holland's manager during the 1978 World Cup finals?

4. Which Second Division club recently signed Nicky Johns from Tampa Bay?

5. Aberdeen's striker Joe Harper has played for two Football League clubs. Name one of them.

6. Which of the following men was Derby County manager Tommy Docherty's immediate predecessor at the Baseball Ground: Jimmy Sirrel, Colin Murphy, Dave Mackay, Brian Clough, Alan Durban?

7. Who scored Spurs' winner in the 1973 League Cup final, and which club is he now with?

8. Who joined Luton from Blackpool last summer?

9. LEFT Their manager last season was a former captain of England. Among his players were John Dempsey and Colin Waldron. Eire's manager played for them too. Which club is it?

10. With which Football League clubs did the following players make their debuts: Steve Kember, Archie Gemmill, Ron Futcher, John Mahoney and Phil Boersma?

11. He joined Burnley from non-League Atherstone. He's now playing for a London Second Division team and has played in goal for his country on several occasions. Who is he?

HOW TO ENTER

504

KICK OFF WITH...

Stuart Kennedy

Stuart forces Rangers' Gordon Smith to cover back in last year's Scottish Cup final.

'I learned a great deal from Argentina. It was an opportunity to study the top sides and the best players in the world and I didn't waste the chance.'

Many critics described Scotland's World Cup adventure to Argentina as a waste of time and effort. But Aberdeen and Scotland full-back Stuart Kennedy certainly doesn't agree.

Kennedy, fast emerging as one of the country's finest international prospects for years, reckons it was part of the reason for his continuing development and improved performances.

He told *Handbook:* 'I've become a better player as a result. I studied the different styles of other full-backs in Argentina and noted points which I have concentrated on since then.

'I used to do the difficult things well and the easy things badly. My crosses were apt to go astray. Now I'm getting the ball over accurately at different angles and levels.

'It's not only because of my experiences at the World Cup. I trained hard when I came back and worked at improving the weaknesses in my game'

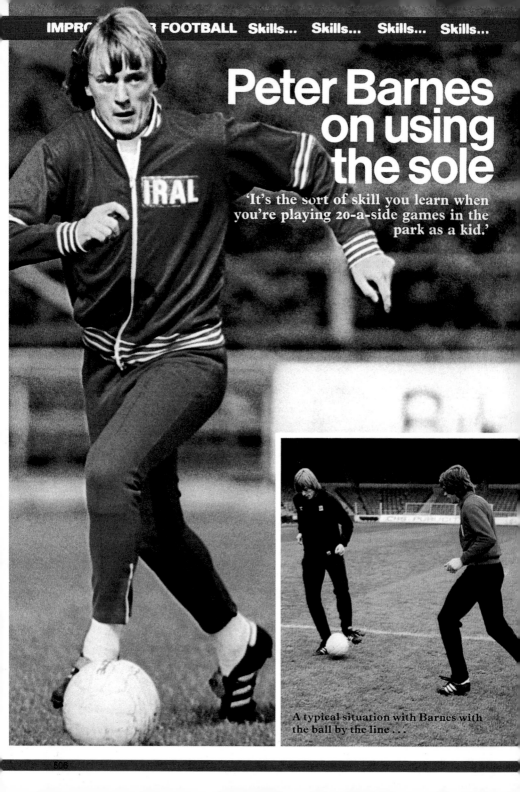

Peter Barnes on using the sole

'It's the sort of skill you learn when you're playing 20-a-side games in the park as a kid.'

A typical situation with Barnes with the ball by the line . . .

The ability to roll the ball around the foot, using the sole of the boot, has always been the trademark of the game's 'ball players'.

It makes opponents feel uneasy because the player in possession is saying, in effect: 'This ball is mine and there's no way you're going to get it.'

Peter Barnes, Manchester City's England winger, says it often. He stands on the ball momentarily near the touch-line and tempts the full-back to lunge for it. The advantage is with Peter because he has possession and can dictate the play.

'I only do it when a defender is trying to get right and pinch the ball,' says Peter. 'Then, if I get past him, he might think twice the next time and give me that vital yard or two.'

Peter is already a hardened pro but he says that it's this type of skill that's the icing

Graham Taylor: Practising with the sole of the boot is one of the best ways of getting the 'feel' of the ball. On your own you can move with the ball in a centre circle and drag it back now and again. The important thing is to maintain control, and you'll find that it's also a question of 'sorting your feet out'.

on the cake for him.

'It's the sort of thing you learn when you're playing 20-a-side in the park as a kid, and it's sad that a lot of that kind of thing is knocked out of youngsters.

'The skill is also useful for switching the play. Anyone who finds himself in a situation where there's 'nothing on' can drag the ball back with the sole and look for other alternatives.'

As the defender gets tight, Peter drags it back . . .

With such a skill, it's very much a question of . . .

. . . now you see it, now you don't—and fly away Peter.

The close up shows how the ball is dragged back the length of the sole without Peter losing possession. Even when it's on the tip of the boot, it's still his—just right to be lifted over the tackling foot and go clear.

Barnes stormer
Peter is the son of the former Manchester City wing-half now the club's chief scout Ken Barnes. He made his debut in a Manchester derby a League Cup tie at Old Trafford in October 1974. City lost... Peter went on to gain England Under-21 honours and a League Cup winners medal, and won his first full cap in the 2-0 win over Italy at Wembley in the World Cup qualifying match in November 1977. With the Czech game he now had nine full caps to go with his nine at Under-21 level. Peter was PFA Young Player of the Year in 1975

From behind you can see how Peter drags back just before the challenge.

'You get the defender to commit himself then shoot past him.'

Graham Taylor:

As nice as it is to see a player using the sole in tight situations—Rodney Marsh was one of the finest exponents of the skill—it's important to see it as a means to an end and not as an end in itself.

It's easy to fall in love with the ball and see it

'The next time he might think twice and give you that vital yard of space.'

as your own personal property, but football is still a team game and if a team-mate has made a good run in anticipation of you slipping past an opponent, it's your job to find him, not dally on the ball or think about beating someone else.

So a good practice is to set up the kind of situation in which Peter often finds himself. The ball is served to the player out wide (left or right) and once he's past the defender [see diagram] it's his job to get to the by-line and get his cross in to the server. Obviously, the defender would feel a bit of a mug by letting the forward get past him every time, so it's best to give him a fairly free role to make the practice realistic— that is, he can try hard to win the ball on occasions, not just let him get past every time.

That way it won't be a wasted exercise for the defender: he'll have the satisfaction of making the odd good tackle. At the same time, he must remember that sole control is the main object of the practice.

Incidentally, don't think the skill is relevant only by the touchline—it can be used all over pitch, simply to change direction or to open up new angles. How often have you seen Liam Brady heading for a dead-end situation and then see him drag the ball back with that lovely left foot of his to probe for another opening?

One last thing: this is not an easy skill and it's probably better to practise it only on your stronger foot. Fluffing it on the weaker one could be a bit demoralising, and no one wants that.

DEREK JOHNSTONE

'I suppose to have played top-class football for nine years and still be only 25 may seem remarkable. In fact, a lot of people think I'm much older.'

Centre-half or striker? That's the dilemma facing Derek Johnstone and Rangers manager John Greig. Fortunately, the man they call 'the new John Charles' has shown that he can be equally effective in either role.

But while Johnstone began the season at the back doubts were soon cast about whether Rangers could afford to play him there on a permanent basis. After Rangers' failure to get goals in their opening League games it was inevitable that the fans and the critics should question the wisdom of the new manager's decision.

After all, they argue, you don't put your top scorer in the back four. Johnstone was Scotland's most prolific scorer last season with 41 goals, two of these counting as the only goals managed in the Home Championship prior to the World Cup.

Johnstone insists that he will play where he is asked, and that's up front in Europe, at least, but his own preference is for centre-half. 'The media said I had put pressure on the club to allow me to play there, but that's not true. I play where the manager says.'

During a summer of uncertainty about his future with Rangers, it was stated often enough by the media—in comments attributed to Johnstone—that he saw himself developing his career in a defensive role.

He went as far as to slap in a shock transfer request on the eve of Scotland's departure for Argentina, and then admitted that a move to America and the lucrative soccer boom there appealed to him.

But with his former team-mate John Greig installed as manager in succession to Jock Wallace and the new season looming Johnstone thought things over, withdrew his

transfer request ('not one club bid for me')
re-signed for Rangers . . . and then took over
the job vacated by Greig as captain.

Now Johnstone faces a fresh and demanding challenge to lead Rangers to a repeat of
last season's treble success—their second in
three seasons.

'But being appointed captain wasn't my
reason for staying with Rangers—and it had
nothing to do with the fact that I began the
season at centre-half, either.'

Irrespective of what course Johnstone's
career takes, whether defender or striker, he
remains one of the genuine star personalities
of Scottish League football.

His strength and determination to win
every ball and his ability to create space for
himself are two outstanding features of his
game, but it is his tremendous power and
class in the air that is his greatest asset. There
isn't a goalkeeper north of the border who
can't testify to that.

He says: 'When I play as a striker nearly
everything I do is inside the 18-yard box.
Most strikers chase out wide for the ball and
create things from outside the box. That's

not my style.

The fact that Rangers have always played
with wingers—and still do—has meant that
the ball comes into me. It's just a question of
climbing higher than the other fellow and
judging the power and direction of your
header through good timing.'

Certainly, there are few more lethal
headers of the ball than Johnstone. But he
still sees scope for improvement in his game.

'I could do with being a bit sharper off the
mark, particularly over short distances. It's
something I'm always working on.'

How did Derek, one of the few really class
Scottish players not to have made the move
to the Football League, come to join
Rangers? 'I played for Fintrey Primary and
Linlachon Secondary in Dundee and won a
Under-15 cap for Scotland.

'Every club seemed to want me and I went
down to have trials for Arsenal and Aston
Villa. I enjoyed the big-time atmosphere but ▷

511

ABOVE *With striker Derek Parlane and the Ibrox silverware. Derek's goal against Celtic as a 16-year-old in the 1970-71 League Cup final ended a four-year trophy famine for Rangers and began the club's gradual climb back to supremacy.*
RIGHT *Seven seasons on and he's at it again, wheeling away after scoring the winner against Aberdeen in the 1978 Scottish Cup final—to give Rangers their second treble in three years.*

◁ got homesick. When I returned Rangers were the first big club in for me, just beating Celtic.

'I've never regretted signing for Rangers but I'm still a wee bit of a Dundee United fan. I used to train with them three times a week on a spare piece of ground outside Tannadice.'

At 25, Johnstone is probably still a couple of years short of his peak, yet he has been a first-team regular for six years—with a pile of honours—and was blooded fairly consistently for two years before that.

'I suppose to have played for nine years and still be only 25 might seem remarkable. In fact, a lot of people think I'm much older. It's understandable when you consider that the average footballer probably only has around a dozen or so seasons at top level at the most.

'But I don't think that by the time I reach 30 I'll be bored with football. With Rangers involved in so many areas every season you don't get a chance to mark time.'

It was as a raw 16-year-old that Johnstone first hit the headlines. Just one week after scoring twice in his debut against Cowdenbeath at Ibrox, the young Dundonian was pitched into the 1970-71 League Cup final

against Celtic at Hampden.

The gamble of playing a virtually untried boy paid off when Johnstone scored the only goal to break a five-year monopoly by Celtic.

Reflecting on that final, Johnstone recalls: 'I don't suppose I really took in what had happened. At that age you're not fully aware of the implications of scoring the winner in a Cup final.'

'Obviously I couldn't have wished for a better start to my career. Rangers hadn't won a trophy for more than four years and it got me noticed early on.'

Later that season Johnstone came on for Penman in the Scottish Cup final, and scored again—though Rangers eventually lost in the replay to Celtic. Those two Hampden goals were the only ones Derek scored for the first team all season outside the League.

'However, I didn't become an automatic first team choice as a result. I was in and out of the team for a couple of years.'

The League Cup winners medal was only

the first of many Johnstone has collected. Two years later he was a member of the Rangers team which defeated Moscow Dynamo 3-2 in the European Cup Winners Cup final in Barcelona, and since then he has gone on to play a key part in League Championship, Scottish Cup and League Cup triumphs, including two 'trebles'.

It hasn't all been a fairy tale for the big Ranger. A fairly experienced international— he made his full appearance as a teenager in the defence against Wales at Wrexham in May 1973 and held his place for four more games—Johnstone did not play in the 1974 World Cup finals.

But he certainly looked set to figure in Scotland's World Cup bid after scoring the only goals of the games against Northern Ireland and Wales prior to the finals.

The illusion was shattered when manager Ally MacLeod left him out of the team for the final Championship encounter against England—and then forced him to spectate as the Scots failed to make any impact in Argentina.

After the defeat by Peru and the draw with Iran the decision naturally evoked strong reaction back home. It made no sense that the top scorer in Scotland should sit on the sidelines while the team failed to get goals. After all, they argued, Joe Jordan had only scored six League goals all season. Derek would even be an improvement on the listless Burns and Buchan at the back.

Rumours of a rift between MacLeod and the player were inevitable. But when Johnstone returned from the World Cup he strongly denied a split.

Why did MacLeod leave him out? Only he knows the answer. But one thing is certain: Derek Johnstone, at 25, has other World Cups ahead of him and new fields to conquer.

Meanwhile, the question remains open— centre-half or striker? Like the legendary John Charles, he may become known as a giant in both departments.

Daly shoots past the onrushing Hughes and Thompson . . .

The Daly telegraph

'From our point of view it was a great free-kick. From England's point of view, I suppose it's something you'd have to talk about afterwards.'

EIRE manager JOHNNY GILES

Entertaining England were once again caught wanting defensively by this set piece goal from the fighting Irish.

It earned the Republic a point when they must have been wondering if they would get any at all—and it kept their hopes alive in the European Championship.

It stemmed from a free-kick just outside the left-hand corner of the England area. Liam Brady elected to take it and a three-man wall —Brooking, Mills and Wilkins—lined up in front of him.

Brady seemed to be looking to cross into the area— with David O'Leary's head the likeliest target.

But Brady and Gerry Daly had seen the best move, even though no visible signal had passed between them.

So Brady side-footed the free-kick to Daly, who was standing completely unmarked on the edge of the area. The England defence woke up to the danger . . . and Thompson and Hughes did their best to close Daly down.

But it was too late. His shot, struck with the outside of his right foot, squeezed into the net between

KEEGAN

CLEMENCE

. . and the ball eludes the desperately diving Clemence.

Graham Taylor's analysis

A striker's job doesn't end when the other side have the ball. In this kind of situation they have to get back and do their share of defending.

To be fair to the England forwards, they did get back. But what they obviously didn't do was sort out between themselves who was marking who. And that means talking—or shouting—to each other . . . letting your team-mates know who's unmarked, who's making a blind-side run and so on.

In any defensive situation, the first priority is to mark the men in the danger area—right in front of goal. The next step is to mark anyone else in a position to receive the ball. Then, only if everyone is marked, should you look for a space to cover, or position yourself to receive a clearance out of defence.

Clemence and his left-hand post.

Why was Daly unmarked? With all the England defenders fully occupied inside the area, it was left to three forwards to pick up the Irish support players. Peter Barnes took Grealish . . . and pointed out that Coppell should take Holmes.

It's possible that Keegan saw Barnes and Coppell sorting out who should mark who . . . and assumed that everything was being taken care of.

Instead, Daly took care of England's hopes of two points.

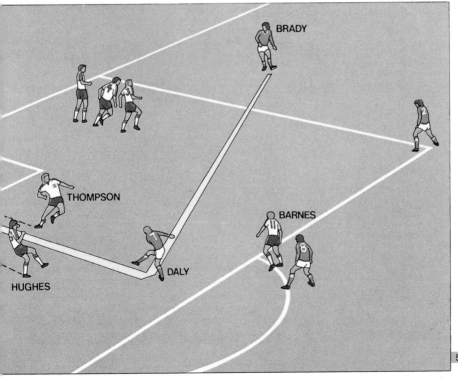

BRADY

THOMPSON

BARNES

HUGHES

DALY

ABOVE **Peter Mellor, then with Burnley, receives treatment during a Chelsea game.**
RIGHT **Leeds striker Mick Jones is escorted from the Wembley pitch after sustaining a broken collar bone in the 1972 FA Cup final.**
BELOW **Knee injuries are among the most common. The victim this time was Motherwell's Bert McCann.**

INJURY!

In the last four seasons over a hundred League pros have been forced out through injury. We analyse the players' biggest curse...

Every season between 25 and 30 Football League players are told the dreaded news: 'I'm sorry, son, your football days are over.'

That means that one in every hundred professionals will have their careers cut short by serious injury—a chilling statistic.

Most players who have to quit the game through injuries suffer under the plain heading of 'knee or ankle'—covering the feared cartilage, ligaments and Achilles tendon.

And, with the game today played at such a pace—'100 miles an hour football'—there is a new 'killer', the arthritic condition that attacks the same joints.

This type of arthritis comes as a result of the constant wear and tear inside the joints. It is literally crippling many of our top players, and some, including Mick Jones (ex-Sheffield United, Leeds and England striker), have been forced to quit the game

> When the trainer runs on to the pitch just what is he carrying in his 'bag of tricks'?
> Although he can't carry too much equipment, his bag will contain a selection of the following: scissors, tweezers, pliers, strapping, pain relieving spray, triangular bandage, cotton wool, plasters, antiseptic cream, Vaseline, butterfly closures (or thin adhesive tape for bringing cuts together), dressing gauze, rubbing oils, inflatable splints, smelling salts, and the 'magic sponge'.

because of it. As of yet, there is no cure.

But players have also been forced to quit prematurely because of injury to almost every part of the body, including the foot and hand. Once on the pitch, they are completely vulnerable.

In the four-year period up to 1977, 104 players were out of the game through injury. Topping the league were injuries to the knee, which finished 63 players. Next came ankle

> The goalkeeper is one of the most 'protected' players on the pitch, but this fact was little consolation or help to ex-Charlton Athletic goalkeeper Graham Tutt.
> Tutt's career was finished at 20 after a horrific kick in the face left him with impaired vision. Seven minutes into an away game at Sunderland, Tutt went for the ball at the split second that forward Tom Finney was poised to strike it.
> The result was a broken nose, a shattered cheek bone and a badly injured eye. Tutt was left with double vision in one eye and an end to the big future in football that had been predicted for him. He says the mental and physical scars of the accident will be with him for the rest of his life.

and Achilles tendon, with 16 apiece.

Few injuries are this serious of course, but what they lack in severity they certainly make up for in numbers.

In the first four weeks of this season, Second Division Millwall had an injury list that read like a busy day in a hospital's accident department.

Physiotherapist Richard Adams treated groins, hamstrings, bruises, knee ligaments, ankle ligaments, foot injuries and concussion. And this he called being 'pretty lucky'.

By far the most common injury is haematoma, or bruising of the muscles. Although painful, this generally heals up quickly and is one of the injuries that a player is likely to carry from game to game.

Carrying an injury is frowned on by physiotherapists—it is easy to aggravate it and prolong the healing process.

But many players do it. Bryan Hamilton, midfield player with Swindon, carried an Achilles tendon injury for six months.

'When you've only got a small squad there's not always someone who can play in your position. So if you can play, you do.

'Players also bear in mind that there are up and coming youngsters after positions.

Injuries know no snobbery. They affect the big and the small alike. Two of today's big-name managers, Brian Clough and John Lyall, both retired prematurely as a result of knee injuries.

In their present role it is their unhappy lot to be the bearers of such tidings to today's players. Little wonder that Brian Clough has called this 'one of the worst jobs in football management.'

One of the youngest and newest 'physios' in the game is 25-year-old Richard Adams, who looks after the lads at Millwall.

Small but square-shouldered, Richard (affectionately nicknamed 'coat-hanger'), says the football physiotherapist is constantly working against the clock. He always has Saturday's game in mind when working with an injured player. The bigger the club, the bigger the physio set-up.

And when you only have a few years left in the game, you just can't afford a long injury.'

Injuries can come at any time but also go with the season. Richard Adams explains: 'At the beginning of the season you always get your players going down with strains and hamstrings. Their bodies aren't used to playing.

'At the end of the season it's the stress injuries, caused by playing so many games, such as inflamed Achilles tendons.'

There's no 'safe' position on the pitch; injuries can generally occur to anyone at any time. But Adams believes referees have a big influence on this.

'It's a hard game and there are bound to be knocks. But the referee has a great responsibility in keeping them down.

'Take goalkeepers. Refs won't let players get near them. They're very well protected. But elsewhere on the pitch, players get away with whatever the referee will allow.

'I can often gauge who will be injured by who he's playing against.'

Modern trends in the game have also taken their toll. Football is faster than it used to be and tackles are much quicker. The old boots that used to support the ankle have

given way to low-cut 'shoes', and ankle sprains are now more common.

Legs have also become more vulnerable as pads have become smaller. And players who take off their pads for the last ten minutes of a game should be 'put up against a wall and shot' according to Mr Adams.

When a body is under such a strain for 90 minutes, it is obvious that it must be prepared for the stresses it is going to meet in the game. No player should ever go on to the pitch without warming up first, for instance.

Every footballer at every level of the game should spend some of the time in the dressing-room stretching his body. The important parts to stretch are the hamstrings, groin and calves. His body is then at least 'made ready' for most of the pulls it will undergo during the game.

But even before this, every professional would have built up to the game with a very stringent training schedule to get 'match fit'.

'The most important part on the road to fitness is pre-season training,' says Adams.

'At Millwall the lads spent five or six weeks on full-day training. The ideal way to start the season is with every player fresh— and no injuries.'

During the season, the training pattern is different. At Millwall, after a Saturday game, the players have Sunday off. On Monday they will have a fairly strenuous work-out, and sprints and stretches on Tuesday.

If there is a Wednesday game, the morning will be spent warming up and the

---

The unluckiest of injured footballers must be ex-Chelsea striker Ian Hutchinson, forced out at 27 after a *fifth* operation on his right knee. His other injuries included broken arm, broken nose, double fracture of left leg (twice), slipped disc, two broken toes, broken left hand and two cartilage operations. Hutchinson came back three times after being told by doctors that he would never play again. Now publicity manager at Stamford Bridge, Ian says: 'I'm convinced I'll be a cripple by the time I'm 40.'

---

afternoon resting. Thursday is a day off, but players who are nursing injuries will go in for their own special session. Friday it's back to sprints and stretches, and so to Saturday.

With all this thought going into his welfare, the professional is still unable to escape injury. So it's little wonder that with the hundreds of thousands of amateur games going on in a season that injuries are colossal.

INJURY	TREATMENT	RECOVERY
CONCUSSION Temporary loss of consciousness due to blow on head	Cold compress to back of neck. Check for bleeding from eyes, ears or nose, and check vision. Gauge mental state.	If any doubt, player must leave pitch
HAEMATOMA Bruising of muscles	Ice, compression bandage ; then graduated exercises	Less than a week
ARTHRITIS Wearing down of joints	Strengthen muscles round joint to slow down erosion process	No real cure
GROIN Tearing fibres by over-reaching for ball with straight leg, especially when 'cold'.	One day's rest. Hydrotherapy pool, ultrasonics, friction and stretches	1-6 weeks
KNEE Tears, partial tears, strain to the four knee ligaments	Depends on severity. Bad tears require surgery or time in plaster	6-8 weeks in plaster. Resume training in 3 months. Strains can vary from a few days to several weeks
CARTILAGES Medial (inside) and lateral (outside). Caused by landing awkwardly or blow to outside of knee as well as wear.	If torn, removed by operation ; followed by course of exercises.	6 weeks to 3 months
HAMSTRING Tearing of some of the fibres of one or more of the three hamstrings at the back of the leg, either a strain or 'pull'.	Ice, strapping, stretches. After 24 hours' hydrotherapy, stretches and ultrasonics. Finally jogging or appropriate activity	1-6 weeks
ACHILLES TENDON Runs from bottom of calf muscle to heel bone. Three main types of injury : 1. Rupture (complete or partial tear) 2. Strain 3. Tendonitis (stress injury)	1. Strengthen calf or surgery for partial rupture. Complete rupture is rare. 2. Reduce swelling 3. Maintain length of tendon, strengthen calf. Inflammation and swelling reduced by ice. Heel raised to take strain. Plaster and drugs in severe cases	1. Complete : doubtful if player will ever get back to peak fitness. Partial : 1-6 months, depending on severity. 2. 1-4 weeks 3. Few days to several weeks
ANKLES Tears and sprains of ankle ligaments	Reduce swelling. Improve balance over ankle. Maintain mobility of joint. Strengthen muscles round ankle.	A few days to a week

But the amateur can at least copy the professional in warming up properly before a match and wearing pads.

As a final warning he can take a piece of advice from a professional physiotherapist. 'At every game there should be a good first-aid box and, just as important, someone who knows how to use it. It's no good at all having one without the other.

'And don't let's belittle the "magic sponge". An ice-cold sponge behind the neck of an injured player will do wonders for waking him up. It can bring round someone who's dazed from concussion. And if used properly it can also relieve pain, limit swelling and close broken blood vessels.'

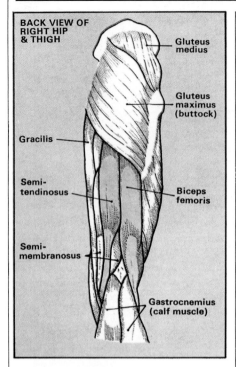

BACK VIEW OF RIGHT HIP & THIGH

Gluteus medius

Gluteus maximus (buttock)

Gracilis

Semi-tendinosus

Biceps femoris

Semi-membranosus

Gastrocnemius (calf muscle)

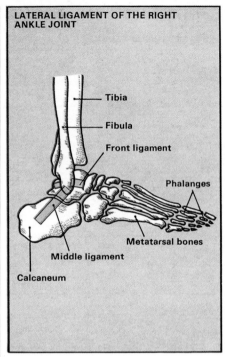

LATERAL LIGAMENT OF THE RIGHT ANKLE JOINT

Tibia

Fibula

Front ligament

Phalanges

Metatarsal bones

Middle ligament

Calcaneum

HAMSTRING

The hamstrings are the five tendons at the back of the thigh, stretching across the knee to the top of the calf. The two main ones—semitendinosus and biceps femoris—are shown in red.

Hamstring strains, caused by over-use or excessive stretching, are contained by a protective muscle spasm and can produce no worse than mild inflammation. With the correct treatment this can heal in a few days.

The more serious tear, which stops a player dead, usually occurs either when a player is very tired or when the hamstring is contracted by an outside force (eg a trapped foot). The tear is usually in the middle of the muscle, a little below its 'point of origin'.

Severe tears can take up to two months to recover—and are always likely to break down again under pressure.

ANKLE

The most common ankle injury in soccer is the spraining of the front and middle bands of the lateral ligament, as shown above, caused by a twist or turn which forces it down. A ligament is fibrous tissue binding the bones together.

Unless the injury is a complete tear—which is not uncommon in football—the recovery period is quite short provided the mobility of the ankle joint is maintained and the muscles round it are strengthened.

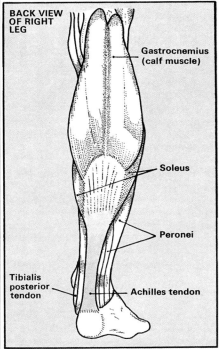

BACK VIEW OF RIGHT LEG

- Gastrocnemius (calf muscle)
- Soleus
- Peronei
- Tibialis posterior tendon
- Achilles tendon

FRONT VIEW OF RIGHT KNEE

- Femur
- Front cruciate ligament
- Back cruciate ligament
- Lateral semilunar cartilage
- Medial semilunar cartilage
- Fibula
- Tibia
- Patellar tendon

ACHILLES TENDON

The Achilles tendon connects the calf with the heel, giving the foot its leverage. It can be bruised or torn in any place, but is particularly vulnerable at the base in football.

The Achilles can be subject to strain, stress injury (tendonitis) or a tear. It is fairly common in sprinting to tear or pull a few fibres of the tendon, but a complete rupture is rare.

As in all tendon injuries, the pain is out of all proportion to the severity of the injury.

CARTILAGE

The cartilage is gristly tissue between the bones, and acts as both a lubricator and a shock absorber. Injury is caused when the knee is rotated while carrying bodyweight, and the twist of the femur on the tibia exerts a grinding force which tears or splits the cartilage. It can also be gradually worn away, causing a cyst .

There are two cartilages in the knee, and it is the medial one (inside of the leg) that is more likely to tear.

All of the cartilage is taken out if possible—if the other one is bad, then both may be removed—but menisoctomy (the removal of the cartilage) can only be done after the knee has returned to normal. This, and the gradual build up after the operation, can make it a costly business in terms of time.

If a damaged cartilage is not removed, it may lead to early osteo-arthritis.

Switching Ipswich's style

Winning the FA Cup didn't stop Bobby Robson looking for new ways to improve his Ipswich side.

And the player he bought during the summer—Dutch international Arnold Muhren from Twente Enschede—showed that Robson was after a new-look Ipswich.

'Well, it wasn't so much a complete change,' he told *Handbook*. 'It was more a question of giving ourselves greater flexibility.

'We were in Europe, the Cup Winners Cup, and there's no doubt that you need greater variety in your play in these international competitions.

'In the last few seasons we've been tremendously strong in the air up front with Trevor Whymark and Paul Mariner. But every side must be ready to improvise.

'That's why I bought Muhren. I also had in mind that in Europe possession is much more important. When you lose the ball you don't usually get it back so quickly. With Muhren, we're likely to keep it longer.'

Match Point traced the tall Dutchman's play against Everton at Portman Road in October and his part in the Ipswich switch is obvious over 90 minutes.

From the left side of midfield, with Brian Talbot moving to the middle,

Muhren played almost everything short—particularly little one-twos with Mick Mills and Clive Woods.

'From a new tactical approach, Arnold's superb left foot gives us a lethal inswinging corner and swerving free kick,' says Bobby.

'Also, we're now able to play with four forwards, moving Clive Woods to outside-right and pushing Arnold wide on the left.'

'One point I would make is that it's just as wrong to play everything short as everything long.

Arnold on his way ... Muhren gets past Sammy McIlroy and Martin Buchan. 'He's giving us more variety,' says Robson.

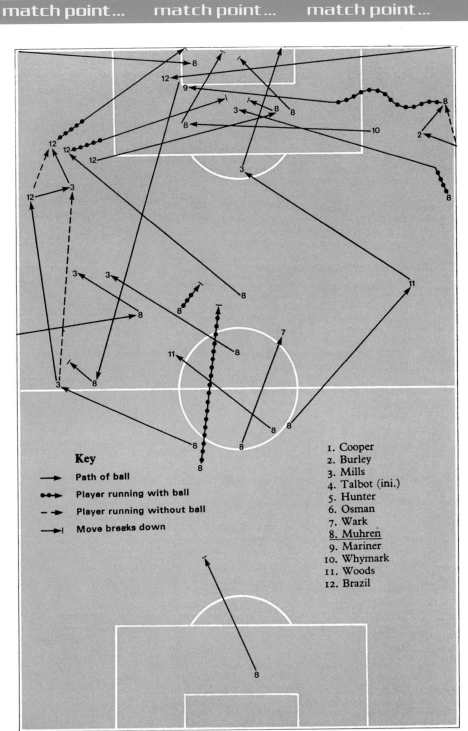

Key

→ Path of ball

•••► Player running with ball

--► Player running without ball

→⊣ Move breaks down

1. Cooper
2. Burley
3. Mills
4. Talbot (ini.)
5. Hunter
6. Osman
7. Wark
8. Muhren
9. Mariner
10. Whymark
11. Woods
12. Brazil

RISING BILLY STAR WRIGHT

The football world has quite quickly adjusted to the news that there is more to the name Billy Wright than the former Wolves lion-heart who made 105 appearances for England.

Mention the name now . . . and more and more people identify it with the youngster turning in astonishingly mature perform-ances for Everton in his namesake's old position.

Young Billy is the latest player to make a dramatic breakthrough from Everton's youth policy. Two years ago it was full-back David Jones who burst on to the scene, going on to win England Under-21 honours before having his progress interrupted by injury. Last season the 19-year-old giant Mark Higgins was introduced to the senior team.

Now it's the turn of 20-year-old Wright, who got his chance in the second game of the season and took it so well that he looks the best bet of the lot.

Hailing from Liverpool's Norris Green area, Billy had three first team games at the end of last season, having earlier made a dramatic first impression when he came on as substitute in a match against Leicester in February. On that occasion he played 30 minutes in midfield . . . and showed such skill in his use of the ball that those who knew of him only as a reserve centre-back began to wonder if it was the same man.

Part-time amateur

It was no mistake. For a central defender Wright possesses enormous skill which, with a cool temperament, makes him such an outstanding prospect.

Certainly Ron Greenwood thinks so. He named Billy in the England Under-21 squad after the youngster had played just eight games in Everton's first team.

Skill and composure are words that are frequently used in connection with Wright, but a third factor—determination—has prob-ably been the key to his progress so far; because this is anything but a story of the well-planned success of a highly promising

Billy Wright, nephew of an Everton star of the recent past and owning the same name as a world-famous Wolves and England captain, is rapidly establishing a name for himself.
ABOVE *Repelling Wolves.*
RIGHT *Under pressure against Bristol Rovers.*

youngster with a top club . . .

Wright was a late developer; as a school-boy he failed to convince Everton's coaches that he was good enough. In fact the club let him go rather than offer him a place as an apprentice.

But Wright, whose uncle—one Tommy Wright—was a member of Everton's 1970 Championship side and an England inter-national full-back, was not to be put off.

'The club fixed me up with a job as a motor mechanic and I carried on playing for them as an amateur,' he recalls. 'I wasn't really happy with the job—I just wanted to play football.

'Then the club took me on as a part-time

'The most eye-catching performance was that of Everton's 20-year-old central defender, Billy Wright. He did his job superbly against David Johnson and Kenny Dalglish . . . obviously one to watch for the future.' FRANK MCGHEE in the 'Daily Mirror' after Everton's first Merseyside derby win for seven years.

Club	Season	League		FA Cup		Lge Cup	
		Ms	Gs	Ms	Gs	Ms	Gs
Everton	1977-78	4	–	–	–	–	–
		4	–	–	–	–	–

pro. I was working three days a week and training two days a week.

'I got a bit fed up with that because I was missing out on the things the other lads were doing. So I went in to see the manager, Billy Bingham . . . and he signed me on full-time.'

That was in January 1977. Signing Wright on full professional forms was one of Bingham's last acts before being dismissed.

Just over a year later, Billy was playing in the First Division.

Winning 6-0—and scoring

He is a player who likes to express himself. His role is far removed from the traditional centre-half's job of simply stopping anything getting past him. He is expected to distribute the ball positively . . . either wide to the left where Mike Pejic and David Thomas are ready to receive, or forward through the middle.

Wright also has the ability to bring the ball upfield himself. And—as you'd expect from someone who has played a few Central League games at centre-forward—he has a useful shot as well.

In fact, he scored in only his third full game in the Everton first team. It was the final match of last season, when Everton beat Chelsea 6-0—and Billy's feat was overshadowed by Bob Latchford's achievement of finishing the season with 30 League goals.

'Billy will play for England'

But Wright is not perfectly satisfied with his own ability. He knows that he has to keep learning all the time. He knows he has to keep working on his game.

'I would like more speed . . . and height,' he told Handbook. 'I'm 5′ 9½″, and though I reckon I get up well, if I was a bit taller I would get up even better.

'But I would like to work on getting that little extra bit of zip.'

Manager Gordon Lee has forecast that Wright will play for England. If he does, then the world will discover that England has another Billy Wright . . . and that Billy mark two is in no way overawed by the reputation of his famous predecessor.

525

Founded: 1886
Address: Gay Meadow, Shrewsbury, Shropshire
Ground: Capacity 18,000; Playing area 106 x 69.5 m
Record attendance: 18,917 v Walsall, Div. 3, 26.4.61
Record victory: 7-0 v Swindon Town, Div. 3(S), 1954-55
Record defeat: 1-8 v Norwich City, Div. 3(S), 1952-53 & v Coventry City, Div. 3, 22.10.63
Most League points: 62, Div. 4, 1974-75
Most League goals: 101, Div. 4, 1958-59
League scoring record: 38, Arthur Rowley, Div. 4, 1958-59
Record League aggregate: 152, Arthur Rowley, 1958-65 (completing Football League scoring record of 434)
Most League appearances: 329, Joe Wallace, 1954-63
Most capped player: 5 (12 in all), Jimmy McLaughlin, Northern Ireland, 1962-63
Honours: Welsh Cup winners 1891, 1938, 1977
League career: 1950 Elected to Div. 3(N); 1951-58 Div. 3(S); 1958-59 Div. 4; 1959-74 Div. 3; 1974-75 Div. 4; 1975- Div. 3

SHREWSBURY TOWN

Are Shrewsbury Town for real? There they are at the right end of the Third Division, challenging for a place on the fixture lists of Sunderland and Newcastle.

The people of Shrewsbury don't seem convinced yet. They recall that last season Shrewsbury were in a similar position until November. They hit a rough patch before finishing in mid-table.

And most of them remember that Shrewsbury have looked like Third Division promotion candidates at least three times before. And each time they were edged out at the finish.

Each time they were under the managership of Arthur Rowley.

Gateway to the First Division . . . ? Richie Barker at Gay Meadow just before joining Wolves as assistant manager to John Barnwell.

Shrewsbury had been elected to the League—from the Midland Counties League—in 1950. But they were regular stragglers in both the Third Divisions (North and South) until Rowley, an England 'B' international and a formidable goalscorer, was appointed player-manager.

In his first season for the West Midlands club Rowley scored 38 goals . . . and Shrewsbury won promotion from the newly formed Fourth Division. In his second season (1959-60) Rowley scored 32 goals . . . and Shrewsbury finished third behind Southampton and Norwich.

But Rowley proved to be more than just the League's all-time record goalscorer. After hanging up his boots in 1965 he put together Shrewsbury Town's best-ever side.

In 1967 they missed out on promotion to the Second Division by three points; in 1968 they missed out by one point. Shrewsbury fans, grown used to a side geared to getting the ball into the penalty areas as quickly and as often as possible in the hope that Rowley could get on the end of it, were now treated to neat, quick-passing build-ups, with a highly accomplished former England international inside-forward—Peter Broadbent—centrally involved.

Many of the team eventually moved on to a higher grade of football. Ted Hemsley, Alf Wood, Frank Clarke and Broadbent subsequently played in the First Division.

But that 1967-68 season was a test of Shrewsbury's nerve—a test that the club failed badly.

The beginning was promising. Northern Ireland international Jim McLaughlin was back on the left-wing. Little Trevor Meredith, once of Burnley, skilful and irrepressible, patrolled the opposite flank. Broadbent had gone, but George Boardman, spasmodically brilliant in midfield, was still there.

Behind them Hemsley and Wood anchored a solid defence. And up front there was Frank Clarke, Allan's elder brother, one of the best of the new generation of backs-to-the-goal centre-forwards. Frank was never great in the air, but he was intelligent, mobile, he turned quickly and he scored goals.

It was an effective, well-balanced team that played to its strengths. And it was good enough to win promotion. But within months it was dismembered.

The first to go was John Manning, a powerful inside-forward who had combined well with Clarke. Before the season was more than a few weeks old he was on his way to Norwich.

But the team didn't falter. They looked like good bets for the championship for most

of the season. Then, with a handful of games to go, the board succumbed to a £34,000 offer from Queen's Park Rangers for Clarke.

With these moves Town robbed them- selves of most of their goal threat. Yet they finished the season only one point and one place in the table away from promotion. ▷

The front runners. Left to right: *Paul Maguire, Steve Biggins and Ian Atkins, the goalscorers Shrewsbury are relying on to get them into the Second Division. They're backed by one of the best defences in the division.*
RIGHT *Ian Atkins in training.*

◁ The sale of Manning and Clarke and the missed promotion chance had a disturbing side effect. It convinced many people in the town—and they remain convinced—that the board doesn't want Second Division football . . . that the small-town club would prefer to remain small-time.

Richie Barker, manager of Shrewsbury until his move to Wolves in November, has heard the rumours, but he doesn't believe there's any truth in them.

'If Shrewsbury don't get promotion this season it won't be for lack of trying,' he promised, just before his move to Molineux as assistant to manager John Barnwell. 'I don't think anyone is afraid of promotion.

Ken Mulhearn, still at full stretch after a long and distinguished career. He began at Everton and was a regular in Manchester City's Championship winning side of 1967-68.

'But there might come a time when—even if we were doing well—it might be necessary to sell a player in the interests of the club.

'I did a deal last year . . . Brian Hornsby. We were in relegation trouble, yet when we had an offer of £45,000 from Sheffield Wednesday for him, I thought it was best that we accepted it.

'The directors balance their books. Whether that's good or bad I don't know. But the point is that's the way the directors want to run the club. So you've got to try and get promotion . . . but it's got to be within a certain structure.'

If that's the club's policy, then in the recent past they haven't done a very good job in convincing the townspeople that it's workable. Last season they attracted an average of under 3,400 spectators to home League games—the lowest in the division— even though they were second in the table as late as Guy Fawkes' Day. Attendances haven't been much better this season.

'And quite rightly so,' said Richie Barker. 'We finished the season quite well, but we had a bit of a slump during it. Then I didn't sign anyone during the close season.'

Attendances have started to improve since, and the 7,500 who saw the Walsall game in November formed Shrewsbury's biggest gate for two years.

This season Sammy Irvine has been sold to Stoke for £60,000 to be replaced by Blackpool's midfielder David Tong for £20,000 and Sammy Chapman from Notts County for £2,500. Barker admitted that he'd also been looking for a target man.

Shrewsbury have done consistently well in the transfer market. Cast-offs from other clubs have often been reconditioned, then sold at a large profit. The classic example is Jim Holton. Signed on a free transfer from West Bromwich Albion, he fetched £90,000 when Town sold him to Manchester United, and he was Scotland's regular centre-half in the 1974 World Cup finals.

Town have also done well out of non-League players. They signed a pair of strikers from Southern League Stourbridge Town in 1974 . . . and between them Ray Haywood and Chic Bates scored nearly half of Town's goals the following season when the club won promotion back to the Third Division under new player-manager Alan Durban.

In the present side there are Steve Biggins, a six-foot striker from Hednesford Town who scored seven goals in nine games when he came into the side at the end of last season, and Paul Maguire, an immensely promising winger who cost just £1,500 from a Scottish junior side.

'Invariably I look at the leagues,' Richie Barker explains. 'There are good players in non-League football. The problem is following them up. We didn't have any full-time scouts . . .'

Barker himself began his career in non-League football, with Burton Albion. His manager was Peter Taylor, who signed him for Derby when the Clough-Taylor partnership took up residence there. Barker, a centre-forward, later played for Notts County and Peterborough before a broken leg ended his career.

He says: 'I saw the value at Notts County of working with the players—Jimmy Sirrel was a very good coach—and at Derby I saw how players should be handled. If you can

Arthur Rowley, goalscorer
Arthur Rowley joined Shrewsbury Town as player-manager in 1958 and immediately led them to promotion in the newly-formed Fourth Division, scoring 38 goals in the process. The following season he hit 32 as Shrewsbury came within one place of winning promotion to the Second Division. And, in his third season with the club—he had played previously with WBA, Fulham and Leicester—he passed Dixie Dean's record of 379 League goals with a header (*above*) against Bradford City at Valley Parade. He retired in 1965 at the age of 39, with a final total of 434 League goals, scored in 619 games. He later managed Sheffield United and Southend.

handle them and work with them you've got a bonus.'

That's the kind of bonus Shrewsbury will be looking for from their new manager. As Barker says, they've got 'a tremendous lot of players, who really put it in week in and week out.' With the right manager, they might even break through this season . . . into the Second Division.

The new manager will have money if he wants to spend it. A small, efficient staff— and a considerable income from the Supporters' Association—mean that Shrewsbury can live comfortably on gates of 6,000.

Says Barker: 'If the people weren't available . . . then I wasn't going to spend money just for the sake of it.'

Graham Turner . . . midfield anchor, record buy, club coach and emergency manager.

529

Calling the shots:

Jimmy Adamson

'It was like a graveyard at Sunderland until I bought Mick Buckley —hardly anyone was rabbitting.'

If every spectator was taken away from a big match, it would still be one of the noisiest games in the world.

The din would come from the pitch as the players kept up a constant stream of advice, encouragement and, yes, abuse.

Before he took on the Leeds job, Jimmy Adamson found himself with an unusual problem at Sunderland: 'It was like a graveyard out there. Hardly anyone was rabbitting.'

So Adamson bought Everton's Mick Buckley to help give Sunderland a voice.

'I see it mainly as feeding information,' says Adamson. 'If someone is making a good run down the line and the player in possession is blind to it, someone else should tell him about it. It's criminal if everyone else keeps quiet.

'Like most things, it's quite natural for some players but difficult for others. I've known players who literally go through matches without uttering a word.'

Confidence is vital in top-class football and Jimmy says that 'good talking' is one of the ways of getting it.

'If you're constantly giving good advice and encouragement you're also telling the opposition, in effect, that you're fully committed to the game. It also gives an extra boost to your own players.

'Mind you, bad calling is probably worse than no call-

Currie in command . . . the Leeds man lays down the law to Frank Gray, Brian Flynn and Trevor Cherry.

Tommy Craig makes his position clear against the club he later joined—Aston Villa.

ing at all. Nobody wants the clown who says all the wrong things at the wrong times.

'In my experience, if you're a good player you'll be a good talker as well.'

Where are the best positions to have a 'talker'?

'Ideally, everybody should be doing their bit.

'But, failing that, you can get by with a talker at centre-half and a couple in midfield.'

What about Leeds? 'No problems—they all talk.'

Graham Taylor:

Talking is probably more important for young players because most pros are looking all around them and don't need that much advice. At 13 or 14 you tend to be looking at the ball more and need to be told what's happening on other parts of the pitch.

But before you start giving that sort of advice—telling the player in possession who's making a run—it's better to concentrate on more basic

calling. *'Man on!'* is the most basic—and often most necessary—piece of advice. It means, if you haven't already heard the footsteps, that someone is coming fast for the ball behind you or less often from the side.

'Turn' tells you there's enough space behind you to turn with the ball. And *'time'* means exactly that—you've got time and space to do what you like. Use these calls and notice the difference!

A Matter of Fact

Ray Clemence and Derby keeper John Middleton went to the same school in Skegness. Before their clubs met at Anfield this season, they agreed that the loser would foot the bill for a meal. Liverpool won 5-0 . . . !

Leeds star Brian Flynn hit goals in international and Cup soccer before he got his first League goal. He scored for Wales v Scotland and for Burnley in a League Cup tie at Hereford in 1975 before scoring in a First Division match at Everton on 31 January 1976, when the Clarets won 3-2.

LEFT Northern Ireland's Terry Cochrane glides past an Eire defender in the historic meeting in Dublin in September. Cochrane impressed Middlesbrough so much that they paid in excess of £210,000 to Burnley for the transfer of the former Coleraine flier—a record for the North-Eastern club, who had earlier failed in their bid for Argentina's Rene Houseman.

Exactly 29 years to the day elapsed between Crewe Alexandra's first hat-trick in the Football League and their second. Their first came in 1892, four years before the Cheshire club dropped out of the League. The long wait was ended by one Albert Winterburn, who bagged all the Alex's goals in a 3-2 victory in a Third Division (North) match at Lincoln in 1921.

With 17-year old Wayne's recent debut for Wolves, five members of the football family Clarke have now appeared in League football. Ex-England striker Allan has put Barnsley among the Fourth Division front-runners in his first season as player-manager; former Carlisle striker Frank retired last summer; brother Derek is at Orient, while Kelvin is with Walsall.

A sign of things to come? San Diego Sockers goalkeeper Alan Mayes, a member of the United States squad which met Scotland's Under-21 hopefuls at Aberdeen in September, always takes the field wearing a protective helmet, an idea he borrowed from the rough and tumble of 'grid-iron' football.

Bristol Rovers' long-serving Welshman Frankie Prince has always said that he sees red when playing against Bristol City, and over the years he's figured in numerous incidents in local 'derby' games with the Ashton Gate club. But all that was forgotten when Rovers were looking for attractive opposition for his testimonial match in November—City readily accepted their neighbours' invitation to play for Prince, who has played well over 300 League games.

When Alex Stuart took over from Ally MacLeod at Ayr he switched round the 'dug-outs'. One of the first steps Ally took on returning to Somerset Park was to ask the groundsman to change the home and visitors signs back. Ayr then launched on a run of victories before Ally left for Motherwell.

There's no place like home . . . all these players have rejoined clubs they once left since the end of last season: Don Masson (now back with Notts County), Derek Hales (Charlton), Frank Barton (Bournemouth), Leighton James (Burnley), Paul Went (Orient), Bobby Campbell (Huddersfield & Halifax), Derek Spence (Blackpool), Mick Moore (Wigan), Joey Jones (Wrexham) and Dennis Nelson and Phil Nicholls, who both rejoined Crewe.

Alan Rough

'No player worth his salt enjoys being second best. But it's something we've all got to accept from time to time. The important thing is to strive that bit harder to ensure that it doesn't happen often.'

That was Scotland goalkeeper Alan Rough's reaction after Middlesbrough rival Jim Stewart had been promoted to the international team in his place for the European Championship tie with Norway at Hampden Park in October.

Jock Stein's first match in charge of the national team was a blow to Rough and his supporters. But the 27-year-old Partick Thistle star, who established himself in the Scottish side two years ago, refused to be dismayed.

'Mr Stein explained the position to me before he made public the team to play Norway.' Alan told *Handbook*: 'Every manager has his own ideas about which players he wants in his squad, and Mr Stein obviously feels that every-one must be given an equal chance to prove his worth. That's only natural.

'There's tremendous competition in every grade at international level and it's important that there is adequate cover.

'I'd be less than honest if I didn't admit that I was disappointed when I wasn't named in Mr Stein's first team after taking over from Ally MacLeod as manager. But I feel —whatever the critics and sports writers might say— that I've done a good job for Scotland in the past and I'll be striving to win back a place by producing top form at club level. That's the only way—to turn in good steady performances and just wait.'

Alan didn't have to wait long. Going for 'international experience', Stein selected Rough against Portugal in Lisbon at the end of November. Scotland lost 1-0.

Part-time player

It's remarkable that a player of Rough's talent and experience should still be playing for a part-time club when so many of his Scotland team-mates are basking in the reflected glory of championship wins and cup triumphs both north and south of the border.

'I wonder now if I'll get a move to England. After all, I have just turned 27 and not many clubs are keen to pay large fees for players of that age. But I haven't given up all hope. They do say that keepers are approaching their peak in their late twenties—and just look at Peter Shilton, Ray Clemence and Pat Jennings, all very experienced and at the top of their profession.

'I've heard it said by certain managers that I'm weak at cross-ball situations. Well, perhaps that isn't the strongest point about my game, but no player who plays 23 times for his country can be especially suspect in any department. Anyway, any weaknesses I have are compensated for by other strong points.'

STEVE HEIGHWAY

Steve Heighway was, in his own words, a late physical developer. He also did well in school—well enough that he eventually won a place at Warwick University.

This probably explains his reluctance even to think of a football at an age when most boys would jump at the big chance. Even at 21, when most footballers have five years of their full-time careers behind them, Steve wasn't contemplating turning pro, never mind becoming part of one of the world's most successful teams.

'I had no intention of becoming a footballer when I was at university,' Steve told *Handbook*. 'I was with Manchester City when I was 17 and, although they gave me every opportunity to enjoy a footballer's life, my education always came first.

'It came as a surprise when Liverpool wanted me.

'People then said I'd begun a new era . . . professional footballers would go out and get

'Heighway is an individualist . . . He can win a match with one flash of genius.' BILL SHANKLY

an education before they began playing. But, as I pointed out at the time, I was a one-off, the first. And not many have followed me.

'It may dent the theory that you have to catch boys young to turn them into foot-ballers, but soccer has to have a good scouting system. If you are any good they'll catch you at any age.'

Steve was playing for Skelmersdale United, a Lancashire club that was earning a growing reputation in the old Amateur Cup, when he was caught . . . and within weeks he was in the Liverpool first team.

'It's fantastic what he's done,' said his team-mate and fellow graduate, Brian Hall. 'I was in my sixth season with Liverpool when I got into the first team—I had three years as an amateur while at university and another two as pro before making it. Steve did it all in his first season.'

Now, at 31, the winger is in his ninth season with Liverpool.

'I'm quite happy at Anfield. England is the place to play if you want to win the things that I do. Kevin Keegan won them once, but wanted to go off and do something else. That's where we differ.

'It's just as important, just as exciting, to win the same things again as it was the first time.

'You could say I was lucky to start with Liverpool—there are better players than me who have never won anything—but you have to remember that to a large extent we make our own luck.

'It depends on whether you want to be the best player in your position . . . or part of the greatest team.'

Heighway has a mere handful of inter-national caps. But it doesn't reflect his value to Eire . . . more his availability.

'I've missed so many because of my ▷

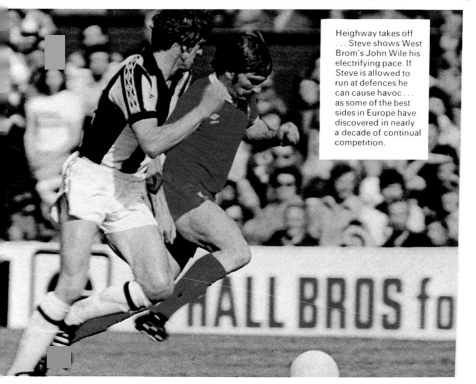

Heighway takes off . . . Steve shows West Brom's John Wile his electrifying pace. If Steve is allowed to run at defences he can cause havoc . . . as some of the best sides in Europe have discovered in nearly a decade of continual competition.

Steve Heighway at Birmingham. Steve's main task with Liverpool has been to provide penetration on the flanks, but he's been a constant factor in a forward line that has often opted to do without an orthodox centre-forward.

Honours: European Cup winners medal 1977, 1978; UEFA Cup winners medal 1973, 1976; League Championship medal 1973, 1976, 1977; FA Cup winners medal 1974, runners-up medal 1971, 1976

Club	Div	Pos	Season	League Ms	League Gs	FA Cup Ms	FA Cup Gs	Lge Cup Ms	Lge Cup Gs	Int'nls Ms	Int'nls Gs
Liver-	I	5	1970-71	31	4	7	2	2	–	5	–
pool	I	3	1971-72	40	4	2	–	3	2	–	–
	I	1	1972-73	38	6	4	–	8	2	1	–
	I	2	1973-74	36	5	6	2	6	1	–	–
	I	2	1974-75	35	9	2	1	4	2	3	–
	I	1	1975-76	39	4	2	–	2	–	2	–
	I	1	1976-77	39	8	7	3	2	–	5	–
	I	2	1977-78	28	5	1	–	8	–	3	–
				286	45	31	8	35	7	19	–

commitments at Anfield. If I'd played in all Ireland's games I'd have quite a collection— perhaps even the record. I've missed whole seasons through injury and club calls.

'I'm happy playing for Ireland. I've never thought about playing for England, although I've got dual nationality.

'I never had to ask myself: "Shall I play for England or Ireland?" Ireland asked me to play before I joined Liverpool.

But then Eire haven't enjoyed all the perks of a successful international side—the world fame, and the big money, a place in the World Cup finals. Last time France squeezed them out of the competition . . .

'The French surprised me in the World Cup. We beat them in Dublin and thought we should have been there instead, but they played a lot better in the finals than they did in the qualifying group.'

Steve is surprised that a handful of top-class foreign players have since signed for English clubs.

'They could probably earn a lot more playing somewhere else,' he points out. 'We're well paid but we pay more tax than in a lot of other countries.

'But maybe they want to play in the Football League because it's the best in the world.

'Foreigners may laugh at British football but they don't laugh at British clubs. We've

Steve challenges Mick Doyle, then of Manchester City. Heighway's not noted for his heading ability, but he has, as Tony Waiters once said, 'tremendous pace and ability.'

Steve at an Eire training session. Though he and his family are English, he was born in Dublin . . . and was chosen for Eire before he'd played in the Liverpool first team, against Poland in Dublin in September 1970. Eire lost 2-0.

dominated European competitions—every cup—for years.

'I don't think Liverpool have found any secret ingredient for winning European Cup competitions. The players have just learned how to play two-legged games. It took an English club—Forest—to break our two-year run.

'There's a lot of difference between playing away and playing at home. The food is different, so is the climate and the attitude of the opposition. The ball can be lighter and swerve more in the air.

'But when you've played in the places we have over the years you don't worry about European matches . . . about any matches.'

So defeat by Forest in the first round of this season's European Cup came as a shock ▷

Merciless Heighway . . . Steve fires—with his weaker right foot—past West Bromwich Albion's young full-back Derek Statham . . . a newcomer to the First Division's unenviable Heighway patrol last season.

LEFT *The Bachelor of Arts with his wife . . . Steve shows Sue—a qualified teacher—round Anfield during his first season. Days later he scored the opening goal in the 1971 FA Cup final.*

◁ . . . especially as not many of the Forest team had had any European experience.

'The best team wins the League, but it's not always the case with cups,' Steve reflects ruefully. 'Bad luck or loss of form in one game and you're out of it.

'But we're still the best-known club in Europe. Just look around the dressing-room and among every player's mail there are letters from France, Germany, Italy—all over the place.'

Steve places a lot of the credit for the Liverpool success story on the players themselves—not just for their ability, but also for their character and attitude.

'They're the ones who make it easy and enjoyable to play here,' he says. 'And they make it enjoyable for newcomers as well. I

don't think it can be like that at all clubs.

'And the fans here play a large part in our success. You can sense an aura at Anfield just by walking around the place. Every player wants to play here, but opponents fear it.'

Steve's degree is in economics and politics. Just the sort of qualifications that the PFA—the players' union—should be looking to recruit for their negotiating team.

'The problem is that we're governed by bodies with whom we have very little contact. Only through the players' union can we communicate with them.

'The union was very responsible over the freedom of contract dispute.

'The major issue has been fought and won. The next one will probably be getting the government to recognise professional footballers as special cases.

'No matter what people think about how much players are paid, their careers are short. We can't opt out of the Pay As You Earn tax system . . . and if a player doesn't get a job for a couple of years after packing up he won't have a cent left.'

Whistle Test

'The game is almost ready for another clean-up . . . I think the time is coming now when all the things I'm inclined to talk about—the gamesmanship, the cheating, the time-wasting—have to be dealt with.'

You'll have difficulty finding references to the Big Clean-Up of 1971 in any of your football books . . . but the fact is it was one of the greatest landmarks in the history of the game in this country.

Jack Taylor was one of the referees involved in drawing up the 'memorandum' that led to the clamp-down on dirty play at the beginning of the 1971-72 season.

He recalls: 'It was brought about because a certain team in the late 1960s brought in tactics that were so revolutionary as far as English football was concerned—gamesmanship, cheating, whatever word you like to call it—we'd almost lost out.

'In the late 1960s ball players were getting hammered . . . and it was then that the Football League said: "Look, we've got to do something about this game because we're losing it". And that was right—we were.

'So the League set up a committee of five people—two referees and three ex-referees—and we met every Sunday for about six months formulating a package that became the 1971 clean-up . . .

'Bill Nicholson's comment was that we'd all be walking around with handbags before we're finished. But it did the game good. It cleaned it up. The ball players were allowed to play. The hacking went. The game needed it.

'I think the time is coming now when it needs it again. The game is almost ready for another clean-up.

Time for another clean-up . . ? Jack Taylor, former international referee, certainly thinks it is.

'I think the time is coming when all the things I'm inclined to talk about have to be dealt with.

'The malpractice that's taking place now is not a physical thing for all to see. It's the sly bending of the rules that isn't so obvious.

'But it's just as important to eliminate these things from the game as it is to get rid of the deliberate chop or the over-the-ball tackle.'

Jack wants the game cleaned up, but he doesn't want to lose all the fire and thunder.

'I recently had three weeks in China, and their game is what you might think every referee would want,' he says. 'You have no dissent. You have no physical contact that's unfair. And you have an appreciative crowd.

'But the end result is that there's nothing to challenge a referee.'

Rangers wreck a record

'This must be our greatest victory in Europe ... especially after that start, when things looked so black for us.' JOHN GREIG

By putting out Juventus and PSV Eindhoven in successive rounds, Rangers have already earned their place among the elite of Europe for 1979.

Their win in Eindhoven was the Dutch club's first home defeat in 23 years of European competition.

But it took them 147 minutes of the tie before Rangers beat PSV's reserve keeper van Engelen.

It stemmed from a long hopeful cross from Tom Forsyth on the left—straight to an Eindhoven defender. The Dutchman made a hash of his first attempt to clear then, under pressure from MacDonald, lobbed his second attempt to Tommy McLean on Rangers' right.

McLean dummied World Cup defender Ernie Brandts out of the way, then hit a low curling cross to the edge of the six-yard box. MacDonald dived in first to head home.

Graham Taylor:
A marvellous result for Rangers —but you've got to point the finger at the Dutch defence on this goal.

I don't know what that full-back was trying to do with Forsyth's cross. A ball from that position—on the touch-line but well away from the by-line, and straight to him—shouldn't have given him any problems at all. Was he trying to bring it down on his instep?

You could also say that the keeper showed his inexperience a bit. But in between Rangers were brilliant. McLean almost dummied Brandts into the photographers, and MacDonald, very sharp, took his chance well.

That dummy—I'm not sure because I haven't seen enough of their football—but it could be that the Dutch are a little vulnerable to orthodox wing play. They've been concentrating on producing all-rounders ... so it's possible that they don't often come across a genuine winger.

In the World Cup final, of course, their national side was up against two wingers (Ortiz and Bertoni).

Alex MacDonald is making quite a speciality out of diving headers . . . he also scored with one against Aberdeen last year.

CDONALD1

MACDONALD 2

Founded: 1898
Address: Fratton Park, Frogmore Road, Portsmouth PO4 8RA
Ground: Capacity: 46,000; Playing area 106.1 x 66.8 m
Record attendance: 51,385 v Derby County, FA Cup quarter-final, 26.2.49
Record victory: 9-1 v Notts County, Div. 2, 9.4.27
Record defeat: 0-10 v Leicester City, Div. 1, 20.10.28
Most League points: 65, Div. 3, 1961-62
Most League goals: 87, Div. 2, 1926-27 & Div. 3, 1961-62
League scoring record: 40, Billy Haines, Div. 2, 1926-27
Record League aggregate: 194, Peter Harris, 1946-60
Most League appearances: 764, Jimmy Dickinson, 1946-65
Most capped player: 48, Jimmy Dickinson, England, 1949-56
Honours: Div. 1 Champions 1949, 1950; FA Cup Winners 1939, Runners-up 1929, 1934; Div. 3(S) Champions 1924; Div. 3 Champions 1962
League career: 1920 Original members Div. 3; 1921-24 Div. 3(S); 1924-27 Div. 2; 1927-59 Div. 1; 1959-61 Div. 2; 1961-62 Div. 3; 1962-76 Div. 2; 1976-78 Div. 3; 1978- Div. 4

PORTSMOUTH

In the autumn Portsmouth became short-priced favourites to sample success for the first time in years.

And even if it was in the comparatively humble regions of the Fourth Division, it was being eagerly anticipated.

Yet 30 years ago Portsmouth were 'Proud Pompey', one of the country's great clubs, their side littered with internationals. Their slide from the pinnacle—League Champions in successive seasons in 1949 and 1950—to their present obscurity is one of the saddest and, to some people, the most baffling stories in football.

And the opening chapter deals with the glory days themselves . . . because that great team already nursed the seeds of its own destruction.

Pompey, unlike the Liverpool of 20 years on, didn't plan for the future. The great players faded out or moved on, and despite a massive staff, the replacements were lesser players.

Championship manager Bob Jackson moved on to Hull in 1952 and his successor, schoolteacher Eddie Lever, enjoyed transitory success in 1955 (when Pompey finished third) before the rot became evident.

Then the board made a fruitless decision. In April 1958, after escaping relegation on goal average, they sacked Lever and called in 'Mr Magic'—Freddie Cox.

Cox, the chubby former Arsenal winger, had created a reputation as a giantkilling go-getter at nearby Bournemouth. But his brief reign at Fratton Park was a time of unfortunate decay.

Cox believed himself a man with the Midas touch, a manager who could transform lower division players into men capable of

Jeff Hemmerman, who failed to make an impression for his previous two clubs—Hull and Port Vale—arrived on a free transfer and became one of the Fourth Division's top scorers.

The pride of Pompey . . . Portsmouth pictured in 1949, the year they won the first of two consecutive League Championships. Left-winger Jack Froggatt recalled: 'It was the half-back line (Jimmy Scoular, Reg Flewin and Jimmy Dickinson) that was the key.'

storming Pompey back up the First Division.

But in the process he laid waste to Portsmouth's crop of young players.

Ray Crawford was told he would never make it and was sold for a song. He went on to win England caps and a Championship medal with Alf Ramsey's Ipswich side; extrovert Derek Dougan was allowed to go before his career had got off the floor; Johnny Gordon and Ron Newman also departed.

And, so local rumour will still have it, even the legendary Peter Harris was in line for the clear-out until illness prematurely retired him.

Harris excepted, these were young players whose careers blossomed elsewhere. And Cox's judgment was again called into question by the quality of the replacements he brought in.

In his first season (1958-59) Pompey finished nine points adrift at the bottom of the First Division. They conceded 112 goals.

Pompey fans . . . looking for something to cheer about this season. After the war Fratton Park was sold out regularly every fortnight; last season average attendance was down to below 10,000 as Portsmouth were relegated to Division 4 for the first time in their history.

*Peter Denyer and, in the background, Peter Ellis
—two products of Portsmouth's revitalised youth
team, playing in the 2-0 win at Aldershot.*

Remarkably Cox lasted more than another disastrous season. Pompey were relegated again . . . but, under the tough disciplinarian George Smith, they came straight back up again as Third Division champions in 1962.

Then, however, the directors were forced to turn the screw. They declared that drastic economies were needed . . . and another decision that ranks high among the reasons for the slide was taken.

The reserves and the youth team were scrapped in 1965. Pompey were reduced to a squad of 17 full professionals.

In the short term it may have made economic sense; in the long term it was almost suicidal.

Among the apprentices sacrificed was a fair-haired midfielder they felt was too small to make the grade. He later joined Ipswich and eventually became an England international. His name was Mick Mills.

Among the promising schoolboys Pompey had turned their back on were Bobby Stokes, who was to win the FA Cup for Southampton, David Jones of Norwich and Wales and, most recently, Malcolm Waldron of Southampton.

The decision also meant that Pompey, the club without money, had to buy all the replacements they needed.

After several seasons of getting by on free transfer players and cheap buys, the fairy godfather the board had been searching for arrived.

John Deacon, a Southampton property magnate, was the board's Christmas present to itself. In his first two weeks as chairman, Portsmouth spent £200,000 on Peter Marinello, Ron Davies and Phil Roberts.

Deacon came up with a three-year plan to transform Portsmouth.

John Mortimore was brought back from Greece as manager . . . and the spending went on. Paul Went cost a record £155,000 and Malcolm Manley accounted for another £50,000.

Then, before the results started coming, it all began to go wrong.

Deacon's three-year plan had to be torn up. The property boom died and the chairman couldn't go on putting money into the club. Debts mounted and Mortimore, 15 months into his three-year contract, was suspended for 'lack of success'.

The new manager, Scottish international Ian St John, arrived expecting that money would be available for new players if he thought they were necessary.

St John had found players approaching the twilight of their careers, players with massive contracts.

> **Mr Portsmouth, MBE**
>
> Jimmy Dickinson (below, coming out for his 750th League game, against Southampton) played for Portsmouth for 20 seasons, making a total of 764 League appearances and winning two Championship medals and 48 England caps. He was never booked or sent off and was awarded the MBE in 1965. He is now Portsmouth's manager.

Bravely he axed them, but had to rely on the free transfer market and the immature products of the club's re-created youth scheme to replace them.

Finally Deacon was forced to admit his failure. He appealed to the public to save Pompey from bankruptcy. The club, he said, were half a million pounds in debt.

The club was saved—but the team was on the slide. Relegation to the Third Division in 1976 was followed by St John's suspension, and in desperation Portsmouth turned to their living legend.

Jimmy Dickinson, giant of the Championship days, took over as manager—the job he had always said would never be his.

His first two matches brought the three points needed to save the club from the Fourth Division in 1977.

But it was a fate delayed by only one year.

CLOCKING

Goals are what the game is all about— but the times they are scored can be just as vital. So *Handbook* charted the times of all the goals scored in the First Division in October —with interesting results . . .

There's nothing more sickening in football than a goal given away just before half-time. That's the moment when both sides have more or less settled the first-half argument and thoughts turn to a breather and the second-half strategy.

But when are the real crisis times for goals? If our chart is anything to go by, goals are most likely around the 30-minute mark in the first half and midway through the second. But why?

Could it be that after half an hour both sides have relaxed mentally after successfully following the pre-match instruction of 'Keep it tight early on'?

As for the second-half peak, perhaps this is the period when the majority of games are won and lost. All

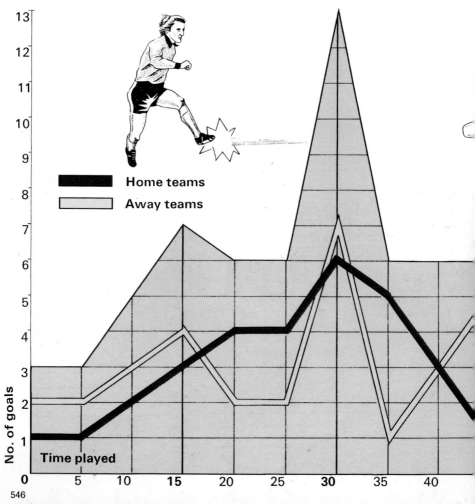

Home teams
Away teams

No. of goals

Time played

0   5   10   15   20   25   30   35   40

THE GOALS

the early tension has gone and every move is for real. The home teams did much better during this period, possibly because their fans—sensing the importance of it—got behind their team more.

Not surprisingly, very few of the goals scored came in the first ten minutes. Pros haven't worked hard all week to give the opposition a goal start!

And more goals were scored by away sides at the 'danger time' around 30 minutes. Then, having 'sneaked one', their goals dropped dramatically before soaring again just before half time. This implies the home team welcomes half time most!

But they have a good period right after the break. Perhaps their team talk is more relevant and they tend

to 'snap out of it'.

But the visitors, being good pros, are ready to score on the break and their effectiveness in the 'danger time' is almost equal.

The last few minutes? A good time for goals—for both sides. Perhaps the home team is piling on the pressure, or maybe the away side 'with character' is fighting desperately to save a point . . .

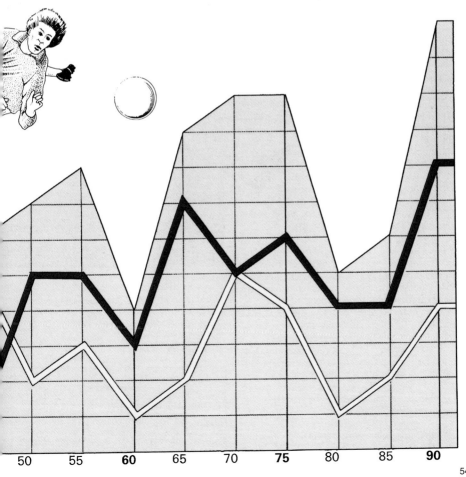

50   55   **60**   65   70   **75**   80   85   **90**

RISING STAR BYRON STEVENSON

Byron Stevenson has only a handful of First Division appearances to his name, but already he looks like becoming a fixture in the Wales team for years to come.

This pencil-slim 6′ 1″ defender won his second full cap in the 7-0 romp against Malta in a European Championship game at Wrexham—and fulfilled the prediction made by former Leeds boss Don Revie when he signed Stevenson straight from school.

Following in distinguished footsteps

Revie reckoned that his Welsh scout Jack Pickard had produced another lad destined to reach the top—a boy capable of following in the distinguished footsteps of other Elland Road favourites from the principality down the years.

Coventry's•Terry Yorath, now the Welsh captain, is probably the best person to judge Stevenson's merit and promise. He was at Elland Road when the tough ambitious youngster from Llanelli was fighting his way through to the occasional first-team appearance via United's junior sides. 'Byron always stood out as one of the fiercest competitors on the park,' says Yorath. 'But his courage apart, what really struck me about him was his skill.

'As he's developed he has become a cross between my old mates Norman Hunter and Terry Cooper—and that can't be bad. At 21 he obviously still has a lot to learn, but he's done enough already to prove that he has a great international future ahead of him.

'His ball control is remarkable for a defender; he can dribble as well as a lot of First Division forwards I could name.

'Like Cooper, he's never happier than when he's going forward on the overlap. But Byron has one asset TC lacked—height.

'And while Byron will never match Norman as a ball winner—who will?—his other qualities more than compensate for that.'

Welsh manager Mike Smith is another who speaks highly of Stevenson, who is a

ABOVE *Stevenson's determination in training helped to set him apart from the other young hopefuls at Elland Road.*

RIGHT *Establishing himself in the first-team . . . Stevenson shows the power which made such an impact on Jock Stein.*

Club	Season	L'gue		FA Cp		Lge Cp		Int'nls	
		Ms	Gs	Ms	Gs	Ms	Gs	Ms	Gs
Leeds	1974-75	1	–	–	–	–	–	–	–
United	1975-76	1	–	–	–	–	–	–	–
	1976-77	10	–	–	–	–	–	–	–
	1977-78	5	–	–	–	–	–	1	–
		17	–	–	–	–	–	1	–

'He's become a cross between Norman Hunter and Terry Cooper ... and he can dribble as well as a lot of First Division forwards I could name.' TERRY YORATH
'Byron is one of the best young defenders I've seen in England. I couldn't possibly have left him in the reserves.' JOCK STEIN

former youth international captain. Before handing the hard-tackling youngster his first cap—against Northern Ireland in the Home International at Wrexham last year—Smith gave his debut boy a vote of confidence.

'He doesn't know what nerves are'

'Byron won't let me down. He doesn't know what nerves are. He might play most of his football before a handful of spectators for Leeds reserves, but I've no doubts whatsoever that he'll step into the big time without any trouble.'

With such an impressive array of admirers singing his praises it seems odd that Stevenson's first-team chances have been so restricted.

Stevenson views the situation with typical modesty. 'I suppose different managers—mainly Jimmy Armfield—felt I wasn't quite ready for regular First Division football,' he told *Handbook*.

'And even though I'd made my League debut as a 17-year-old under Don Revie I could hardly say the boss was wrong, could I?

'Fortunately for me assistant manager Maurice Lindley took charge for our summer tour of Holland and Germany. And he made it clear it was my big chance to really show what I could do.'

Great strides

During Jock Stein's 45-day sojourn with the Yorkshire club Stevenson made great strides towards making the right-back slot his own. The current Scotland manager was suitably impressed.

'Byron's one of the best young defenders I've seen in England—I couldn't possibly have left him in the reserves. He had one poor match when I first came, but that could happen to the most seasoned campaigner.

Stein may have gone, but Byron Stevenson feels he has finally arrived.

'Now it's up to me to play well enough to secure a regular place.'

'The dummy'

Bryan Robson & David Cross

'How you dummy is up to the individual. It might be a jump over the ball or just a dip of the shoulder. Kidding your marker is the object of the exercise.' WEST HAM manager JOHN LYALL

Like the two central defenders, twin strikers have to get on the same wavelength to make an effective partnership.

They have to co-ordinate their movements—often by instinct.

And, when it's 'on', the dummy between them can be a killer combination.

West Ham's 'front two' Bryan Robson and David Cross have become one of the most lethal double acts in the Second Division.

After a training session at Chadwell Heath, they demonstrated typical dummy situations for *Handbook*.

'It's on when Pop goes looking for the ball and David gets in a position beyond him,' says Hammers' manager John Lyall.

'The pass to Pop has to be played with pace so that he can dummy and the ball will go through to David at a good speed. Then all it takes is a touch from David to send Pop clear.

'How you dummy is up to the individual. It might be a jump over the ball or just a dip of the shoulder. Kidding your marker is the object of the exercise.

'And, like most of the best football moves, it's full of alternatives. Pop can take the ball himself and David can shoot first time if he fancies his chances or use Pop's run as a decoy, turn on the outside of his right foot and crack one in with his left. He'd love to do that!'

1. Pop shapes to take the ball . . .

2. But dummies and lets it go through . . .

Strike force . . . West Ham's double act up front—David Cross and 'Pop' Robson—spells danger to Second Division defences.

3. David comes to meet the ball and all it needs is a touch . . .

4. A neat side-footed pass into space by David . . .

5. And there's Pop, having 'lost' his marker, in a shooting position.

6. Now it's up to the striker to make sure the move wasn't wasted.

GRAHAM TAYLOR:
As John Lyall says, the value of the dummy is that it gives you alternatives, adds a new dimension to your play. If you get known as a player who always takes the ball, that can only help defenders. But if you mix up your game, it's bound to make them think twice. It follows, of course, that too many dummies are likely to make a dummy out of you! The surprise element would be lost.

It's not only the dummying player who's got alternatives—the player behind him has as well. The obvious and easiest ball is the touch to the runner, but the possibilities are almost endless. A snap shot on the turn by the second player could surprise the keeper. And the biggest surprise of all would be a second dummy.

Players like Pop Robson are ideally built to take the ball themselves—as an alternative to dummying—because they've got a low centre of gravity and the sharp turn that's needed to get past a tight-marking defender comes easier to them. Another player who's excellent in these tight situations is Derek Hales, once with West Ham but now back at Charlton.

Dennis Tueart...
Manhattan transfer

Maine Road to Meadowlands ... the first current England player to go Stateside had a great season in New York, culminating with two goals in Cosmos' win over Tampa Bay Rowdies in the Soccerbowl (right)

Dennis Tueart shook the soccer establishment in this country when he opted for the rich pickings of America instead of the sweat and endeavour of the English First Division.

While the States provided a golden opportunity for players from the lower echelons of the Football League and a grazing patch for ageing European stars, it had failed to lure any of England's top stars away to a life in the sun.

Capped six times and still a candidate for an England spot—especially in view of Ron Greenwood's liking for wingers—Tueart felt he was striking a blow for the individual by accepting Cosmos' offer to try his luck in the USA.

'I was 28 when the Cosmos came in for me, and I'd just about achieved everything I wanted to in England,' he explains.

Those achievements include an FA Cup winner's medal for his first club,

Sunderland, in 1973, and the League Cup victors' medal he clinched with Manchester City with a spectacular goal from an overhead kick against the team he supported as a boy, Newcastle United.

As well as a fresh challenge, the move to New York brought him financial security. ▷

**Early glory—Tueart
with scorer Ian Porterfield after
Sunderland had beaten Leeds 1-0 in 1973 to
become the first Division 2 FA Cup winners in 42 years.**

Dove-grey Cadillac and penthouse apartment—some of the trimmings of a lucrative Cosmos contract.

Training in the £35 million Meadowlands Stadium—Astroturf, electronic scoreboards and 70,000 seats.

'I'm not one of those players who is content to stay with one club, breaking the appearance record . . . but winning nothing. I need to be searching for something else. Ambition is the key word for me.

'GOING PLACES'

'The Cosmos are one of the greatest clubs in the world—certainly the only American one I would have dreamed of joining, although there are clearly other clubs here who are going places.'

Tueart was dogged by a nasty hamstring injury when *Handbook* visited him. Despite a lone battle to get fit, he was forced to miss Cosmos' next game against the Toronto Metros.

It was the first match after Cosmos—they dropped the New York prefix when they moved to New Jersey—had clinched the Eastern Conference of the North American Soccer League.

Not surprisingly for a player of his calibre, Tueart made an explosive impact in his first US season. He was the star of the play-off final in which Cosmos defeated Tampa Bay Rowdies—complete with that other refugee from Maine Road, Rodney Marsh—3-1 for their second successive title.

The foundations of the victory against the Rowdies were almost exclusively an English affair. Tueart scored twice while Steve Hunt—playing his last game before his £40,000 move back to England with Coventry—laid on the 'killer' goal for Italian ace Giorgio Chinaglia.

It was a tremendous climax to the season for Tueart, compensating for the frustration of missing games through injury.

'The Cosmos have marvellous facilities for treating injuries, but nature has to do some of the work too,' Tueart told us.

GETTING BURNED

Knocks weren't the only problem he had to overcome on arriving in the States. For a start, Cosmos play on Astroturf, which requires specially studded boots for gripping purposes.

'I must admit I've found it difficult to adjust to the pitch here. There's no give in the surface as there is with grass. Real turf gives you greater mobility . . . but when you're standing on Astroturf you're stuck rigid.

'It can also give you skin burns, though that doesn't stop defenders from tackling you just as hard. I've been sent flying by defenders over here just as I was at City. This league is every bit as competitive as any I've ever played in.'

DIFFERENT ROUTINE

Tueart has also had problems adjusting to the time zones that have to be crossed.

'I've had to adopt a different preparation routine. Back home I geared myself to 3 o'clock or 7.30 kick-off times. But here they can be 9 pm, 7.30 pm or even 1 pm. Los Angeles time is four hours behind New York for instance . . . and sometimes it's hard for your body to cope.'

Tueart up against Danny McGrain in the last of his six full England games, as sub for Ray Kennedy in the 2-1 defeat by Scotland at Wembley on 4 June 1977.

With wife Joan ... and proof of helping Cosmos to retain the American soccer title.

Newcastle to New York

Dennis was born on 27 November 1949 in Newcastle . . . He was in the Sunderland team that won the FA Cup in 1973, and was transferred to Manchester City for £250,000 in March 1974 . . . His flashing overhead scissors kick was City's winning goal in the 1976 League Cup final against Newcastle at Wembley . . . He scored twice in his one and only England Under-23 appearance—a 3-0 win over Scotland at Aberdeen in December 1974 . . . He made his full international debut five months later in a 1-0 win in Cyprus, coming on as substitute for scorer Kevin Keegan . . . Cosmos paid £250,000 for him . . . He scored six goals in six play-off games last summer, including two in the Soccerbowl final against Tampa Bay Rowdies at Meadowlands.

In the 'whirlpool' in Cosmos' treatment room. Warner Bros' money means no expense is spared for success.

But if the enormous distances between clubs in the States are an irritation, the strain was hardly etched on Tueart's face as he left the super-modern £35,000,000 Meadowlands Stadium and climbed into a Cadillac.

Tueart had just finished a training session. Seemingly unburdened by the intense humidity, stars of several nations and the club's home-grown prospects breezed through a light session with coach Eddie Firmani on a bed of dazzling green Astro-turf under a brilliant sky.

'SUPERB TRAINER'

One small boy was kicking around with some friends. The fierce shooting, the impeccable balance and ball control . . . it came as no surprise to learn that he was Pele's six-year-old son!

Nearby, Franz Beckenbauer jogged around the track with an almost condescending air; Carlos Alberto, who led Brazil to their 1970 World Cup triumph, arrived ages after his colleagues; and Chinaglia just about raised enough enthusiasm for a game of head-tennis.

Tueart's attitude contrasted sharply. 'He's a superb trainer,' volunteered one of the Cosmos coaching staff. For Tueart, physical fitness is of paramount importance —whether you're a New York superstar or a Rochdale reserve.

Meadowlands Stadium— which Firmani hopes will become the Wembley of America — is a 20-minute drive from Tueart's apartment, which overlooks the Hudson River.

His new home is ample proof of just how luxurious life can be in the States. Manhattan's famous skyline dominates the view from the window. Known as the Galaxy, the apartment block is indeed fit for the stars.

'We simply drove around with Cosmos officials until we saw a place we liked—and bang, it was ours,' he says.

TWO SWIMMING POOLS

The violence which has now become a depressing part of New York life hardly touches Dennis and his wife Joan. They're virtually barricaded in their flat with a host of television sets to pinpoint any would-be intruders at the flick of a switch.

The flat, complete with

A touching moment with Leeds' Peter Hampton at Maine Road in April 1977. Dennis won a second Wembley medal with City—scoring spectaculaly against Newcastle.

two swimming pools and a gymnasium, comes courtesy of the Cosmos.

Despite their new-found affluence, the Tuearts have no plans to stay beyond Dennis's three-year contract.

'I like the lifestyle,' he told us, 'but I don't think we'll stay. I'd like to return to England and go into business eventually, though what kind of business I don't really know yet.'

It was a rare moment of uncertainty for a man who seems to know exactly what he wants—and how to get it.

Honours: FA Cup winners medal 1973; League Cup winners medal 1976; Voted 'Most Valuable Player of the NASL play-offs' 1978.

Club	Div	Pos	Season	League Ms	League Gs	FA Cup Ms	FA Cup Gs	Lge Cup Ms	Lge Cup Gs	Int'nls Ms	Int'nls Gs
Sunderland	I	17	1968-69	10	2	1	–	–	–		
	I	21	1969-70	39	4	1	–	1	1		
	II	13	1970-71	20	4	1	–	–	–		
	II	5	1971-72	42	13	4	–	1	–		
	II	6	1972-73	40	12	9	3	1	–		
	II	6	1973-74	27	11	2	–	3	1		
Manchester	I	14	1973-74	8	1	–	–	–	–		
City	I	8	1974-75	39	14	1	–	2	–	2	–
	I	8	1975-76	38	14	2	2	7	8	–	–
	I	2	1976-77	38	18	4	–	1	–	4	2
	I	4	1977-78	17	12	2	1	5	2	–	–
				318	105	27	6	21	12	6	2

(Cosmos 1978: 26 matches, 16 goals)

A Matter of Fact

ABOVE Jack Charlton (left) and Mike Summerbee were no strangers to referees' notebooks during their illustrious careers. Now, as managers of Sheffield Wednesday and Stockport, they must set a standard—but Summerbee was still sent off against Barnsley last year.

Halifax Town officials were shocked when only 985 fans turned up at The Shay for the goalless draw with Crewe recently. It was the lowest crowd for a Saturday match there since Town were founder members of the Third Division (North) in 1921, and the third smallest attendance in their history.

Strange but true ... Shifnal defender Peter Cosh was sent off before half-time in a recent West Midlands League match at Rushall. Nothing very unusual about that you might think. But his manager Ken Jones was dumbfounded. 'It was the first time I had ever seen a player dismissed for swearing at one of his own team,' he said after his ten men had hung on to win 2-1.

Manchester City's Kazimierz Deyna's biggest fan is none other than John Paul II, the newly elected Pope who, like the midfield ace, comes from Poland.

Johan Cruyff's testimonial game in November was something of a disaster. His old club, Ajax, crashed 8-0 to Bayern Munich and the great man was substituted 20 minutes from time—a decision greeted with a hail of cushions and a storm of boos by the 65,000 crowd in Amsterdam's Olympic Stadium.

Sheffield United had high hopes of young Irish midfielder Peter Dornan when they bought him from Linfield in 1976. But after one full game and 25 days at Bramall Lane, he returned to Ireland because of homesickness. Now, with several English clubs on his trail, he's ready to try again.

When John Shaw saved a Jimmy Greenhoff penalty at Old Trafford in October it was a case of 13th time lucky. Of the previous 12 spot-kicks the Bristol City keeper had faced, 11 beat him outright while the other, from Wolves' Willie Carr, hit the bar only for Alan Sunderland (now with Arsenal) to score from the rebound.

What's up Doc ? In the first eight League games of the 1977-78 season Derby's Tommy Docherty called on 20 players—almost two whole teams. Yet when the Rams won the League title in 1971-72 and again in 1974-75, they used just 16 players in each campaign.

Hungary's defeat at the hands of West Germany in the 1954 World Cup final not only cost them that great trophy, but also ended a record of 29 internationals in succession without losing. Their run stretched back four years to when Austria won 5-3 in Vienna. Hungary scored 27 goals in only 5 games in those 1954 finals!

Nottingham Forest boss Brian Clough's spell as manager of Leeds United lasted only 44 days before he was sacked. How ironic, then, that Jock Stein should choose to leave the Elland Road club just 45 days after taking over from Jimmy Armfield, the man called in to replace Clough.

Alan Gowling

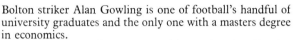

'The footballers' environment has its own fascination. You don't have to discuss Marx to have a good chat with someone.'

Bolton striker Alan Gowling is one of football's handful of university graduates and the only one with a masters degree in economics.

So what's it like for someone with an education like that to spend his days in the pro football atmosphere, which is not renowned for its discussion of world events?

'No problem at all,' Alan told *Handbook*. 'The point is that whatever job you choose you have to fall in with the way things are—on the shop floor, anywhere.

'I've talked about this with Steve Heighway (another graduate) and he agrees. And anyway, the footballers' environment has its own fascination. You don't have to discuss Marx to have a good chat with someone.'

Alan has had very much an up and down career at Manchester United, Huddersfield, Newcastle and now at Burnden Park.

'I've had to get used to different training methods but all clubs have the same basic standards. Looking back, I think I trained harder by myself when I was an amateur with Manchester United.'

Alan, not surprisingly, is a big believer in players having 'something to fall back on'.

'Let's face it, football's an insecure profession. You might not make it. You might get injured. So young players with time on their hands would do better to learn a trade, or improve their academic qualifications, than spend it in snooker halls. That's not easy to do—but it's worth the effort.'

An educated pass ... Alan Gowling doing his 'A' level best for Bolton.

561

RI **S** ING **S** TAR VINCE HILAIRE

Standing a mere 5′ 6″, Crystal Palace's young forward Vince Hilaire has become a regular target of Second Division cloggers.

But Palace manager Terry Venables says: 'It takes a lot to bring him down. He's got this knack of stumbling through tackles and coming out the other side with the ball.'

Still only 19, Vince—already takes the hustle and bustle of pro football in his silky stride. But some say that stride should be nearer goal, not so deep in midfield . . . suggestions that are put down by Venables.

Roving role

Vince explains: 'I'm a more confident player this season now that Terry has given me a roving role which enables me to go anywhere on the park and not have to worry about being out of position. 'It's a good role to have because you see so much more of the ball.'

Born and bred in Forest Hill just down the road from Selhurst Park, Vince was signed by ex-Palace boss Malcolm Allison on schoolboy apprentice forms.

Time out with Mal

'Malcolm was a great influence on my career. He used to come and watch our schoolboy games in the morning before the first team played in the afternoon. This gesture helped us a great deal—none of us forgot it.

'Big Mal was a completely different

Vince the subject of hot pursuit during this season's Palace-Brighton meeting at Selhurst, which Palace won 3-1.

'It frightens me sometimes when I think how good he might end up. Vince has a combination of power and balance that I've seen in very few players.' TERRY VENABLES

Club	Season	League		FA Cup		Lge Cup	
		Ms	Gs	Ms	Gs	Ms	Gs
Crystal	1976-77	3	–	–	–	–	–
Palace	1977-78	30	–	–	–	2	–
		33	2	–	–	2	–

manager to Terry, although the end product was still the same. Malcolm seemed to have difficulty in getting his point across to you, but taking time out to talk to you at the age of 13 helped to make Palace the friendly club it is today.'

From then on Hilaire has gone from strength to strength, winning two FA Youth Cup medals with Palace's highly promising young side, and being the subject of an ITV documentary three years ago.

After a successful season in the reserves came Vince's rather unexpected debut. 'Palace gave me my chance much earlier than I expected, as a substitute against Lincoln in March 1977.'

Hilaire impressed with his one appearance. Two more outings in the senior side, one against Brighton and the other against Port Vale, rounded off Vince's season.

A start to the 1977-78 season which would have pleased any 18-year-old was severely criticized by one person . . . Vince Hilaire. 'I wasn't playing well at all in our first 14 games, but it didn't really show because the team were playing so much good football.'

Playing for promotion
Vince's stiff self-examination test seems to keep him up to scratch—as Terry Venables will testify. 'It sometimes frightens me when I think to myself how good he might end up. But that doesn't mean he's an automatic choice—I had to make him the sub for a while last year.'

Palace, a side which have been on the verge of promotion since a step up from the Third Division in 1976, can boast a team of good young international talent—one which seems to have the ingredients for elevation to the First Division.

As Vince says, 'If there's one big ambition in the club it's got to be promotion.' With players like Vince Hilaire it shouldn't be long until Palace are up there.

Brighton rock Wrexham:

'Brighton look ready for promotion—if this goal is anything to go by.' GRAHAM TAYLOR

Brighton owe much of their success in recent seasons to their captain and midfield anchor man Brian Horton.

The former Port Vale half-back played an important part in the Seagulls' League win over Wrexham in November, culminating with a well-taken winning goal.

Mark Lawrenson, another key figure in Brighton's pro-motion push, started the move when he intercepted a Mel Sutton pass intended for Bobby Shinton deep on the right of Albion's defence.

Lawrenson knocked the ball forward to Teddy May-bank just inside his own half, and Maybank laid it off first time to Peter O'Sullivan, who hit a long, raking pass for Horton to run on to.

Two Wrexham defenders and keeper Dai Davies con-verged . . . but Horton—known as 'Nobby' to his

Graham Taylor's analysis

Certainly Brighton look ready for promotion—if this goal is anything to go by.

All four players involved did extremely well. It was one of those goals where everything comes right, all the training is suddenly worthwhile.

And it's a tremendous boost to a side when a goal like this goes in. You can see them looking at each other and saying : 'Look at that. *That's* how good we are.'

I liked the way Lawrenson won the ball and was confident enough to turn with it and hold it. Every back four needs at least one player like that, who's quick to cover and can use the ball. And O'Sullivan did well, not only seeing the gap in the Wrexham defence but being quick and accurate enough to expose it.

Horton saw it too, of course. He found himself in yards of space with a clear run at goal. You could see him signalling for the ball—and probably he couldn't believe his luck . . .

Because you've got to say that the defence wasn't entirely blameless. You can forgive them for not picking up Horton immediately. After all, an attack had just broken down . . . and Horton was probably about on the halfway line when it happened. He didn't present any immediate danger . . .

Wrexham's first priority was to sort themselves out at the back. Instead they left that great gap—between Joey Jones and Gareth Davis, wasn't it?—which Brighton used so well. O'Sullivan's through ball was perfect . . . and there was nothing wrong with Horton's finishing ; he was very cool, even under considerable pressure. He kept his head, got to the ball first, waited for the right moment, then stuck it away well.

O'SULLIVAN

MAYBANK

LAWRENSON

team-mates—just got there first, knocking the ball with the outside of his right foot over Davies.

It gave Brighton a 2-1 lead —a lead they preserved until the final whistle—and two more vital points in the close-fought Second Division promotion race.

HORTON

> 'I've become part of a great tradition at Newcastle. The days at Forest are already no more than a memory ... it's all about the future now, and I want to earn the right to be talked about in the same breath as the great Newcastle number nines of recent years—like Jackie Milburn and Malcolm Macdonald.'

There can't be many players who start their career in the Football League with Southport, then move on to Barrow (two sides now operating in the Northern Premier League) . . . and end up leading the League Champions' scorers and being signed by a top club for £200,000. Yet that's exactly what's happened to Peter Withe, now knocking 'em out at Newcastle.

Along the way he played for seven clubs, one in South Africa and one in America, collecting a League Cup medal and Championship medal with Forest before leaving the club after a much-publicised row 'over money' with Brian Clough.

So now Withe's undoubted talents are hard at work in the Second Division, committed to the cause of lifting Newcastle United back to what their supporters see as their rightful place in the top flight. And he is leading the Magpie's front line so well that he is already the hero of the fans.

Not that he has achieved an impossible feat—the fervent Newcastle fans have always idolised the man in the Magpies' No 9 shirt.

'Best interests'

Jackie Milburn was a super-hero; so was Malcolm Macdonald. Now Withe is hoping to follow in their footsteps after giving up the chance of European glory with Forest to go to the North-East.

Newcastle manager Bill McGarry had been trailing the bearded six-footer for some time, but had to wait until the season had already started before finally signing him. He had to do some convincing talking to persuade Withe that his future lay with a club in a lower division, but Withe took the plunge.

As he explained to *Handbook*: 'True I, had my differences with Forest, but I believe I was on the point of settling them when I was told they'd agreed terms with Newcastle for my transfer. I felt then that it was in my best interests to leave.

'Mr McGarry offered me very good terms. Newcastle are a big club with tradition and ambition, and I'm happy to be with them.'

Yet when Withe started in football there were few signs that he was going to become a top striker. He played just three games for Southport in Division 4, and only one for Barrow, before leaving for one of South Africa's best clubs—Arcadia Shepherds.

Dougan finds a lost sheep

He didn't have a League goal to his name at that point, but his game developed to the point where Derek Dougan spotted him while visiting South Africa and tipped off his Wolves boss, Bill McGarry, who paid out £13,000 to bring Withe home. But their first association as manager and player was not a success—though Wolves did make a £27,000 ▷

LEFT *Glory days with Forest.*
RIGHT *Withe turns away after scoring for Birmingham City v Burnley on 9 September 1975—his first League goal for the Blues.*

Honours: League Championship medal 1978; League Cup winners medal 1978

Club	Div	Pos	Season	League		FA Cup		Lge Cup	
				Ms	Gs	Ms	Gs	Ms	Gs
Southport	IV	8	1970-71	2	–	–	–	–	–
	IV	7	1971-72	1	–	–	–	–	–
Barrow	IV	22	1971-72	1	–	–	–	–	–
Arcadia Shepherds (*not known*)									
Wolves	I	12	1973-74	3	1	–	–	–	–
	I	12	1974-75	14	2	–	–	–	–
B'ham City	I	19	1975-76	32	9	2	–	2	–
	I	13	1976-77	3	–	–	–	1	–
N. Forest	II	3	1976-77	34	16	5	1	–	–
	I	1	1977-78	40	12	6	2	8	5
				130	40	13	3	11	5

Slow starter

Withe, now 27, made a slow start to his career. A Liverpool lad who used to sell programmes at Goodison on match days, he was ignored by the big two on Merseyside. He joined Southport as an amateur, then broke into the Barrow first team just before they were kicked out of the League. Derek Dougan spotted him playing in the South African League: 'He looked like my natural successor in the Wolves team,' said the 'Doog' of the tall, dark, naturally left-footed centre-forward—and persuaded Wolves to sign him on a three-month trial. Withe's manager there was Bill McGarry, who is now his boss at Newcastle United.

ABOVE *Bill McGarry has now bought Withe for a second time—though on this occasion the fee is 15 times the amount he paid for him in 1973.*
RIGHT *Up against John Lacy of Spurs. Newcastle fans would be more than happy if Peter could repeat his two great seasons with Forest: promotion, League Championship and League Cup.*

profit when he moved on to Birmingham in the summer of 1975.

At Birmingham, nine goals in 35 First Division matches were enough to bring him to the notice of Brian Clough, the man with the talent for developing players to the very limit of their potential. A £42,000 fee took him to the City Ground—and the start of a classic success story. He developed a fine partnership with Tony Woodcock. Forest were promoted from Division 2, Withe netting 16 times from 34 games.

He retained his place for the whole of Forest's Championship season, despite the occasional threat from Clough that he would be dropped unless his performance improved further, playing an essential part in their success. McGarry was delighted to get him, describing Withe as 'brave as a lion'.

Withe, while certainly brave, doesn't see that as his main attribute. 'I'm the type who likes to be involved throughout a game,' he told us. 'It's nice to score goals but I don't

> **Clough's criticisms**
> The outspoken Brian Clough didn't mince words about Withe, the centre-forward who was Forest's top scorer last season when they won the championship.
> After the League Cup final against Liverpool at Wembley Clough said: 'He didn't turn his man once in two hours. Unless he proves he can do it on Scarborough prom in training, the kid (Steve Elliott) will get his place in the replay.'
> Then, when Withe looked as though he was on the way out at Forest: 'I cannot tolerate Withe any longer, because I don't know when I can expect him to last 90 minutes. I'm only interested in players who can be relied on to do their stuff.'

like to be out of the game for 89 minutes then grab one in the last minute.

'Naturally, my main job is scoring, but it's also important to create chances for others. If we won 3-0 and I hadn't scored, but made a couple, I'd be well pleased.

Bluff Clough

'I don't really worry if I'm not scoring regularly, because I've always been a confident type of player. Still, I hope the fans don't start comparing me with Malcolm Macdonald. He lives for goals and I regard myself as more of a team player . . . a rover who will work in all areas of the field. Hard work doesn't bother me.'

Peter is happy to give credit to Brian Clough for his new-found confidence. 'I learned so much from him,' he says. 'I must have done because he sold me for five times what he paid for me! His instructions were simple. He told me to run into the opposition half, not my own. He said he paid defenders to do that.'

'The right move'

When Peter arrived at Newcastle they had lost their two opening games—but he soon changed all that. In his first match he really turned it on; his partner Jim Pearson scored the vital goal and Luton were beaten 1-0. He scored twice against Blackburn after Newcastle trailed at half time but went on to win 3-1, and made sure of the fans' affection when he scored Newcastle's goal against arch-rivals Sunderland in a 1-1 draw.

He told *Handbook;* 'I've made the right move in coming to Newcastle. They're an ambitious club and the aim is promotion. It happened for me at Forest—and I'm going to do everything I know to make sure it happens here as well.'

THE EXILES

Every week in the football season small bands of supporters leave London to watch matches all over the country. These are The Exiles, people who have moved to the capital but still prefer to shout for their home town team. They all belong to APFSCIL (the Association of Professional Football Supporters' Clubs in London) and rival fans actually travel by train together to the same game—more often than not in complete harmony.

Football Handbook joined the congregation for the Coventry-Middlesbrough game at Highfield Road and found a group of fans who can get carried away at a match . . . without being carried away by the coppers.

It was a foggy day in London town when the two sets of supporters met near platform six at Euston Station for the 12.10 to Coventry. They're all on the quiet side—apart from Ivy—but there is still that air of anticipation. For everyone this is another Saturday, another game . . .

They're the best behaved supporters in the land!

At the station; on the train; at the ground; even on the journey home after a defeat, their behaviour is straight out of a policeman's dream.

As Pete Johnson puts it: 'We've never been news because we never wreck shops or beat up bystanders.'

Pete's a big bloke, too. He could look after himself if he had to. But he's got a collective reputation to look after. He's social secretary of the Middlesbrough Supporters Club in London and organises the train trips to far off places—including Ayresome

An unlikely but happy combination . . . Middlesbrough and Coventry 'exiles' on the same train to the First Division game at Highfield Road. All pals together, and they were even happy after!

Park 'back home'.

'When I first came to London I went to various grounds down here but I couldn't really enjoy it. There was no real interest, no involvement.'

With lots of other Boro exiles feeling the same way, it wasn't long before they got themselves together—literally. Ads in programmes did the trick and now there are 80 members in London.

'We've got a strict code for people who join—no hobnail boots, no skinhead haircuts, things like that,' says Peter. 'We have a few drinks on the way home but it never gets out of hand. We've got this indemnity clause with British Rail. If there's any damage, we have to cough up a thousand quid!'

Everyone is safely in their seats—and it's time to meet Ivy. Ivy's as London as Big Ben but she travels every week with the Boro boys and girls. She's a social worker, nearing 60, and is known as the Angel of Harrow, where she works with young and old alike.

'This hooligan problem,' says Ivy, 'it's because kids haven't got enough to do. They turn to football and it gets them into trouble. But I still introduce them to football in my work, and old people too. You've got to get involved in this world.

'Take me. I didn't go to football until my husband died five years ago. I wanted to, but my husband wanted to stay in and watch John Wayne. Now I follow the England team as well.'

Sitting with Ivy is her friend, Eric Bardell. He agrees with Ivy that kids 'at a loose end' are likely to disturb the peace in one way or another, but he also thinks that a 'clip round the ear' wouldn't go amiss now and again.

On arrival at Coventry station, Eric finds himself— along with the others—in the ▷

SKY BLUES 1 (8)
MIDDLESBRO 0

The writing's on the electric scoreboard for Boro . . . although Micky Burns scored, Garry Thompson nodded the late winner. It was all quiet on the Coventry front on the train home, but two Sky Blue exiles (below) enjoyed the triumph in silence.

ludicrous position of getting the evil eye from Coventry constables. Eric's a police sergeant!

There's time for a pint and a bite to eat in the Coventry supporters' club, a good walk from the ground.

Geoff Grainer, an artist, explains what supporting the Boro means to him. 'I was at college in Birmingham and living 50 yards from Villa's ground, but I preferred to go into town on Saturday afternoons. If I lived 50 yards

> Jill Barnett was in at the beginning of the Boro club in London.
>
> 'I left Brotton, a village near Saltburn, because I didn't get on with my stepfather,' says Jill, 22, who works for the GLC.
>
> 'I stayed at a Church of England hostel. It was a bit lonely and, as I'd been taken to games as a kid, I went to a Spurs match.
>
> 'Unbelievably, I met a lad from Brotton and later he introduced me to someone who wanted to start the supporters' club. We put an ad in a programme and the response was great.

from Ayresome I'd never miss a game.

'When we go to home games we catch the 7.40 and get there about 10.30, so I go home for lunch and go to the game with my dad or brother-in-law. Then, if I fancy it, I stay for a night out and return on the Sunday—make a weekend of it.'

Geoff goes to lots of mid-week games, too, because he's got a flexible job. 'I paint theatre scenery and I can do my 40 hours any way I like, so I work to fit in football.'

He also takes full advantage of APFSCIL's social life. 'I play for the association's football quiz team every week. It's not just an excuse for a good drink. If you drink too much you'll let your team down. We take it very seriously. We beat Manchester City by 30 points last week!'

Another Geoff—one Geoff Barrass—is a Labour councillor from Lewisham. 'It's a complete break from committees for me. I'd go bananas without it, and the link with the old town is important to all of us.'

The game itself: Boro ripped off their 'boring' tag in a cracking encounter. But the Blues won after a late, neat nod by yet another emerging black star, Garry Thompson.

On the train home the Boro band are as sick as the proverbial parrot: 'well worth a point' is the general consensus. The Coventry crew are amazingly quiet: no expected choruses of 'Two-one' to the tune of 'Amazing Grace'.

The train flies. Soon it's up the slope at Euston. Thoughts turn to next week and a trip to Ayresome: 'Great—can't wait!'

A Matter of Fact

West Bromwich Albion's best win in 11 years—the 7-1 drubbing of Coventry in October —had a local radio commentator so excited that he didn't realise an eighth Albion 'goal' had been disallowed, and the station's results slot gave the score as 8-1.

The hottest soccer property in Iceland in recent years has been Petur Petursson, who has now joined Dutch aces Feyenoord. But he almost came to England to play for . . . Rochdale ! The then Rochdale manager Mike Ferguson, who introduced Petursson into Icelandic League soccer when he was in charge of Akranes, was pipped at the post in a three-club race which also involved Ajax.

Above The day the lights went out at QPR . . . after the electricity failed in the dressing-rooms, Frank McLintock, then Leicester manager, had to give his half-time talk on the pitch. But it didn't do much good—QPR won 3-0.

Claudio Coutinho, the man at the centre of so much controversy during Brazil's last World Cup campaign, has finally been replaced as national team manager. His successor is Mario Trabaglini, who has promised to assemble a team of 'very young players' for the 1982 World Cup.

Leeds United's League Cup visit to their Yorkshire neighbours Sheffield United earlier this season helped to produce new record receipts for the Bramall Lane ground. A crowd of 40,899 paid £60,003 to see Tony Currie's return to the ground where he made his name as Leeds strolled to a 4-1 win. Strangely enough, a visit from Leeds for a 5th round FA Cup tie in 1936 was also responsible for the Blades' record attendance : 68,287 fans turned up to see Sheffield triumph 3-1, a record which is unlikely ever to be broken since the capacity is now 49,000.

Queen's Park had been in existence nearly nine years before they conceded their first goal, to Vale of Leven, in 1876. Their first ever defeat in Scotland was also at the hands of Vale of Leven, who triumphed 2-1 in a Scottish Cup fifth round tie later that year on their way to winning the trophy.

Life can be cruel when your team is anchored to the foot of the League . . . especially when your nearest rivals are comfortably placed. Among the taunts that Birmingham fans had to endure from their Villa counterparts earlier this season was the jibe that Blues were the only team in history to fail to score a League goal throughout the reign of a Pope!

When Bristol Rovers played the Zambian National XI at Eastville recently, midfielder David Williams was substituted at half-time, but decided to watch the second half without changing out of his kit. With 15 minutes left, Phil Lythgoe took a knock. Since it was a friendly, the Africans agreed to let Williams come back on, and he promptly scored a 30-yarder.

Founded: 1893
Address: Dens Park, Dundee, Angus
Ground: Capacity 38,500; Playing area 100.6 x 68.6 m
Record attendance: 43,024 v Rangers, Scottish Cup 2nd round, 7.2.53
Record victory: 10-0 v Alloa Athletic, Div. 2, 8.3.47 & v Dunfermline Athletic, Div. 2, 22.3.47
Record defeat: 0-11 v Celtic, Div. 1, 26.10.1895
Most League points: 54, Div. 1, 1961-62
Most League goals: 113, Div. 2, 1946-47
League scoring record: 38, David Halliday, Div. 1, 1923-24
Record League aggregate: 111, Alan Gilzean, 1960-64
Most League appearances: 341, Doug Cowie, 1947-61
Most capped player: 24, Alex Hamilton, Scotland, 1961-66
Honours: Div. 1 Champions 1962, Div. 2 Champions 1947; Scottish Cup Winners 1910, Runners-up 1925, 1952, 1964; Scottish League Cup Winners 1951-52, 1952-53, 1973-74; Runners-up 1967-68
League career: 1893-1938 Div. 1; 1938-47 Div. 2; 1947-75 Div. 1; 1975-76 Premier; 1976- Div. 1

DUNDEE

To Dundee fans the glory days of the early 1960s, when their side invaded Europe with a scintillating brand of skill and goalscoring flair and overcame such big names as Cologne, Anderlecht and Sporting Lisbon, must seem a lifetime ago.

Nearly always the major football power on Tayside, Dundee have drifted into the background while rivals United have grown in strength and shot to the top.

European Cup semi-finalists back in 1963, the Dens Park club face the very real danger of sinking into part-time obscurity in much the same way as Dunfermline, twice Scottish Cup winners and three times finalists a decade or so ago.

It's a frightening prospect for the club's directors, who have gambled in excess of £100,000 to keep the club on a full-time footing.

The cash flow can't be maintained indefinitely. After twice failing to win promotion from the First Division, Dundee are fast approaching a crisis. A third failure would almost certainly spell the end of their plans for a quick re-birth.

Yet chairman Ian Gellatly remains optimistic in spite of the pitfalls; with losses totalling £110,000 in the past two years he can't afford not to be.

'Yes, I suppose we are taking a big gamble,' Gellatly admitted to *Handbook*.

Left to right, back: *Shirra, Ian Redford, Iain McPhail, McCormack, Scrimgeour, Davidson, Caldwell*. Middle: *Gemmell, Eric Ferguson (physio), Lamb, Turnbull, Phillip, Donaldson, Allan, Gavin Redford, McIntosh, Pirie, Hugh Robertson (coach), Willie Wallace (trainer)*. Front: *Schaedler, Morris, John McPhail, Sinclair, Glenny, McGeachie, McKinnon, McDougall, Williamson*.

'But we're not acting simply for ourselves and the shareholders.

'No prudent businessman would conduct his affairs in the same way as running a football club. But we're acting more as trustees of the club on behalf of the city.

'It would be an absolute disaster for the area if the club failed to win back a place in the Premier League, and we're doing everything in our power to maintain our status as a full-time team geared to achieving success.

'We pay what we consider to be good wages and the incentives for success are there for everyone to see. But it's not enough just to win promotion. We must ensure that the team is good enough to hold down a permanent place in the top league.'

Deeper in debt

Gellatly added: 'Two years ago our net loss was £59,000. Last year it was £51,000. Next time the figure could be much more; it certainly won't be less.

'But if we are successful in winning promotion we'll get a fair proportion of that cash back in just one season.

'I'm not prepared to say at the moment whether we would remain full time if the club failed to go up this season. Obviously, the whole question of our approach and the financial implications would have to be re-examined closely before a decision was taken.'

Ironically, Dundee's record as a First Division club is impressive enough. Since being relegated in 1976 they have twice failed to be promoted by just one place.

And they have continued also to enjoy a larger support than their Premier League neighbours a few yards away, despite

Tommy Gemmell, here clearing a Motherwell attack, had a short spell as a player with Dundee before taking over as manager. Motherwell's No. 4 is Bobby Watson, later manager of Airdrie.

United's superior performances in recent seasons.

It's a fact which has brought justified moans from Tannadice—and the realisation that, for the time being at least, Dundee remain the city's more established club.

The task of leading Dundee back to the big time fell to Tommy Gemmell at the end of the 1976-77 season . . . when Davie White was sacked after failing to win promotion at the first attempt.

After an honest return

Gemmell, former Celtic and Scotland star, the man who scored the equaliser in the 1967 European Cup final, has lost none of the confidence and forthright manner which characterised his play as a full-back.

In the 18 months or so he has been in charge Gemmell has never hesitated to impose severe penalties on players who fail to give an honest return.

There are no players of the calibre of Billy Steel, Alan Gilzean or Charlie Cooke on the Dens Park scene nowadays, but Gemmell still believes that there is enough ability in his squad to complete the basic job.

'Dundee used to have a reputation for classy football, but they lacked something in the way of hardness and competitiveness,' says Gemmell. 'I have tried to change things in that direction.

'That's not to say we have willingly ▷

Marathon win

Dundee's one Scottish Cup triumph was way back in 1910. Even then, it was a long struggle. After taking three matches to dispose of Hibernian in the semi-final, they were taken to three games by Clyde in the final. Dundee have been runners-up three times.

The one and only Billy Steel

Billy Steel played for Great Britain against the Rest of Europe . . . after just nine Scottish League games! What's more, he scored—with a spectacular volley from 30 yards. After leaving Morton this immensely skilful but unpredictable inside-forward had a short but successful career with Derby before joining Dundee in 1950—for a Scottish record fee of £24,000. He led the club to two successive League Cup triumphs . . . before emigrating to California.

abandoned skill. But you've got to work hard and play hard to achieve results in this league. Players who aren't prepared to give 100 per cent effort are no use to me.

'Any player who gives me everything he's got and has a bad game has nothing to fear. He'll still get his place in the team the following week. It's those who cheat and play badly who have to worry.

'I've never hesitated to drop non-triers because work-rate and bite are two of the qualities needed for success. Any club which has ever achieved anything worthwhile has had both.

'Perhaps the skill factor has suffered a bit, but there's no shortage of ability here.'

Cup-tie pressure

Gemmell has played against the best in the world at every level, but has rarely experienced the pressures now being made on him.

He knows that if Dundee fail to climb out of the First Division this season he'll be termed a failure by demanding fans.

'Certainly, there are increased pressures on me. All I can do is make the effort required.

'Every First Division team wants to beat Dundee because of the club's former standing in the game. Every game is like a cup tie for us. It's something we must live with.

'The boot will be on the other foot next season when we win promotion. We'll lift

Champions
Dundee have won the Scottish League championship only once in their history—in 1962. The following season they reached the semi-finals of the European Cup.

Their manager was Bob Shankly, brother of Bill. He inherited a side full of good young players built up by his predecessor Willie Thornton, to which he added three experienced players, including winger Gordon Smith, who had already won championship medals with Hibs and Hearts. They won the title with a three-point margin over Rangers, clinching it with a 3-0 win at St Johnstone (the team group picture on the far right was taken immediately afterwards). They then took the continent by storm, beating FC Cologne 8-5, Sporting Lisbon 4-2 and Anderlecht 6-2, before going out on a 5-2 aggregate to the eventual European champions AC Milan.

Almost immediately, the side began to break up. Centre-half Ian Ure (near right) joined Arsenal for £62,500 and Alan Gilzean (middle right)—111 goals in 135 League games, plus eight in the European Cup campaign—moved to Spurs for £72,500. Dundee haven't finished in the top four since, and they now find themselves in danger of becoming the city's number two club.

our game against Celtic, Rangers, Aberdeen and Hibs because there will be bigger crowds and a more stimulating atmosphere.'

Not that top-scorer Billy Pirie could hardly be more stimulated than he was last season, when he hit 35 goals in 39 League games . . . 13 more than his nearest rival in the Scottish First Division and the best in Scotland.

Gemmell has worked hard at rebuilding the club, buying players like Billy Williamson from local rivals United, Jim Shirra and Jocky Scott (pictured far left) from Aberdeen, former Scottish international Erich Schaedler and Alex McGhee from Hibs and Willie Watson and Stuart McLaren from Motherwell.

New faces

In a little over a year he completely altered the face of the team. Yet he says: 'I would like to strengthen one or two departments before I'll be completely satisfied. At the moment I feel we can do at least as well as last season's promoted sides, Hearts and Morton, maybe better.

'But our progress mustn't be allowed to stop at promotion. We've got to go on improving from there.'

It's a refreshing outlook—one which conjures up memories of the club's last major success, when they beat Celtic 1-0 on a cold December day in 1973 to win the League Cup.

Since then times have been hard. And if they slip at the top of the table, they could get harder still.

Lisbon Lion's new den
An hour of the 1967 European Cup final had gone . . . and Celtic, despite almost unremitting pressure, were 1-0 down to the great Inter-Milan. Then full-back Tommy Gemmell struck with a 20-yard blast through the packed Italian defence. The Cup was on its way to Scotland after 11 years of unbroken Latin dominance. Celtic eventually won 2-1 when, six minutes from time, Steve Chalmers deflected Bobby Murdoch's shot into Inter's goal.

Tommy Gemmell was a powerful pillar in that Celtic side that ruled Scottish soccer for nearly a decade. He won every honour going with the club, plus 18 Scottish caps. Now he's manager of Dundee, and his ambition is unimpaired, though somewhat more modest: his first task is to take the Dark Blues back to the Premier Division . . .

THE APPRENTICE

Putting himself about . . . training for Paul is all involvement—'I just think to myself that I'm lucky to be doing this job.'

The story so far: Paul Allen signed for West Ham last summer and *Football Handbook* **is following his career as an apprentice. Paul is a cheerful kid with the natural enthusiasm that coaches see as the first requirement of a good pro. And the signs are that, give or take a fluffed pass, things are going to plan . . .**

Ten minutes from the end of West Ham Reserves' game against Plymouth Reserves, Paul got the nudge.
The nudge told him to get up and warm up; he was going on. Only a few hundred people were at Upton Park but for 16-year-old Paul it was another little milestone in his pro career.
'I hardly touched the ball but it was still nice to get out there. We were winning 4-1

so there wasn't much danger of losing, was there?'
Paul, from Aveley in Essex, had been sub for three other Hammers reserve games and played seven times for the colts in the South-East Counties League.
'I'm enjoying it. Ronnie Boyce [the youth coach] is hard to please but he tells you if you've done well. He makes you work hard and explains to you what

A RUDDERLESS RESULT

'My family thought we'd done well, but we knew we hadn't.'

you're doing wrong.
'I'm still having problems about playing sideways on, but it makes sense and I'll stick at it. I'm also having a little bit of trouble about when to run with the ball and when to lay it off.

'Happy'
'But I'm happy with the way things are going. I enjoy the training, even on Monday when we do lots of running.' His one full game at Upton Park, an FA Youth Cup game against Southend, was a night to remember .. ! the team played terrible.
'About ten of my family went to the game and it was a bit of a let-down really. We were 3-0 down in no time and it looked like a disaster. We got it back to 3-1 by half-time but Ron wasn't all that happy in the dressing-room.

'Disappointed'
In the second half it was all us and we finished 4-3 winners. My family and aunts and uncles thought we'd done well but we knew we hadn't—and Ron told us we hadn't. We had a long team talk and it was all a bit disappointing.'
Some of the Counties' results wouldn't look good in a League context either—Gillingham, lost 1-0; Orient, lost 3-1; Portsmouth, lost 5-2. 'But we've been doing better lately. We beat Orient away and beat Charlton twice.
Paul, signed last summer, won't fail for lack of effort. He puts it all in during training and if the two teams in the five-a-sides weren't wearing bibs, you could get

the impression it was Paul against the rest.
Just after he signed Paul, manager John Lyall saw him as an 'Alan Ball type.' If he ever plays regularly in the Football League, his opposite number will have to be prepared for a breathless afternoon.
Lyall smiles. 'He gets about, doesn't he ? And does he get geed up! Some players you have to give a little bit of devil to, but with Paul you wonder if you should ask him to ease up a bit. We don't want him to burn himself out before he's 18!'
Because he's beavering away most of the time, Paul tends to play lots of little one-twos

and his 'vision' is not what it might be.
'That's right,' says Lyall, 'but it's not a problem really. We'll get his head up. Anyway, who wants the finished article at 16 ? We don't. There's a lot of natural development to go on yet. We're just here to help out on the small things.'

Quiet word
The Boyce way on match day is also about the small things.
'He usually has a quiet word with each of us,' says Paul. 'You know, telling us what he expects of us. It gets you in the right mood for the game and makes things nice and clear.'

'There's a lot of natural development to go on yet,' says boss John Lyall. 'We help on some of the small things.'

Don Givens on the near-post header

'Defenders are more aware of the danger these days but there's nothing they can do about it if you get there first. The keeper hasn't got a lot of chance if you get a touch from a yard or two ... and the touch can be very slight.'

Givens getting there first—this time against Northern Ireland for the Republic of Ireland in the European Championship.

Although it no longer shocks defences the way it did a few seasons ago, the near-post header is still one of the most favoured ways of finishing an attack.

It's quick—and it can be a killer. Often it's just a question of getting the slightest touch to find the net.

Birmingham City's Don Givens, always dangerous in that area, says: 'The important thing in such situations is getting there first.

'Defenders are more aware of the danger these days but there's nothing they can do about it if you get there first. And the keeper hasn't got a lot of chance if you get a touch from a yard or two.'

Timing the run is all important and City coach Norman Bodell—who acted as the defender for our session—made the point that although getting there first was vital, it was equally important to 'arrive late' at the point of contact.

'That sounds like a contradiction but it's not really,' says Norman. 'The near-post header is very much a split-second thing and to be effective the header has to be made at speed, so the last thing you want is to get to the position too early and find yourself almost waiting for the ball'.

Don gets half a yard on the defender—and for the near-post header that's enough . . .

Very often the ball is played in low and the striker has to stoop to conquer . . .

The ball had been only inches from the defender but Don got there first to score.

On his own Don shows how it's very much a question of sticking your neck out and leaving it there . . .

Just a touch and Don sends the ball goalwards.

From behind the net you see the defender's dilemma.

Don is there first and there's no chance for the defender who's 'blind' and helpless behind him.

Graham Taylor:

The near-post header has become an accepted part of British football because it fits perfectly into the pace of our game. Everyone talks about early balls from the wings—'get it in early'—and that's become a standard move in the League because there are so many players willing enough to keep getting into those situations. As Don says, it's primarily about getting to the ball first.

Often it's a case of getting your nose in front of your markers, and the actual header is usually not much more than a touch. If you need to glance the ball towards the target, I always think of that type of header as little more than raising the eyebrows—if you can picture what I mean.

But, as the ball will tend to run away from you, it's best to aim for the near post—then, if it does brush off the forehead, there's still a good chance of it hitting the target inside the far post.

So, the practice. You need three of you really—one to feed the ball, one to get in the header and the third to make it as difficult for him as possible. I think it's best, at least at first, for the server to throw the ball —otherwise it could develop into a frustrating and unrewarding exercise.

It should be a flat, pacey throw—as much like a cross as possible. Because defenders are more aware of the danger— as Don points out—it's up to the forward to find ways of getting in front of the defender.

The forward has the advantage because he chooses when to go. The defender has other responsibilities, like keeping goal-side of his opponent and watching out for other dangers.

Also, the forward can duck inside his marker—getting on his blind side—then nip back outside to get that valuable half yard on him. Once the forward is in that position he's in business. All he needs is that early ball . . .

20 COPIES TO BE WON!

From Cochran to Clapton, from Holly to Hendrix—all the great pop & rock guitar idols are featured in this unique book.

- Biographies & discographies
- Instrumentation & amplification
- Styles & techniques

1. Kevin Sheedy, John Ridley and Paul Barron were all Third Division players in the 1977-78 season. Since then each of them has been transferred to a club in a higher division. Which clubs did each join?

2. Bolton, Blackburn, Villa and Sunderland are all famous clubs. They're also the surnames of four men who turn out regularly in the Football League. For which teams do they play?

3. Which two of the following clubs have not won the Second Division championship since 1960: Leeds, Liverpool, Huddersfield, Chelsea, QPR, Newcastle?

4. LEFT It's there! The shot which won the FA Cup in 1971 has just hit the net. Name the scorer and his present club?

5. Manchester United celebrated the start of their centenary season with a win over which famous European club?

6. Eire international Joe Waters plays for them. Bill Shankly & Lawrie McMenemy have managed them. Who are they?

7. In Peru's 4-1 win against Iran in Cordoba during the last World Cup, which player scored a hat-trick?

8. Stoke's Roger Jones once played for them, as did Norwich star Tony Powell. Their fans still refer to them as Boscombe, although they dropped that part of their name in 1971. What is their correct current name?

HOW TO ENTER

List your answers to the questions on a postcard, add your name and address, cut the 'Part 21' flash from the cover and attach it to the postcard (entries that do not bear the flash will be ineligible), then mail to: Football Handbook, 600A Commercial Road, London E14 7HS. Entries must arrive by 6 February, 1979, the closing date. The senders of the first 20 correct answers scrutinised after that date will each be awarded a copy of 'GUITAR HEROES'. The Editor's decision on all matters relating to the competition is final and binding. All winners will be notified as soon as possible and a full list of prize winners to date will be available from *Football Handbook* on request.

INDEX

KEY: 20-21 Major feature; *20* Picture reference; 20 Text entry in copy or caption.